DAUNTLESS HELLDIVERS

A DIVE—BOMBER PILOT'S EPIC STORY OF THE CARRIER BATTLES

HAROLD L. BUELL

ORION BOOKS · NEW YORK

*Some of the material in this book originally appeared, in different
form, in other publications under the following titles:*

"Death of a Captain," reprinted from U.S. Naval Institute *Proceedings* with
permission. Copyright © 1986 U.S. Naval Institute.

"Elimination Base Training," reprinted from Naval Aviation Museum *Foundation*, Fall 1987, courtesy Naval Aviation Museum. "Yorktown's Crucial Dash to
Midway," reprinted from Naval Aviation Museum *Foundation*, Spring 1988,
courtesy Naval Aviation Museum.

"Coral Sea Aftermath," reprinted from *The Hook*, Vol. 17, No. 2, Summer 1989,
courtesy *The Hook* and the Tailhook Association.

Published by Orion Books, a division of Crown Publishers, Inc., 201 East 50th
Street, New York, New York 10022. Member of the Crown Publishing Group.

ORION and colophon are trademarks of Crown Publishers, Inc.

Manufactured in the United States of America

Library of Congress Cataloging-in-Publication Data

Buell, Harold L.
    Dauntless helldivers / Harold L. Buell.
    Includes bibliographical references (p. 332) and index.
    1. Buell, Harold L.   2. World War, 1939–1945—Aerial operations,
  American.   3. World War, 1939–1945—Naval operations,
  American.   4. World War, 1939–1945—Campaigns—Pacific
  Area.   5. World War, 1939–1945—Personal narratives,
  American.   6. Fighter pilots, United States—Biography.   7. United
  States. Navy—Biography.   I. Title.   II. Title: Dauntless helldivers.
D790.B77   1991
940.54'5973—dc20   90-27243

ISBN 0-517-57794-1

Book Design by Shari de Miskey

10 9 8 7 6 5 4 3 2 1

FIRST EDITION

*Dedicated to
my beautiful wife Molly Lang Buell,
who has
stayed with me on my wing
all the way*

CONTENTS

ACKNOWLEDGMENTS

THE AUTHOR wishes to acknowledge contributions to this book by certain former colleagues, historians, writers, and publishers.

First, I want to thank Adm. Roy L. Johnson, combat friend and respected senior, for his excellent foreword, which sets the tone of the work.

I have used the words of that fearless Cherokee, the late Adm. J. J. "Jocko" Clark, several times to emphasize certain points of the story; all are from his autobiography, *Carrier Admiral*, written with Clark G. Reynolds and published by David McKay Company (1967). These quotes enlighten the reader regarding decisions made at high levels—choices which affected the lives of all Dauntless Helldivers during that exhilarating summer and fall of 1944, when we met and defeated the Japanese carriers in two final battles.

I am grateful to the Belote brothers, James and William, for their historically solid book *Titans of the Seas* (Harper & Row, 1975) and to William Y'Blood for his definitive work on the Philippine Sea battle, *Red Sun Setting* (Naval Institute Press, 1981). These two fine accounts are cited to provide historians' opinions concerning my squadron's attack on the Japanese carrier *Zuikaku* on 20 June 1944. Leading this attack, and surviving, was the apex of my combat efforts against the Japanese enemy.

I am indebted to five naval aviator comrades for providing me with their stories to include in this book—Vernon Micheel, Jefferson Carroum, W. B. Webb, E. John Weil, and Edwin Wilson—and to several others for memorabilia and encouragement, including Howard Crews, Bill Emerson, Ralph Yaussi, Dave Stear, Ken Glass, George Searle, Tom Ringe, George Shoemaker, Benjie Nelson, and Phil Kelly, to name only a few. God bless you all.

I wish to remember Eugene Burns, that gentle Associated Press correspondent and friend of those fearful days in 1942 aboard the Big E, with his news story about two Dauntless Helldivers hitting a Japanese carrier at the Battle of Santa Cruz. He lost his life more than thirty-five years ago when he was torn to pieces by a howling mob of Iranians during a coup in Teheran.

Last, my sincere appreciation to three fine editors and their publications: Fred Rainbow of the U.S. Naval Institute's *Proceedings*, Vice Adm. Chris Cagle of the National Museum of Naval Aviation's *Foundation*, and Robert Lawson of the Tailhook Association's journal, *The Hook*. All of these gentlemen published at least one portion of *Dauntless Helldivers*, in years past, for which I am truly grateful—thank you for your confidence in the mission of this story.

FOREWORD

IN RECENT years there have been several fine books written describing personal experiences of Navy pilots flying fighter planes in combat against the Japanese in World War II. Two that I have read are *The Jolly Rogers* by Tom Blackburn and *Skipper* by Hugh Winters. These books give well-deserved tributes to the heroic exploits of skilled and dedicated fighter pilots in the Pacific war.

To my knowledge there has never been a comparable literary effort devoted to the accomplishments of the many brave dive-bomber pilots who participated in the major, crucial carrier battles of that war against the Japanese Navy. It was the dive-bombers who provided the offensive Sunday punch (in coordination with the torpedo planes) that was so effective in destroying the enemy carrier threat. What better example than the Battle of Midway, when the dive-bombers won the day, completely devastating the Japanese task force, sinking four of their major aircraft carriers in one day of action.

America's development of the aircraft carrier and the powerful carrier task force concept are of great historical importance. But no history of this development by our Navy is complete unless we include recognition of the dive-bomber. I believe it is correct to say that dive-bombing as a weapon is a 100 percent invention of

U.S. naval aviation, starting in the late twenties with fighter squadrons using the rugged F4Bs to originate and develop the concept.

The technique was a relatively simple one—a seventy-degree vertical dive on a target so that, when a bomb was released, its trajectory would carry almost exactly to the target point. Release altitude varied but was usually in the 1,500- to 2,500-foot range. As the concept gained acceptance in American naval aviation, special aircraft were built to implement the idea. Aircraft such as the SB2U, SBC, SBD, SB2C, and AD were developed, each improving the basic design from lessons learned.

For the above reasons, plus some others, I am delighted to see that Hal Buell has produced a book dedicated to our dive-bomber pilots and crews. And I feel honored that he has asked me to write a foreword for this dramatic book. But I wish to emphasize that nothing written can do justice to the men who gave their all in those fierce air-sea battles almost half a century ago; it is fitting and appropriate that this book document further their exploits and pay tribute to their bravery and loyal devotion to duty.

I can think of no one better qualified for this task than my good friend Dr. Hal Buell. I am well acquainted with his outstanding career as a dive-bomber pilot in World War II, which included active participation in four out of the five major carrier battles of that war. We first met when he came to VB-2 at Quonset Point, Rhode Island, in the summer of 1943, when I was commander of the newly formed Air Group Two. Just back from extensive combat in the Pacific, he provided valuable training guidance to the new dive-bomber pilots of VB-2; later, as both Commander, Air Group (CAG) and air officer in *Hornet* during a six-month combat cruise of AG-2 in 1944, I watched in admiration as Hal led his "Buell & Company" in the destruction of numerous Japanese warships, support vessels, and tough ground targets at Truk, the Jimas, Marianas, and the Philippines. He survived with many honors and decorations and has lived to tell of his experiences, and those of other Dauntless Helldivers, in this exciting book.

The dive-bomber no longer exists in today's powerful nuclear carrier navy. It has been replaced by what is known as "attack" aircraft, in the rapidly moving technological process of aircraft design, instrumentation, and weapons, including smart bombs, a variety of air-to-ground missiles, sophisticated target detection and acquisition, as well as effective guidance systems exploiting radar, infrared, and laser.

Yes, technology spelled the demise of the dive-bomber as we knew it in the past. But it did not and never will erase the memories and place in history of the dive-bomber. When two or more old VB pilots meet they will reminisce about the good times they shared, the hairy experiences they went through, and certainly the trustworthy men of skill, courage, and intelligence they were closely associated with in the supreme tests of air-sea combat against a cunning adversary. Finally, they will raise their glasses in a toast to the memory of those who were not as lucky as they and did not return.

I highly recommend this book for your reading enjoyment. It is instructive from a historical point of view, and brings into proper perspective the role of those Dauntless Helldivers in the proud history of U.S. Navy carrier aviation.

Roy L. Johnson
Admiral
U.S. Navy (Ret.)

PREFACE

THIS IS a story about dive bombers, their pilots and gunners, and some of the missions they flew against the Japanese in the Pacific during World War II. Thus it seems appropriate to use the names of the two carrier-based dive-bomber aircraft of that war in composing the title—Dauntless, the Douglas SBD, and Helldiver, the Curtiss SB2C—and so we have Dauntless Helldivers. This title is descriptive of both the aircraft and the men who flew them.

Since it is about dive-bombers, this account emphasizes these aircraft and their airmen exclusively. Appropriate treatment of the escapades of fighter and torpedo pilots and aircraft are woven in to enrich the main fabric only. This is not done to slight these great comrades-in-arms, both Marine and Navy, nor their exploits. But I was a dive-bomber pilot and this tale is about close friends and me—shipmates both living and dead—and our roles in that dramatic carrier war almost fifty years ago.

The aircraft carriers in this saga are the ones from which I flew in the conflict or became involved with in the many sea operations and battles described. Three of these CVs were among the finest ships that fought the Japanese Navy. *Enterprise* was the greatest U.S. combat carrier that ever sailed in harm's way; she survived more engagements, and received more honors, than any other warship of that time. *Yorktown* was a fine ship that did not live long enough to attain full stature; however, her two major battles, Coral Sea and Midway, were so significant that she established an enviable place in U.S. combat naval history by her role in them. The new *Yorktown* continued this fine tradition. As for the new *Hornet,* she proved equal to a proud name and reputation as one of the best of the Essex class carriers that took the battle back to the Japanese homeland itself. She also gained fame as the flagship of that tenacious Cherokee, Adm. J. J. "Jocko" Clark.

My wartime squadrons were three of the best. Scouting Squadron Five (VS-5), Bombing Squadron Ten (VB-10), and Bombing Squadron Two (VB-2) all compiled remarkable combat records, and the list of heroic airmen who served in them, and their air groups, is too long to catalog here. It will suffice to say that, in the truest sense, we were a "band of brothers."

I have emphasized the five carrier-versus-carrier battles of the Pacific war—Coral Sea, Midway, Eastern Solomons, Santa Cruz, and First Philippine Sea—for two reasons. First, the battles in many ways represent the very heart and soul of the U.S. Navy's conflict with the Japanese Navy. These crucial struggles, four fought in 1942 and the last in mid-1944, were the essence of a new form of sea warfare exemplified by an exchange of offensive and defensive weapons by both aircraft carrier task forces and their planes.

My second reason for this emphasis is a personal one: I was present, as a naval aviator in one capacity or another, in all five of these battles. A few historians have told me that I am the only carrier naval aviator, Japanese or American, that lived through this experience. I do not know if this is true or not; I do know that after several frustrating close calls, I finally got to dive on a major Japanese aircraft carrier (every dive-bomber's dream), leading an attack on *Zuikaku,* 20 June 1944, that damaged her seriously with eight hits. It had taken over two years for this bridesmaid to finally become a bride!

So this book is a combination of personal experiences and factual history arranged in chronological order. It presents events from an eyewitness viewpoint for each action, with summaries and historical analyses that are, for the most part, my own—I accept full responsibility for them. It is a sea story, but not a fantasy; I have tried to keep every person and happening as historically accurate as possible. Basic research materials were my personal diary, notes, orders, letters, battle reports of squadrons and ships, memoranda, newspaper clippings, pictures, presentations, speeches, early writings, and other assorted memorabilia. Occasionally I have left a person unidentified—this does not make that person (or the event) any less real, but reflects personal feelings in the matter.

A cherished resource is my own memory, which I have been fortunate in retaining through the passage of time. Valuable original materials came from old friends—many of them surviving naval aviators like myself—who generously gave of their memories and memorabilia. Some have written contributions that, with their permission, are included where appropriate to the overall story.

I have listed numerous secondary resources in the bibliography. This list contains much of the best historical writings, and some fictional works, related to the carrier-versus-carrier war, and the people who fought it, written during and since that war.

In the process of reviewing these works through the years, it is natural that some have emerged as more accurate and interesting to me than others. This preference is logical as I have a benchmark to compare these historians' accounts—my own memory. This does not mean that I consider myself infallible, or that my memory does not have its gaps and inaccuracies. It does mean that when an account meshes with my own recollections, or fills a logical gap, and the author has done his research carefully, that work tends to extend and join with my own memory of the event. When the opposite happens and I read an account filled with errors I can spot—errors that do not fit into my recall or research—I discard that version. Any materials cited in this book have passed this personal set of selection standards.

Thus all accounts are factual; any criticism is meant to be constructive; there is no intent to injure anyone personally. Admiral Clark stated this concept very well in the preface of his autobiography *Carrier Admiral:*

I have endeavored to stick to facts. . . . Everyone makes mistakes, and I made mine. After all, we did win the war, and therefore it is not proper to shoot our naval heroes. The naval writer must, however, call the shots as he sees them, not only for the sake of bringing out the truth, but for the benefit of students of naval warfare.

In putting together this account, I have sometimes used language that is not part of my normal vocabulary. Some readers may be offended by certain four-letter words or an occasional profane one. Please understand why these words are used: they are an accurate expression of the times and situations pictured—to change or omit them would not be historically honest. I have discussed many controversial persons and subjects, and have stated certain viewpoints relative to them that are my own as well as those of others. Be considerate—I do not ask you to agree with me—just be tolerant of an old historian and let him tell the yarn his way!

This book represents many years of work. In a sense it began back in my youth when the world was young and, while there was right and wrong, there was no heinous evil in my American midwestern part of it. World War II was to change my life and the lives of millions of my generation, our families, and friends. All of them are a part of this effort, and many are no longer here to accept my deep appreciation for their contributions. To those of you who are here to read this—my beloved wife Molly, my children, my sisters, relatives, friends, comrades (old, new, and wartime), and all the others who encouraged me and contributed to this effort through the years—thank you from the bottom of my heart.

And last I especially want to thank those Dauntless Helldivers with wings of gold, both living and dead, for their special input into this book. After all, without their efforts, trials, tribulations, joys, and victories, there would not have been a story to tell. God bless all of you.

A Naval Aviator

I want to be a Naval Aviator when I grow up because it's
fun and easy to do. Naval Aviators don't need much school.
They just have to learn numbers so they can read
instruments. I guess they should be able to read maps so
they can find their way if they are lost. Naval Aviators
should be brave so they won't be scared if it's foggy and
they can't see or if a wing or motor falls off they should
stay calm so they'll know what to do. Naval Aviators have
to have good eyes so they can see through clouds and they
can't be afraid of lightning or thunder because they are
closer to them than we are. The salary Naval Aviators
make is another thing I like. They make more money than
they can spend. This is because most people think airplane
flying is dangerous, except Naval Aviators don't because
they know how easy it is. There isn't much I don't like,
except girls like Naval Aviators and all the stewardesses
want to marry them so they always have to chase them
away so they won't bother them. I hope I don't get airsick
because if I do I couldn't be a Naval Aviator and would
have to go to work.

A fifth-grader

THIS LITTLE gem of composition was allegedly written by a fifth-
grader, time and place unknown. It was sent to me by an old dive-
bomber friend, William "Bill" Emerson of Columbia, Missouri, who
received it from Dick Hanecak, a retired Navy fighter jock. Please
keep its message in the back of your mind as you read this sea
story.

1

ALPHA

I

DOG DAYS in the midwestern plains of Iowa are an experience that any native son born and reared there never forgets for the rest of his life. The memory is seared into his brain forever by the almost unbelievable heat of the summer sun. This heat, combined with timely summer rains, is necessary for the huge grain crops, especially corn, that make this area America's breadbasket. The sun beating down transforms rolling prairie farmlands from frozen, windswept, barren acres into fields of plenty in the relatively short period of a few weeks; a bountiful crop grows, matures and is harvested; then the spinning planet shifts back on its axis, the heat dissipates, the cold returns, and another annual cycle of nature is complete.

During a typical summer growing season in the twenties the days were long and work never seemed to end. Every adult male and female had more work than they could do in the hours of daylight there were to work by. Even the children had assigned chores, for this was summer vacation time from school classroom boredom. The almost frantic pace continued for six days, then there was a pause for one day. These devoutly religious people took a well-earned day of rest on Sunday, performing only necessary work on the sabbath.

A favorite method of cooling off from the heat of dog days, before air-conditioning and swimming pools, was the old swimming hole. Almost every Iowa community had one of some kind—it might be a small lake or pond, an abandoned rock quarry filled with water, or simply a deep hole in the bend of a creek or river. Some of them were not too sanitary, many were rocky or muddy, and a few were dangerous. These drawbacks were forgotten when dog days heat reached its zenith.

The swimming hole for Plymouth was located under a railroad trestle that passed over Shellrock Creek on the northern edge of town. Here this small stream formed a slight bend that created a large hole with gently sloping, sandy sides. An eight- to ten-foot depth in the center allowed the more adventurous to jump or dive from the trestle down into the hole, a distance of about fourteen feet. Because of the shallow as well as deep features of this swimming hole, its cleanliness, and the slow current during summer, children and adults of all ages, male and female, flocked to its cooling waters.

On this particular day in late afternoon, the noisy, colorful crowd had left as supper time was nearing. Only one swimmer lingered, compelled by the cool waters to delay his homeward trek back down the railroad tracks to the cluster of houses that made up the town. The nine-year-old youth continued to splash about, taking an occasional cannonball jump from the trestle for excitement. He finally pulled himself from the water for the last time, slipped his battered sneakers on, donned his straw hat, and was taking one final look down at the water from the tracks when he heard the sound.

It was a sort of droning, much like that made by a large insect, coming from some distance away, and increasing in intensity as it moved closer. The sound was not a common one, as airplanes were not common in 1928, but the boy instantly recognized it as an airplane engine, and he eagerly scanned the skies for a sight of the craft. With eyesight already much keener than that of his peers, he spotted the plane to the south of town, still just a speck in the clear summer sky but growing larger as it approached.

The pilot was obviously following the railroad tracks—an iron compass heading north toward Minnesota's Twin Cities. Flying at about 1,500 feet of altitude, he cut back his engine and glided his craft in a diving spiral around the town water tower; the large

PLYMOUTH, IOWA painted on its sides gave him an exact fix as to his location. Applying throttle again, he resumed following the tracks, headed toward the boy standing on the trestle.

As the open-cockpit biplane came nearer, its red body and blue wings gleaming, the boy took off his straw hat and began waving it over his head, while jumping up and down and letting out long, loud whoops. This was the closest he had ever been to an airplane in flight. Did the pilot see him? This question was immediately answered as the craft suddenly nosed over into a shallow dive directly toward the boy. The pilot then veered course slightly to his right, cut the engine back to idle, and glided the plane around the boy, with wheels almost touching the tracks. When abreast of the lad he banked up sharply to the left and shouted above the idling engine:

"Hi there young feller! How's the water?"

There, almost close enough to reach out and touch, was a glistening plane. The pilot was smiling, a leather helmet encased his head, and sunlight flashed from huge square goggles covering his eyes. A gloved left hand was raised in a sort of salute as he swept by, and his white scarf streamed behind him like a banner in the wind.

The young spectator was struck dumb by the majestic splendor of the encounter. This was a knight in shining armor passing by from another world, his aircraft a giant bird free to take him anywhere in the world that he chose to go. The boy answered the salute with more waves of his straw hat as the pilot applied power to his engine, reversed to a climbing right turn, and continued his northerly flight along the railroad.

The boy watched the plane until it disappeared—a fading dot in the azure evening sky. He felt a sadness, almost like a heavy weight upon his mind. Why can't that free spirit be me? Why can't I be that bold aviator flying through the skies without a care in the world?

As the lad turned toward his foster home, he set his young jaw in determination. "I can do it," he said to himself. "If I work hard my chance will come. Someday I will be a pilot!" With an important decision made, the weight lifted from him, his steps quickened, and he broke into a trot as he moved down the tracks.

The young Iowa orphan boy of nine who made his decision after a chance encounter with an unknown flyer from that world of sky, clouds, wind, rain, snow, and sunshine, was me. The decision was final—I never seriously considered any other early direction for my life, and never looked back.

II

It was my last day at Garfield School. Taking my final exam as a seventh-grader, I was confident that I would pass with good marks. Next year would find me attending Washington Junior High School for the eighth grade, in preparation for further movement into Ottumwa High School.

Garfield was one of five elementary schools in the public school system of Ottumwa, Iowa, in 1932. A child went to the one nearest home through the first seven years of schooling, spent one year in junior high, and then moved into a final four years of public education in Ottumwa High School. Known as one of the finest high schools in the state, its new educational plant had been built just before the Great Depression, an economic condition we were then in the midst of, with no relief in sight.

My mother had been killed in an accident when I was four, and for the past two years I had been living with a guardian, Dr. Donald McElderry, and attending Garfield. Our house was six blocks from the school, in what was called the East End. A large meat-packing plant, John Morrell and Company, was located there, and the school had a heterogeneous student body that came from many ethnic, economic, and religious backgrounds. In addition to these differences, our school had one other distinction: The young men from Garfield had a reputation in the rest of the town as being tough, and quick to resort to their fists to settle an argument. It was generally good advice to not engage an East Ender in a quarrel past a certain point but to walk away instead.

Personally I did not like fistfighting as a means of settling differences of opinion. And I had never been attracted to boxing or wrestling as sports. Football, with its violent physical contact, was my favorite sport, followed closely by both baseball and basketball. Thus team sports involving physical contact were what I engaged in—I had little time or interest for such luxury games as golf, tennis, or bowling. Yet you didn't live where I did and go to Garfield unless you learned how to take care of yourself, so I had developed some ability in the rudiments of street fighting—enough to get by, I hoped—but most of the time I smiled a lot.

4

On this last day of school in May the summer heat was already upon us, and all the windows were open throughout the school. We seventh-graders were taking our final exam in a classroom on the second floor. Our teacher told us to bring finished papers to her at the front of the room, then leave by going out a large window and down the fire escape.

I completed the exam with time to spare, turned in my paper, gathered my belongings, and started down the fire escape. From this vantage point I could see a large mob of students gathered on the playground. The noise coming from the group could mean only one thing—a fistfight was in progress.

As a paperboy for the *Ottumwa Courier*, with a delivery route of over one hundred daily customers, I had no time to hang around to see the outcome of a fight, as it was already time for the afternoon delivery. As I started down the street away from Garfield, I heard a voice from the crowd behind me call out: "Hey, Tommy, there goes Buell now." Turning around, I saw the mob coming toward me.

Leading the group was a short, stocky boy with a grimy appearance—a former student named Tommy Roberts. A troublemaker with a foul mouth and quick to use his fists, he was known for his truancy and unreliability. As he had not been around the school for many weeks, I guessed he had been expelled for his incorrigible behavior. But he was here now, coming my way with something in mind that might be injurious to my health.

Apparently Roberts had been warming up on some poor victim while he waited for me to come out of the school. As I was still close to the school, I could simply head for the front door and go back inside. Once there, I would receive assistance from the school superintendent, Miss Ann Wilson, gracious, charming, intellectual, but tough as nails; she would handle Roberts, at least for the present. Unfortunately, within my set of standards of conduct, this course of action seemed cowardly and would not solve the problem, but only delay it for a time. I stood and waited.

Roberts came up to me and stopped. He had a mean look on his face and had rolled his shirtsleeves up, revealing his muscular arms. He was at least two years older than I and, while short in stature, his muscle development was far superior to mine. More important, he knew something about boxing, especially how to hook and jab from a stance. He spoke:

"Buell, several months ago you punched me in the gut, then someone stopped me before I took you apart. Do you remember that happening?"

His statement caught me by surprise. Then I recalled that I had, indeed, punched him in his stomach months before during a quarrel while playing marbles on the playground. As I remembered, he had run off crying that I had "hit him low." At this point I made the biggest mistake of my young life—I took my eyes off him and looked down while considering a reply.

When I looked back up, his right fist was inches from my face and coming inbound at full velocity. It crashed into my nose and left cheekbone, breaking the nose, closing my left eye, and dropping me to my knees. I had been sucker-punched. Struggling to rise, I saw his right boot coming for my head. I grabbed it and threw him off his feet as I got back up on mine. He bounded back up and the fight began.

Recently at my fiftieth high school reunion I talked with Joe Orman, who saw that fight long ago on the Garfield playground. He has lived in Ottumwa all of his life, and he told me that people still talk about it. The ferocity of this battle between two boys barely in their teens is hard to understand. Having no knowledge of boxing, I simply kept making bull-like rushes at an opponent who was not only stronger but smarter. Tommy Roberts kept dancing about, hooking and jabbing at my eyes, until both were closed. In one of my rushes I caught him flush on his nose, breaking it so that his blood also flowed. But there was no doubt that he beat the hell out of me. The reason the fight went as long as it did was because I didn't know when I was thoroughly whipped. It finally stopped when spectators, realizing that I could no longer see my opponent through my battered, swollen eyelids, did not allow it to continue.

I was led away from the scene by a boy who lived near me. He took me to a well pump where I bathed the eyes with cool water. Then he helped me around the paper route. My guardian's wife, Sadie McElderry, a gentle, tiny woman, almost fainted when she saw my battered countenance. The good doctor packed my nose and put ice packs on my eyes to reduce swelling. I ended up with a permanently crooked nose, and the biggest pair of shiners ever seen in the East End.

That beating became a major turning point in my young life. I was determined it would never happen to me again. I began learning how to box and later I studied the fundamentals of hand-to-hand combat. I started a program of gymnastics to build myself up. I purchased both light and heavy punching bags for workouts and slugged away until I had developed a pretty good hook, jab, and one-two. I collected a library of written materials on self-defense. I also learned how to avoid a confrontation without loss of face or pride.

Later, when I became a combat pilot, I never forgot the lesson I learned on the Garfield School playground: Hit the first lick, with everything you have—and watch out that your opponent doesn't sucker-punch you first!

III

After graduation from high school in the summer of 1937, I had no plans to attend college in the fall. The reason was a simple one —I had no money to pay even the low entrance fees common at many private colleges scattered throughout the area.

I was living with my guardian and his wife on a small farm on the eastern edge of Ottumwa. The doctor and I made a deal: If I worked at the farm, did all the chores, drove for him on night calls —in short, worked as a hired hand without pay until the fall of 1938—he would pay my first year's expenses to attend Parsons College the following year. As there were no jobs available for seventeen-year-old boys, I accepted the offer with gratitude.

I had my own room in a small garage building, got three generous meals a day, and was allowed to use the car for occasional dates. The doctor gave me a few dollars' spending money from time to time as needed. It was not a bad deal considering the economic conditions of the time.

The year passed swiftly, because I had many interests to keep me occupied. My routine chores kept me on a rigid daily schedule that was excellent discipline for a still-maturing young man. I also picked up a few dollars working jobs for other nearby farmers (one, Fred Smith, became almost like a father to me). There were Saturday night dances at the YMCA, and the traveling big bands of that era would often stop while passing through to play a quick gig at the city armory for expense money. There was no shortage of dates, because even though I had hardly any money, I often "had wheels," and so was seldom turned down. I found time to carve two fifteen-foot cedar-wood totem poles, which were erected as an entrance gateway to Overlook Farm, the name Dr. McElderry gave to his home. Best of all, I succeeded in getting an athletic scholarship to nearby Parsons College; it would pay tuition and provide me with a campus job to earn my meals, leaving only room and books as major expenses.

In September 1938 I moved twenty-five miles east of Ottumwa to Fairfield, Iowa, to enter Parsons College. This small city of approximately ten thousand souls, in the southeastern part of the state, is at the center of a circle of large midwestern cities, 250 miles from St. Louis and Omaha, 275 miles from Minneapolis–St. Paul, and 245 miles from Chicago. It was, and still is, a typical Iowa farm country village filled with beautiful people. Birmingham, and the Maple Hill cemetery containing my parents' graves, was only fifteen miles south.

That year Parsons College had a total enrollment of about four hundred students. A Presbyterian church–associated facility, it was struggling for existence as it had since it was first incorporated on 24 February 1875. It was a typical midwestern, private, church-related, four-year college with classroom buildings, chapel, library, gymnasium, several administration buildings, some faculty homes, a football field, and a steam plant to provide heat in the cold winter months. Its fifty-five-acre campus was beautifully landscaped with many species of trees and shrubs.

Like most small private American colleges in the thirties, Parsons had limited student housing on campus. There was one three-story dormitory for women with approximately one hundred beds, and two sorority and two fraternity houses on the edges of the campus. Six athletes lived in cubbyhole rooms at the gym as part of their athletic scholarship benefits. At least half of the student body commuted to the campus from their homes in Fairfield or the nearby countryside by automobile, bicycle, or "shanks mare." This left some male students with a real problem—where to live.

This housing need was met in part by local citizens who resided near the campus and rented extra rooms in their homes to students. Often the space available was the result of their children having left to start homes of their own. Such a house was Rody's Manse, the residence of Mr. and Mrs. A. P. Rodenmayer, located a block south of the campus. In the fall of 1938, this warm home became the shelter of four young men living two to a room and sharing a bath. Jack Mayo and Ed "Noot" Noonan from Fort Madison had one room, while Pat Smith and I from Ottumwa shared the other. All four of us were on some form of scholarship and at different stages of our college education, with Jack Mayo and I the freshmen in the group. As Jack, Ed, and I were on athletic scholarships, while Pat was an academic merit student, we represented one brain and three jocks.

My campus job turned out to be waiting tables, three meals a day, at Ballard Hall, the women's dormitory. Most of the waiters and other male kitchen help were athletes on scholarship—it was a great place to work. I toiled at my job every day the college was in session until I left in December 1940. President Ronald Reagan had a similar job in his Eureka College days in Illinois. He once said it was the best job he ever had, and I agree.

Then there was football. Because I had no extensive experience in this sport in high school, it was particularly hard work for me. I shall never forget those grueling fall afternoon battles on the practice field at Parsons College. At the time, nothing was more brutal than a serious scrimmage, between friends and teammates, just before a big game; if you could get through the scrimmage, the Saturday game became almost easy. After a scrimmage one day, Coach "Bear" Bryant of the University of Alabama said it this way to his players:

> There is that time when you go out on that practice field and
> you're tired and hot and you think you're gonna die. You gotta
> suck your guts up, reach down and get something, and if you do
> that then you know how. You'll not only do that in practice, and in
> a game, but also when you're out trying to make a living and
> everything is going wrong; you'll do the same thing. To me, that's
> what this game is all about.

Coach Bryant linked the game of football to later struggles in life to make a living. It can also be associated with meeting the trials of combat in war. I think I could have had no better preparation for the rigors of naval aviation cadet training than my football experience at Parsons under the stern tutelage of Coach Fritz Faurot. It was something I carried with me to the battles in the Pacific against the Japanese. When the going got tough at Guadalcanal, I found myself more concerned with not failing my ship-

9

mates than afraid for my own life. Just as one could not let his teammates down on the football field, so he could not fail to meet his obligations in combat. After all, as the "Bear" said, if you have sucked your guts up before, it's easier to do the next time.

All four of us at Rody's Manse were destined to be active participants in World War II. Jack Mayo would serve as a chief petty officer in the Navy until the war's end in 1945, then return to Parsons to finish his degree work. Pat Smith would serve in the Army and have a successful career in computers after the war. Ed Noonan and I would become ensign naval aviators with wings of gold—both of us would go to the Pacific—and one would not return.

2

PREPARATION ONE

I

MY SECOND year of college began in the fall of 1939, with money earned during the summer working for Ray Dixson's Farm Implements Company at Mason City, Iowa. The war in Europe was a continuing topic of conversation in the many bull sessions held at the frat houses, Rody's Manse, and the campus hangouts such as the Jail Cafe, Red and Ruth's Restaurant, or Martin's Drug Store. When will the United States go to the aid of the Allies against the Axis? Each of us asked himself: With a draft coming, what should I do?

Within the college population a small number of men began a move toward aeronautical careers when nine students were accepted for flight training in a new college course sponsored by the federal government. Ed Noonan and I from Rody's Manse were two of the nine. Known as the Parsons College Civilian Pilot Training Program (CPTP), the course consisted of academic course work and flight training that would lead to a private pilot's license to fly light, single-engine aircraft. The program, including forty hours of flight time, cost the candidate nothing—in fact, he received a small remuneration for his efforts.

The aircraft used in the CPTP was a Piper Cub two-seater, fore and aft cockpits, stick-controlled, with a sixty-five-horsepower engine. Our flight instructor was Clifford "Oley" Oleson, a short, dark, wiry man with a foul mouth, who ran a small private flying operation from the Ottumwa airport north of the city. This airport was little more than a cow pasture with one tiny office shack and a weather-beaten hangar housing four aircraft. Oleson was a veteran pilot with years of flying experience in many types of airplanes of the time, having learned to fly in the Army Air Corps. He ran a military-style operation with continual emphasis upon one theme: If you want to live to be an old pilot, never make a mistake, especially a big one!

The fact that CPTP flights were starting just as winter weather was moving into the area did not ground our enthusiasm or our aircraft. Oleson, by equipping one of the Piper Cubs with skis, continued flying instruction even in heavy snow conditions. I remember taking off with him one crisp, shining morning after a night blizzard. The earth was covered with a heavy blanket of new snow so white and gleaming from the sun that it hurt one's eyes. We flew about over the countryside—everything was clean and pure. We were glad to be alive. Selecting a farm field of unbroken snow, Oley decided to show off his flying skills. The field was fenced and appeared like a giant square to us from the air. He dropped down over one corner and, lined up with the opposite corner, flew diagonally across the field, carefully dragging one ski along in the snow through the field. He then banked sharply around and repeated the pattern between the other two corners; the result was a giant X inscribed in the exact center of the field. I was properly impressed with the skill of my tutor.

By early spring all nine of us had soloed and were busy building up the required flight time before making an individual cross-country navigational flight for the final air test of the course. This flight was the first time we would be flying more than ten to twenty miles from the home field alone. Each of us laid out a preflight triangular course running roughly from Ottumwa northwest almost to Des Moines, then eastward to Iowa City. After landing, refueling, and eating lunch, each pilot took off and flew back to Ottumwa. We were allowed to use landmarks on the ground to check our position, but the main idea of the flight was to navigate using compass headings and timed legs, properly taking into account any wind drift. Our main map was a standard aeronautical chart published by the government, but I remember getting the latest automobile road map, drawing my course lines upon it, and carrying it with me as a backup for the chart. The Shell Oil road map was actually more accurate, with more discernible landmarks than the aeronautical one, and it got a real workout on my solo cross-country flight, due to a strong wind from the northwest that made all of my time estimates wildly inaccurate. I refused to allow myself to get even slightly lost, and used the Iowa highways as flight guides, with towns and cities as checkpoints, to complete my final exam successfully.

Financial remuneration, combined with several hours of college-level credits for course work completed in ground school, and the sheer joy of flying, made the federal CPTP one of the most popular courses of the time at Parsons College. Passing this flight course and getting a private pilot's license in early 1940 convinced me that I could fly and make aviation a career. It had the same effect on Ed Noonan, so we decided to spend Easter break from college classes looking into the possibilities of naval aviation training by visiting the U.S. Naval Reserve Aviation Base in Robertson, Missouri.

After hitchhiking to the St. Louis area, we gathered with a group of young men from the Ninth Naval District to take the tough flight physical required for entrance into the naval flight program. After about five hours of tests, there were only two other men besides Noot and myself left of the original thirty-five or so candidates who had started the tests together that morning. The Navy recruiter wanted to sign the four survivors to an immediate on-the-spot enlistment. I could not sign because I had not completed the required two years of college credits, and Noonan wanted to finish his present courses to get his bachelor's degree in May before signing up. So we left St. Louis feeling both sad and elated—sad because we had to return to a drab college study routine for the rest of the semester instead of continuing flying, yet happy that we both now knew we could pass the demanding physical requirements for entering naval flight training.

The forty hours of flight instruction in a Piper Cub, flying from a cow pasture in Iowa under the tutelage of a discarded Army Air Corps pilot, was the beginning of my flying career of more than twenty-five years. I would circumnavigate the globe, survive three major airplane crashes and two wars, and fly from aircraft carrier decks in all the world's oceans both day and night. During this career, I would fly many different types of fighter, attack, and transport aircraft, from open-cockpit biplanes to swept-wing jets, and experience the thrills of test-piloting experimental aircraft. Through it all I never forgot the basic flying skills taught me by a tough, profane little man who first instructed me in the art of flying: Oley Oleson started me right as a pilot and, in a real way, I owe my life of aerial survival at least partly to him.

II

By the fall of 1940, many young men in colleges and universities throughout the country—including our Parsons College group—began to think seriously of flying in the Royal Air Force (RAF) or the Royal Canadian Air Force (RCAF) in the Eagle Squadrons. This interest was generated by the highly successful federal CPTP programs provided by the Civil Aeronautics Authority (CAA) at selected academic facilities.

Becoming an Eagle took more than just stepping forward and enlisting as a volunteer: Neutrality restrictions prohibited open recruitment of Americans for such service. Early attempts to procure U.S. pilots for both the RAF and RCAF were conducted by individuals who used considerable effort to maintain a low profile and keep their operations secret.

Major recruiting efforts came through an organization known as the Clayton Knight Committee. Backed by the RCAF, this recruiting committee was set up in Ottawa (and also New York City) under the command of Air Vice Marshal Billy Bishop. Bishop was a famous Canadian World War I air ace who was credited with downing seventy-two aircraft in that conflict. He induced an American flying buddy of that war, Clayton Knight of Rochester, New York, to assist him in the endeavor. Knowing that many unemployed pilots lived in the western states, especially California, Knight and a working partner, Homer Smith, conducted extensive recruiting in the larger cities of that state—San Diego, Los Angeles, and San Francisco. Because of neutrality restrictions, they proceeded cautiously, using word of mouth and personal contacts at key airfields to meet pilots. Interest in the efforts of the Knight Committee became so great that offices were set up in other major cities.[1]

The "unrecruited" applicant, to be eligible to join the RCAF as a pilot, had to have (1) at least three hundred hours of certified flight experience, (2) a CAA license to pilot a two-place airplane, and (3) the equivalent of a high school diploma. Unlike the U.S. Army and Navy in their flight-training programs, the Canadians did not care about college credits, marital status, or perfect eyesight. They allowed corrective glasses for 20/20 vision, and took both older and younger men. They required the consent of a parent or guardian for those men under the age of twenty-one. Of course, the main concern was flight time—they wanted licensed pilots who could be trained for immediate combat.

Why would young American pilots—many of them barely more than boys—volunteer to leave the comfort and security of the United States to cast their lot with England, a country fighting for its life? These postdepression youth were hungry for excitement, adventure, and a chance to fly; they were eager to prove themselves. What better way than to fight Germany's best in the air, for a cause that was just? After all, Americans had always identified with an underdog. Regardless of individual intentions, one thing is clear regarding these early Eagles: they were not mercenaries in any modern sense of the term. As stated by the Right Honorable Lord Martonmere, formerly Wing Comdr. J. Roland Robinson, M. P., of the RAF: "The pay offered to these young men, who were prepared to sacrifice their lives, was pitiful, so much so that at the end of the month some of them had difficulty in meeting their mess bills."[2]

Looking back to that fall in 1940, I came very close to volunteering for the RCAF. While I never actually joined up, in my desperate attempts to get into the air as a military pilot I was ready to lie about my total hours, or do almost anything within reason, to get into military pilot flight training. My first choice was naval aviation cadet training in my own country, but if that kept eluding me, should I go to Canada? Would the RCAF accept me? After all, Ottawa was relatively nearby. I decided to prepare a letter of inquiry to Ottawa.

At that time, October 1940, I received my first encouraging news from the U.S. Naval Reserve Aviation Base in Robertson, Missouri. Lt. J. K. Averill wrote that the Navy was still interested in me as a candidate for flight training if I would send in the required transcript from Parsons College.

15

I replied immediately to this letter, telling Averill of my continuing intense interest in naval aviation and that I would send the transcript as soon as the college released the three hours of English credits, now ongoing, that stood between me and naval flight training. Three days after my twenty-first birthday, I received another letter from Lieutenant Averill:

7 November 1940

Mr. Harold L. Buell
603 North Third Street
Fairfield, Iowa

Dear Sir:

You are advised that if we receive your educational record by the 28th of December, your papers will be forwarded to the Navy Department for training in the class commencing 15 February 1941. The January group is now in the process of being selected and their papers will leave this office the latter part of this month.

We suggest you obtain the transcript as soon as the college will release it and forward same to us promptly. Your application will be given every consideration at such time as you can meet the educational requirements.

Your continued interest in Naval Reserve Flight Training is appreciated and we hope you will be one of the successful candidates.

Yours truly,

J. K. Averill
Lieutenant, USN
Commanding

Clutching this latest letter in my hand, I went to see the two most powerful faculty persons on the Parsons College campus— Dean of Men Dr. Fred J. Hinkhouse and Dean of Women Dr. Dora Dexter. My plea to them was a simple one: Would they use their influence with my English professor, Dr. Hugh Brower, to get an early release of my transcript with the vital three hours of English credit added to it? Perhaps I could take a special examination? If the college would release the transcript, including the English credits, before 28 November, my application process might move ahead one month and I could make the January 1941 elimination class now forming.

My request was successful and Deans Hinkhouse and Dexter induced Dr. Brower to give me an early examination for credit. As this course was a makeup for one that I had dropped in my freshman year, I passed the special test without trouble and the required transcript left the college by registered mail the morning of 19 November 1940.

With the required papers on their way to the base in Robertson, I decided also to send off a letter of inquiry to the RCAF, using the Alpha Kappa Chi (AKX) frat house as an address—a letter I had spent several days preparing. With two applications going, perhaps one of two paths to military flight training would open up to me. One thing was definite: I was determined to continue a flying career in the coming new year. The day before leaving the campus for Christmas vacation, an answer to my RCAF inquiry came in the mail:

DEPARTMENT OF NATIONAL DEFENCE
"Air Force"

Ottawa, Ontario, 11 December 1940

H. L. Buell, Esq.
Alpha Kappa Chi
Parsons College
Fairfield, Iowa, USA

Dear Sir:

Acknowledgment is made of your letter of 19 November wherein you request particulars of the procedure to be followed in making application for entry into the Royal Canadian Air Force.

The regulations governing enlistment require that representation should be made personally at one of the Recruiting Centres on the list attached. A candidate undertaking the journey to Canada proceeds at his own expense with no assurance of eventual acceptance. It is important that he should take with him the supporting documents enumerated in Paragraph 1 of the enclosed bulletin outlining the general requirements. Upon completing an application at a Recruiting Centre and successfully passing the required medical test a candidate should be prepared to return to his home to await a call, as immediate enlistment cannot always be effected.

Your keen interest in this matter is greatly appreciated.

P. T. Chapman, F. O.
For: A. deNiverville
Group Captain
Chief of the Air Staff

III

In what was to be my last Christmas holiday vacation from Parsons College, I left Rody's Manse on 14 December 1940 for the McElderry residence at Ottumwa. My plans included visits with my sisters and their families.

I did not discuss with anyone how near I was to going into military flight training. After receiving the "invitational" letter from Ottawa, I was determined that I would leave in January for the RCAF if I had not heard from the Navy by that time. However, the necessity for making a final decision never materialized. Five days before Christmas I received a telephone call at the Mc-Elderry home from Mom Rodenmayer at Rody's Manse in Fairfield:

"Buelly, this is Mom Rody. I'm calling to tell you that a telegram has arrived here for you from the Navy people down in Robertson, Missouri."

My heart leaped and I thought it would jump right out of my chest. At last I would have an answer!

"Thank you for calling me, Mom. Please read me the message."

Her soft, calm voice came to me across the telephone line:

"To Harold Lloyd Buell, six-oh-three North Third Street,
Fairfield, Iowa. You are directed to report to commanding officer,
U.S. Naval Reserve Aviation Base, Robertson, Missouri, on six
January nineteen-forty-one, for enlistment into the United States
Navy. Elimination flight training as a member of the January class
will begin immediately upon completion of enlistment procedures.
You will be reimbursed for expenses incurred in carrying out
these orders. J. K. Averill, Lieutenant, U.S. Navy, commanding"

There was a short pause, then her voice continued: "Buelly, does this mean that you are going to be leaving us?"

"Yes, Mom Rody, it looks like my prayers for military flight

18

training have been answered. I'll be over later this week to clear out my things. Thank you for getting this message to me—and Merry Christmas!"

In the typical fashion of youth, I hastily hung up the telephone and sprinted away to tell everyone—my sisters, my foster parents, and all close friends—the exciting news. I was going to become a naval officer and aviator!

At the other end of the line, Mom Rodenmayer hung up the telephone and began crying into her checkered apron. The first one of her college boys was leaving to enter military service. With the wisdom that comes with age, experience, and memories of World War I, she shivered as she asked herself: How will it all end?

IV

On a bleak, cold winter day, 6 January 1941, a group of thirty eager young men gathered at the U.S. Naval Reserve Aviation Base in Robertson, Missouri. The men were reporting as prospective naval aviation cadets and had enlisted in the Navy as seamen, second class, V-5, USNR. These bases were known as E bases because of the elimination training being done—training that ran from four to six weeks while each recruit was observed carefully to see whether he possessed the combination of aptitude and attitude required to warrant spending thousands of tax dollars to transform him into a first-class pilot. While at an E base, each seaman was paid thirty-six dollars per month and subsistence of one dollar per day; uniforms and housing were furnished free.

With the passage of the Naval Aviation Reserve Act of 1939, all cadet aviators who completed flight training were commissioned A-V (N), USNR or USMCR, and received both wings and commissions upon completion of 465 hours of ground school and 300 flight hours in an eight-month period. To get a chance at this prize one first had to get by E base.

The new candidates were a varied group of young men from all walks of life and family circumstances. But because of naval aviation requirements, they had several traits in common: good health, unmarried status, youth (ages ran from twenty to twenty-six), two to four years of college education, and an intense desire to fly airplanes. Most came from modest financial backgrounds with some wealth here and there; they were white, middle-class

19

men from the rolling prairie heartland of mid-America. Among their native ancestors could be found almost any European strain, with a heavy majority of Anglo-Saxon Protestant heritage evident. One striking feature shared by most of these fledgling pilots was blue eyes—almost every shade of blue could be found represented in the steady, straightforward gazes. The Navy used numbers to designate these diverse blues—my eyes were #6.

Although we were to be aviation cadets for flight training, we were required to enlist in the Navy for four years as seamen. I was given my first military designation: seaman second class, V-5, 411-42-46, USNR. We were treated firmly and well—it was much like a Marine boot camp without the harassment. We were issued Marine-green uniform shirts and pants made of heavy wool, garrison caps, and lined winter jackets with no insignia of any kind. For flying, each man wore a heavy flight suit with white silk scarf, wool-lined boots, and leather gloves.

Living quarters at Robertson were an old enlisted personnel barracks, with ten double-deck bunks per room, and a clothing locker for each man. Toilets were adequate, with open showers and numerous sinks for washing and shaving. Up to twenty men lived and slept in very close quarters, with little privacy or space for personal possessions. As there was no mess hall at Robertson, we ate meals off base at the nearby cafes and restaurants, using food allowance money from the Navy; one of our favorite cafes was the *Winnie Mae*. For those interested in aviation trivia, this was what the great one-eyed aviator Wiley Post called his airplane —the one that he and Will Rogers crashed to their deaths in Alaska in 1935.

We were in the military and had plenty of chances to become aware of our new status. Reveille came before daylight with formations, marching, physical exercises, and classes on various naval subjects following each other in rapid order until taps and lights out ended the ordeal for the day. We were in quarantine: This meant no booze, no dates, no liberty trips into St. Louis, and very little free time.

Among the new skills of a military nature that we had to develop were sending and receiving messages by signal flags and by telegraph in Morse code. To learn these procedures required long hours of rote practice and memorization. Telegraphic code practice was particularly dull; it consisted of your sitting in a small

20

booth with a steady stream of dots and dashes coming through earphones while you frantically tried to determine the individual letters and thus the message being sent. As certain levels of proficiency had to be attained, these practices continued for as long as it took to "qualify." It took me months to pass.

Flight training at Robertson was a short, compact ten hours of dual-instruction hops leading to a one-hour solo flight checkout. Flying was done from Lambert Field in the freezing cold of an open-cockpit Stearman N3N biplane nicknamed the *Yellow Peril.* Concentrating on takeoffs, landings, aerobatics, spins, and stalls to recovery, these first flights were for both training and the simple determination of whether a prospective pilot was afraid of flying, or would become ill when doing the aeronautical maneuvers involved. Instructors were ensigns and lieutenants (jg) who enjoyed deliberately trying to make us embryonic aviation cadets airsick by wringing out the planes with every type of violent aerial maneuver known. They were often successful to the extent that men would return to the flight line from a hop with full "barf bags."

A few could not adjust to this new environment and dropped out voluntarily after a few flights, leaving the flying Navy and returning home. As for myself, the rougher my instructor made the flights the better I liked it! I was in my element in the sky and solo came after the minimum number of dual flights. I presented my instructor with the traditional fifth of booze (he liked Ballantine scotch, in the square bottle).

Quarantine lasted four weeks before the Navy turned us loose for liberty in St. Louis. In my personal case, it was just as well because until we got our first naval paycheck at that time, I had no money. As a new group of seamen had arrived for training and needed the facilities and attention we had been getting, it was time for the Navy to move us on for further training in the Naval Air Basic Training Command.

Normally this next assignment would have been no mystery; all seamen from the sixteen national E bases had always collected at Pensacola, Florida, to continue their flight training. However, a new large basic aviation training complex had just opened at Jacksonville, Florida, so there were now two possibilities for our next orders. A majority of us were hoping to be sent to Pensacola— logically, an old, established base had to be better than a new, undeveloped one.

Orders came, and on 8 March 1941 those of us who had no car or other transportation boarded a train for Jacksonville. Excitement ran high, for although we had not received the preferred Pensacola assignment, we were taking another step on the way toward our final goal.

In March 1941, Jacksonville Naval Air Station was not an impressive place. Expert planning and a lot of work were changing a huge tract of sandy land on the banks of the St. Johns River into a major aviation training base, but there was still much to be done. The influx of our group, combined with those from other E bases, created an overload on the instructors and training aircraft available, and we got a big break; we were ordered west across the Florida panhandle to the finest basic flight training base in the world—the cradle of naval aviation at Pensacola.

In Pensacola I was discharged as a seaman and appointed an aviation cadet, USNR. Our group joined others to become flight class 4A-41-PC (166-C). A long hot summer of hard work was ahead; as most of us would receive commissions, wings, and first assignments before the 7 December 1941 day of infamy, we were a war class of destiny.

What motivated us in those days long ago? Max Gregg, from Wilmette, Illinois, an old friend from the flight class just ahead of mine, wrote me shortly before his death in 1986: "Hal, do you sometimes think about 1941 and our striving to earn those Navy wings? That was certainly the goal of our lives at that time, and a worthy one we might add."

Max, old friend, you said it all—we just wanted wings of gold!

V

In April 1941, Pensacola Naval Air Station possessed a charm and dignity that came from age and permanence. From its imposing main gate entrance, to the brick hangars along the bay front, this base exuded a pride peculiar to naval aviation. It was a complete base, with distinctive officer housing on the hill overlooking Chevalier Field, a large overhaul and repair facility, a beautiful beach and officers club (with tennis courts), and a large naval hospital of high quality. There was even an eighteen-hole golf course of regulation size. A new aeronautical ground school complex had just been completed with auditorium, movie house, armory, and classrooms equal to the finest college or university in the country. Compared to the wooden frame buildings and blowing sand of the new Jacksonville Naval Air Station, we newly designated aviation cadets agreed that we had arrived in paradise for our flight training.

After we were assigned to cadet quarters and we got clothing and other gear, our indoctrination training began in earnest. For a period of two weeks, as new cadets, we did not fly or attend aeronautical ground school. This time was spent removing our last civilian characteristics and filling us with information about the naval service. Classes were held daily in seamanship, naval command and procedures, naval courts and boards, fundamentals of the naval service, and military drill, and radio code practice continued. These two weeks completed our development from ex–college men into naval aviation cadets.

One particular event that occurred during this indoctrination period has remained in my memory. Our entire class of about 150 cadets was seated in the auditorium for a lecture. The young naval officer speaking wanted to impress upon us the difficulty of the training we were undertaking. He told all of us to look to both our left and right sides, carefully noting the men sitting next to us. Then he said, "By the time you graduate from naval flight training, if you do, one or both of the men alongside you now will be gone." The man on my left that morning was Jack Arnold from Danville, Illinois; on my right was Harry Ball from Columbia, Missouri. Jack Arnold washed out within a few weeks, and Harry Ball transferred to the nonflying surface Navy after having flight difficulties.

Upon completion of the indoctrination period, ground school began and filled all our working hours for the next six weeks. The syllabus was designed to give each cadet a basic knowledge of the major technical requirements of his new aeronautical profession within a background of naval methods and procedures. We covered four main subdivisions—aircraft engines, navigation, aircraft structures, and communications. Navigation included both celestial and plotting board dead-reckoning methods. Engines and structures dealt with performance of aircraft under all conditions, and how to get maximum performance from both engines and airframes. Radio code, semaphore, and blinker methods were included in communications. A course in meteorology gave us a working knowledge of weather, clouds, high- and low-pressure areas, and how to read a weather map.

The total of all aeronautical and naval ground school academic hours taken by a cadet during a six-month period was equal to approximately one academic year of college at a level of difficulty equivalent to bachelor's to master's degree requirements in aeronautical engineering. It was a grueling grind, which did not officially end until one was commissioned and designated a naval aviator. While all cadets had at least two years of college, and many were college graduates, some failed to pass the naval aviation academic program and were dropped at that point.

As I began serious training at Pensacola as a newly designated cadet, I became caught up in the tremendous pride and spirit that permeated the naval aviation organization. It was clear that, like marines, this group considered itself an elite group. A famous naval aviator, Adm. John W. Reeves, Jr., put it this way: "Naval aviators, like most specialists, believe that there is something extraordinary about their chosen field. They recognize that this requires of them something above just average in their concept of responsibility and duty."

Where did this concept of dedication, valor, pride, respect, and loyalty that we were being exposed to daily—the idea that naval aviators were the best pilots in the world—get its start? In looking for the answer, I came upon some words written after the war by one of my favorite commanding officers, Rear Adm. Clifford H. "Dutch" Duerfeldt: "Through the efforts of a few dedicated men with great foresight, aviation found a role in the mission of the Navy. From a humble beginning as the eyes of the fleet, naval aviators soon proved their ability and machines as worthy of a front rank position in 20th Century sea power." Dutch was one of those early few who created an organization that continues to grow in prestige to the present time—wearers of the wings of gold are still the best combat aviators flying in the world today.

Personally I had no problems adjusting my life-style and objectives to comply with the high standards of naval aviation being presented to us at Pensacola that summer of 1941. I do not mean that I understood all of it, or that I agreed with some of the trivial rules and regulations directed by a few petty tyrants who were now a part of our daily existence. I had few difficulties because I wanted those wings, and would do anything within reason to attain them.

VI

My flight training at Pensacola started with primary land planes Squadron One, which was divided into three units, A, B, and C. Assigned to One-C, I began learning the basic flying concepts and techniques that had given the Navy its reputation of producing the finest aviators in the world.

Primary flight training was conducted at Corry and Saufley fields, both located a short distance from the main base. Major fields around Pensacola in those days were named after past naval aviators who had died accidentally while flying with the fleet, or had made an important contribution to naval aviation, or both. Saufley Field was named for Lt. Richard C. Saufley, USN, Naval Aviator #14, who set early records in both altitude and endurance flights with Curtiss pusher-type seaplanes; he was killed in an accident in 1916. In addition to these two major training fields, several smaller outlying fields were used for practicing simulated emergencies and landings to a circle. They had strange names— Bell's Farm, Clearing X, Clay Pits, Site Four—and each had its own involved maze of course rules, landing patterns, and hidden hazards.

After checking out as safe for solo, each pilot began working toward his first real hurdle—the twenty-hour check. This first major check tested a cadet's abilities to handle an airplane in emergencies—stalls, spins, recoveries, and simulated emergency landings. These landings required the pilot to hit a circle marked on the ground (it looked about the size of a dime) with engine power cut back to idle in a simulated dead-engine emergency. Fortunately for all of us potential naval aviators, we were flying the Stearman N3N or N2S trainer biplane we had first met at E base. With open fore and aft cockpits, a frame of rugged construction, and a reliable radial engine, the *Yellow Peril* was forgiving of errors.

Our instructors were mostly ensigns, lieutenants (jg), and an occasional lieutenant, who varied greatly in their abilities and dispositions. But they had one thing in common: the flight curriculum was exact in every detail and they insisted it be followed to the letter the Navy way. Thus while instructors might vary in their abilities to teach cadets to fly, the methods and routines of flying the Navy way did not, and a consistency of purpose resulted.

There were also godlike individuals called check pilots. Some of these were known to cadets as Santa Clauses because they had feelings, realized we neophyte aviators were only human, and often gave an up check to a marginal cadet (in other words, passed him) providing he did not do anything particularly dangerous to himself or others while flying a check flight. Cadets were known to state in reverence, "God bless the Santa Clauses!"

In most organizations day-to-day gossip is a part of the life of the group. Rumors and gossip were called scuttlebutt in the Navy, and could be harmless, serious, morbid, or humorous. Scuttlebutt stories often became a permanent part of the history surrounding a particular place or person. An example of a typical scuttlebutt story follows:

Probably the greatest Santa Claus in Squadron One was Lieutenant Blank. Recently he was giving a twenty-hour check to a cadet who was a marginal flyer. This cadet had already been given all of the extra board time allowed; a down on this check meant that he had washed out. After finishing all basic air work, they landed at Clay Pits and Blank got out of the airplane. Blank said: "If you hit four out of five dead-stick landings to this circle here, you've got an up." He retired to one side to watch.

The cadet hit the first two circle landings, then missed one, and hit his fourth. On his fifth and last approach, he was high and started to overshoot. In desperation the cadet stalled the N3N about twenty feet in the air and dropped straight down into the circle's center. The aircraft struck the ground in a flat stall attitude; both wheels broke off; the wings and tail buckled; the engine broke away from the firewall; the crash was total strike damage.

All Lieutenant Blank could see was pieces of broken airplane amid a cloud of red clay dust. He ran to the crash, where the dazed cadet was struggling to climb out of the cockpit. With blood streaming from a broken nose, the cadet said to Blank: "Well, sir, at least I hit the circle."

Lieutenant Blank made history that day with his reply: "That's right, boy, and that was our agreement. You just earned an up!"

The opposite of a Santa Claus was a Down Checker. These instructors had reputations for rarely giving even the best cadet pilots an up in twenty-, forty-, or sixty-hour checks. If your name appeared opposite a Down Checker on the schedule blackboard, your friends would give you condolences before you took off for the check ride. Why Down Checkers acted as they did was beyond the understanding of mere cadets. One fact was certain: no cadet ever questioned the decision of a Down Checker and survived.

After a successful twenty-hour check, I moved into the most interesting phase of training in Squadron One-C—acrobatics. With little time to prepare for the next check, we had to learn how to do snap rolls, loops, wing overs, the Immelmann, split-S, and falling leaf. It was not enough to perform these maneuvers safely —they had to be done smoothly and with precision. Again, the Stearman N3N proved to be a plane without peer for limited-experienced cadets. Forgiving and solid, even with rough handling and gross aeronautical errors, the *Yellow Peril* made it almost impossible for a cadet to kill himself unless he hit something—the ground, trees, power lines, or another *Yellow Peril* occupying the same airspace. Cadets could find ways to make all of these very permanent mistakes and thus might leave the program in a box addressed to their next of kin. Bad weather was also a dangerous factor, and the blue-and-white-striped recall flag was often seen when fog or rainstorms came in from the Gulf of Mexico.

A pitifully few hours of solo practice on all maneuvers learned in previous phases brought me to my final check flight in Squadron One. It was a comprehensive one-and-one-half-hour hop, covering everything learned in the squadron—and a personal confrontation with a Down Checker.

On a typical day of flight operations we would arrive at the field by open bus, called a "cattle car," as dawn was breaking. We had already done calisthenics, made up our rooms, had breakfast, and ridden the several miles to the field from our barracks. Leaving this transportation, each cadet hurried to an assigned hangar area to see when he was scheduled to fly. Flights were listed by time, name of pilot, aircraft number, and type of flight on large portable blackboards in the hangars. If it was a dual-instruction or check flight, the assigned instructor's name was also listed. If the weather was good, first flights would take off at daylight.

On a beautiful June morning I was approaching the hangar to look at the schedule board for my final check listing, when a fellow cadet came running up to me, concern clearly showing on his face:

"Hal, I've just seen the schedule board. You are assigned Lieutenant (jg) Downer [a pseudonym] for your final check. What a tough break!"

Fate had dealt me the most notorious Down Checker in Squadron One. Soon other cadet friends were gathering around me to offer their advice and express concern for my situation. One suggested that I should leave the hangar area immediately for sick call, as if stricken with a sudden illness. The emergency was real —Downer had a solid string of downs going back so far that no one could remember when he had last given an up. To use a cadet expression, I was a dead gosling.

With my heart in my boots, I prepared myself for flight and waited, my parachute at my feet, at the assigned N3N airplane. Short and stocky, with a perpetual half-sneer on his pockmarked face, Lieutenant (jg) Downer strode up, threw his parachute into the front cockpit, and began a preflight inspection of the assigned plane. I saluted him and said "Good morning," which he ignored.

Without a word we both climbed into the cockpits, the engine was started, and we taxied away with Downer at the controls. As we left the parking apron, the silence was broken by his harsh voice booming into my ears through the gosport telling me to man the controls and take off. A gosport was a one-way form of communication in which the cadet received his orders and instructions from the front cockpit through his earphones, with no way to comment in return. With Downer's voice droning in my ears, often to a point of near hysteria, I flew as best I could for more than one hour of sheer hell. Before even allowing me to finish the flight with the traditional precision landings to the circle, Downer took over the controls, returned to Saufley Field, and landed.

I was both hurt and angry as we taxied up to the chocks. What right did this man have to treat me or any other cadet in this way? After we had descended from the airplane to the apron, Downer turned to me and in a loud voice said:

"Buell, I don't have to tell you that you have just flown a down —I'm sure you know it. I thought when I read your flight-training jacket that you were some kind of hot pilot, but you just flew one of the worst check rides that I have ever had. I hope you enjoy meeting the hearing board and that they decide to give you extra time—you need it."

I was crushed. I made no reply to this outburst, but remaining silent took all of the restraint that I could muster. I realized that one wrong word might find me facing more serious charges than flying a down. As I glanced around the area, I noticed an unusually large number of cadets were standing around taking in the scene, including several of my friends. Something must be up, but what?

The lieutenant had turned away from me, and was moving around the starboard wing of the airplane, when he was confronted by the CO (commanding officer) of Squadron One-C. The commander had years of carrier experience in the fleet, flying both dive-bombers and fighters, and was highly regarded by both officer-instructors and cadets. He was Downer's commanding officer and evaluator.

In a voice dripping with sarcasm he said: "Well, Mr. Downer, I presume that Cadet Buell just flew a down for you, is that right?"

The lieutenant's mouth fell open in surprise, and he was visibly shaken by the unexpected appearance of his CO on the flight line. "Yes, sir, he flew a down—just wasn't his day I guess." He tried to smile, but the piercing stare of the CO froze his expression into its usual half-sneer.

Coldly the commander spoke again: "I intend to check this cadet's flying abilities myself. When I return we will discuss this matter in my office. Please do not put any write-up into Cadet Buell's jacket of record until we have had our discussion, is that clear?"

Downer's face had turned crimson during this short exchange. He had come to attention during the remarks; he gave a short "Yes, sir," saluted, and walked away toward the hangar offices.

The CO now approached where I was standing by the side of the airplane. Disheveled, my flight suit covered with perspiration, I came to attention in a cadet brace.

He smiled and spoke: "Cadet Buell, how would you like to take another check ride with me? I realize that you have just finished a grueling flight—do you think you can handle another check ride now?"

"I would appreciate the chance to fly another check, sir."

"Fine. Go get yourself a coke while the line crew gas this plane for us. We will leave in fifteen minutes."

The commander moved off the apron. I was immediately surrounded by cadet friends, who slapped me on the back and pumped my hand, expressing their congratulations for my good luck. That magical circuit, scuttlebutt, had spread the word about the CO being on the flight line waiting for Downer, and explained the large number of cadets present for the showdown.

My second check ride was probably the best flying under stress that I did during my entire naval flight-training program in the summer of 1941. The CO had the ability to get maximum performance from a cadet without causing a high level of anxiety during the check. After shooting five perfect landings to the circle at Bell's Farm, with him watching from the edge of the field, I taxied up for pickup. Over the engine's idle roar, I heard him tell me to move into the front cockpit, while he settled himself into the back one. Then he said the magic words: "It has been a fine check ride, Cadet Buell. Take me home."

Almost in a daze, I flew us back to Saufley Field. As we taxied up to the chocks, the fact that I was in the front cockpit told everyone I had passed my final check in One-C. Check pilots traditionally had the cadet fly from the front on this last hop. The commander added to the festive (for me) occasion by grinning broadly as he held aloft his gloved hand with the thumb extended upright in the standard signal of an up ride.

There are certain events in life that the human mind remembers acutely, and deliberately, and with satisfaction. My second check ride that day in June 1941 is right up there with first solo, first carrier landing, first combat mission, and first bomb hit among the fondest remembrances of my naval flying career. Like the newspaper editor told Virginia long ago—there really is a Santa Claus!

VII

A night-flying checkout with an instructor was my final flight in Squadron One. Class 4A-41-PC began its second phase of flight training in the appropriately named Squadron Two. Here cadets were introduced to both service-type aircraft and their fleet mission uses.

Squadron Two was based at Chevalier Field, the main field at Pensacola Naval Air Station. This field was named in honor of Lt. Comdr. Godfrey de C. Chevalier, USN, Naval Aviator #7; as an ensign he was one of the first three flying officers assigned to Pensacola when it became an air station in 1914. He also made a place for himself in naval aviation history when, on 22 October 1922, he became the first naval officer and aviator to land an aircraft aboard America's first carrier, the *Langley*.

Squadron Two's flight program continued the naval flight-training principle of precision flying requiring judgment, coolness, and decision-making from the pilot at all times. Flying in the fleet was based on perfect formation work as second nature, so this squadron stressed development of a good formation flyer. Tricky flight work in three-, six-, and nine-plane units, with crossovers, vees, and echelons occupied many hours of training time in the air.

One major point regarding formation flying was stressed continually: any mistake leading to a midair collision was likely to be the last one made by either the sinner or his victim. While parachutes might be useful, midair collisions often killed pilots upon initial impact—thus no bailout. The only answer was perfection: fly formation so that you never hit another aircraft in flight.

Up to this point in our training, all flights had been made in the Stearman N3N and N2S biplane trainers. Squadron Two aircraft were O3Us and SBBUs, which were ex-fleet aircraft, heavier and with larger power plants for propulsion. To fly these service aircraft a cadet had to use a number of new engine controls and instruments—variable-pitch propeller, mixture control, manifold pressure, cylinder head temperature, and RPM gauges, to name only a few. These controls and instruments became a part of his increasing flying knowledge and, used with takeoff and landing checkoff lists, a part of his precision approach to flying. Precision became the watchword in both preparation for flight and the actual flight itself.

For the cadets, the most important thing about Squadron Two activities, other than flying, was being selected for a fleet-type assignment. By the time a cadet reached this stage of training, he had certain facts about the three types of fleet naval aviator billets: a carrier-type (VC) squadron assignment was the most coveted, followed by multiengine seaplane or transport (VP) and battleship/cruiser seaplane (VO-VS) assignments.

There was one other type of assignment that no red-blooded naval aviation cadet would allow himself even to think about. Due to the expanding naval air-training program in 1941, some new ensign aviators were being assigned to shore duty as basic instructors. Cadets derisively called these officers "plowbacks." Except for a few nonaggressive types, most cadets considered instructor duty the equivalent of a death sentence, to be shunned at any cost.

No one, not even scuttlebutt experts, had any valid ideas how the Navy made these important selections. Obviously the needs of the service at that particular time must have had a big impact upon selections. Cadets also wanted to believe that their indicated preferences had some effect. As we were less than halfway through the total flight program, we really couldn't be selected for a particular fleet-type assignment on the basis of our ability to fly the type of aircraft or mission required, since none of us had reached that level of expertise. The logical conclusion was that these assignments, like many other military decisions, were in the hands of fate—a power far greater than that of mere mortal naval aviation cadets.

I had been in Squadron Two for more than two weeks when the selections were revealed. On the bulletin board were posted the names of Flight Class 4A-41-PC cadets in alphabetical order, followed by their assignments: Cadet Harold L. Buell was assigned to VC! Thanks to my guardian angel, and other powers beyond my comprehension, I had been selected for carrier-type training. It was the only choice I had ever allowed myself to think about since enlisting back in St. Louis on that cold, snowy January day. Many cadet friends also received VC assignments, among them Dave Chaffee, Bob Gibson, Ed Kinzer, Herbert Shonk, and John Wesolowski. Little did we imagine that in less than one year, on the other side of the world in the South Pacific, we would be fighting for our country, and our lives, in aircraft carriers like *Lexington, Yorktown, Enterprise, Hornet, Saratoga,* and *Wasp,* and from a jungle island called Guadalcanal.

Several changes occurred in Squadron Two that made life more livable for us lowly cadets. As survivors of Squadron One, we were considered a step above the new recruits arriving each month, and we wore a small two-bar insignia over our left shirt pockets to indicate this status. We were allowed overnight liberty on Saturday night, which meant we could go to exotic places like Mobile, or to Tallahassee to attend dances held by the sororities at the women's college there. Our living quarters were less crowded, with two-man rooms equipped with individual beds, desks, lockers, and closets. Flying began taking precedence over ground school, and one could feel a slight easing of pressures from battalion officers; although still cadets, we were beginning to receive small doses of officerlike treatment from the mighty naval establishment.

As we proceeded through Squadron Two, all of us who had received VC assignments began to anticipate leaving Pensacola for final training in carrier-type aircraft at Miami Naval Air Station in Opa-Locka. Before that wonderful day, we had one last hurdle to clear—instrument flying in Squadron Three, using the SNJ single-wing trainer. This required flying in the rear cockpit by instruments, completely hooded, with the instructor as safety pilot in the front cockpit.

I came closer to real trouble during this phase than at any time in my entire naval flight-training program. While I never received a down, and thus kept my training record clear, I disliked instrument flying from the start, and that affected my performance.

There were two reasons for this. First was the hours we had to spend in the Link trainer. The "black box" was nothing short of a torture device in those early days of its development. Although roughly shaped like a small airplane, the *Iron Maiden* was really a mechanical sweat box, and nothing remotely like a real airplane at all except for the instruments on its panel. I knew that it wasn't an airplane, but simply a ground device in which to learn radio beam flying procedures. But as soon as the lid was closed on me, and a radio problem started, I found myself trying to fly the box by feel like an airplane. This invariably led to overcontrol and the resulting errors which the table recorder showed on its course tracings. I learned to fly the box mechanically in order to complete this training phase, but I never liked what was required of me. I found out later that the more natural-reflex feel a pilot had for an aircraft's controls (a God-given talent very valuable to a combat fighter or dive-bomber pilot), the more trouble he had flying the black box with no control feel.

The second reason I disliked instrument flight training was the feeling of claustrophobia that I would get while under a hood in an airplane, or closed up in a Link trainer. I am one of those people who don't like small, tight places, or being jammed up in a crowd. Night flying or actual instrument conditions never bothered me; the imitation environment of hooded flying and the black box did.

However, I learned a considerable amount of self-discipline during my instrument training in Squadron Three. Some of the basic procedures—needle, ball, airspeed, and flying the beam—would save my life more than once in later years. But I never went under a hood or into a Link during my entire flying career unless required by regulations after a layoff from flying. I flew under all conditions and kept my instrument capabilities sharp by actually using them, rather than just by practicing them.

The morning that the instrument check pilot, a Marine first lieutenant, popped the hood open over Mobile range station, and I looked out to see the plane in position for landing, was a red-letter day. It was my last check ride at Pensacola and one of the most satisfying. That night I allowed myself an extra shot of Old Grand-dad at Mustin Beach, went back to the cadet barracks, and packed my gear for Opa-Locka.

VIII

Miami Naval Air Station was located at Opa-Locka Field, north-west of the city, an area of sand, scrub brush, and rattlesnakes under a blazing tropical sun. It consisted of two beautiful new fields, one for planes taking off and one for those landing. Here I was to go through my last stage of naval flight training before receiving the coveted wings of gold, a commission as ensign, USNR, and orders to a fleet carrier squadron. I would receive advanced training in gunnery, dive-bombing, fighter tactics, aerial navigation, and fleet-type formation flying. The aircraft used here were older fleet-type models that had been replaced by newer craft, and the instructors were mostly veteran fleet pilots doing a tour of shore duty.

This final stage of training was even more ruthless and profes-sional than intermediate training had been at Pensacola's Chevalier Field. A cadet could leave Opa-Locka in one of three ways: in a coffin, washed out and disgraced because finally he lacked the right stuff or commissioned with wings and operational orders. This was the place where a hot cadet pilot could become an even hotter naval aviator, where final selections for the first team were made, where for the last time men were separated from boys.

Several well-known naval aviation characters, all academy-trained regular-navy officers, were the backbone of the Advanced Training Command program at Opa-Locka. Holding the rank of Navy lieutenant or Marine captain, this group of hard-flying pilots was the epitome of what was regarded as everything that a fleet or marine pilot should be. There was Joseph "Jumping Joe" Clifton, who taught fighter gunnery; J. T. "Tommy" Blackburn, who was an expert in fighter tactics; and H. P. "Bags" Bagdanovich, chief flight instructor and considered to be a dive-bombing expert. Commanding officer of the entire operation was Comdr. G. F. Bogan, a long-time fleet pilot and aircraft carrier commander; executive officer was Comdr. A. O. Rule. Men like these set the tone and character of the final training that each Navy and Marine fighter, dive-bomber, and torpedo bomber cadet received prior to getting wings, and they had a tremendous influence in forming attitudes that would soon be tested by combat.

The flying equipment at Opa-Locka may have been old fleet types to the pros but they were all we cadets could handle and then some. Several of the fighters, such as the Grumman F2F, F3F, and Brewster Buffalo F2A were really fun to fly. These were the last of the Navy biplane fighters and possessed all of the wonderful flying characteristics of a high-powered biplane for doing acrobatics and dogfight maneuvers. Their twin 50-caliber guns, firing through the propeller, were relatively easy to control—even the neophyte fighter pilot found that he could get some hits on a towed target sleeve.

After getting thoroughly checked out in these heavier aircraft we began using them as weapons for the first time. The F2F introduced us to both dive-bombing and gunnery. What an airplane! As we took off and started to retract the wheels by hand-cranking them, the airplane would weave and bob about like a punch-drunk boxer. Flying the F2F, and later its replacement F3F, while fun, had a serious intent—we were learning to use an airplane to kill or injure someone other than ourselves.

During our acrobatics phase in Squadron One at Pensacola, we had been taught a maneuver called the split-S. To do this particular stunt, the pilot simply rolled the aircraft over on its back and then let the nose fall toward the ground, giving it some assistance with back pressure on the stick. The result was a long swooping dive toward the ground at almost any angle that the pilot wanted to allow his plane to dive. Obviously one did not let the dive continue too far, and provided ample room to pull out safely.

As a start to dive-bombing, we were taken out to a target area in the nearby Everglades. The target was a large bull's-eye outlined in a small clearing in the swamp. It had a solid white center and an outside ring also in white. Our instructions were to line up with the target at an altitude of eight thousand feet on a course heading, fly over the target, and at the right time do a split-S. Then plunging down on the target, you were to use your sight for aiming and trigger off a small practice bomb, which would explode with a puff of smoke when it struck the ground. If everything went as planned it was a beautiful maneuver, and the bomb would strike inside the bull's-eye, sometimes right in the solid white center.

For the novice, this relatively simple exercise could be fraught with dangerous problems. Almost anyone could get a split-S dive started, but finding the target, controlling the plunge, and avoiding the ground on pullout were more difficult aspects to be mastered. Some pilots never got their plane under control in the dive: the result was a wild ride with the pilot hanging from the seatbelt, a gut-wrenching pullout with moments of blackout, and a smoke bomb tossed almost anywhere—even into a Seminole Indian village miles from the target.

After a couple of wild rides almost out of control, I sat down with one of the instructors to "get the word." I was not content simply to get by in this stage of training—I wanted to hit the target and, if I didn't, I wanted to know why not.

I do not recall by name the instructor who took the time to help me, but I do remember several of his hints. He stressed the importance of *flying* the plane in the dive—being in control—and especially of avoiding a skid, as this determined where the bomb hit relative to your aim. Do as much as you could before diving—set the power, all flaps and tabs, RPMs—get everything done before the plunge began. And never go too low, thinking that you could get a better hit—striking the ground while pulling out of a dive was a permanent error.

In addition to these helpful hints, I figured out a couple of procedures for myself that made my efforts at dive-bombing a success. I noted that if I moved my initial path over the target (at altitude) a little to the right, thus keeping the target in sight under my port wing, I could start the dive in more of a high wingover than a split-S, thus getting into the dive under better control. I was beginning to realize that a dive could be ruined by an improper start at altitude even before getting into the actual plunge. This technique, combined with a steady seventy-degree dive, not too steep or too shallow, helped me start to get hits on each practice hop.

Probably the most important concept of dive-bombing that I determined for myself was that of firing a bomb like a bullet rather than dropping it like a bomb. As I dove, I began thinking of my plane as a large rifle or cannon, with my sight the same as one on a regular gun. At the instant of release, I visualized my bomb as a bullet leaving the muzzle, moving at the velocity of my dive, and speeding to the target exactly as a bullet does when fired. With this concept it became easy to select a point of aim where a missile should and would hit. One quit thinking of a bomb dropping on a target—instead it was a bullet fired at a target. As simple as this concept was, I never heard anyone talk about firing bombs—only about dropping them. It would be years before, with my own division of planes trained in the idea, I would be able to prove it in combat by sinking ships, especially when they were under way, at a higher rate than ever before.

I did well in the dive-bombing phase at Opa-Locka. I have no idea if this talent got me assigned to a scout-bombing squadron or not, as I also did reasonably well in the fighter phase, getting my share of the gunnery hits on a towed sleeve, and showing the right stuff in the simulated dogfights with fellow cadets and instructors. I do know that when fleet orders arrived, mine were to Scouting Squadron Seventy-one, a scout dive-bomber outfit in *Wasp,* and I was not unhappy with the assignment. This purely chance assignment to dive-bombers, rather than fighters or torpeckers (torpedo bombers), made it possible for me to make a greater combat contribution in the coming war than I would have in either of the other types of assignments.

The flying at Opa-Locka was so much fun and our status as advanced naval aviation cadets about to get both wings and commissions was so officerlike, I found myself almost wishing that the idyllic days would never end. The officers' club was still under construction that summer, but that was not a problem. The Hollywood Beach Hotel, a short distance away on the ocean, set up a special club for us that provided cheap drinks, access to their many facilities, and all kinds of special events and parties that kept us busy every weekend. In addition, we would receive invitations to attend private parties, dances, and outings of all kinds. The Miss

Florida contest was held at the hotel that fall and several of us acted as escorts to the contestants—very good duty indeed!

The important ingredients in a naval aviation cadet's existence were his flying, his recreation, especially drinking, and his luck and ability with the girls. The combination of superior weather, exciting aircraft, and challenging tactical flying made our work as much fun as our play. With plenty of places to drink and dance, and beautiful girls all around, Opa-Locka was almost perfect from a cadet's point of view.

IX

Almost as an anticlimax, the great day finally arrived. Graduation exercises were simple and to the point. Each Saturday morning the cadets who had completed their final flights gathered at the administration building. As I recall, there were about two dozen in my group on 1 November 1941. Each of us had been given a pair of ensign shoulder boards and a set of shiny new gold wings. Helping one another, we removed our cadet boards, put the ensign boards on the shoulders of our whites, and pinned the wings over our left breast pocket. My helper that morning was my roommate, Johnny Lough from Geneseo, Illinois.

After that was done, we stood in an informal group at attention, raised our right hands, and repeated the oath of allegiance before the commanding officer, Commander Bogan. We then exchanged congratulations and handshakes all around before moving into the personnel office for our papers. Our new commissions, aviator designators, and orders delivered, we were officially logged out and free to depart on a fifteen-day leave, plus travel time, before reporting to our new duty assignments. The great ordeal was over.

As Johnny and I strode away from the administration building we took part in one last traditional act. Each of us had procured a silver dollar specifically for this event—our first salute. A young seaman standing by the sidewalk moved forward, came to attention, and saluted me. It was my first official salute as an officer in the Navy. I returned the accolade, tossed him the silver dollar, which he deftly caught, and we shook hands.

3

ODYSSEY

I

WITH SHINY new wings of gold on my chest, ensign bands of gold on my sleeves, and a set of flight orders to Scouting Squadron Seventy-one (VS-71), a scout dive-bomber squadron based in the aircraft carrier *Wasp*, I departed Miami Naval Air Station for a fifteen-day leave before reporting to Norfolk, Virginia, home port of the ship. I had just been commissioned Ensign Buell, A-V (N), USNR, Serial Number 0104297, and designated Naval Aviator (Heavier-than-Air) Number 9095. These twin achievements had come after approximately ten months of intensive work and discipline, three days before my twenty-second birthday, and thirty-six days before the 7 December 1941 attack on Pearl Harbor by the Japanese Navy. With sea duty orders I was going to be able to follow the advice given me by one of my instructors at a farewell party. Lt. Tommy Blackburn said to me with a grin: "Hal, your new wings are no good until you get some salt on 'em!" The date was 1 November 1941.

Accompanying me north from Opa-Locka on U.S. Route 27 the next afternoon was another new ensign-aviator, Johnny Lough from Geneseo, Illinois. Roommates and close friends during our final advanced flight training, we departed in a gray 1936 Dodge convertible roadster, which I had just bought a few days before for $250 cash. This car represented the largest purchase of my depression-ridden life, and was made possible by an advance on my Navy pay, some cadet pay savings, and my cash uniform allowance. Loaded with all our worldly goods, Johnny and I had nonstop objectives of his farm home just east of Geneseo and my home in Ottumwa, for reunions with our parents, relatives, and friends. We would divide the cost of gasoline and driving shifts between us.

John Lough and I came from similar backgrounds that had a lot in common. We were midwesterners from small-town, rural, frugal, religious (WASP) upbringing. We both attended local colleges —Illinois Wesleyan and Parsons College. Lough was a small- to medium-sized man, about five foot eight inches and 145 pounds, darkly handsome with straight black hair and heavy eyebrows. A quiet man, his face was serious yet serene, and he seldom smiled or showed any emotion even to his friends. His voice, like his demeanor, was low and calm, and he listened much more than he talked. We became as close as two brothers, and I would grieve his loss at Midway as if I had lost a member of my own family.

Rolling along in the Dodge, we were ecstatic as we savored our first real freedom from the flight-training grind of almost a year. Gone for the moment were fears of engine failure, midair collision, structural failure, high-speed stall, fire in flight, stall during landing approach, bad weather—all of the multitude of things, both simple and complex, that could go wrong and kill one while flying high-performance military aircraft.

I still remember details about that trip with Johnny Lough as we returned to the midwestern farmlands of our origins. We alternated driving over the sometimes almost impassable roads, stopping only to refuel, to use a bathroom, or to have an occasional sandwich and cup of coffee. We bypassed Atlanta to the west, struggled over Lookout Mountain in the dark, and, after driving all night, rolled into Chattanooga at dawn's first light. Spotting a small cafe advertising home cooking, we stopped for our first real meal since Miami—and what a meal it was! Eggs, sausage patties, hotcakes, grits, biscuits, and honey, with both milk and hot coffee —all we could eat—while a steady stream of nickels kept Glenn Miller's "Chattanooga Choo Choo" blaring from the jukebox into our eager eardrums. The large motherly proprietress of the cafe let us use the men's room to shave and wash up, and we left refreshed and ready to proceed.

Some time later we crossed the Ohio River and moved onto the flat, rolling prairies of mid-America. As it was November, and we were moving north and west, the ride became colder. The wind was picking up and we were heading into it, the wind chill factor bringing the temperature below freezing. We finally pulled off the highway, dug out the new sheepskin-lined leather flight gear we had been issued at Opa-Locka, and resumed our trip wearing leather flight jackets, gloves, and flying boots. We got more wear out of our winter flight gear on this leave trip than during the entire war in the South Pacific.

It was dark and more than thirty hours after we left Miami when we pulled into the farmyard of the Lough home. By steady nonstop driving we had averaged over forty miles per hour. Johnny's mom was ready for us with a supper fit for kings. Fortified with this home-cooked feast, including cookies and apples to take with me, I headed west alone, crossed the Mississippi River at Rock Island–Davenport, and arrived at the McElderry homestead about 0200 on 4 November 1941.

It was my twenty-second birthday and I had been gone ten months. During that period I had matured more than in any previous time of my life. While some of this change was physical as reflected by an almost ramrod straight posture and carriage, a lean muscular body with reflexes honed to perfection, and crisp new tailored Navy uniforms, the greater changes were mental, unseen and unspoken, but felt deeply.

I had just finished naval flight training and not been found wanting. I was now a member of that close-knit fraternal group known as naval aviators and, with orders to an aircraft carrier, was about to join that most elite of all naval pilot groups—the tailhookers. I had been trained by the Navy to be ready for a showdown with our enemies—many felt that action was coming very soon. As Tom Wolfe said in *The Right Stuff*, all the wealth in the world could not buy men to take the place of those who had the uncritical willingness to face danger, those who, in short, had the right stuff. By earning the golden wings I had now joined that group.

I split my leave time between visits to the Dixsons' home at Plymouth and runs over to the Parsons College campus and

Rody's Manse at Fairfield. At Plymouth my old working buddy, a mechanic named Sparky, tore down the engine of the Dodge and gave it a complete repair job. When he finished he advised me to trade the car for a later model as soon as I got to Norfolk as the previous owner had apparently put many more miles on it than showed on the odometer. He had it in as good a shape as possible but what was really needed was a complete engine change.

When my leave ended I picked up Lough at his home, and we headed east for the Norfolk Naval Base and reported to the commander of the Advanced Carrier Training Group (ACTG) for temporary duty involving flying under training until our carriers and squadrons arrived from sea. (There were two ACTGs in the Navy at that time—one at Norfolk and the other at San Diego.) We flew, had some drinks, played, and waited for our squadrons to come home.

II

7 December 1941.

To the American people, it was the day that Japanese aircraft attacked Pearl Harbor and started, for them, World War II.

To the Japanese people, it was the day their glorious Navy struck a devastating blow against the hated Yankee fleet—a force standing in the way of their expanding Greater East Asia Co-Prosperity Sphere; it was a strike for the freedom of all Asians.

To President Franklin D. Roosevelt, it was a date that would live in infamy.

To 1,123 crewmen aboard *Arizona,* an American battleship at anchor near Ford Island, it was the last day of their lives.

To the Japanese Navy, under the command of Adm. Isoroku Yamamoto, it was the day his Plan Z, representing more than one year of training efforts, was realized.

And to the U.S. Navy, under the command of Vice Adm. Husband E. Kimmel, Pacific Fleet Commander, it was the day of the greatest disaster ever inflicted upon a U.S. fleet—and the end of his distinguished career.

One can see that the attack on Pearl Harbor by the Japanese First Air Fleet had varied meanings to its many participants. Historically it was a unique battle—the first large-scale use of carrier task force aircraft as a weapon against a target. The air attack caught the U.S. military forces completely by surprise at the very time that diplomatic discussions were being conducted in Washington, D.C., between the two protagonists.

Using 353 carrier-based fighter, dive-bomber, and torpedo bomber aircraft from six aircraft carriers, Japanese pilots attacked in two flights of 183 and 170 planes each. Targets were in three categories—aircraft in the air and on the ground, ships in the harbor, and facilities at the airfields. At a cost of twenty-nine aircraft and fifty-five aircrewmen, the Japanese aviators sank the battleships *Arizona, California, Oklahoma, Nevada,* and *West Virginia,* three destroyers, and the target ship *Utah.* Heavily damaged were the battleships *Maryland, Pennsylvania,* and *Tennessee* and the cruisers *Helena, Raleigh,* and *Honolulu,* plus the seaplane tender *Curtis.* It would take a year of repair before any of the heavier ships would go back to sea. Approximately three hundred Army, Navy, and Marine aircraft were destroyed, most of them on the ground. The Japanese air strikes set afire and demolished hangars, storage shops, warehouses, barracks, piers, munitions dumps, and other valuable installations. They killed 2,844 and wounded 1,178 members of the U.S. military forces, as well as numerous civilians. Fortunately, submarines and fuel storage farms were spared.[1]

The Pearl Harbor attack was a disaster to the U.S. Navy, yet like many historical events it was also a blessing in disguise. While the assault knocked out a major part of the Pacific Fleet, it did not knock out the United States. On the contrary, it united the American people as nothing else could have done; they forgot about isolationism and dedicated all their resources and energies to war. No U.S. aircraft carriers were lost simply because none were in port at the time of the attack. With heavy losses of battleships, the Navy was left with only its carrier forces afloat for either offensive or defensive actions. A dramatically new and effective naval air weapons system, the carrier task force, had entered the naval warfare scene.

III

The Japanese attack on Pearl Harbor was more shock than surprise to the young naval aviators of the ACTG at Norfolk. The ease with which Japan's naval flyers had destroyed much of the battleship component of the Pacific Fleet was a bitter blow to our pride. There was a sense of relief that none of the aircraft carriers had been in port and thus had missed destruction, but why had naval aviation been of no apparent consequence in the battle? The stories we were getting talked of total destruction by the Japanese pilots of all Navy and Army Air Corps aircraft at all of the fields in the islands. Such a complete success, even though a sneak attack without warning, made the Japanese flyers look like supermen and their aircraft indestructible.

Our group had been expecting a declaration of war for some time, but against a different enemy—the Axis. We had orders to Atlantic Fleet carriers—*Yorktown, Hornet, Wasp,* or *Ranger*— where the enemy was German submarines, with possible clashes against the German Luftwaffe or Italian Air Force if action came in the Mediterranean Sea or English Channel areas.

Thus the Pearl Harbor attack, and President Roosevelt's response, and the declaration of war by Congress did little immediately except to speed up the already ongoing preparations of all ACTG pilots to be ready for their squadron assignments. *Yorktown* came in, stayed briefly for resupply and repair, and departed on reassignment to the Pacific. She took with her new pilots like my friend John "Yogi" Jorgenson, who had orders to her squadrons. For those of us waiting to go aboard *Wasp, Hornet,* and *Ranger,* training was accelerated to prepare us for joining our squadrons when these ships next came into Norfolk from sea. This preparation centered on two main areas of flight operations: field carrier landing practice to enable safe carrier landings, and dive-bombing practice further to develop our abilities to use an airplane as a weapon.

In those days of January 1942 there were three outlying fields running down along the Atlantic Ocean coastline just east of the main naval air station at Breezy Point: Oceana (Virginia Beach), Pungo, and Creeds. Both Oceana and Pungo had short, paved runways, but Creeds was little more than a farm pasture with a pair of bombing targets nearby. Pilots also used a point of marshland known as Troublesome Point as a target for bombing and strafing.

Aircraft assigned to the ACTG for training in dive-bombing and field carrier landing practice were the SBN and SB2U. The former was a scout bomber that had been developed and produced by the Naval Aircraft Factory in Philadelphia from 1938 to 1940. Thirty of these aircraft had been constructed when it was decided to abandon the model as a fleet dive-bomber. The SBN served briefly in *Hornet* before coming to the ACTG as a training plane. It had a rigid single wing, perforated dive and landing flaps, and was powered with a Wright R-1820 engine developing 950 HP (horsepower). One unusual feature of the plane was its landing gear—it was identical to that of an F2A fighter. It also had one tricky flight characteristic—a tendency to stall suddenly and fall off on a wing when power was reduced at the landing touchdown point. To avoid a potential crash on landing, the pilot had to keep power on until the wheels were on the ground. This was not a desirable landing feature for a Navy carrier–type aircraft so the SBN was discontinued as a fleet dive-bomber. Unfortunately, the very experience necessary to handle this airplane safely was lacking in the new ensigns assigned to fly it. Several ground loops and hard landings resulted, including one in which the engine broke away from the airframe and went bouncing down the runway like a huge rubber ball (no one was seriously hurt). However, the SBN was quite reliable in the air and during a dive-bombing run on a target.

The SB2U Vought-Sikorsky scout bomber was the major aircraft made available to me for fleet preparation training at the ACTG. Those of us who were assigned to VS-71 needed as much time in this type as we could get for it was the airplane being used by the squadron. The decision to equip all carrier scouting and bombing squadrons with the Douglas SBD Dauntless had been made and was well underway, but priority for receiving these improved dive-bombers had been given to those squadrons on board carriers in the Pacific. Approximately one hundred SB2Us had been manufactured in 1937 and 1938; it had a standard Pratt and Whitney "Twin Wasp Junior" fourteen-cylinder engine, which developed one thousand HP and up to 235 MPH rated speed; it could carry a one-thousand-pound bomb or two five-hundred-pounders, and a crew of two.

The days passed swiftly in January with a dive-bombing flight in the morning and a field carrier landing practice in the afternoon for a week, then a reverse of the schedule the next week. It was an exciting time, with lots of flying during the week, and parties at Breezy Point Officers Club and Virginia Beach Cavalier Hotel on the weekends.

During these happy days I was driving a sporty new set of wheels. The old 1936 gray Dodge had performed well on the trip from Iowa to Norfolk. But remembering what Sparky had told me about trading it in, I began looking around for another car as soon as I was squared away at the base. I found exactly what I wanted at Bruce-Flournoy Motor Company. It was a 1938 Ford V-8 convertible coupe, robin's-egg blue, with a rumble seat, wire wheels, and low mileage. The asking price was $475. When the salesman, an Irishman named McCarthy, offered me $230 trade-in for the Dodge that had cost me $250 in Miami a month before, it was an offer I couldn't refuse. On 26 November 1941, I made the best car deal of my life—I wish I still had that little blue baby!

Training flights continued, with a little fun thrown in. One of my favorite instructors at the ACTG was Art Decker, a tall, thin, blond lieutenant who really could bomb on the practice range. We would bet drinks, and sometimes a dinner out, on who could get the most hits on a practice hop. A short diary note dated 6 February 1942 brings back a memory: "Dive-bombed Creeds target below Virginia Beach. Scored five hits in five drops with two bull's-eyes. Good for a free steak dinner from Decker." Then on 8 February 1942 is the note: "Qualified on aircraft carrier *Long Island* in Chesapeake Bay off Wolf's Head Point; made three arrested landings without trouble." This latter achievement was sufficient reason for a huge party at the main base officers' club, where all of us newly qualified ensigns, who were waiting for our CVs to come in, organized our own private group called the Norfolk Deck Dodgers.

IV

It took only a week after carrier landing qualifications on the *Long Island* for the Navy to change the destinies of twenty-two Norfolk Deck Dodgers. After morning muster on 16 February 1942, Lt. C. W. Crawford, CO of the ACTG, called all pilots together in the ready room. He had a dispatch in his hand and a serious look on his usually smiling countenance:

"Gentlemen, please give me your careful attention. This dispatch I am about to read to you came during the night."

He then read a BUNAV (Bureau of Naval Aviation) dispatch ordering twenty-two of us to scouting and bombing squadrons based in three major aircraft carriers of the Pacific Fleet. I was the sixth name on the list, assigned to Scouting Squadron Five (VS-5) aboard the USS *Yorktown*.

When Crawford finished reading the dispatch, an excited murmur passed through the assembled pilots. It began dawning upon the group that what they had just heard were orders for twenty-two pilots to proceed immediately and directly to squadrons aboard Pacific carriers, where action against the Japanese carrier fleet was expected at any moment. It was the first such orders from BUNAV since the war's beginning and meant that those selected were the top scout- and bomber-trained pilots available to bring existing fleet squadrons to combat personnel readiness levels. Cheers, shouts, and laughter rang out amid handshaking and backslapping from ACTG instructors, the twenty-two Norfolk Deck Dodgers, and the other pilots.

After a brief time, order was restored and Crawford said:

> This is an important day to us here at the Advanced Carrier Training Group. This dispatch ordering twenty-two of you to combat squadrons in the Pacific is only the first of many that will come here before our enemies are defeated. We have known some of you for only a short time. During that time we all have worked very hard to prepare for the carrier battles that are to come. You have only six days, including today, to get yourselves across the country to the Twelfth Naval District headquarters in San Francisco, California. Each of you is responsible for reporting to those headquarters prior to 1400 this coming Saturday 21 February 1942. I have the entire office force working on your orders so you will be able to check out of here by noon. Good luck to all of you as you depart upon this most serious mission.

Immediately after the meeting I got with Johnny Lough to make plans. We decided to leave as soon as possible in my car for our homes. From there, after farewell meetings with families and close friends, we would catch the train out to California.

Everything was moving at a heady pace. It was not difficult to pack our few belongings at Breezy Point BOQ (bachelor officers' quarters) as we had little but our uniforms and a few personal effects. Once more we drove nonstop; I dropped Lough in Geneseo and continued on to a girlfriend's home in Newton, arriving in the early morning of 18 February 1942.

I would leave my car with the friend and catch the westbound Union Pacific Challenger at Newton. Johnny Lough would already be aboard, having got on the train at Rock Island. This gave each of us approximately twenty-four hours in which to say farewells to loved ones.

The Dixsons came down from Plymouth to see me off to war, and I called my three sisters and the McElderrys at Ottumwa to bid them farewell. These goodbyes were typical of the times—they came on short notice, were extremely emotional, and were often the last time that loved ones would be together in this lifetime—one of the grimmer aspects of war.

V

I climbed aboard Challenger for the two-day trip across the United States covered with lipstick, tears, and perfume. Lough and I were aboard a famous train, following the Union Pacific railroad to the Pacific Ocean on tracks that had been laid in 1867–69. Leaving Omaha, they ran across southern Nebraska, briefly followed the Platte River Basin, and the old Oregon Trail, then along the Wyoming-Colorado border past Cheyenne and Laramie, through the Rocky Mountains to Salt Lake City. We passed the Great Salt Lake, then crossed northern Nevada, paused briefly at Reno, went downhill through the Sierra Nevada Range to Sacramento and finally San Francisco, with its Golden Gate Bridge gleaming in the morning mists.

To an Iowa farm boy going West for the first time the experience was ethereal. The sweeping countryside flowing past the coach windows was barren and snow-covered for the most part, but still beautiful and spectacular in its magnitude. The Rockies were raw and powerful. It was a rewarding trip.

Right on schedule and according to plan we arrived at 0900 on 21 February and went immediately to the Twelfth Naval District headquarters. From there everyone was taken to the dock area, where we loaded our possessions aboard the transport ship *Castor*. We were given that night for a final liberty, which was spent roaming the streets of Chinatown and the Barbary Coast, with drinks in the Persian Room and final toasts to our future at the Top of the Mark overlooking the bay and bridge.

Castor left the dock the next afternoon and anchored in the harbor. We sailed with the tide the morning of 23 February 1942, and passed under the Golden Gate at 1000 heading southwest—one of a six-ship group. On the twenty-fourth we joined five more ships for a convoy total of eleven and continued on a southwesterly heading. Our destination was Pearl Harbor.

This was my first real voyage on a ship at sea. The ship's captain fit us into his officer's watch schedule, and I stood four-hour main-top watches three times during the passage. We became a part of the ship's routine: watches, sleep, meals, cardplaying or reading, and pacing the decks for exercise. About two days out the weather picked up a bit and the *Castor* began rolling and pitching in heavy seas. It was hard to keep our gear secured, and difficult to eat our meals with dishes moving about. Some of the passenger group became victims of mal de mer, and I was pleasantly surprised to find that I had no signs of this common malady.

After eight days at sea, the *Castor* arrived at Pearl Harbor. Although almost three months had passed since the December attack, there were still signs of devastation in the harbor and shore installations. Most depressing were the battleships resting on the harbor bottom with only their masts sticking out of the water. On Ford Island many buildings had sustained bomb damage, and hangars were still being repaired.

Vice Adm. Chester W. Nimitz had relieved Vice Adm. Husband E. Kimmel, the victim of the Japanese sneak attack, on 31 December 1942 in a brief ceremony aboard the submarine *Grayling* moored at the submarine base. Kimmel had emerged from the Pearl Harbor debacle a forlorn figure carrying the blame for the tragedy. One story of the day described Kimmel as he was watching some of the last Japanese attacks upon his exploding ships in the harbor. A spent bullet crashed through his headquarters window, striking him in the chest and leaving a dark red splotch on his white uniform. As he bent down and picked up the .50-caliber machine-gun slug, in sorrow and despair he was heard to say: "It would have been merciful had it killed me."[2]

Nothing much had been accomplished since the change in command. There had been a few hit-and-run raids by our carriers upon Japanese-held island bases, while the Japanese military forces had enjoyed success after success in the South Pacific and Indian Ocean areas. About the time of my arrival on 3 March, Commander in Chief, Pacific (C in C Pac) Nimitz was beginning to feel some concern about how things were progressing in his new assignment; in a letter to his wife Catherine on 22 March he wrote:

I have not seen anything of K. [Ernest J. King] recently so believe he is lying low. I am afraid he is not so keen for me now as he was when I left—but that is only natural. Ever so many people were enthusiastic for me at the start but when things do not move fast enough, they sour on me. I will be lucky to last six months. The public may demand action and results faster than I can produce.[3]

Fortunately for the American people, the United States Navy, and an insignificant young ensign naval aviator named Buell, this great naval leader prevailed; using his limited forces wisely and with consummate skill, he survived and hurt the Japanese Navy at every opportunity. By the end of the first year (1942) he was recognized by both superiors and peers as a sea warfare genius; he never had cause to fear his position in the Navy—or in naval warfare history—again.

Leaving the *Castor* with all gear, I reported to the personnel office of the naval air station, located on Ford Island. I was told to take the rest of the day off, check into the local BOQ, and return for orders the next day. I looked up Bill Branham, my old friend from E base days, who was stationed with a local utility squadron on Ford Island. He gave me a whirlwind tour of downtown Honolulu, Waikiki Beach, and the Royal Hawaiian during the rest of the day and into the night. It was a big day, full of new sights and fun with old friends.

Back at the BOQ at midnight I was too hyped up to sleep. Everything was blacked out, but there was enough light from a waning moon to get about. I walked from my room across a well-kept lawn to a small dock at the water's edge. Out in the water, a stone's throw away, were the twisted, blackened remains of *Arizona*, most of the ship resting on the harbor's bottom. Deep within her bowels were the remains of over one thousand Americans—men who had been her crew. I felt an eerie silence at the sight, like that in a cemetery, broken only by the sound of bubbles of oil still rising to the surface around the sunken dreadnought.

As I thought about how these men had died just a short time before, I found myself saying a quiet prayer for their peaceful rest —it was combined with a deep desire for revenge: "Please God, allow me to be a killer angel, an avenging force, to crush these enemies who so callously took the lives of *Arizona*'s crew. Give me the courage and strength to go all the way down the perilous road stretching ahead of me." I went back to my BOQ bed and a peaceful sleep.

The wise men who decided to make *Arizona* a permanent memorial to our heroic dead of that terrible attack must have been guided by a higher power. Make a pilgrimage: go visit this hallowed place yourself. Then I think you will know what I mean.

VI

The next day, 4 March 1942, I was ordered to Bombing Squadron Three (VB-3) based at Kaneohe Bay across Oahu to the northeast of Honolulu. Under the command of Lt. Comdr. Max Leslie, it was a squadron without a carrier. Its previous home, *Saratoga,* was being repaired in the States for a torpedo hit it took before ever getting into action. They had SBD Dauntlesses, the type of aircraft that all of the Norfolk Deck Dodgers had to get some experience in before reporting to the new squadron assignments we had been given. So I joined several of my old friends on temporary duty for training—Johnny Lough, Bob Edmundson, Spike Conzett, J. D. Bridgers, J. Q. Roberts—in new quarters in the Kaneohe BOQ.

At Kaneohe, the Norfolk Deck Dodgers were together for a final time before separating to go to our various squadron assignments. We soon became aware of the fear bordering on paranoia that still hung over the islands from the Japanese attack of the previous December. We found VB-3 on battle alert, with several aircraft armed and ready for immediate takeoff and attack, twenty-four hours a day. Everyone was on edge, no leave or liberty was being granted, all based upon rumored Japanese fleet movements and daily intelligence reports. An occasional night air raid alarm would get everyone out and into shelters, but after a couple of these false alarms, most of us in the BOQ simply turned over and went back to sleep.

As we checked out in the SBD Dauntless and got a few hours of formation, dive-bombing, and field carrier landing practice under our belts, we went on the squadron duty roster along with the regular squadron pilots. This assignment required staying overnight in a bunkhouse on the airfield near the ready aircraft when on standby pilot status. I have often wondered what would have happened if I had been in the duty section when an actual alert hit. A midnight launch with a bomb to go attack Japanese warships in the darkness might have been more than an inexperienced ensign could have handled at that stage of his flying career.

The days flew by, with one or two hops each day, including lots of dive-bombing and strafing practice. We would take off, fly across Kaiwi Channel east to Molokai, where a target was located on Ilio Point. There were trips to Ford Island for airplane parts and to pick up whiskey rations from the officers' clubs there. We finally started getting liberty in Honolulu, where the favorite overnight place was the Moana Hotel out on the beach.

On 23 March, VB-3 exchanged places with VS-6 in *Enterprise,* as the ship was preparing to go back to sea after a brief stay at Pearl. None of us knew then that the Big E was going out to escort *Hornet* on the famous Doolittle Tokyo raid. VS-6, under the command of Lt. Comdr. Bill Gallaher, became our new temporary home. Here was another fine dive-bomber squadron that had seen considerable action in the first raids against the Japanese bases at Kwajalein, Roi, Wake, and Marcus. Getting to fly with this great outfit on temporary duty let me learn still more about combat tactics.

VB-3 and VS-6 were two of the finest dive-bombing squadrons that flew in World War II. As two of the three squadrons that would destroy four Japanese carriers at Midway in June, both were loaded with great dive-bombing pilots—Leslie, Gallaher, Bottomley, Cobb, Holmberg, Elder, Lane, Pittman, Isaman, McCarthy, Patriarca, Micheel, and Schneider, to name a few. And several of my buddies in the Norfolk Deck Dodgers ended up in these two squadrons, including J. Q. Roberts, Johnny Lough, Ray Miligi, Carl Peiffer, and John Ammen; all of these young ensigns would be lost.

The all too brief four weeks with VS-6 came to an end for several of the Norfolk Deck Dodgers who had not yet left for their squadrons. The order was simple and abrupt: Report to Hickam Field with all personal gear in bags ready for air transportation to wherever the *Yorktown* might be.

VII

Waiting on the parking apron at Hickam Field in the predawn darkness of 24 April 1942 was U.S. Army Air Corps B-17 number 2633, Captain Bullock, pilot, Second Lieutenant Hoff, copilot, and Second Lieutenant D'Angelos, navigator. All gear was loaded and we were airborne by 0700 heading southwest. Approximately eight hours later we landed on a small speck in the Pacific called Christmas Island. After a restless night spent in tents by the runway—our sleep was disturbed by huge land crabs the size of dinner plates scavenging about in the moonlight—we again took off for another speck in the vast Pacific, Canton Island. It was a relatively short flight of five hours. Another restless overnight break before continuing on to Viti Levu, Fiji Islands. Getting from the airfield to the dock area of Suva (the capital) required a short flight over the island mountains in an antiquated, single-engine cabin biplane piloted by an Australian bush pilot. By 1800 on 26 April we reported aboard the destroyer *Sims* for the final leg to a rendezvous with *Yorktown* somewhere in the Coral Sea.

Three days later, 29 April 1942, the dawn was bright and clear in the Coral Sea and a young ensign aviator was nearing the end of his odyssey. Rendezvous was made, and *Yorktown*'s crew brought a motor launch alongside *Sims,* gear and personnel were loaded aboard, and a short, heaving ride to the carrier was completed with little discomfort except some salt spray.

This short ride by motor launch concluded a trip that started more than halfway around the world at Norfolk on 16 February 1942: automobile travel to Iowa; train to San Francisco; transport ship to Oahu, Hawaii; Army Air Corps B-17 to Fiji via Christmas and Canton Islands; a bush-piloted commuter plane to the port of Suva; and naval destroyer and motor launch to the quarterdeck of *Yorktown* in the Coral Sea. I had finally completed a trip of approximately eleven thousand miles to arrive at my first squadron flying assignment just in time to take part in the first carrier-versus-carrier sea battle in the history of naval warfare.

And the happy ship *Sims,* filled with brave American mariners who had brought me to this rendezvous, had only eight more days to live.

4

CORAL SEA

I

AT THE time of my arrival to join Scouting Squadron Five in
Yorktown, the Japanese high command had nearly completed their
first-phase operations. Their naval forces now roamed both the
Pacific and Indian oceans with little opposition, and their army
units held strategic bases throughout the South Pacific. The Japanese called this newly acquired empire the Greater East Asia Co-
Prosperity Sphere.

The area was so vast it almost defied description. Stretching
five thousand miles east, south, and west of the home islands, *Pax
Japonica* included Formosa, the Philippines, Indochina, Thailand,
Burma, Malaya, Sumatra, Borneo, Java, the Celebes, the Kurils,
the Bonins, Ryukyus, Marianas, Carolines, Palaus, Marshalls, Gilberts, northern New Guinea, and most of the Solomons. All of the
coastal cities of China worth having, including Hong Kong, were
occupied and there were also two Alaskan islands within this vast
domain. It was probably the largest combined earth's surface area
—if you included the oceans—ever under one flag, surpassing
Alexander's conquests and the Roman Empire, and rivaling those
of the Great Khans, the Spanish, and the British. The sphere
contained the oil and other raw materials needed by Japan to maintain her new status as a world power, but it would require the

Japanese Navy and Air Force, as well as the Army, to hold the whole package together.

In establishing this new empire, the combined military forces of Japan had suffered relatively minor losses and the Japanese carrier task force, with its aircraft, had emerged as a major sea weapon. Aircraft carrier successes had replaced the prewar concept held by most naval high commands of the battleship, with its big guns, as the backbone of a fleet. While this had not yet disappeared, it was becoming increasingly clear that the idea that surface ships— even heavy cruisers and battleships—could control sea areas without also controlling the air above those areas was a false concept. As the Japanese success at Pearl Harbor had not destroyed a single American carrier, the movement of our CVs into the southwest Pacific was setting the stage at Coral Sea for a clash between these new titans of the seas—a battle that would determine the nature of sea warfare in the Pacific for the remainder of World War II.

II

There was an air of excitement and expectancy among the officers and men of *Yorktown* and VS-5. As I became acquainted with my new shipmates, this fever moved into my thoughts and feelings, too. The scuttlebutt was that a major Japanese carrier task force was also in the Coral Sea, although no one knew just where. Here we were, in company with *Lexington,* heading for our first real challenge of the war. Raids were scheduled against targets with strange names like Tulagi, Gavutu, and Tanambogo. There was a good possibility that our forces might get a crack at the mighty Japanese carrier fleet—those ships that had brought death, destruction, and disgrace to the U.S. Navy on a December Sunday only a few short months before.

My new squadron skipper was Lt. Comdr. William "Bill" Burch, a tall, slim, fair-skinned man with thinning blond hair and piercing, pale blue eyes. He had an intense, yet mild manner and normally talked in a low voice, which would increase in intensity and volume as he became excited. I am sure that he was shocked when he learned of the limited flying experience of the four new ensigns who had come so far to join his squadron for the impending struggle. He immediately decided that he would not fly us unless circumstances made it absolutely necessary, and told us so. My first squadron duties consisted of manning standby planes for respot on deck, engine warmups, and striking below.

This decision was a letdown that my ego found hard to accept. After all, I was a naval aviator and wanted my chance to fight the Japanese, too! My anxiety became more acute when two buddies, Tom Brown and Dave Chaffee, were told by their new VB-5 skipper, Lt. Wally Short, that they would fly in rotation with the rest of the squadron pilots. Using this information as a basis for argument, we kept pressuring the older pilots of VS-5 to intercede in our behalf to convince Skipper Burch to allow us to fly in turn. Burch finally weakened a bit and agreed to let the new pilots fly antisubmarine patrol (ASP) around the task force; we would have the ship in sight at all times, and there would be enough time for wave-off landing approaches if necessary. This was a happy compromise—after all, flying ASP was better than no flying at all.

There were several old friends in my new squadron. Yogi Jorgenson had joined the squadron at Norfolk and was flying wing on Burch. Ed Kinzer, who had been in 4A-41-PC at Pensacola, welcomed me as his new roommate. And there were two Norfolk Deck Dodgers who had also made the long odyssey—Walt Brown and Skip Ervin. VS-5 was a great bunch of guys who welcomed four well-traveled newcomers with open arms. Unfortunately, I was going to know some of them for only a week, including my new roommate. The war was coming closer with each passing day, and the days of wine and roses were over.

To a dive-bomber section or division leader in combat, good wingmen were more precious than diamonds. My first flying assignment in VS-5 was as a wingman on Lt. (jg) Art "Goocher" Downing. Art was one of the great dive-bomber pilots of World War II, but he was tough on wingmen. He flew his airplane in a rough, aggressive way, showing little concern as to whether he was maneuvering in a manner that might confuse or embarrass his wingmen. After all, their job was to stay in formation no matter what happened. Because of inexperience, few young ensigns could stay with him all the time. I hung on like a pit bull, determined that he would not lose me from a formation, and he never did.

I was impressed with Art from the first time we met. Tall and dark, with rugged, handsome features, he had a direct, positive manner that was straightforward and honest. And he was full of subtle humor. In one of my early conversations with him, he told me about the squadron's first raids back in February against Mili, an island in the Marshall group. He was flying with Lt. Wally Short, executive officer (XO) of the squadron, with six planes. They could not find targets worth anything and were becoming frustrated by the entire operation. About this time Art saw some small tanks in a palm grove below. After bombing the area and getting no secondary explosions of fuel or oil from the tanks, Art came to one conclusion: He had destroyed the freshwater supply of the local native population, and so reported back at *Yorktown*.

The squadron had more luck in the Lae-Salamaua raids off New Guinea in March, when they contributed to the sinking of *Kongo Maru* and *Tenyo Maru*, and damaged several other Japanese destroyers and transports. The combined attacks from *Lexington* and *Yorktown* inflicted more damage to Japanese fleet units by dive-bombing than any American action had accomplished since Pearl Harbor, and was done with only one SBD lost from VS-2. Captain Buckmaster and Vice Admiral Wilson Brown, Jr., were so delighted with these first positive results that many medals, mostly Navy Crosses, were given to the participating aviators.

III

It was with this battle experience that the carriers *Lexington* and *Yorktown* approached the Guadalcanal area for still another hit-and-run raid. However, this time the Japanese fleet, in the form of three carriers, was also present in the Coral Sea, and the serious business of carrier-versus-carrier fighting was about to be introduced into the Pacific conflict. Intelligence reports indicated that Japanese fleet units could be expected near Tulagi; what was not known was that the Japanese were building an airfield on Lunga Point. They were also bringing down an invasion force to occupy Port Moresby, New Guinea.

On the morning of 4 May 1942, the first action of what history would call the Battle of the Coral Sea began with a maximum strike effort on Tulagi from *Yorktown*. In spite of rain squalls and winds up to thirty-five knots, a force of twenty-eight dive-bombers were launched at 0700. VS-5's contribution was thirteen planes, led by the CO, Bill Burch; the remaining fifteen were VB-5 aircraft led by new CO Wally Short. All were armed with thousand-pound general-purpose bombs. Twelve of the old, slow TBD torpedo bombers, each carrying a Mark 13 torpedo, were also a part of this first strike against Japanese forces at the Tulagi base.

Approaching the target, the pilots looked down on what appeared to be a sizeable Japanese fleet. Not yet experienced at ship recognition, pilots reported a cruiser, two large transports, three small transports, two destroyers moored together, and numerous gunboats and small craft. Burch led his group in from nineteen thousand feet, moved to an angle of seventy degrees at about ten thousand feet, and made drops at twenty-five hundred feet. The AA guns put up a heavy, inaccurate fire and no planes were hit. When he returned home, Burch reported four bomb hits.

An old problem recurred during the dives. The SBD telescope sights and windshields fogged over, starting at about seven thousand feet, causing many pilots to lose sight of targets and release high. This was not the first time that fog-up had developed during a dive and some way had to be found to stop the condition. Someone suggested a lower approach altitude—fifteen thousand feet or so—to see if a temperature difference would help. Approaches at about twelve to fourteen thousand feet were used for later strikes, and no fogging occurred. A few weeks later, new sights and coating of windshields ended the problem completely. By that time we never went higher than about fifteen thousand feet unless forced to by AA or the presence of fighters. One could go to fifteen thousand feet safely without oxygen, which was an advantage. When leading, sixteen thousand feet was the maximum altitude I ever used.

IV

I wish to digress briefly here in the middle of the Battle of Coral Sea to discuss an important issue relative to all the Pacific battles that are to come. If you do any research on the Pacific carrier-versus-carrier conflicts, it does not take long before you note that there is a big difference between the kills of enemy planes and ships claimed by pilots after combat from what records show actually happened at the time. These discrepancies are found in both Japanese and American combat reports. Fleet battle reports of both sides, when studied after the war's end, clearly show that large numbers of claimed hits and sinkings of ships simply did not happen. This same phenomenon occurred in almost every air fight, with a larger number of aircraft claimed shot down by pilots of both sides than records show as actually lost. Why?

This is not a simple question to answer. Many dive-bomber or torpedo bomber pilots attacking heavily defended warships—carriers, battleships, and cruisers—in debriefing upon their return would report a hit. Both American and Japanese attack pilots showed a compulsion to believe that their attacks, made at high risk and great cost, were personally successful. Any hit made just had to have been the result of their attacks. In many cases errors were caused by pilots and aircrewmen observing battle damage that actually happened but was insufficient to destroy the target under attack; although damaged, sometimes seriously, the ship would escape from the fight and live to fight another day.

As for the fighters, it was quite easy for these pilots to claim a plane shot down more than once, sometimes with camera shots to back it up. This could happen because two pilots making runs on an enemy plane at the same time (a leader and wingman for example) might both hit the target with destructive bursts, see fire and pieces of aircraft flying off, and watch it go in or blow up. In an air battle, too much would happen in a few brief moments of time for every pilot to remember exact details of how or when he made his runs; the net result could be two planes credited as shot down for one actual, with no intention by either pilot to make an inaccurate claim.

Hits or kills claimed often had no camera photos to back them up. An aircraft might not have camera equipment; cameras might not function properly; there might not be any film. Claims were largely based upon pilot accounts at debriefings, with hits and kills verified by other pilots. This backup was not difficult to get with wingmen as anxious as their flight leaders to give or receive credit for hits and kills after heavy action, especially when squadron friends did not return from the battle.

Both American and Japanese pilots liked to make their combat efforts look worthwhile even in defeat. A convenient way to do this was to relate losses to enemies shot down—a favorite ratio of four or five to one made that one loss more acceptable, at least for the moment. Japanese pilots had the additional burden of loss of face if they admitted that American pilots and planes were good enough to defeat them in equal combat. So they claimed they were outnumbered, and listed their kills at a high ratio to their losses.

In fact, early in the war the Japanese outnumbered our aircraft in fighters, especially on strike escort, and the Zero could outperform our aircraft on a one-to-one basis. But their desire always to be listed as outnumbered became reality after early 1944 and continued to the end of the war.

Hits by dive-bombers, and claims for them, is a subject on which I profess some expertise, based upon observations in actual combat, first as a wingman flying on others and later as a section, division, and flight leader. Before discussing hits and how they were made, I must clarify the types of hits involved. Any dive-bomber pilot, even those of poor ability and doubtful boldness, could hit such targets as airfield runways or installations, groups of buildings, and other stationary land targets. Ships at anchor in a harbor and aircraft parked along runways of an airfield required some ability, but the fact that they were not moving simplified their destruction. Providing ground support to troops by dive-bombing was more difficult than hitting ordinary nonmoving targets as there was the danger of missing a designated enemy target area and hitting friendly forces instead. Usually neither friendly nor enemy personnel and equipment could be observed from the air by the pilots providing the requested air assistance. Many support attacks were made upon targets identified only by smoke markers placed upon them by friendly ground forces or from grid coordinates on a map or chart—the enemy was never really seen or recognized.

The real test of a naval dive-bomber pilot was hitting a moving target—a ship at sea going full speed and maneuvering. Different enemy ships posed relatively more difficult targets. Aircraft carriers were the largest and most vulnerable warship targets, followed by battleships, cruisers, and destroyers in that order. Transport ships were the easiest to attack and hit, partly due to less speed of movement and less AA fire. This latter factor (AA fire) became a deterrent to a hit on a warship because it was heavier from these ships than from a support vessel.

Those who insist that AA fire was no factor in causing bomb misses must not have dived very much on warships in a task force formation. It required mental discipline, as well as courage, for a dive-bomber pilot to ignore heavy fire and press home his attack while also selecting the precise point at which it was necessary to aim his bomb in order to secure a hit. With the ship moving at full speed and maneuvering wildly, it took the same qualities of marksmanship as a sharpshooter to put a shot into a target consistently.

When one considers the heterogeneous variables at work in a typical dive-bomber attack upon a moving target, it was amazing that hits occurred at all. (And sometimes they didn't!) Attacking a gyrating ship with great maneuverability (a destroyer, for example) has been compared to trying to hit a cockroach racing across a kitchen floor with a small flyswatter. Like any shooting problem where movement is involved, point-to-point aiming does not work because the projectile will strike where the target was at the time it was fired. The key to hitting a moving target is knowing where the target will be when the projectile arrives after firing—this is commonly called "lead." But unlike a fighter pilot shooting at another aircraft, the dive-bomber pilot had no shotgun effect when he fired and couldn't use tracers to change a point-of-aim and "walk" his projectiles into a target. He had only one shot in the gun. Thus his aiming point, like that of an old single-shot Kentucky rifleman, had to be right at the moment of firing to get a hit.

Selecting the right aiming point and smoothly firing a bomb required the finest coordination of reflexes and eyesight. A favorite defensive tactic of both Japanese and American carrier captains was to put their ship into a maximum turn either to port or starboard as the dive-bombers came streaming down, continuing the turn at full rudder for a complete circle, stopping only after the bombing attack was finished. This simple ploy gave the attacking pilots several problems when selecting a point-of-aim, not the least being that the ship was moving in several directions at the same time—a ship in a turn also slides sideways on its track. This skidding effect was not only potent when used by a target, it was a serious deterrent to a hit when it happened to an attacking dive-bomber. Probably the single most common mistake by a diving pilot was firing a bomb with his plane in a slight skid; this would throw off the point-of-aim just enough to cause a close miss instead of a hit by a bomb.

Often the error of the inexperienced pilot, a sudden last-moment attempt to correct a dive could cause the most experienced to miss by throwing the bomb off aim. An example of this problem was related by Rear Adm. Earl Gallaher to Robert Barbe in an interview on 29 June 1966 regarding the Battle of Midway. A former Marine Corps officer, Barbe was a student of Gordon W.

Prange at the University of Maryland and working on a doctoral dissertation at the time. On 4 June 1942, Gallaher, as CO of VS-6 flying from *Enterprise,* led the morning attack and hit *Kaga,* which soon sank. In the afternoon he led another attack down on *Hiryu.* Describing this second attack, Earl stated: "An unbelievably swift turn of the carrier threw off my aim, and in endeavoring to throw the bomb rather than drop it, I wrenched my back and the missile dropped harmlessly off *Hiryu's* stern." He returned to the Big E with severe back pain caused by the unorthodox maneuver in his dive.[1]

Earl Gallaher was one of the great dive-bomber pilots of the war and an excellent teacher and flight leader. I was fortunate to get to fly practice dive-bombing flights under his tutelage several times while on temporary duty with his squadron (VS-6) in March and April 1942. He taught me refinements in the art of dive-bombing; if Skipper Earl could throw a bomb so badly that he injured his back in the process, anyone was capable of the error.

There was still another way a pilot could unintentionally "toss" his bomb and cause a miss. At the exact moment of release, it was essential that the aircraft remain in the dive as the bomb separated from its carrying shackles on the plane. If the pilot instinctively or carelessly started his pullout at this moment of separation, the bomb could be affected in its flight path and would not hit the spot aimed at. The electrical release helped solve this problem as it removed the chance of coming back on the stick with the right hand while pulling the manual bomb release with the left. You simply pushed down a bomb release button mounted on top of the control stick while concentrating on smooth stick pressures and exact point-of-aim. However, like the man who wears both belt and suspenders, most veteran pilots also pulled the manual backup release after pushing the stick release button, to be sure that the bomb left the plane before pullout. And, don't forget, all of these procedures had to be followed precisely and smoothly amid varied amounts of AA fire, with every instinct dictating to get the hell out of there!

I have tried to give an honest interpretation of how hits and kills were determined in the Pacific war with Japan. However, to be completely honest I must add one last factor: the false, dishonest, and self-glorifying claims of some pilots. There were certain pilots, often leaders (I wish I could say only a few), who always claimed hits or kills after an action. These men were so intent on their own self-interest that they took credit for the work of others; they exaggerated actions they took part in; they made claims that were often denied by their own comrades. All confidential action reports contained the instruction "Do not 'gun deck' this report. If data cannot be estimated with reasonable accuracy enter a dash in space for which no data is available." Dishonest pilots ignored this instruction especially in the "Results (Certain)" area, where any claim might be found. Most of these pilots were known to their shipmates, who held their actions in contempt, but higher officers often went along with the claims in their own desperate efforts for recognition. The final irony of this despicable conduct was when these men received decorations and promotions that furthered their careers.

At Tulagi on 4 May, scouting Squadron Five made three attacks against harbor ships, a total of thirty-eight aircraft sorties. Combined with VB-5 and VT-5 sorties, pilots claimed two destroyers, a light cruiser, a cargo ship, and four gunboats sunk, and a destroyer, heavy cruiser, cargo ship, and aircraft tender damaged. Five floatplanes were claimed as shot down. However, the actual ship bag "was far less impressive, considering the prodigious expenditure of 22 torpedoes [no hits] and 76 1,000-pound bombs, 12,570 rounds of .50-caliber and 7,095 rounds of .30-caliber ammunition fired: [*Yorktown* aircraft] sunk *Kikuzuki,* three minecraft and four barges, and inflicted various degrees of damage on *Yuzuki, Okinoshima, Azumasan Maru* and *Koei Maru,* at the cost of six SBDs and two TBDs damaged; one TBD and two F4Fs lost."[2]

There was a positive result of these raids for the Japanese— they now had a valuable piece of intelligence. The attacks had been made with carrier aircraft. Thus U.S. carriers were definitely in the Coral Sea. Based upon general knowledge of aircraft ranges, they had an approximate location of our CVs, while we still had no concrete information regarding any Japanese carrier's location. If they closed in quickly, some surprise might be obtained in attacking our carriers before we knew their position.

V

As junior ensign in a new squadron, my chance to fly and fight the enemy at Coral Sea would be limited. There were eighteen aircraft in the squadron, of which usually only fifteen or sixteen were flyable at any one time, with twenty-one pilots now on the personnel roster. This meant that my assignment to fly a strike would come only after all the others had made a first strike, and only if the squadron commander would let me go. My intense desire to become a part of the action led to an event that brought a granting of my wishes to fly.

All VS-5 pilots and gunners had manned the ready rooms when flight quarters sounded at 0540 on the morning of 6 May 1942. In the first launch at dawn, our squadron was to provide two planes for antisubmarine patrol around the force, and four planes for two search sectors. There were also two standby aircraft to be manned, and taxi pilots for all other squadron aircraft on deck. Much to my delight I was assigned standby duty by the squadron flight officer, Lt. Roger Woodhull, to man one of the extra aircraft; this meant that I would at least get to start the engine and taxi on the deck.

Yorktown regulations required any pilot who manned a plane to be fully dressed and equipped for combat flight. When the order came to man planes, I hurried topside in full flight gear, including my plotting board with all relevant flight data on it, even though I was only a taxi pilot of an extra plane on the deck. A young gunner by the name of Barton Woods also manned the Dauntless I was assigned. In the predawn light, we found our assigned plane, started the engine when ordered, and sat watching the first search planes take off.

There was complete radio silence in those early war days—a quiet to be broken only in actual combat. All operations on deck were conducted by hand signals and an occasional chalkboard order that would be displayed at the primary fly (PriFly) area of the ship's bridge. We even carried small bean bags with a message pocket to drop handwritten messages onto the deck instead of using the radio.

The launch continued in the early morning first light when one of the deck plane directors began giving hand signals to me to move my aircraft. The first inkling that something unusual was going on was when this director brought me out of my spot past a VS-5 aircraft scheduled to fly. I realized then that I was being positioned for takeoff. Apparently the other aircraft was a dud, and the deck crews thought that I was a standby. Unless I gave a thumbs-down signal for a faulty plane I was being taxied forward for launch!

I was directed into the takeoff spot with my mind in a turmoil. If I took off, even though it was a mistake, I might be blamed for not stopping the directors. But why stop them? I was about to be given a chance to fly! I had worked more than a year, and traveled halfway around the world, to be here at this moment.

I looked up toward the PriFly area and what I saw there gave me an answer. The *Yorktown* air officer, Comdr. Murr Arnold, was holding up his chalkboard. Written upon it was a message: "You will fly west sector ASP—good luck." He was grinning down at me as he lifted his right hand in a thumbs-up gesture—the signal that one pilot gives to another when indicating that everything is OK. I replied by raising my right hand and patting myself on the top of the head—the signal that I was accepting the assignment.

The launch officer began twirling his launch flag. I advanced full throttle against the brakes; all engine gauges indicated ready. I nodded my head, and the launch officer's arm went down and forward, pointing up the deck. I released brakes and thundered down the deck on my first operational, and combat, flight from *Yorktown*.

I took up station on a bearing of 270 degrees from the task force at an altitude of one thousand feet and began the standard ASP flight pattern outside the screening destroyers. The weather was perfect, with bright sunshine and calm waters; occasional white cumulus clouds drifted by like icebergs floating in a sea of pale blue sky. I felt like an angel flying the assignment while maintaining a westerly bearing from the speeding task force formation.

Getting back aboard an aircraft carrier required flying to signals from a Landing Signal Officer (LSO). Using paddles, the LSO indicated whether a pilot was approaching the deck too high or low, too fast or slow, or off line. The final signal—a movement of the paddle across his throat—was called the "cut"; a pilot then closed his throttle and landed. A waving of the paddles was a "wave off"; a pilot applied power and went around again. The cut and wave off were mandatory. I landed back aboard on the first pass with a slight high, a little fast, and a cut from Lt. Norwood "Soupy" Campbell, the LSO of *Yorktown*. My first accidental carrier mission was a success.

VI

On the morning of 7 May 1942, Vice Adm. Takeo Takagi, commanding Carrier Division Five and in charge of Operation MO (the invasion of Port Moresby), was concerned. He knew that American aircraft carriers were somewhere near him in the Coral Sea and had been for several days, as evidenced by the raids of 4 May against Japanese land and sea forces at Tulagi. While continuing search efforts, his invasion force of eleven transports, four heavy cruisers, the escort carrier (CVE) *Shoho,* and escorting destroyers proceeded on a direct course toward the invasion site.

So it was with some elation that Takagi received an early morning report from the pilot of a cruiser-based floatplane on search that he had sighted "a carrier and escorting cruiser." In reality the scout had found, and misreported, the U.S. oiler *Neosho* and its escort destroyer *Sims.* The admiral hastily ordered his two big carriers, *Zuikaku* and *Shokaku,* to launch an all-out attack; by 0830 thirty-six Val dive-bombers and twenty-four Kates with torpedoes, escorted by eighteen Zero fighters, were on their way to the scene of the contact.[3]

When this seventy-eight plane group arrived at the target and found two unprotected ships and no U.S. carriers, they attacked and sank the unfortunate quarry, wisely using only bombs, as no Long Lance torpedoes were needed. After an easy victory, the Japanese aircraft returned to their carriers.

Meanwhile Rear Adm. Frank Jack Fletcher in *Yorktown* was as concerned about locating the Japanese carrier force as his opponent Takagi was about finding his. The morning search soon reported a contact: Lt. John Nielsen of VB-5, after encountering a Japanese reconnaissance floatplane and shooting it down, sent an encoded report to *Yorktown* about six ships he had located. Somehow this report of two cruisers and four destroyers became two carriers and four cruisers when decoded back at *Yorktown.* Like his Japanese opponent, Frank Jack immediately ordered a strike to be launched for what was believed to be an enemy carrier target, and by 1030 Air Group Two (AG-2), fifty aircraft from *Lex,* and Air Group Five (AG-5), forty-three from *Yorktown,* were headed for the reported ships.

My squadron, VS-5, had been assigned the attack standby on this day. In a perfect launch, the squadron got seventeen SBD-3 Dauntlesses airborne, each with a thousand-pound bomb with a one-hundredth of a second delay fuse. This was a truly maximum effort, with every experienced pilot in the squadron headed for the enemy. Only the four new pilots remained behind in a deserted ready room.

Lt. Comdr. Bill Burch led his charges on a slow climb toward a new position report that was sent to him from *Yorktown* control. At a range of 150 miles, he came upon a force of the CVE *Shoho*, four heavy cruisers, and one destroyer. [He reported later that the force consisted of a carrier (CV), a battleship (BB), three attack cruisers (CA), and one light cruiser (CL).] From eighteen thousand feet, as three Zeros tried vainly to intercept his squadron, and in spite of a plea from his academy classmate Lt. Comdr. Joe Taylor, who was leading his lumbering TBDs of Torpedo Squadron Five (VT-5) toward the target and wanted to coordinate the attack, Burch took his seventeen dive bombers down on *Shoho*.

Apparently AG-2 had already completed their attacks and scored some hits, as *Shoho* seemed unable to turn and was holding a straight course at high speed. Historian Robert Cressman describes the combined AG-5 attack:

> Six minutes after *Yorktown*'s planes had commenced their attacks, the order went out on board *Shoho* to abandon ship. Within five more minutes, though, the carrier sank, taking with her all but 255 of her 800-man crew and having suffered hits from at least 13 bombs and seven torpedoes before the keeping of records of such massive destruction became superfluous. To Bill Burch, watching from his SBD, *Shoho* "just ploughed herself under." LCDR Robert E. Dixon, commanding the *Lexington*'s VB-2, reported laconically, "Scratch one flattop."[4]

This attack against one Japanese carrier was the largest concentration of bombs and torpedoes expended against a single warship during the Pacific war. Approximately sixty dive-bombers and two dozen torpedo planes combined simply to blow the small CVE to bits. It is sad that the object of all this armament could not have been the twins, *Zuikaku* and *Shokaku*.

Burch reported nine direct hits and two near-misses by VS-5 with no losses. VB-5 lost one plane that became short of fuel after leaving formation to chase a Japanese airplane, and ended up in the drink with the crew finally making it to land in their raft. One VB-5 pilot who had just arrived with our group from Fiji, Ens. Tom Brown, a Norfolk Deck Dodger, got to go on the strike. He admitted at his debriefing that he had not bombed the doomed carrier at all, but had dived and dropped his bomb on a heavy cruiser instead. The next thing he knew he was being credited with hitting and sinking the vessel!

Brown became an instant celebrity, acquired the nickname Cruiser, and was properly decorated with a Navy Cross later. Japanese reports of the battle have no record of a cruiser being hit, much less sunk during the action, so Brown's cruiser becomes one of those unsolved mysterious sinkings that fill the pages of American battle reports. I remember that we ensigns who knew Tom and his abilities as a dive-bomber found the story incredible at the time—as the expression goes, Tom would have had trouble hitting a bull in the ass with a bass fiddle. I never saw or heard of him in action again after Coral Sea; I guess he went back to the States instead of reassignment at Pearl after the battle.

Both sides spent the rest of the day trying to no avail to pinpoint each other's positions for further attacks on the big carriers. Squalls and rain helped us remain hidden from the prying eyes of search planes. Late in the afternoon the Japanese launched a combined search-strike mission of twenty-seven Vals and Kates, hoping to find the U.S. carriers for a dusk attack. These planes never made contact, but American radar picked them up and carrier air patrol (CAP) fighters were vectored out to intercept. In the ensuing melee, Lt. Comdr. Jimmy Flatley shot down one Val, and his other pilots got a couple more. Lt. Comdr. Paul Ramsey, CO of VF-2, and his men also made kills on the Japanese attack group. Vice Admiral Takagi ended up losing nine planes—one third of the ill-advised strike—without a single attack against an American ship. We lost two fighters, one of them becoming disoriented and disappearing in the extreme weather conditions in the area.

The almost freak experiences of this day of combat were not over. The Japanese and American task forces had managed to get within twenty-five to thirty miles of each other in the rain and approaching darkness. At about 1900, as Soupy Campbell, *Yorktown*'s LSO, was bringing our last fighters back aboard, three Japanese airplanes joined our traffic pattern and tried to come aboard! When this activity was reported by bullhorn, several of us scurried to the port-side catwalk to watch the show. In the frenzy of the moment, with gunners firing at both friend and foe, some of us got caught up in the excitement and drew our .45 Colt automatics to join in, blasting away at the red meatballs as they flew past the ship—an offensive gesture about as effective as throwing rocks. Fortunately, no one shot themselves or a friend. There was considerable speculation later as to what would have been the reaction in high places, especially Pearl Harbor and Washington, if LSO Campbell had been able to bring a Japanese carrier plane aboard *Yorktown* that night.

So ended the near-chaotic events of 7 May 1942. While getting closer together than would ever occur again in the war, the American and Japanese fast carrier task forces still had not found each other.

VII

The events that occurred on 7 May saw ships sunk on both sides, with the Americans destroying their first Japanese carrier —albeit a small one—all action undertaken and destruction accomplished with carrier fighter and attack aircraft. But the battle so far had not been a true carrier-versus-carrier one because a most important ingredient was missing: an exchange between carrier task force groups against each other. This deficiency was about to be eradicated in a blazing interchange on 8 May 1942.

The air operations (ops) plan for the next day, delivered to the VS-5 ready room after the evening meal, was short and to the point:

U.S.S. YORKTOWN

AT Sea
7 May 1942

AIR DEPARTMENT MEMORANDUM

Subject: Flight Operations, Friday, 8 May 1942.
0540: Flight Quarters.
0620: Pilots man planes.

When directed launch attack group as follows:

    9 VT—Torpedoes.
    12 VB—1,000-pound bombs.
    12 VS—1,000-pound bombs.
    8 VF—Protective Patrol.

Launch 5 VB plus 3 VS as anti-torpedo plane patrol as directed.

Launch 8 VF Combat Air Patrol when ordered.

Additional attacks may be launched during day.

> M. E. ARNOLD
> Commander, U.S. Navy
> AIR OFFICER

It also contained a requirement that had been the subject of some disagreement among dive-bomber pilots: The plan called for eight SBD Dauntlesses to be used as "anti–torpedo plane patrol," with our squadron to provide three of the required planes.

The concept of using SBDs to augment F4F fighters in defending a task force against attacking enemy torpedo planes was an old one going back to prewar fleet battle problems. Just how good the concept was had never been proved, but with the prospect of heavy enemy attacks, people pretty high up were quite concerned with the defense of the precious carriers, and ready to try anything. Both Rear Adm. Aubrey "Jake" Fitch, Commander Tactical Air, and Capt. Frederick C. Sherman, CO of *Lexington,* were recommending not only the anti–torpedo plane patrol, but a 360-degree search around the task force at dawn as well. Rear Admiral Fletcher acquiesced to these requests for the coming morning launch schedule.

Eighteen SBDs of AG-2 in the *Lex* took off for the morning search, and eight Dauntlesses from VS-5 left *Yorktown* for anti–torpedo plane patrol. With fighter CAPs in place, and all hands at general quarters, Task Force Seventeen (TF-17) was ready for action.

It was not long in coming. Lt. (jg) Joseph G. Smith of VS-2 found Takagi's main task force at approximately 0830 and placed the enemy of two CVs, four CAs, and numerous DDs (destroyers) on a bearing of 028, distance 175 miles. At about the same time, PO1c. Kenzo Kanno, a scout from the Japanese Operation MO

Striking Force, found and reported the position of TF-17. Both the American and Japanese forces began launching maximum strikes against each other. The Americans dispatched seventy-five aircraft (fifteen fighters, thirty-nine dive-bombers, and twenty-one torpedo planes) from *Yorktown* and *Lexington;* the Japanese strike was composed of sixty-nine aircraft (eighteen fighters, thirty-three dive-bombers, and eighteen torpedo planes) from *Zuikaku* and *Shokaku.* The first carrier-versus-carrier exchange in history was airborne.[5]

Only seven VS-5 aircraft were available for the attack strike after we had provided the eight for the anti–torpedo plane patrol earlier. Led by our CO Bill Burch, they were joined by a maximum-effort seventeen SBDs of VB-5 led by Lt. Wally Short. Upon returning to *Yorktown* after the attack, Bill Burch reported the action:

> Launched at 1000, sighted enemy formation of one BB, two CV, and many cruisers at 1130, range 175 miles. Waited for VT to arrive, attacked at 1150. Started dive from 17,000 feet with releases at various altitudes. Telescope sights fogged very severely during dives, starting at 8,000 feet. Bombing accuracy considered reduced 75% by this. Immediately after pullout all planes were attacked by many Zero fighters. Used cloud coverage to escape fighters [individually] as were unable to completely rendezvous. Jap fighters very vulnerable and they did not work well together. All planes returned to own CV; one landed in water on return with landing gear shot away. Six other planes had numerous 7.7 mm and 20 mm holes in wings and fuselages. Five out of seven planes were saved by leak-proof tanks; armor saved one pilot and two rear gunners. [Estimate] three direct hits on CV, four Zero fighters shot down, seven Zero fighters damaged.

The usually astute Burch erred grievously in waiting for his Academy classmate Joe Taylor to arrive with his slower nine TBDs instead of attacking the Japanese carriers immediately. A delay of almost half an hour circling above allowed *Zuikaku* to take protective cover in nearby rain showers, and both carriers had time to get all defensive Zeros airborne. This loss of initiative was more costly than any advantage gained by a coordinated attack. The torpedo runs were unproductive with no hits, and the combined attacks of both VS-5 and VB-5 scored only two hits on *Shokaku*—damaging but not fatal.

Miserable as this showing was, it was superseded by that of *Lex*'s Air Group Two strike group. Led by Lt. Comdr. William "Bill" Ault, air group commander (CAG), this group got lost near the target. Ault, with three wingmen, finally found *Shokaku* and dove on her, scoring one more hit. All twelve of VT-2's torpedo planes attacked and dropped their loads, but no hits were made. The remaining SBDs, still lost, jettisoned bombs and returned home without ever finding the rain-obscured Japanese task force. CAG Ault, with two wingmen, never returned—lost to both weather and enemy Zeros.

The three hits on *Shokaku* were enough to knock her out of the battle. On fire, with her flight deck holed, she could no longer conduct flight operations. Vice Admiral Takagi ordered her to retire, she headed for Japan, and it would be late summer before she would fight again in the eastern Solomons. The undamaged *Zuikaku* remained to recover surviving aircraft and continue fighting.

While our aircraft were attacking the Japanese carrier twins, the Japanese striking force under command of Lt. Comdr. Kuichi Takahashi arrived over Task Force Seventeen. The Japanese flight leader, a veteran of years of carrier combat, wisely split his force and attacked both *Lexington* and *Yorktown* with dive-bomber and torpedo Kates and Vals. The results were possibly three torpedo hits on *Lex* and one direct bomb hit with two grazing near-misses on *Yorktown*. Surviving the initial blows, the *Lex* continued flight operations until about 1400, when a tremendous internal explosion of gasoline vapors from ruptured lines led to uncontrollable fires and an eventual call to abandon ship. At about 2000, the U.S. destroyer *Phelps* fired five torpedoes into the stubborn Queen of the Flattops, who was refusing to die. Then, with a huge explosion, she plunged over two miles down to a final resting place on the bottom of the Coral Sea.

Professor E. B. Potter of the Naval Academy summarized the battle:

> The Japanese had won a tactical victory. Their loss of the converted 12,000-ton *Shoho* and a few small vessels sunk off Tulagi was a small price to pay for the sinking of the *Neosho,* the *Sims,* and the 33,000-ton *Lexington.* For the United States, however, the Battle of the Coral Sea was definitely a strategic victory; the main Japanese objective, the capture of Port Moresby, had been thwarted.[6]

VIII

On the evening of 8 May 1942, the officers and men in *Yorktown* were jubilant, sad, and apprehensive. They were jubilant because they had just taken the worst that the enemy could hurl against them and survived. The first carrier-versus-carrier naval battle—the Battle of the Coral Sea—was now history. They were sad because many good friends and shipmates, both in the air and in the ship, had given their lives during the process. The apprehension came from the condition of their beloved ship—*Yorktown* was bleeding, leaving a trail of oil in her wake from numerous wounds in her starboard side. Such a marker might be spotted by Japanese search aircraft or submarines and bring another pack of aerial wolves to finish off a wounded adversary, sending her to join her sister ship already in Davy Jones's locker.

We were especially sad in the Scouting Squadron Five ready room. Four empty chairs were grim reminders of four pilots lost on the infamous anti–torpedo plane patrol during the morning attack. In compliance with a direct order, Lt. Comdr. Burch, against his better judgment, had to provide eight planes from his squadron for this patrol.

Lexington squadron VS-2 and VB-2 had provided another fifteen aircraft for the patrol, and fared considerably better than VS-5. The results of the entire patrol of twenty-three SBDs were four enemy aircraft shot down (seventeen claimed) at a cost of nine Dauntlesses, five pilots, and six gunners. Three of our SBDs had to be jettisoned because of battle damage. Ens. Red Austin's was one of these; the plane was shot up (Red was wounded slightly), and he then crashed into the island while trying to land. John B. Lundstrom, in his excellent book *The First Team,* summarizes:

A total of twenty Grumman F4F fighters and twenty-three Douglas SBD dive bombers participated in the defense of Task Force 17. . . . From a correlation of Japanese and American sources, it appears reasonable that the F4Fs actually shot down no Zeros, but perhaps splashed three dive bombers and one torpedo plane, while the SBD crews accounted for no Zeros, but downed one dive bomber and three torpedo planes—total eight Japanese aircraft destroyed by aerial engagement.[7]

Numerous decorations were given to these gallant pilots who tried to perform an impossible task of defending the task force using slow dive-bombers as fighters. Lt. (jg) William E. Hall of VS-2 was awarded the Medal of Honor for his efforts, although wounded, joining Lt. John "JoJo" Powers of VB-5, who was killed while delivering his bomb against *Shokaku* at point-blank range. These two Dauntless divers received the nation's highest decoration for valor in this epic first carrier-versus-carrier battle.

Taking nothing away from the valorous conduct of the courageous men who performed this hazardous mission, I feel compelled to comment in some detail about it. Admirals Fitch and Fletcher, and Captain Sherman, made a tactical error of grave and almost fatal consequences when they used SBDs as interceptors of Japanese aircraft attacking TF-17 on 8 May 1942. In an act that bordered on defensive paranoia, these leaders were so concerned with the safety of their carriers that they influenced the outcome of the battle in a negative manner, making it almost impossible to achieve victory.

The outcome of this battle might have been radically changed in America's favor if the twenty-three Dauntlesses used as defensive fighters in an anti–torpedo plane patrol had been sent against *Shokaku* and *Zuikaku* in their normal attack roles. Many of the same pilots who overhit and sank *Shoho* the day before might have hit or sunk either or both Japanese carriers in the same manner as the Japanese attack aircraft did *Yorktown* and *Lexington*. By using for defense twenty-three of the limited SBD aircraft available for attack, the ability to destroy the enemy carriers, and thus win the battle, was compromised. The U.S. Navy was fortunate that its aircraft and ship losses were not greater.

Some historians try to rationalize this extremely bad tactical decision by U.S. leaders at Coral Sea as necessary because of a shortage of fighters aboard our carriers. In their view, SBDs became "better than nothing" for carrier defense. They also give credit to the SBDs for stopping additional damage to *Lexington,* apparently referring to the successes of several pilots in both shooting down and diverting a number of Japanese torpedo planes in their attacks. The actions of all the dive-bomber pilots in their role as fighters were heroic but the fact still remains that *Lexington* was lost and *Yorktown* damaged by Japanese carrier aircraft used in their designated roles, while twenty-three aircraft that

should have been hitting enemy carriers offensively (thus performing their proper role) were being misused as defensive fighters.

In considering this decision made by our naval air leaders in this
battle, one must remember that it was the first carrier-versus-
carrier engagement of the war, and some of the prewar planning
and tactics used proved not relevant to this new type of sea struggle. The mistake of using dive-bombers as interceptors was
never repeated again in a major battle. Thus 8 May 1942 saw
the only anti–torpedo plane patrol of SBDs ever launched in defense of an American CV. Carrier defenses were enhanced by increasing the number of VF fighters carried, better AA guns and
more of them, proximity-fused shells, improved fire control systems, and more effective fighter direction and squadron tactics
in making contact and downing incoming enemy attack aircraft of
all types.

It has been said that Rear Adm. Frederick Sherman remained a
champion of the tactic and "when he took command of *Enterprise's*
Task Force Sixteen he incorporated the use of SBDs on anti–
torpedo plane patrol in his December 1942 air defense doctrine."[8]
I was aboard the Big E at the time in VB-10. If such a policy was
in the doctrine, it was never mentioned, discussed, or practiced
by the SBD squadrons aboard, during a war cruise that lasted until
May 1943.

One thing I do know: Rear Admiral Sherman regretted the
decision made at Coral Sea, and the loss of good dive-bomber
pilots and gunners who had been ordered into a situation where
there was so little chance for either success or survival. I know
this because he told me so when he apologized to me aboard
Enterprise, in January 1943, for the loss of eight shipmates from
VS-5 in that bloody summer of 1942.

IX

After finishing off the *Lexington,* Fitch and Fletcher agreed that,
due to numerous serious problems including lack of fuel, a damaged carrier, and a shortage of fighters, it would be best to leave
the Coral Sea immediately. As Lt. Wally Short put it: "We were
running scared, if the truth were told." Faded diary notes, written
in pencil as I sat in the ready room that night in May 1942, reveal
the unspoken fear that rode in *Yorktown* as she headed southeast
to the shelter of American and Australian bases:

USS Yorktown, 8 May 1942, at sea. Today was it. Our VS and
VB planes left about 0900 to attack enemy carriers. At 1130 our
forces were hit by a large group of Japanese torpedo, dive-
bomber, and Zero fighter aircraft. All hell broke loose. My
squadron lost four pilots and gunners out of eight that were on
anti–torpedo plane patrol. A very good buddy from St. Louis
E base days, Ens. Dave Chaffee, was shot down while attacking
the Jap carrier *Shokaku* with VB-5. Our boys on the ship's guns
were magnificent, sending about fifteen Jap plane crews to join
their ancestors. The ship took a bad hit near the #2 elevator—a
delayed-action bomb which penetrated to the third deck down
before exploding in compartment C-402-A—killing many of the
crew. [Forty men were killed and twenty-six wounded.] We owe
the ship's life to our skipper, Capt. Elliott Buckmaster, who
maneuvered between many bombs and torpedoes [thus avoiding
further damage].

The bomb hit described occurred in an aviation storeroom and
started a fire there. However, the main damage to personnel took
place one deck above in C-301-L, where many of Engineering
Repair Party V were killed. This group was led by Lt. Milton
Ricketts, Naval Academy class of 1935, who died fighting the fires
about him, earning a posthumous award of the Medal of Honor.

Because of the large numbers of casualties, both wounded and
dead, caused by the direct hit, the ship's hospital and sick bay
areas were quickly filled to overflowing. Backup space in such an
emergency was the officer's wardroom, where mess tables became operating ones. Seriously wounded men waited in wire basket stretchers in the surrounding passageways and officers'
staterooms for their turn with the doctors, some dying during this
time in line. It was a scene from Dante's *Inferno* and reminded
one of photographs of Civil War field hospitals sometimes seen in
history books.

With no wardroom for dining, sandwiches and hot coffee were
brought to the ready room for our evening repast. Still keyed up
from the horrible events of the day, I had no appetite, but tried to
eat a little, knowing one needed something to keep up strength.
More than food I wanted rest, since I had been up since about
0430 and was nearing complete exhaustion. Many pilots were
dozing in the ready-room seats, but what I craved was to stretch
out in a bunk.

The ship was still without power (and thus no lights) in many areas. We had been told that much of the "officers' country" was uninhabitable due to emergency use for the wounded. In spite of this advice, I decided to try to get to my room and bunk, before I collapsed.

Using a small flashlight, plus illumination from battle lanterns in the passageways, I slowly made my way toward the room. As I neared my goal, I saw that the aisles were crowded with dead and injured men in the baskets. I carefully worked my way around these obstructions, trying not to notice the terrible misery all about, and finally arrived at room number 208.

The door was partly open. In a gloom faintly lighted by dim rays of the flashlight I could see that the room was already occupied. There was someone in the lower bunk (previously the preserve of my late roommate Kinzer) and a small deck area contained a basket with another occupant. The upper bunk—mine—was empty. Carefully stepping around the basket I climbed up into my berth, took off my shoes, loosened my belt, lay back on the pillow, and was out of this world within seconds.

I do not know how long I had been asleep when I was roused by hands grasping me and lifting me from the bunk. It was still dark, and I had no idea what was happening so I asked in a rather loud voice what the hell was going on. At the sound of my voice I was immediately dropped halfway out of the cubicle, and a rather startled voice said: "My God, Doc, this one ain't dead!"

It seems that Captain Buckmaster, with approval of Rear Admiral Fletcher, had ordered that all dead crewmen be prepared for burial at sea off the fantail during the night hours in preparation for further fighting in the morning. The corpsmen had removed the two other occupants of room 208, both deceased, and were about to prepare me to join them. Needless to say I convinced the doctor that I was not one of his casualties—only a tired ensign pilot who had no other place to rest than his assigned quarters. Everyone finally left me alone and I was able to get a few more hours of sleep before flight quarters at 0530.

5

MIDWAY

I

GOING INTO Sydney or Brisbane, Australia, for R and R—rest and relaxation—proved to be wishful thinking. On 15 May the entire task force put into Tongatapu, where divers determined that the *Yorktown*'s underwater hull damage was relatively minor and the ship was essentially seaworthy. The air group flew many of the flyable planes into Tonga airfield. VS-5 had ten planes in this flight; I flew 5-S-8 as wingman on Goocher Downing flying 5-S-15.

My old diary notes describe this flight into Tongatapu:

> *15 May 1942.* Arrived at Tonga airport about 0830, squared away, and proceeded to see local sights. Native troops are wonderful physical specimens, tall and muscular with bushy hair and tough bare feet. Local residents live in grass and board huts, are very friendly, and like to trade *tapa* cloth, seed beads, coconuts, bananas, oranges, and other fruits for our cigarettes and anything else we want to swap. During our stay we got some rest and much-needed exercise. There was no flying, only early morning standby. A good time was had by all hands. We left in the afternoon of 19 May, landing back aboard *Yorktown Maru* at 1700.

78

As CV-5 cleared Tongatapu bound for Hawaii rather than the United States for repairs, it was clear that something important was afoot. Admiral Nimitz had summoned Rear Admiral Fletcher back to Pearl Harbor at "best sustained speed"—another way of saying as fast as possible without maximum effort. Unknown to the officers and men of *Yorktown*, Nimitz and the U.S. Navy needed the wounded carrier's services immediately. Comdr. Joseph Rochefort, chief of the Combat Intelligence Office at Pearl Harbor, had broken enough of the Japanese Navy operation code JN25 to deduce that a large Japanese naval force was going to move against our installations at Midway Island the first week in June. This enemy force would have four large aircraft carriers as its heart, to be opposed by *Enterprise, Hornet,* and, everyone hoped, *Yorktown.*

At about 1030 the morning of 27 May 1942, off the Pearl Harbor entrance, *Yorktown* launched forty-two flyable planes to precede her to Ford Island. She then stood into Pearl with her rail manned, and moored at Berth 16, Repair Basin, 101 days after leaving in mid-February.

Rear Adm. Frank Jack Fletcher was summoned to meet with Admiral Nimitz immediately at his headquarters. At this meeting, Fletcher was briefed about the coming battle at Midway, based upon the decoded messages of the Japanese, and the need for *Yorktown* and him to return to sea as soon as possible. After hearing the news, he expressed concern about *Yorktown*'s air group. In the Battle of Coral Sea, many pilots had been lost, been wounded, or gone through the ordeal of landing in the sea and being rescued. Fletcher recommended to Nimitz that the *Yorktown* air group be kept intact, filling empty seats with replacement pilots. Nimitz understood but overruled him. He felt that bringing three *Saratoga* squadrons—VB-3, VT-3, and VF-3—aboard *Yorktown* would be better. After all, *Saratoga* had been out of action since taking a torpedo hit in January and many of her aviators had been training on the beach for weeks. (There were four squadron designations used on U.S. carriers at this time. Fighters were VF, torpedo planes were VT, and dive-bombers were VB and VS. The VS was used to designate the scout searchers while VB was for bombing.)

Saratoga's VB-3 was considered a sharp squadron, and came aboard for VS-5. *Yorktown*'s own VB-5 would remain on board, but would be redesignated VS-5 (a decision resented by almost everyone involved). This arrangement added one replacement dive-bomber squadron, giving us an experienced one for the upcoming battle.

Saratoga's VT-3 was less ready but well organized. However, the squadron was still flying the ancient TBD-1 Devastator. VT-3 was to suffer terrible losses along with VT-6 and VT-8 in this all but useless aircraft. Out of a total of forty-one TBDs launched from three aircraft carriers on 4 June 1942, thirty-seven would not return. Of the eighty-two men flying in these planes, only eight pilots and six crewmen survived.

VF-3, led by Lt. Comdr. John S. Thach, was strengthened by sixteen combat-experienced pilots from VF-42. The squadron's talent also included an admired and skilled executive officer, Lt. Comdr. Donald A. Lovelace, whose expertise added much to the squadron's strength. Also joining VF-3 were eight new and inexperienced pilots who had not yet landed on a combat carrier.

Thus *Yorktown's* mix and match air group for the Battle of Midway was composed. Aboard the ship the impossible was being accomplished—a three-month overhaul became a three-day patch job. Navy yard crews had worked frantically to get dry dock #1 ready to receive the crippled flattop. Early on the twenty-eighth the ship passed through the entry caisson gates, they closed behind her, and pumps began evacuating the water.

By late Wednesday afternoon, *Yorktown* stood high in the dry dock. Admiral Nimitz put on rubber boots and waded beneath the giant carrier to see for himself the damage that one direct hit and two near-misses from Japanese bombs had caused. Sprung seams along the ship's hull could be welded closed and one huge steel plate could be patched to her skin quickly, but the worst damage the direct hit had caused (not to mention the associated lesser damages) would be difficult if not impossible to repair in three days.

But Admiral Nimitz said it had to be done. Fifteen hundred workers poured aboard; huge lights were rigged around the dry dock to let the patch job begin despite the Pearl Harbor blackout. More than 150 welders and shipbuilders began round-the-clock work. The ship's crew also helped to heal the wounds and brought stores, food, and ammunition aboard.

Yorktown was out of dry dock on the twenty-ninth. Fueled and provisioned, she sailed at 0930 on 30 May 1942 with her hastily gathered new air group and veteran crew while her band cheerfully played "California, Here I Come." They had chosen this tune for a reason—Admiral Nimitz had made the officers and men of *Yorktown* a promise. He directed Captain Buckmaster to tell the crew that he apologized for sending them back into action immediately, but urgent work had to be done, and they were needed. After the Battle of Midway was over, he pledged that he would send the ship to her home port in Puget Sound, Bremerton, Washington, for a long liberty.

At sea that afternoon, *Yorktown* took her air group aboard. During the recovery, a tragic flight deck accident occurred. One of VF-3's new ensigns, making his first-ever carrier landing, came in high and fast. After touchdown, he bounced over the barrier and crashed on top of the aircraft that had landed before him. Don Lovelace, the new squadron executive officer, was killed—a grievous loss and an ominous beginning for the cruise.

Sunset found the gallant ship bravely steaming, with a bone in her teeth, toward Point Luck and then a rendezvous with the enemy. One patched-up aircraft carrier, flying a maverick air group, was destined to give her life to make the difference between defeat and victory in the greatest carrier naval battle of the Pacific war with Japan.

This would be her finest hour.

II

It may be the greatest sea battle of all time. Certainly it is the most significant one in U.S. naval history. Historian Gordon W. Prange named it the "miracle at Midway," Walter Lord entitled it the "incredible victory," and the dean of naval historians, Rear Adm. Samuel Eliot Morison called the Battle of Midway "six minutes that changed the world." I wish to join this elite group and call it "six immortal minutes."

The date was 4 June 1942 and the six minutes were from 1024 to 1030. The place was the open sea, a little more than one hundred miles northwest of Midway Island. Here, steaming in a box formation, were four of Japan's finest flattops—*Akagi, Kaga, Soryu,* and *Hiryu*—under the command of Vice Admiral Nagumo.

The carriers, spearhead of an invasion force headed for the occupation of Midway, had already launched an early-morning attack of over one hundred aircraft, recovered the survivors, and were preparing to send in a second attack against the island. At about 0930, a series of U.S. torpedo plane attacks began: VT-3, VT-6, and VT-8, a total of forty-one TBD aircraft, struck the Japanese force in waves, without escorts or dive-bomber diversion. Defending Zeros on CAP, and devastating AA fire, shot down thirty-five of the gallant attackers—an aerial "charge of the light brigade"—with no damage to any of the carriers.

Suddenly in the excitement, with the Japanese savoring this successful defense of their carriers, at 1024 the dreaded cry "enemy dive-bombers!" arose from three of their flattops. In those six immortal minutes, approximately forty-six Dauntless SBDs of VS-6, VB-6, and VB-3 from the U.S. carriers *Enterprise* and *Yorktown* dove from eighteen thousand feet and destroyed *Akagi, Kaga,* and *Soryu.*

It was an attack of unbelievable quickness, completeness, and luck. The Japanese carrier leaders literally did not know what hit them. In almost an instant, this dive-bombing attack ended Japanese dreams of a Greater East Asia Co-Prosperity Sphere.

It was a battle full of enigmatic events:

- The leader, CAG Wade McClusky from *Enterprise,* almost missed the enemy carriers completely; he found them by following a Japanese destroyer that was speeding to rejoin the carrier formation.

- CO of VB-3, Lt. Comdr. Max Leslie, and three of his charges lost their bombs en route to the target because of faulty arming systems in the aircraft; they dove anyhow as part of a seventeen-plane attack.

- Two squadrons of Dauntlesses from *Hornet* (over thirty aircraft) never found the Japanese carriers and lost several aircraft due to lack of fuel while searching beyond fuel range.

- A complete strike of *Hornet* fighters became lost and landed in the water without contacting the enemy.

- The three dive-bomber squadrons each attacked a different Japanese carrier in the immortal six minutes, but insisted later that they had attacked only two of them—no one wanted to claim the smaller *Soryu.*

- The Japanese carriers were caught with their decks loaded with both aircraft and armament. Thus each American hit started a chain reaction of explosions that made damage control impossible.

- The fourth Japanese carrier, *Hiryu,* was found and sunk in the afternoon by twenty-four Dauntlesses from the same three squadrons that did the job in the morning attack. Unfortunately, by that time this carrier's aircraft had hit *Yorktown,* putting her out of action.

- Although hit by Japanese aircraft torpedoes and bombs, *Yorktown* was making progress toward survival when struck with a spectacular spread of submarine torpedoes, fired from extreme range—a most fortunate break for the Japanese.

- Nimitz had a fourth carrier on the Midway scene as backup if needed; *Saratoga,* loaded with 107 aircraft of all types and a mixed bag of experienced and new pilots, became the new flagship for Rear Admiral Fletcher and his staff on 8 June after *Yorktown* went down.

One can see that there were numerous problems mixed in with the successes at Midway. But overall, the ambush set up at Point Luck by Nimitz, based upon information compiled by his intelligence people at Pearl Harbor, led him to say afterward: "The Battle of Midway was essentially a victory of intelligence." (And some damn good dive-bombing!)

While the total cost in lives was relatively small in proportion to the magnitude of the victory, it was hard on the aviators, especially the new young ensigns. Morison says over "three score" naval aviators were lost of the more than three hundred that participated, somewhat above 20 percent of the total. But some individual squadrons lost over half of their rosters—and to the survivors this was grievous indeed. These figures pertain only to the carrier squadrons; the Marine squadrons at Midway also suffered greatly. These figures for the carrier groups would have been much higher without the tremendous rescue efforts that were conducted in the battle area for several days after the Japanese withdrawal.

Coral Sea and Midway, back-to-back battles in thirty days, brought home to all naval pilots the irrevocable finality of death. It was so sudden—one moment a friend was in the ready room or wardroom or on liberty, the next he was gone forever. Historians say that the high number of casualties at the Battle of Shiloh in 1862 made men of both the North and South realize that the War Between the States was real. Midway was the Shiloh of the Pacific war; never again would naval aviators and their gunners consider the war a big adventure—a game to be played for the sport of it —but rather a serious business that, even when you were winning, could exact a terrible toll.

Speaking for the carrier aviators of those mid-1942 days, Ed Stafford says it very well in *The Big E:*

> To some extent they transferred their normal daily affection for their families to the companions in adventure who shared their meals and staterooms and bull sessions and ready rooms, their acey-deucey games and knowledge of their planes, the sky over the sea, the pride in the neat and deadly formations and the unspoken imminence of death.
>
> Then at the end of a certain day half had died or were lost, and to each one of the other half perhaps none or one of his close friends was left. It was sudden, unexpected and devastating.[1]

Personally I was never again the same after I began to realize the enormity of those fateful thirty days. To me, losing Dave Chaffee and Ed Kinzer at the Coral Sea, followed by one of my closest personal friends, Johnny Lough, and other Norfolk Deck Dodgers such as J. Q. Roberts, Gene Green, John Ammen, and Carl Peiffer at Midway, was like losing members of my own family.

There was never another dive-bombing victory quite as crystalline and pure as those few moments in June 1942 at Midway. Every 4 June we should pause then and remember the six immortal minutes and those, living and dead, who made them possible.

III

Vernon "Mike" Micheel and I go back almost half a century. Both of us were born and reared in Iowa (Mike in Davenport and I in Ottumwa), went to Iowa schools and colleges, and left the midwestern prairies by way of St. Louis's Lambert Field in search of wings of gold. As new ensigns in April 1942, he joined VS-6 and I arrived at VS-5, and we would later serve together in VB-2 for about a year and one-half, including a six-month combat tour in *Hornet* in 1944.

In spite of close associations during those years I never really knew much about Mike's experiences at the Battle of Midway. Modest, almost reticent about them, he had never told me the details of those eventful days in June 1942 when the Japanese Navy lost four of its finest aircraft carriers in one day to America's dive-bombers. So it is with gratitude that I give this account, utilizing materials given recently to me by Mike, which tells his heroic tale. He begins the story:

"On 17 April 1942, as a new ensign with a group of several other reserve aviators, I reported for duty involving flying in VS-6 at Pearl Harbor. At that time, like my colleagues, my flying qualifications were not too impressive: I had a total of 360 hours of flight time of which 87 were in the Dauntless. We new pilots immediately began tactical, bombing, and field carrier landing flights and on 30 April, with sandbags in the rear seat, I qualified aboard *Enterprise* (three landings).

"After a short cruise into the South Pacific to deliver a bunch of marine fighters and pilots to Efate in the New Hebrides, and missing the Coral Sea battle, we arrived back at Pearl on 26 May. Frantically refueling and replenishing, we departed in two days with *Hornet* as Task Force Sixteen; our destination was a spot at sea northeast of Midway Island someone named Point Luck. After a couple of days we were joined by Task Force Seventeen with the carrier *Yorktown*. We loitered and watched."

Mike Micheel was a part of the clever ambush that Nimitz set to attempt to surprise the Japanese forces coming to seize Midway. The intelligence coup turned out to be real, and on 4 June the stage was set for the most famous naval battle of the Pacific war. Mike continued:

"At 0730 we took off and rendezvoused for an attack on a reported four enemy carriers. CAG was Lt. Comdr. C. Wade McClusky leading a formation of fourteen SBDs of VS-6 and fifteen from VB-6. I was flying in the second section of the second division. All our aircraft were loaded with one five-hundred-pound bomb on the centerline rack and a hundred-pounder on each wing; VB-6 aircraft carried one thousand-pounder on the center rack only.

"With the weather clear and visibility unlimited, McClusky took

Air Group Six to twenty thousand feet. On arriving at the estimated enemy position, the ocean below was bare as far as the eye
could see. At this point we were about at our range limit, but the
CAG kept going, changing direction while searching for the enemy
carriers. I failed to jot down the new course heading and time, and
this was to affect my navigation back to the Big E later."

Mike is referring here to the famous turn that CAG McClusky
made to the heading of an enemy destroyer that was observed
racing northeast on the ocean below. Following this hunch, which
led the dive-bombers to the enemy fleet, is considered to be one
of the luckiest breaks ever to occur in a major carrier-versus-
carrier battle.

Mike went on: "Shortly after turning we found the enemy task
force consisting of four carriers, several heavy and light cruisers,
and many destroyers. One carrier was assigned by the CAG to
VB-6 [*Akagi*] and one to VS-6 [*Kaga*]. At about 1025, I followed
Lieutenant (jg) West into the dive, with Ens. Johnny Lough right
after me. We dove lengthwise along the target. How nice it was
to have a big red dot in the center of the flight deck for an aiming
point! During the dive I saw two fires burning on the carrier, one
forward and one on the starboard quarter. I released my five-
hundred-pound bomb and pulled out to the right. In my excitement
I forgot to release the wing bombs and this caused my Dauntless
to react sluggishly. I soon corrected that error by releasing the
bombs at a cruiser as I passed it broadside; I'm sure that I missed
this target as I was jinking so much trying to avoid AA fire. I never
saw an enemy fighter.

"When I arrived at what I thought was the rendezvous spot, no
one was there. With no section or division leader to take me home,
I took a guess as to the course back to the Big E and left. After a
short time on my heading, two SBDs from VB-6 crossed in front
of me going about twenty degrees to the left of my course. I
tagged along with them, figuring three together was better than
being alone.

"After flying about two hours we sighted the task force. As we
were coming up the wake of *Enterprise,* about seven to ten miles
astern, the two VB-6 planes ditched (out of fuel); I kept going and
landed on deck. I went to the bridge and reported to the captain
where the two pilots went down. As I was leaving I noticed the

nearby *Yorktown* was under attack and saw black smoke rising from several hits."

Mike had survived with a combination of luck and ability. He had landed back aboard with only four gallons of fuel remaining. Eight of his fellow pilots on the strike did not return, including his wingman—our mutual friend Johnny Lough. As none of the three aircraft in the third division returned, he was the last plane in his squadron to dive on *Kaga* and successfully return to *Enterprise*. A follow-up strike using all available aircraft was readied to go after the one remaining Jap CV.

Mike said: "Volunteers were asked to go on the second strike. I knew better than to volunteer for anything in the Navy, but after seeing *Yorktown* getting hit, I wanted off the ship if more attacks were coming—so I volunteered for the late afternoon strike.

"This group was led by my CO, Lt. W. E. Gallaher, and consisted of six planes from VS-6, four from VB-6, and fourteen from VB-3. We departed at 1745 and climbed to an initial altitude of thirteen thousand feet. We sighted the Jap force of one CV, one BB, one CA, and three DDs at about 1845. Gallaher took us to nineteen thousand feet as we circled to dive from the setting sun, with ceiling and visibility unlimited. Diving on the carrier *Hiryu* I saw a hit scored by a plane ahead of me in the dive. This carrier maneuvered radically as opposed to the morning one, which held course during the entire attack. Fairly heavy AA fire was encountered during my dive and after pullout. Japanese fighters were reported by other pilots in the flight, but I didn't see them. All VS-6 planes returned safely from this attack. For the entire battle, VS-6 lost seven pilots of nineteen assigned, six of which were new ensigns."

Taking part in two attacks against enemy carriers in one day, with both targets sunk, is a feat very few naval aviators accomplished during the Pacific war. To follow this achievement with two more major attacks against fleet units, a long search, and two life-saving carrier landings, one at night, is a flight record that might be the best compiled by any pilot in the Battle of Midway. For these exploits Mike Micheel received a well-earned Navy Cross.

Unlike others, Mike does not claim and never has claimed a hit for himself in these actions. After careful study of Japanese reports of hits on *Kaga,* I am certain that he scored one of the hits made that day. The bomb hits recorded by Japanese survivors coincide with the time that the West-Micheel-Lough section made their drops. In my opinion, one and perhaps two hits were made by that trio. Of course, this detail is not of great importance now, almost fifty years later, except for personal satisfaction; it is the achievement of the sinking of *Kaga* that is historically relevant.

IV

Those of us fortunate enough to be selected to fly the remaining ten VS-5 planes into Ford Island ahead of the *Yorktown*'s entrance on the morning of 27 May found ourselves caught up in a fever of activity. After all, we were the survivors of the first carrier-versus-carrier battle, in the Coral Sea, and the local pilots wanted to hear the latest sea stories about what really happened out there, how our SBDs performed against the Japanese fighters, what worked and what didn't—all the things that combat aviators talk about while imbibing a little of the grape after sundown. Serious planning for rendezvous later that night at favorite watering holes in the area had hardly begun when orders came at the flight line to check into the local BOQ and report back to the ship when it docked.

Late in the afternoon, as we lounged about in the *Yorktown* ready room, the decision as to our immediate fate came from higher authority: All VS-5 personal gear and squadron effects were to be removed from the ship as fast as possible. A work force was set up to get the job done and everyone turned to. The more senior officers packed their personal gear, told the working party ensigns where it was and in what amounts, and then left the ship. The junior officers, of which I was the lowest, were given assignments to direct the activities of the various working parties, who had the task of actually getting footlockers, bags, boxes, spare parts, tools, and what-have-you down the gangways, into trucks, and safely stowed into assigned hangar spaces across the airfield from the dock areas.

There was an urgency to the evacuation of VS-5 from *Yorktown.* Instructions were to get everything off as soon as possible so that the ship could go into dry dock. One thing was clear—our sister squadron, VB-5, was not leaving when we were. What was up?

To a young ensign assigned to direct a working party, there

was no time to sit around questioning what was happening, or why. And as a former Iowa farm boy, I knew that when there was work to be done in a hurry, you took off your shirt and pitched in physically to help. I found myself working side by side with the squadron enlisted personnel as we heaved, dragged, and toted gear from the *Yorktown*'s decks to the waiting trucks, where others took it away to the storage site. As the hours passed, thoughts of a planned liberty at the Moana faded slowly away.

Midnight came and went while we toiled away. Sandwiches and coffee were provided somewhere along the line. At about 0300 the last of the gear was gone and we junior officers staggered off to the waiting BOQ beds nearby. All that was in our minds was some sack time for our exhausted bodies.

As we approached the BOQ in total darkness, we were met by Goocher Downing and told to follow him. We soon found ourselves inside the blacked-out tennis club bar, where a fine party was in progress by candlelight. It was obvious that many of our senior squadron mates had not gone into nearby Honolulu, but had stayed at the tennis club because it was convenient and (I like to think) so they could keep the bar open for us until we finished. I managed to forget my fatigue after a couple of shots of bourbon blend, and it was dawn before I found my way to a bunk, to sleep until noon.

We did not know it at the time, but the decision to replace VS-5 with VB-3, a *Saratoga* dive-bomber outfit temporarily stationed at Kaneohe while their ship was being repaired back on the West Coast, had been made at the top levels of the Nimitz staff. Rear Admiral Noyes had convinced CinCPac to use the fresh VF-3, VB-3, and VT-3 squadrons in *Yorktown* for the coming action, holding out only VB-5 with its dozen veteran pilots augmented by eight replacement ensigns. Air Group Three was available after weeks of training at Kaneohe; the *Saratoga* had been torpedoed on 11 January 1942 while operating five hundred miles to the southwest of Oahu, and had left her squadrons behind while she went to Bremerton for repairs.

VB-5 was bitter, and justifiably so, when selected to remain aboard while we got to go ashore. They, too, had suffered losses at Coral Sea, although not as heavy as VS-5. It was a life-and-death decision as all squadrons, especially the dive-bombers and torpeckers, were to suffer grievous losses in the coming battle; being selected for removal from *Yorktown* gave my fellow pilots

89

and me a temporary reprieve from another exposure to death. We were to get some replacement pilots, go aboard *Saratoga* on 7 June, and arrive at the battle scene just after the heavy fighting was completed.

Five new ensigns reported aboard—Spike Conzett, Redbird Burnett, G. G. Estes, Dog Barker, and Rich Richey. With a new allotment of aircraft, we began a heavy schedule of flying from Ford Island, with liberty runs into the Moana and Waikiki Beach at every opportunity. *Enterprise* and *Hornet* left port, followed a day later by *Yorktown,* and the scuttlebutt was that a big battle was about to take place out by Midway. In spite of tight security on all news, too much was happening among the naval aviation squadrons and ships for the coming action to be kept in total secrecy. Combat aviators can smell a fight and nostrils were quivering.

By 30 May Nimitz had his three available carriers at sea and stationed at Point Luck in ambush. And he had one more card up his sleeve that no one knew about: *Saratoga* repairs had just been completed and she was available for participation if she could arrive in time. She had a new commanding officer, Capt. Dewitt C. "Duke" Ramsey. Rear Adm. Aubrey W. Fitch, late resident of the *Lexington* at Coral Sea, was returning home from that adventure aboard *Chester;* he was ordered by Nimitz to move his flag aboard the *Saratoga,* as commander of Task Force Eleven, as soon as he reached the West Coast.

But time was running out for CinCPac and, on 30 May, he ordered Ramsey to get to Pearl as quickly as possible. Loaded with F4F-4s, and SBD-3s, and a few of the new TBF-1 Grumman Avengers, a detachment of VF-2 and VS-3, and several ensigns fresh from ACTG, *Saratoga* headed west at more than twenty-five knots, arriving at berth F-2 off Ford Island the morning of 6 June.

The big carrier refueled, took on provisions, off-loaded passengers, and was back to sea the next morning as Task Group 11.2. Ramsey was in command as Fitch was still trying to catch up with the fast-moving units. With five DDs and the oiler *Kaskaskia,* the *Saratoga* landed her improvised air group at about 1100. No less than parts of five air groups made up the impromptu group that included my squadron VS-5 as well as VF-5, VS-3, VF-72, and detachments of VF-2, VT-5, and VT-8; a total of 107 aircraft (forty-seven fighters, forty-five dive-bombers, and fifteen torpedo planes). Some of these aircraft were meant to be replacements for *Enterprise* and *Hornet.*

Known as the Midway Relief Force, our group rendezvoused with TF-17 on 8 June. *Yorktown* had gone down the previous afternoon, so Fletcher moved his flag aboard *Saratoga* and we became Task Force Seventeen. We conducted the usual APSs and searches looking for enemy stragglers and downed pilots. Many of the latter were found during the next few days, but no enemy ships were in evidence.

I took part in the flying activities during those exciting days. By now everyone knew that our dive-bombers had sunk four Japanese carriers at the cost of *Yorktown* and the destroyer *Hammann.* I recall that a short, stocky lieutenant (jg) by the name of Bill Godwin was LSO, and he was a good one. VS-5 flew ten SBDs to *Enterprise* on 11 June—the beginning of a new assignment in Big E and for me the start of almost one year of combat in two squadrons flying from the greatest carrier of World War II. Looking back, I remember that we were happy to leave the "Floating Dry Dock" and "Torpedo Junction," as the poor old *Saratoga* was known to pilots in those hectic days of 1942, for the much sharper-operating "Galloping Ghost"—the Big E.

But credit should be given where it is due. Recorders have almost totally ignored the important role that *Saratoga* played in the Battle of Midway. One of the few complete accounts about this assignment has been given by historian John Lundstrom in his fine book *The First Team.*[2] It clearly shows that *Saratoga* was summoned to the battle by CinCPac before any action took place, moved into a vital backup role with 107 aircraft and the required pilots as swiftly as possible, and thus provided Nimitz with four aircraft carriers, not just three as indicated in most battle accounts.

Early in the morning of 13 June, the victorious aviators from *Yorktown, Enterprise, Hornet,* and *Saratoga* began arriving at the fields around Oahu. Then the carriers and their escorts entered the harbor to go to assigned berths amid the acclaim of both ship and shore personnel. It was the moment to rejoice—this time there was no doubt that the Japanese had been given a real beating —but the victory had not been without price. America had lost the carrier *Yorktown* and one destroyer, 147 aircraft, and 307 men killed. There had been extensive damage to installations at Midway and Dutch Harbor, and Attu and Kiska were occupied. However, the Japanese losses of four carriers and 322 aircraft with their valuable crews were severe enough to reverse the tide of the Pacific war. In addition, one heavy cruiser was sunk and one seriously damaged, with minor damage to a battleship, oiler, and three destroyers. Approximately twenty-five hundred men were killed in action.[3]

V

One of the great tragedies of the Pacific naval air war was the terrible loss of torpedo planes at Midway. And from the first attempts to hit Japanese warships with the lumbering TBD Devastator at the Coral Sea, through the later battles of the Eastern Solomons, Santa Cruz, and Guadalcanal utilizing the TBF Avenger, the record of gross inefficiency of the U.S. Mark 13 aerial torpedo was appalling.

Many brave naval aviators and aircrewmen went to their deaths while trying futilely to use these inadequate weapons to sink a Japanese warship. The fate of Torpedo Squadron Eight at Midway, under command of Lt. Comdr. John C. Waldron, is well-known. Leading fifteen TBDs with torpedoes against *Akagi*, he lost all aircraft and men except Ens. George "Tex" Gay, who survived a crash into the sea near the Japanese carrier target. What is not as well known is that a total of forty-one TBDs were sent to attack Japanese carriers that day and, of this group from three torpedo squadrons, not a single Mark 13 hit a target. All but six aircraft were shot down by enemy fighters and AA fire while trying to do the impossible with a torpedo weapon known to be all but worthless. What a waste!

American torpedoes were breaking up on contact with the water, running erratically, and not exploding when they struck a target. This dismal performance had been noted in the Tulagi raids and the Coral Sea battles in May, but over-enthusiastic claiming of hits in these missions glossed over the Mark 13's real performance, which bordered on chaotic. With the possible exception of the *Shoho* sinking, which was so overwhelming it defied accurate hit accountability, torpedo hits just didn't happen. But naval air commanders kept using them, and sent fine young torpecker pilots and aircrewmen to Valhalla carrying them at Midway and in later battles. Why?

It is not enough to say that these weapons had to be used because they were all that was available. Better never to have flown torpedo planes except for searches, ASP, and shore base bombing, or to have replaced them on the CVs with additional Dauntlesses, than to send them with an utterly inadequate torpedo weapon system to make torpedo runs on warships. The probable reason for persisting with the Mark 13 was an attempt by American commanders to duplicate successes the Japanese were having with their Long Lance torpedoes, both as aircraft and surface ship weapons.

Long Lances were responsible for much of the serious damage done to U.S. warships early in the war. Starting with remarkable success in the shallow waters of Pearl Harbor against anchored battleships, the year 1942 saw *Yorktown, Hornet,* and *Wasp* sunk, and *Saratoga* put out of action twice by these torpedoes. (*Lexington* did not sink from torpedo damage alone but from huge explosions caused by vapors from broken aviation fuel lines in the ship.) During this same period not a single major Japanese warship was lost to American torpedoes, whether airborne or from submarines or destroyers. Our admirals could not seem to accept that it was the excellence of the Long Lance that made Japanese torpedo tactics so fruitful, while American torpedo efforts, no matter how valorously pressed, failed because of an inadequate weapon.

When the Japanese battleship *Hiei* was sunk off Savo Island on 11 November 1942, it was hailed as the first such ship sunk by U.S. carrier aircraft. Major credit for the feat was given to Lt. Scoofer Kaufman and his VT-10 Avengers from *Enterprise;* known as the Buzzard's Brigade, they were credited with several torpedo hits that brought about the sinking.

Taking nothing away from this courageous squadron, Japanese battle reports reviewed after the war indicate that *Hiei* received only three torpedo hits during the entire day-long battle. But she had suffered dozens of shell-fire hits in a night action, followed by many direct bomb hits from Dauntlesses during the lengthy engagement. It was the cumulative effect of all these injuries that finally did her in, not torpedo damages alone.

Historians James and William Belote point out that had U.S. Navy and Marine aircraft "been equipped with Japanese 550-pound delay-fuse bombs and [Long Lance] torpedoes with reliable Japanese contact exploders, they would have finished off *Hiei* as ex-peditiously as their rivals had disposed of *Repulse* and *Prince of Wales* on the third day of the war."[4]

What a sad commentary on American torpedoes and bombs, but what a compliment to the valor of wearers of the wings of gold!

6

EASTERN SOLOMONS

I

AFTER THE short cruise in *Saratoga*, it was with unabashed happiness that Scouting Squadron Five left her upon return to Pearl Harbor from the Midway victory. She was overcrowded, and her crew, with its limited combat experience, lacked the spirit and vitality that we had grown used to in *Yorktown*. We set up housekeeping at Kaneohe while awaiting further orders for return to combat.

A squadron with the experience and talent of VS-5 was not homeless for long in the summer of 1942. My diary for 8 July states: "Flew aboard Big E for a few days of practice attack tactics. *Enterprise* is a fine ship, which operates aircraft quickly and well. I am rooming with Walt Coolbaugh in 0117, which has a porthole (a good room!). Flew two hops today for a total of seven and one-half hours—the most I have ever flown in one day—I am dead tired."

Something big was in the wind, but what? The next day saw more intensive flying from *Enterprise*. We took off, landed at Maui Field, then went back out to the ship in a simulated dive-bombing attack. We came in from sixteen thousand feet on oxygen and were intercepted by our own fighters, as we practiced various formation maneuvers to foul up their dummy gunnery runs. A second hop in the afternoon brought the total time for the day to six hours.

The three-day workout with Big E finished with a bang. The final part of the exercise had VS-5 attacking a bombing range on the southern coast of Hawaii with live five-hundred-pound bombs. I flew number two on Art Downing on a predawn launch coordinated with shelling from cruisers and destroyers and made a good drop in the target area. The whole affair was practice for something coming, but no one was talking about what or where the action would be.

It wasn't all work and no play. In typical Navy fashion, we went ashore for as much liberty as possible before departing on a war cruise. As I recall, Birney Strong was married during these days and the entire squadron got roaring drunk at the reception. On a final two-day blast, I had a great time with the Goocher. We used the Moana Hotel as a base and even had a steak fry with two local girls who lived in an apartment across the street from the hotel. We were a happy, carefree bunch under the command of a great skipper, Turner Caldwell—good men with high spirits and an intense desire to engage the enemy. Just how good we were would be tested soon.

On 15 July 1942, the squadron left Pearl Harbor and Oahu in *Enterprise* heading south, destination as yet unknown. With good sailing and flying weather, everyone flew practice dive-bombing and gunnery hops, including tactics with the fighters flying cover to prevent interception. Rumor had us headed back to the Tonga area for rendezvous with a large force, but there was still nothing definite, and we continued heading south under fair skies.

Finally the waiting and wondering were over when the Big E joined two other carriers, the *Saratoga* and *Wasp,* as well as dozens of cruisers, destroyers, and support ships of all kinds. The presence of more than twenty transports loaded with marines and their battle gear made it clear that the coming action was not another hit-and-run raid of a Japanese base but an invasion of some consequence. The announcement was then made: The huge force gathered together was headed for an island called Guadalcanal where invasion landings were planned against a Japanese force already there. Landings would be made at Tulagi as well as part of Guadalcanal where a new airfield was being built. VS-5 was familiar with the area from the May raids.

In those early days of the Pacific war, radio silence was strictly followed. VHF radios, with their many channels for both pilot and ship use, were still a thing of the future. Only division leaders were allowed to talk during a strike—other pilots could get on the air only if necessary during combat or in case of emergency. The pilots were identified by nicknames. Our skipper was "Stinky," J.T. Barker was "Dog," and so on. I was simply "Hal."

II

As this first large invasion force of U.S. ships moved toward the target, tension mounted. My diary continues:

5 August 1942: We have had no bogey contacts yet but can expect some tomorrow as we close with the target. I am scheduled to go in on the first attack wave, which will be launched just before daybreak. I am flying right-hand slot on the skipper with Walt Coolbaugh on the other wing. Our target is the AA gun positions and radio station installations on the south shore of Tulagi. We have been issued small maps for our plotting boards and briefed thoroughly for this strike mission. I feel ready for whatever this invasion brings and am hoping that I can be lucky and get through the air support raids OK. I am not worried or scared—just hoping for the best.

The big day—7 August 1942—finally arrived. At 0545 I took off in the darkness with a thousand-pound bomb load. Flying number three on our CO, Caldwell, was a thrilling moment for me. Walt and I made the rendezvous in the predawn without trouble but others were not so fortunate and many wingmen, even whole sections, got lost trying to get together in the black with no horizon to guide us. My diary describes this first invasion support mission:

As we approached the target at fourteen thousand feet, I saw the big guns flashing as battleships, cruisers, and destroyers shelled the Japanese beach installations. There was sufficient light at the target to clearly see it as we dove. I dropped my bomb right alongside the Skipper's in our assigned area. After strafing enemy positions, we returned to the ship for another bomb and ammo load. I made three strikes during this day and by nightfall the Marines had taken Gavutu and Tulagi. While strafing an ammo dump, I got a secondary explosion directly in front of me with debris flying up all around but not striking the plane. We had a fighter make a run on the formation, but the gunners poured such a hail of lead into him that he fell away seriously hurt. Several seaplanes, including float Zeros, were destroyed at their buoys on the water in the first strike.

Our ships covered the waters below—dozens of them as far as eye could see. From the transports flowed a steady stream of landing barges that were putting marines and their gear ashore on the beachheads of Guadalcanal, Tulagi, and Gavutu. From my grandstand seat in the sky, everything appeared to be proceeding in good order and as planned.

III

We did not expect enemy fighter opposition, but were taking no chances, making quick breakups and rendezvous and flying tight formations. A few float-fighters had been destroyed on the water. The new airfield being constructed on Lunga Point was not yet operational and had no aircraft. There had been no reports of Japanese aircraft carriers at sea anywhere near the invasion area, and the nearest Japanese airfields in operation were at Rabaul, 560 nautical miles away. This distance was considered out of range for enemy fighters. And we had our fighter escorts with us from our carriers—shipmates who were itching for something airborne with meatballs on it to shoot down. We were confident.

While rendezvousing after our second air support strike in mid-morning, an exciting "Tallyho, many bogey bombers" came crackling into my radio headset. Several twin-engine Betty bombers were inbound to attack the transports still busily unloading in the harbor. As our F4F fighters took after these planes, there came another call: "Watch out for Zero fighters with the bombers."

We tightened our formation of SBDs, rear gunners alert and ready with their twin-mounted .30-calibers, and all hands began to swivel heads with eyes scanning the skies for enemy fighters. We were a disciplined group who realized that our main chance for survival against fighters was in sticking together so that the combined firepower of our gunners could be brought to bear on any fighter making a run on the formation. Dive-bomber pilots had found out at Coral Sea and Midway that a lone straggler, especially an SBD or TBD, was the first target of Japanese Zero fighter pilots.

At approximately five thousand feet altitude, as our eight-plane formation was turning onto a heading back to the carriers, we spotted an enemy fighter at five o'clock, slightly below, coming in at high speed. A quick "tallyho" with bearing and distance alerted the group. All pilots concentrated on maintaining a tight formation while gunners waited for the enemy plane to come into range before firing in unison. Quickly he closed the distance. Nearer and nearer he came, until at less than two hundred yards the thought flashed through my mind: "My God, he's going to ram the formation!"

At that instant the Zero's 7.7 guns began twinkling, followed by the slower puffs of a twenty-millimeter cannon, and shells came flying into the formation in lazy arcs. As one man, our eight gunners returned the fire, and the power of sixteen .30-caliber guns struck the incoming Zero at point-blank range. The aircraft shuddered as if it had flown into a wall, pieces flew from the wings and fuselage, and it dove under the formation in a roll. Completing the roll, it emerged on the other side, rose slightly, then fell off into a slow left spiral toward the sea below. There was no fire, but it had been badly hit and appeared to be done for. As no one saw the damaged Zero strike the water, or explode, only a probable kill was credited to the gunners when they were debriefed back at the ship.

This determined and courageous solo enemy fighter attack pressed to point-blank range on a formation was the first one I had experienced, and I wish to venture an opinion about it. I believe that the Japanese pilot who made this rash attack on our formation was Saburo Sakai, a samurai superace who has been credited with sixty-four aircraft shot down during an incredible combat career spanning more than five years. I came to this conclusion after reading Sakai's book *Samurai!*[1] His description of an attack at Guadalcanal in which he almost lost his life matches that made on my formation exactly as to time and place.

Some historians have stated that the formation Sakai attacked was a VB-6 group of SBDs led by a Lt. Carl Horenburger. This may be true—there were several formations of SBDs in the area at the time, and some were hit by enemy fighters. But after reading Sakai's own description of his quest, I feel that the formation he attacked consisted of VS-5s; I guess we'll never know for sure.

Personally, I learned an important lesson from this mission: The best, and perhaps only, answer for dive-bombers to an attack from a Zero was a tight formation and good gunnery.

American naval pilots got a major break from the Sakai wounding at Guadalcanal; many probably lived longer because they did not face him again until the war was almost over. By then the odds would be in our favor.

IV

Our carriers and supporting ships stayed in the invasion area for three days, fighting off enemy air attacks and providing close air support. During that time I flew seven close-support bombing missions, which was the average of all pilots of VS-5 during the period. Then everyone pulled up stakes and left, with the marines supposedly in charge of the situation. What we pilots didn't know was that our admirals and captains were leaving without off-loading much of the supplies and equipment needed by the men ashore. Disagreements that had begun weeks before the actual landings were now threatening the success of the postinvasion follow-up.

The carrier task force moved to the south and remained at sea watching and waiting. Japanese surface units—cruisers and destroyers—began coming into the invasion area at night; one engagement saw the loss of four CLs, three American and one Australian. On 20 August a presentation was made in the *Enterprise* wardroom by Lt. Comdr. Slim Townsend, a ship's officer who had been with the invasion forces during the landings. He told us that the Japanese soldiers and sailors found dug in on Tulagi and Gavutu had died to the last man. Our marines suffered heavy casualties because the Japanese had constructed elaborate bomb shelters that protected them from both bombing and shelling, leaving them alive to fight. Over on Guadalcanal it was different— there the enemy simply moved back into the hills and jungle, where they were now being reinforced piecemeal until they reached a buildup great enough to attack the marine lines and take back the airfield.

Two days after Slim Townsend's briefing about the Canal (as we called Guadalcanal), intelligence reports were received stating that the expected counterattack was in progress and that a Japanese carrier fleet was at sea and on its way. Ashore, a Japanese special force of nine hundred men attacked the eastern perimeter at a place called the Tenaru River. During a night action the marines held, killing over 670 of the attackers with a loss of twenty-eight killed and seventy-five wounded.

In spite of some negative aspects, the overall results of the Guadalcanal invasion had to be considered highly successful. American marines captured an airfield almost ready for flight operations and two smaller fighter support fields already laid out. The main field was prepared for Marine planes, which began operations on 20 August 1942 with nineteen F4Fs of VMF-223, and twelve SBDs of VMSB-232, arriving from the *Long Island;* it was to become the focal point of heavy fighting for the next six months. No one had the slightest idea that controlling this island airfield would bring heavy losses to both American and Japanese ground, naval, and air forces, and would include two more carrier-versus-carrier battles, and the sinking of *Hornet* and *Wasp.*

V

The morning of 23 August 1942 brought light fog, limited visibility, and a restless sea. Things were also restless in the Big E: nervous tension among the crew increased as word was passed that the Japanese were at sea with their carriers and headed for our new beachhead at Guadalcanal.

Flying wing on the skipper, I took off from *Enterprise* at dawn. We had been assigned a northerly search sector to look for the Japanese fleet, and each plane carried a five-hundred-pound general-purpose bomb. Under an overcast sky with intermittent rain-squalls, we departed at eight hundred feet altitude on the first leg of the search sector.

At 0725 we sighted a small ship on the water dead ahead that was coming toward us at considerable speed. More than one hundred miles from the force, in waters where any contact would be an enemy one, the surface bogey looked much like a large motor launch as it plowed through the moderately heavy seas, taking water over its bow and leaving a long, white wake aft. It was a Japanese submarine running on the surface on a southerly heading toward our task force.

We had no time to organize an attack, but simply pushed over into glide-bombing runs on the sub as it approached. Its lookouts must have either seen or heard us coming at about the same time that we started our dives and they crash-dived their boat. Caldwell released his bomb, which hit abeam on the starboard side near the conning tower. The sub already had its decks awash and was moving under the surface so that only a direct hit would have damaged or destroyed it at that point. Following Caldwell, I was in a poor position to bomb effectively, so I did not release, but waited to see if the first bomb would bring the target back to the surface for another attack. The boat disappeared completely; there were no signs of any damage; the skipper's bomb probably did little but shake up the occupants. My disappointment in being so ineffective in this, my first enemy ship contact, was almost unbearable.

This early morning enemy submarine encounter was the first of six contacts that Dauntless pilots of VS-5 were to make during the three-day period of 23–25 August 1942. About one hour after this contact, squadronmates Lt. Birney Strong and Ens. Rich Richey had a similar one at a point approximately eighty miles northeast of the first. Their attack was more successful in that the bombs initially forced the sub back to the surface. However, it then dove again and escaped with little apparent damage. In the afternoon, VS-5 Ens.'s Emool Maul and Rastus Estes caught yet another Japanese submarine running on the surface. The pattern of attack and close hits was observed as the vessel crash-dived, and these pilots noted an oil slick on the water after the target submerged. They claimed it "probably sunk." During the next two days, three more enemy subs were attacked by VS-5 pilots—one on the twenty-fourth and two on the twenty-fifth. Ensign Estes was involved in both attacks on the latter date and received credit for a "definite sinking."

Japanese postwar naval records show that their three submarines lost during August 1942 were all sunk by allied surface destroyers. Thus VS-5, while not actually sinking any of the six enemy subs attacked, certainly set a record for sightings and attacks on such boats by a dive-bomber squadron during this three-day spree in late August 1942.

That brief meeting by dawn's early light on 23 August was the first and only enemy submarine I was to see during three years of combat flying at sea in the Pacific. The seriousness of several enemy submarines converging upon Task Force Sixteen in this battle was vividly illustrated shortly after these contacts, with the damaging of *Saratoga* the first week in September and the sinking of *Wasp* on 15 September by submarine hits. These successful attacks were probably carried out by enemy submarines sighted and attacked by VS-5 during the 23–25 August period. Ironically, if our SBDs had been armed with aerial depth charges, rather than the standard five-hundred-pound bombs carried at that stage of the Pacific war, some of the six attacks might have resulted in kills or serious damage to the targets. A near miss with a depth charge was often better than a bomb's direct hit because it opened a submarine's seams and flooded it. For a general-purpose bomb to be effective, a direct hit before the sub went underwater was required. Once the bomb hit the water, much of its explosive effect was lost due to the muffling effect of that medium. This was true only of small bombs—1,000- to 2,000-pound bombs were known to cause severe damage to the sides of ships by near-miss concussion.

By mid-1943 all ASP planes flown from carriers were armed with aerial depth charges. Unfortunately I was never to see, much less attack, another enemy submarine during the rest of the war, although I would spend hours on ASP patrol missions around our task forces with a depth charge hanging serenely from the belly of my dive-bomber.

During 1942, the overall effectiveness of Japanese submarines against American carriers was phenomenal. They sank *Wasp* outright and *Yorktown* while it was being saved after battle damage. *Saratoga* was put out of action twice during this crucial period by submarine torpedo hits. American submarines did not so much as damage a single Japanese carrier during this same period.

VI

The morning of 24 August 1942 found *Enterprise* and her air group still searching for the Japanese carriers that were rumored to be at sea in the area. However, right at this crucial time, Rear Adm. Frank Jack Fletcher made one of the strangest decisions of many unwise ones during several major actions against the Japanese fleet: he dispatched *Wasp* and several destroyers south of the main force to refuel. By this act he effectively reduced his strength by one-third in the face of an enemy force of three carriers and supporting ships. In addition, he disregarded contact reports made by our long-range patrol seaplanes (PBYs) that they had sighted one small carrier shortly after daybreak. He was unsatisfied with their past performances and chose to ignore this most important contact. To complete this odd series of decisions, he did not launch the usual dawn search, but waited until afternoon to do so. Meanwhile the Japanese were determining the American position and would attack our main body in force, while we would find only the small *Ryujo,* a decoy purposely exposed by Admiral Yamamoto and a ruse that had worked previously in the Coral Sea with *Shoho.*

In fairness to Fletcher, I must note that he was in a position of peril not entirely of his own making. The previous day, late in the afternoon, he had launched a major strike of thirty-one Dauntlesses and six new TBF Avengers at extreme range, based upon a patrol plane report. This force found nothing and had to fly to the new Henderson Field in Guadalcanal for the night. Until he got those aircraft back aboard *Saratoga,* he was caught with too few planes to conduct a large search and also still have aircraft for a major strike.

The errant strike group was back aboard *Saratoga* by 1130 from the overnight stay and Fletcher was now able to launch a search. He assigned the job to *Enterprise,* which needed seven SBDs from VS-5, eight from VB-6, and seven TBFs from VT-3 to cover a search area from 290 degrees to due east—a large area that reflected his concerns and those of his staff, and revealed how little was known of the Japanese position. All were off by 1315.

It did not take VS-5's Lt. Birney Strong and Ens. Rich Richey long to find *Ryujo,* which was precisely what Yamamoto had planned. The bait was taken, and a strike group of twenty-eight SBDs and eight TBFs left *Saratoga* at 1430 on a heading of 320 degrees, distance 215 miles, under the direction of Comdr. Don Felt in an SBD called "Queen Bee." Thus, while the entire American strike group headed for a small decoy light carrier (CVL), the main force of *Shokaku* and *Zuikaku* were preparing maximum aircraft strikes against *Saratoga* and *Enterprise.* We had been outsmarted strategically with the tactical battle still to be fought—it was Coral Sea all over again.

Air Group Three found and attacked *Ryujo* at approximately 1610. Lt. Comdr. L. J. "Bullet Lou" Kirn dove with fourteen planes of VS-3 and six of VB-3. CAG Felt, watching from above, saw waterspouts rise one after another as all twenty pilots missed —only two bombs were close enough to do damage.[2]

Things were getting serious. Felt then ordered Lt. Harold S. "Sid" Bottomley with seven VB-3 Dauntlesses to halt an attack on *Tone,* a Japanese cruiser, and switch to the *Ryujo.* Then Felt himself dove, claiming a direct hit. Three more hits were made by Bottomley's seven, turning *Ryujo* into a funeral pyre.

At this point in the attack, five new TBF Avengers of a reconstituted VT-8 made torpedo runs at the shattered warship. "Though AA fire was brisk and both Zeros and Kates harried them, the pilots raced in at 200 knots, twice the speed possible for the old Devastators, to drop their tin fish from 200 feet [altitude] at 800 to 900 yards range." One possible hit was claimed, but the Mark 13 torpedo's performance was still dismal. "Despite the poor bombing score, the *Saratoga* attack group had finished *Ryujo,* ending the remarkable career of the veteran 10,000-ton CVL. . . . As Yamamoto had anticipated, using the ship as a sacrificial pawn had cost him the carrier and part of her air group but had diverted from *Shokaku* and *Zuikaku* most of Fletcher's planes." Japanese casualties were 7 officers and 113 men killed and 138 wounded.[3]

An incident some distance away from the *Ryujo* attack almost changed the results of this short carrier-versus-carrier exchange. At 1545, in another search sector, VB-6 Dauntless scouts Lt. Ray Davis and Ens. R. C. Shaw spotted Nagumo's main force of *Shokaku* and *Zuikaku.* Undetected by either radar or lookouts, the pair climbed to fourteen thousand feet and dove on *Shokaku.* Both five-hundred-pound bombs were near misses, with Davis's so close on the starboard side aft it killed six men with splinters and concussion.

The big Japanese carriers had already launched their main strike groups against *Saratoga* and *Enterprise.* However, *Shokaku* was respotting her flight deck and had eight aircraft midships and twelve parked aft. If either Davis or Shaw had scored a direct hit, the chances of a conflagration on deck similar to the ones at Midway was a real possibility. Lady Luck was not riding with our Dauntlesses this time, and nothing but another missed opportunity came from the encounter. To top off the bad luck, Ray's radio reports did not get through to the Big E: Flight 300 would fly far to the northwest without new, accurate position information; Caldwell's group of eleven SBDs would end up jettisoning valuable bombs and flying to Guadalcanal without ever finding the fortuitous Japanese twins.

VII

On *Enterprise*, VS-5 had seven SBDs armed and ready for launch as a part of a second attack group. By about 1630 those of us on strike standby in the ready room began to think that the action was over for the day. Then radar picked up incoming bogeys, and the order came to man ready aircraft on the double. Racing to the armed SBDs, we cleared the deck just as the first of the Japanese Vals started their dives on the Big E. When rendezvoused, there were seven from VS-5 in formation together: Walt Coolbaugh and I were flying wing on Skipper Caldwell; Walt Brown and Dog Barker were flying on Rog Woodhull; and Spike Conzett was a seventh plane in the formation. A four-plane group of VB-6 aircraft, led by Lt. (jg) Gil Guillory with Harry Liffner, Buck Manford, and Chris Fink as wingmen joined the formation. Everyone had his regular gunner except me; a young Tex-Mex A3c. from VB-6 named Johnny Villarreal manned my Dauntless, replacing Barton Woods. This flight of eleven Dauntlesses, brought together by fate and the Japanese attack, was to be known in history as *Enterprise* Flight 300. A dozen TBFs, including Lt. Comdr. Max Leslie as CAG, and two SBDs from *Saratoga,* as well as all available F4Fs, were launched in a deck-clearing frenzy before the Japanese dive-bombers hit.

As Flight 300 circled just outside the task force screen, I saw two Japanese bombs hit the Big E's flight deck, but could not tell how badly she was hurt. Then Caldwell received his orders: "Proceed to the enemy carriers and attack." Each plane was carrying a thousand-pound bomb and full ammo loads for fixed and free guns. The formation departed toward the northwest on a heading of the last reported position of a Japanese carrier; unfortunately this position was not the twins *Zuikaku* and *Shokaku.*

Two hours of daylight remained. Comdr. John Crommelin, air officer of *Enterprise,* watching us fly away into the afternoon sun, made an observation: "They'll never make it back. They won't find their target before dark, and if they do they'll not be able to return to this carrier. They're expendable."[4]

In spite of Commander Crommelin's prediction for Flight 300, as we flew into a beautiful South Pacific sunset I did not feel fear. At last I was getting the chance to dive-bomb a Japanese warship —if I was lucky it would be an aircraft carrier. As a combat pilot I recognized few of my faults or limited flying experience. After all, I was with my squadron buddies—Walt, Spike, Woody, Dog, and Brownie—and flying wing on the greatest skipper in the Navy. What could possibly happen to me other than to get a share of the fame and glory?

The formation of eleven dive-bombers flew northwest over a calm sea as the shadows deepened to purple in the east and the golden light faded in the west. Passing the expected contact point, Caldwell continued another fifty miles or so but saw nothing. By this time we were more than three hundred miles from *Enterprise,* if she was still afloat, with barely enough gas to make it back to attempt a night landing. I had a sense of frustration: Where were the bastards? "Please, Lord, give us a chance to avenge our dead comrades and stricken ship."

But finding the now-fleeing Japanese carrier task force was not in the cards for Flight 300. The Skipper directed us to jettison bombs and turn our engine settings to a lean fuel mixture for maximum range, as he headed the formation to an alternative destination—Henderson Field, Guadalcanal. It was completely dark, with a new moon rising, when the flight neared the jungle airfield. Coming in from the north over the sea, a few guns opened fire, thinking the aircraft had to be enemy ones. But the word spread quickly: "Don't fire, these are American planes!" As we circled the field, faint lights appeared in the darkness below. Marines on the ground were setting out flare pots to outline the runway. From above, these pots gave the illusion of a large letter L in the jungle.

Two of the planes landed downwind, then all was squared away. One by one each pilot dropped wheels and flaps and, using the last of his gasoline, landed in the darkness on the dusty, gravel-topped runway. On the final approach I was startled to see treetops just below me, illuminated by my engine exhaust flares; several tall trees had not yet been cut down by the Marine and Seabee Construction Unit, Battalion (CUB-1) personnel. Fortunately, not a single mishap occurred during this hazardous termination of a search-strike mission of better than four hours.

Flight 300's arrival at Henderson Field was received with considerable jubilation by the flying marines already present. Pilots from VMSB-232 came running up to our planes as we taxied into parking areas west of the runway. 2nd Lt. Tom Moore greeted me as I jumped down from the wing; we had been in advanced training together at Opa-Locka in the fall of 1941. Here, less than a year later, we were meeting again on the other side of the globe on a coral airstrip in a five-mile-square patch of jungle just taken from the Japanese.

Since we had not eaten since lunch time on *Enterprise,* we were introduced to Marine-type food in the field. I do not remember what was given us that first night—I do know that it was barely palatable and came as a shock to carrier pilots who were used to the excellent cuisine served in a carrier wardroom. Decent food was already starting to be a problem on the Canal; this shortage, and dysentery, would strip about thirty pounds from my already lean frame in the next four weeks while I flew combat missions with the Cactus Air Force.

7

CACTUS

I

THE INVASION of Guadalcanal by the First Marine Division, Reinforced, on 7 August 1942, was given the code name of "Cactus." During the resulting three-month Battle of Guadalcanal, a small group of Army, Navy, and Marine flyers, operating against tremendous odds from a battered airstrip called Henderson Field, became known as the Cactus Air Force (CAF).

Henderson Field, named in honor of Maj. Lofton "Joe" Henderson, a Marine dive-bomber pilot killed during the Battle of Midway, had been in operation only four days when Flight 300 arrived from *Enterprise*. Official flight operations had started on 20 August, when VMF-223 with nineteen F4Fs and VMSB-232 with twelve SBDs arrived from the CVL *Long Island*. From this date through 15 November, a period of eighty-eight days, a total of eight fighter, twelve dive-bomber, and two torpedo squadrons from U.S. Army, Navy, and Marine air forces fought the Japanese Eleventh Air Fleet, based at Rabaul. The prize for all the air, sea, and ground fighting that took place was a piece of coral and gravel about 3,800 feet long and 150 feet wide. The arrival of Flight 300 on 24 August immediately doubled the number of dive-bombers available to Major General Vandergrift at a critical time; the eleven pilots were the first carrier flyers to operate from a land base against the Japanese in World War II.

There were three types of combat aircraft flying with the Cactus Air Force during the three-month battle for control of the skies over Guadalcanal and the surrounding seas. The principal fighter type was the Grumman F4F Wildcat, a stocky, midwing, single-seat plane that could fight almost on a par with the Japanese Zero, but only on specific terms. Its main strength was an ability to absorb punishment and still keep flying—a feature of all American combat aircraft when compared to Japanese models. Armor plate protecting the pilot and self-sealing fuel tanks, combined with solid construction and engines that seldom failed, made up for a lack of speed and maneuverability, both enjoyed by enemy Zeros. These features saved pilots' lives. Rarely did American aircraft explode and burn from enemy fire, but this was a common fate for Japanese pilots. A few rounds into their fuel tanks and they would go down in flames.

In addition to the F4F, the Army Air Corps's Sixty-seventh Pursuit Squadron operated several P-400 fighters from Henderson. With an operational ceiling of about fifteen thousand feet, they could not get high enough to intercept incoming Japanese fighters and bombers. They ended up performing low-level strafing missions, with an occasional dogfight at low altitudes when opportunity or necessity made it expedient.

The Douglas SBD Dauntless was the attack dive-bomber flown by both Marine and Navy pilots at this early stage of the war. A rugged plane carrying a pilot and gunner, it had one bad fault—it was slow, even in a dive. But like the F4F it was tough and could take heavy punishment and keep flying—characteristics that pilots loved. It was rock steady in a dive, and forgiving of small errors caused by the lack of piloting experience of a majority of those who were flying combat that first year of the war.

The Grumman TBF Avenger torpedo bomber arrived toward the end of the period and made a contribution to the box score of ships sunk, including the first Japanese battleship destroyed in the war. Flown by a reorganized VT-8, VT-10, and VMSB-131, this aircraft replaced the old TBD and went on to become a dependable attack plane for the rest of the war.

After finishing a beggarly first meal, the pilots of Flight 300 were taken by their Marine dive-bomber hosts to the bivouac area for the night. We split up among several tents that were set up for shelter in the Lever Company palm groves northwest of the field. As there was a shortage of cots, most of us prepared to sleep on Japanese matting spread on the ground.

Everyone turned in. Before sleep came we were routed out by shelling from Japanese warships in the harbor. We took to air raid shelters with our Marine friends and received a first lesson in sweating out "incoming mail." When the shelling stopped, all pilots loaded into trucks and went to air operations located in a temple-like building built by the Japanese on a knoll overlooking the airfield. Called the pagoda, it was handmade of wood with joints held together with wooden pegs—a beautiful job of woodworking.

Headquarters had decided to send out a three-plane SBD flight to attempt to hit the shelling warships. The first hop was made up of three marines—the CO of VMSB-232, Lieutenant Colonel Mangrum, and Lieutenants Iverson and Baldinus; in the darkness they attacked a group of destroyers with bombs with no apparent success. At about 0400, VS-5 sent out Lt. Rog Woodhull with Ensigns Coolbaugh and Brown to continue the harassment of the now-fleeing ships. The three were also unsuccessful. Brownie became lost in the darkness, and did not return from the strike. We were to hear a few days later that Brown had ditched his plane in a lagoon off Malaita Island nearby and, with the help of friendly natives, returned to Cactus.

Just before sunrise, as we sat around the pagoda awaiting further orders from our leaders, a seaplane made a strafing run on the area, sending everyone running wildly to the slit trenches nearby. All of this enemy activity was coming from a third Japanese force under command of Rear Admiral Tanaka, a troop reinforcement convoy that was the final part of Operation KA. Flying his flag in the light cruiser *Jintsu*, Tanaka's force was three transports with four older destroyers as escort and five newer ones that had done the night shelling. His part of the operation was to land one thousand of the Yokosuka Fifth Special Naval Landing Force—the Japanese equivalent of marines—outside American perimeter defense positions around the airfield.

A position report from a PBY shadowing the enemy force placed it one hundred miles northwest of Henderson Field just before dawn. Major General Vandegrift ordered his small Cactus Air Force dive-bomber group to attack this incoming force and at daybreak, eight SBDs took off.

At 0830, 25 August 1942, the striking group found the enemy and the first dive-bombing attack by the CAF was initiated. Mangrum led the Marines down on *Jintsu;* three near misses and a direct hit by Baldinus seriously damaged the flagship cruiser. Caldwell led down on *Kinryu Maru,* the largest of three transports. Chris Fink scored a direct hit amidships, starting a fire, which got ammunition to exploding. The ship went dead in the water and began to sink. The selection of this particular transport to attack was fortunate as she was carrying the main reinforcement force personnel.

The Japanese formation broke up and headed for safer waters. The *Jintsu,* with an injured Tanaka, left immediately for Truk. The destroyer *Mutsuki* put herself alongside *Kinryu Maru* and began taking off survivors, with both ships dead in the water. At that exact moment a flight of B-17s from Espiritu Santo arrived overhead. A stationary target like the one below was the kind that could be hit using high-level bombing. Three bombs of a cluster struck the helpless *Mutsuki* and she sank in a few minutes—one of only a few times these tactics worked against ships at sea during the war.

All eight SBDs of Striking Group One returned safely to Cactus and preparations began to send a second strike. In spite of difficulties in both refueling and rearming without adequate pumps and hoists, the CUB-1 ground unit had nine SBD aircraft ready by 1130.

My aircraft was one of those prepared for this strike and I went on the assignment. We found only one DD of the force about 150 miles northwest of Guadalcanal. Six of us attacked this ship. I saw two bombs miss as I dove; also, when coming down, I observed a good bit of AA being shot straight up at me. My bomb was a close miss on the starboard side and two others hit close on the port side—one of these was Barker's. The ship was badly injured by the near misses but did not sink. We observed oil slicks and floating debris in the general area of the first attack as we returned to base without mishap.

These two strikes brought to a close Japanese Operation KA— the first major effort of the enemy to land reinforcements on Guadalcanal after its capture. The three-day engagement, including a carrier-versus-carrier exchange on 24 August 1942, became known at that time as the Battle of Stewart Islands. In fact it was so listed in the Presidential Unit Citation awarded to the *Enterprise* in early 1943. Later this fight was renamed the Battle of the Eastern Solomons; why this change in designation was made is unknown to me.

Eastern Solomons must be listed as a minor victory for the United States, in that the Japanese lost the small carrier *Ryujo,* while we had damage done to the Big E but did not lose her. We also stopped a major attempt to reinforce existing Japanese ground forces surrounding our beachhead on the Canal. But it had been a frustrating bag of missed opportunities, individual errors, and some of the worst dive-bombing done in the war by *Saratoga*'s air group. We came out ahead in the category of pilot losses as Japan lost the better part of two carrier air groups, while our carrier pilot losses were low. A shortage of pilots was to become a key factor in lack of efficiency of Japan's carrier forces later, as she did not have either a backlog of reserve CV pilots, or a functioning training system to replace the heavy losses suffered at Coral Sea, Midway, and now Eastern Solomons. The coming battles of Santa Cruz and the final Guadalcanal defense would drain off still more of Japan's most precious resource, her combat-experienced aviators, while America's naval pilot–training production line was in operation and the results would soon be felt. More pilots and aircraft carriers would spell the doom of Japan by 1944.

II

It was now clear that we had been abandoned by the Navy,
and were to serve the Marines for an indefinite time.
We settled into whatever routine we could.

LT. TURNER F. CALDWELL, CO, VS-5

By 26 August 1942, Flight 300's second day on Guadalcanal, it was obvious we were not leaving Cactus soon. We got word that the Big E had been badly damaged and was on her way back to Pearl for repairs. As we were desperately needed here, that probably meant we would remain for some period of time. Probability became reality when carrier TBF aircraft landed and unloaded a

113

bag of personal belongings for each of us. We settled down to stay.

As for the Japanese, they were beginning to realize that the loss of Guadalcanal was an event of some magnitude—a mistake that they could only rectify by taking the area back. A pattern was emerging as to how they planned to retake Cactus. First, there would be a softening-up process by daily bombing raids. The Betty bombers were coming from Rabaul, and the arrival time was consistently at high noon. They were usually accompanied by Zero fighters for protection against our defensive F4Fs. We received advance notice of their coming by radio messages from coast-watchers located on the various islands of the Solomon chain along the flight path of the bombers.

For example, on the twenty-sixth a force of twenty-one bombers with Zero escorts made the daily noon raid. Our fighters were waiting for them at maximum altitude. In the ensuing fight, eight bombers and six Zeros were shot down with a loss of two F4Fs; a third made a dead-stick landing from altitude. While the fighters were handling the attacking planes, all flyable SBDs took off and flew away from the bombing and destruction. This way we kept from losing our valuable dive-bombers on the ground.

The second part of the Japanese plan for retaking Cactus was to build up existing ground forces by landing reinforcements at night from destroyers, both east and west of the Marine defensive perimeter lines. In addition to unloading troops, both these ships and accompanying cruisers would toss a few shells into the general area held by the Americans. To assist in the shelling, cruiser float-type planes would drop flares on targets they might see in the darkness. The shelling ships would use the flares as aiming points —an old system that still gave good results much of the time.

Defense against the Rat Patrol, as these troop-carrying destroyers were called, was to fly a late-afternoon patrol up the slot (the area between islands of the Solomons Chain running northwest) to see if any ships coming down were within range for an attack in the remaining daylight. The Japanese knew our intentions and usually kept out of range during daylight hours. We also tried night attacks but really only succeeded in harassing them. Operating from a primitive field like Henderson, with taxiing and takeoff often under shell fire, made night work quite hazardous with little in the way of rewards.

It did not take long for Flight 300 personnel to get caught up in the frantic pace of activities at Cactus. In a real sense, all of us were involved in frontline combat operations. Fighting against Japanese ground units was taking place only short distances from the bivouac and aircraft parking areas. Japanese snipers crept close to the field to fire at planes and aircrews both on the ground and during takeoff and landing. Everyone was living under siegelike conditions, with soaring temperatures, torrential rains, and humidity for weather, and powdered eggs, Australian sheep's tongue, captured Japanese rice, and hardtack for food. Maintenance and service of the fighters and dive-bombers vital to our survival was a never-ending chore for personnel assigned to these duties. With all of these adverse conditions, it was not surprising that pilots and aircrewmen burned out in a relatively short time. Commanding officers gave each pilot a combat efficiency period of about thirty days on Cactus before relieving them (when possible); the miracle was that so much was accomplished with so little.

Sometimes Japanese bombers could not get through the weather and we would get a day off from the noon bombing. We also had normal off-duty time to do personal things. During one off period, several of us visited the battle area near the Tenaru River to see where the fight had taken place. By then it was cleaned up, with enemy dead buried in a mass grave (using bulldozers) and ours individually placed in a cemetery. The marines on the line let us pick souvenirs from the piles of stuff taken from those killed. I ended up with a rifle, bayonet, helmet, canteen, short knife, flag, and other small personal items. I carried this loot with my own few possessions when leaving the Canal, taking it all the way back to Ford Island. When I got back, a supply officer talked me into loaning him the rifle, bayonet, helmet, and canteen to mount and hang on the walls of the tennis club next door to the BOQ at Ford Island—I never saw them again.

The flag (framed), a Samurai sword, and a cup that I made out of a coconut shell still hang among my personal things, in silent memory of those days that I spent doing hard time in hell.

III

The fourth day of Flight 300's coexistence with VMSB-232 in the Cactus Air Force, 28 August 1942, passed in what was beginning to be a familiar pattern—nighttime harassment from surface ship shelling followed by a large bombing raid at about noon by Japanese twin-engined Betty bombers escorted by Zero fighters. Our dive-bomber pilots would fly a morning search up the slot, depart the field during the noon raid, and later in the day head up the slot again to search for any incoming Japanese surface ships. Then the cycle would be repeated. Any sightings called for attacks, and we flew night defensive missions, too.

This day was to see a change in the routine when the afternoon search, flown by Barker and Liffner, reported contact with four Japanese destroyers near the southeast tip of Santa Isabel Island, a relatively short 125 miles northwest of Henderson Field. Although it was late afternoon there was still enough daylight left to attack this four-ship force before darkness. Since the successes of 25 August, and because our bombers had a 250-mile range, the Japanese had been careful to stay outside that range during daylight hours. Because the need for reinforcements for their ground forces around the American-held beachhead was becoming desperate, the four heavily laden ships were probably attempting to make a large delivery and needed extra time. There was also the chance that someone in command had made an error.

Whatever the cause, the Japanese captains must have realized their relatively simple tactical error of getting too close to Cactus in daylight, when eleven Dauntless dive-bombers arrived overhead at 1830 as the sun was setting. Japanese records show that we dove on the destroyers *Amagiri, Yugiri, Asagiri,* and *Shirakumo.* The handwritten diary notes that I carefully prepared when returning from this successful strike, now yellow with age, describe it as follows:

28 August 1942. Late this afternoon we received a radio message from Barker who was out on a slot search. He and Liffner had found four enemy DD headed this way. It was about 1800 and we had just finished evening chow. Immediately eleven of us took off, five Navy and six Marine dive-bombers. Enemy was found about 1830 just off Santa Isabel Island heading north trying to get away. We split, the five Navy planes swinging around and coming in from the east, the Marines came from the southwest. We dove first; I dove number four. Their high antiaircraft fire was lousy, not getting within two or three hundred yards of us.

I dove through a cloud on the second ship from the right,

released at less than 2000 feet, and pulled out. Heavy 20-mm fire from the third and fourth ships came very close to my tail but did not hit me. As I turned I saw my bomb explode almost midships —a direct hit. She started exploding in her magazines and I saw heavy red fire burst out of her. The first ship had been hit by Fink, one of our gang, with a 1,000-pound bomb, and was sinking as was the one I hit. A third ship was also hit by the marines. One Marine pilot, 2nd Lt. O. Mitchell, Jr., and his gunner, Pvt. P. O. Schackman, were shot down and lost while strafing—all other planes returned safely. This was a very successful attack against the Japanese—we caught them with their pants down.

One thing about fighting at Guadalcanal: there never was a shortage of action. The next day we were all feeling pretty good about our success of the night before when the coastwatchers radioed that bombers and Zeros were on the way again. Several of us took off with all flyable SBDs—it was a good thing we did because the Japanese bombardiers placed their bomb patterns right on the airfield and its parking and repair areas. A direct hit was scored on one hangar with a five-hundred-pound bomb that destroyed two aircraft being worked on and burned a Navy chief badly when he tried to save them. The eight marine F4Fs did well, shooting down fourteen Zeros and two probable bombers without loss. The Army P-400s also got into the fight but lost four while shooting four down—a bad swap not good enough to survive here.

Marine Fighting Squadron 223 was the outfit doing the heavy intercept work during this period in late August. Led by Maj. John L. Smith, one of the truly great fighter pilots of the war, this squadron developed the tactics used so successfully with the inferior F4F in shooting down both Zeros and Bettys in large numbers with relatively few losses. The basic concept was to use the time before the Japanese arrived—time provided by the coastwatcher warning system—to get located over Henderson Field with as much altitude as possible. When the Japanese bombers and fighters arrived, the F4Fs would plunge down in pairs from above through the enemy formations, firing as they passed through, then zooming back up to make a second run. No one engaged in individual dogfights: if an enemy got on an F4F's tail, the best defense was to push over into a dive and leave the scene. The Zero (supposedly) could not hold together structurally in a dive with an F4F. These simple tactics were extremely effective, with Smith, his

XO, Maj. R. L. Morrell, Jr., and ops officer, Capt. M. E. Carl—three pilots—shooting down more than fifty enemy aircraft. The original squadron of twenty-one pilots suffered six killed and three wounded in an approximately six-week combat tour at Guadalcanal. Smith received the Medal of Honor for his actions, while Carl and Morrell each received the Navy Cross.

IV

Night harassment flights continued. We would hardly get in the sack when word would come down to man aircraft. On the twenty-ninth, about midnight, I took off with several other dive-bombers to investigate a report of Japanese ships unloading troops on the beaches to the northwest of our positions. The next thing I knew planes began joining up on me—a lowly ensign—and I became a flight leader with eight planes flying on me! There was nothing I could do in the dark to straighten out the leadership problem, so I led the group to the designated area but found no enemy ships. We all landed about three hours later and everyone told me what a good job I had done as night division leader!

Even though we would often see nothing, it was still dangerous work flying over the Rat Patrol while they were unloading troops and supplies. The next night, 30 August 1942, several SBDs again took off to look for enemy intruders. Spike Conzett, a close personal friend from Dubuque, Iowa, was flying with Capt. Fletcher Brown of the Marines. They flew over an enemy destroyer in the darkness; the Japanese opened fire and a twenty-millimeter shell came up through the deck of Spike's plane, a fragment striking him in the calf of his right leg, lodging by the shinbone. In severe pain and losing blood, he had a bad time getting back to the field. He went out of control as a result of the concussion shocks from more shells fired near him in the night, and for a while he was disoriented, but he made it back.

V

Like a broken record, the routine of noon bombings, morning and afternoon searches, night shellings, and harassment missions went on day after day with little variance. Once in a while, something would happen to break the routine. As we had no laundry service, we had to wash our own clothes. The place to do this was the Lunga River, which ran through our position north to the ocean at Lunga Point. The best method was to combine the washing of both one's body and one's clothing in a single operation. On one such occasion, I was stark naked standing in waist-deep water, washing my clothes on a fallen log, when a sizeable Japanese bombing raid arrived after we thought they weren't coming. Everyone got out of the water, and took cover as best he could— each bare as the day he was born. While the field was the target, and we were more than a mile from it, we knew from experience that Japanese bombs could fall anywhere inside or outside the perimeter. Sure enough, a cluster of bombs fell very close, shaking us up and scaring the hell out of us. Walking back to finish washing, I stepped on a hot piece of shrapnel that had fallen among us. Meanwhile, one bomb hit an ammo dump, causing a fireworks display rivaling any Fourth of July celebration I had ever seen.

I mention this incident because it scared me. Fear is a constant companion of men in combat and, although it may vary in degree, it is always close by. It is a normal emotion that each man learns to handle in his own way.

Fear varies in type and intensity depending upon the experience and training of the man involved. For example, a typical "grunt" marine would be more apprehensive if he found himself facing the enemy in the form of Zero fighters making runs on his gun position in a dive-bomber than he would behind the same gun in a position located on the ground. Enemy fire in the form of AA coming toward his aircraft would be of greater concern than artillery fire coming into his dug-in position. When you reverse the roles, the opposite becomes true: nothing is as frightening to an airman as being subjected to bombing or shelling on the ground.

As a carrier aviator flying with the Cactus Air Force from Henderson Field, I never really became used to enemy bombing or shelling, especially when it came at night. No shelter was deep enough or covered well enough to displace the cold fear that the next shell would hit directly upon my personal hiding place. Perhaps the worse part was that there was nothing that one could do about the shells coming in but accept them as a necessary evil associated with ground fighting.

Feeling fear under these circumstances also brought its companion—cowardliness—to all of us, no matter how good we might be at covering up our innermost feelings. Adm. Bull Halsey had this to say about an overnight stay that he made on Guadalcanal on 8 November 1942:

Archie [Maj. Gen. A. Archer Vandergrift, USMC] put us up in his shack that night. Soon after we turned in, an enemy destroyer somewhere near Savo Island began lobbing over shells, and our artillery started an argument with the Japs. It wasn't the noise that kept me awake; it was fright. I called myself yellow—and worse—and told myself to "go to sleep, you damned coward!" but it didn't do any good; I couldn't obey orders.[1]

VI

The hectic pace continued for the dive-bombers, who had scouting hops to do, as well as attack flights both day and night. It was logical that my luck would run out eventually, and it did on 1 September 1942. Several of us were ordered to take off under fire and attack the ships shelling the field from the harbor. It was about 2100 with no moon and some overcast. I swung out onto the runway and started to take off as shells were coming into the field area. About halfway down the runway, an explosion occurred under the plane, and turned me off course to the left. I did not know just what had happened, but could see that I was getting over the lights running down the port side of the runway and was headed toward two SBDs that were taxiing to take off. I lifted the plane into the air but did not have sufficient flying speed and stalled.

A crash was certain, so I cut back the throttle from full power, turned off the magneto switches, and rode her in. The plane hit a small steamroller parked by the taxiway—this probably kept me from hitting Barker and Manford in the taxiing planes. Careening off the steamroller, the plane began breaking up around Villarreal and me as it flew, slid, and rolled for another fifty yards or so before coming to a stop.

I was out of the crash almost before it stopped moving, fearing fire. There had been a five-hundred-pound bomb underneath—it separated from its rack back at the steamroller contact point but did not explode. The engine tore free of the firewall after contact and was neatly rolled up into a ball of metal some distance from the cockpits. Both wheels were broken off, struts too, and wings were gone, leaving only stubs. Fuel from the ruptured tanks was everywhere, but the only fire was back at the steamroller, where the first contact had occurred.

Johnny Villarreal was slightly stunned and dangling by his gunner's safety belt from what was left of the aft cockpit. I helped free him from the belt, he fell to the ground, and together we staggered a short distance away from the crash remains. Blood was streaming from around my left eye, and I could hardly walk because the control stick had beaten my inner thighs when the wings were torn off, and my muscles were battered. I was covered with fuel and would have become a torch if fire had started, but I was conscious and knew what was happening around me.

About that time a jeep came roaring up with three marines in it. One of them jumped out, ran over, and by shining a ray of light from his flashlight he could see my bloody face. His first words were: "My God, lieutenant, you've gouged your eye out, sir." Of course these words got my attention; I took the end of the silk scarf that was around my neck and felt around my left eye. Something was sticking out of the eye socket—it was a sliver of glass more than an inch long that had broken off my goggles. I pulled the sliver out, blotted the eye, and asked the marine to shine his light on my face. Through a film of blood I could see light and knew that the eye was okay, apparently just cut a little.

The marines loaded Villarreal and me into the jeep and took us to the main field hospital. It was a wild ride through the palm groves, with an occasional shell whistling overhead. When we arrived I was immediately hustled into a bunkerlike shelter for a doctor to look me over. Apparently pilots were considered valuable persons, because a doctor stopped what he was doing and started examining me right away. I kept telling him that I was okay and wanted to get back to the squadron. He looked into my eyes, then turned to a couple of aides and said: "Get this man up on that table—he's about to go." He was right—I passed out cold.

When I came to, I found myself lying in a metal basket–like stretcher on the floor of a porch of the hospital building. It was starting to get light and the shelling had stopped. Painfully I struggled to my feet. My left eye was covered with a bandage. My body was a mass of contusions and scratches, and mammoth bruises stretched from my crotch to my knees on the insides of both legs, and along each arm from wrists to elbows. Every muscle in my body hurt; I felt like I had been physically beaten to a pulp.

The more I walked the better I felt. After I'd had some coffee, the doctor came around to check me. He said that he had never seen a man with so many contusions and bruises, and not even a single broken bone. I had been very lucky with the eye as the glass sliver had gone into an area that did no harm to the eyeball or to my eyesight. However, if I had made that jeep ride with the piece of glass still in the socket, I would probably have injured the eye permanently, so my first-aid removal had been a lucky solution. The doctor told me to take it easy for a few days, and that I could remove the eye patch the next day and fly again when I felt like it.

Walt Coolbaugh had brought me a change of clothing from my gear at the squadron bivouac area to replace the flight suit that the doctors had cut off me the night before. I also needed shoes, as the lightweight chukka boots I had worn ashore from *Enterprise* on the twenty-fourth were coming apart from the hard knocks of field living. One of the medics took me over to a large bin full of marine "boondockers" that were tied together in pairs by their laces and told me to pick myself something that fit. The shoes were all used, with many almost new. I found a pair that fit perfectly, so new they were still stiff. Now I had adequate footwear for the remainder of the time on the Canal. I was, of course, wearing some dead man's shoes as they were too valuable an item simply to bury with the remains. A man might die on Cactus with his boots on, but if he was at the field hospital he wouldn't be buried in them.

While I was hobbling around getting ready to leave, I noticed a quiet native man in walking shorts, who was covered with half-healed wounds and a few bandages, watching me with a smile on his face. The man was Sgt. Maj. Jacob Vouza, one of the most famous survivors of an act of Japanese barbarism on the Canal. We exchanged introductions in sign language.

Vouza was recovering from serious wounds inflicted upon him by a Japanese patrol of Col. Kyono Ichiki's force that captured him on 19 August just before the Tenaru River battle. After Vouza was tied to a tree for questioning, the patrol beat him with rifle butts, stabbed him several times with bayonets, and slashed his throat with a sword. As he was a scout for the Marines, the

Japanese were trying to get information about our positions and troop strength from him, but he refused to say a word. They left him for dead, still tied to the tree.

This forty-eight-year-old superman gnawed his bonds open, freed himself, and then staggered and crawled for three miles back to our lines. Arriving in the midst of an attack by Ichiki's forces, he gave his coastwatcher leader Martin Clemens and marine leaders valuable information about the enemy before allowing himself to receive medical attention. Our marines used the information from Vouza to flank the attack group, killing almost nine hundred elite Japanese soldiers with a loss of about forty Americans. This battle on the Ilu River became known as the Battle of the Tenaru River and was the first successful defense of our position, and of Henderson Field, against repeated Japanese attacks in the next three months.

When I got back to the squadron I found out that 2nd Lt. Tom Moore of the Marines had also crashed on takeoff shortly after I had, but he wasn't as lucky. His engine failed and he went into the trees at the end of the runway. He was badly injured and was taken away by air transport that morning. When I saw the remains of my airplane, I thanked my guardian angel for looking out for me.

VII

I had already missed one day of flying while recovering from the night crash, when I heard about a mission forming up that I could not allow myself to miss. The morning search patrol found a small detachment of enemy landing barges moving men and materials from Santa Isabel Island via Savo to the western tip of the Canal. This new type of reinforcement effort in broad daylight came as a surprise. Unknown to American commanders, the Japanese high command had decided that the Tokyo Express was moving too slowly and the whole operation had to be speeded up. The decision to use barges and landing craft between islands was made, and operations got started. On 3 September we countered this new threat with a sixteen-plane SBD mission against a landing group near San Jorge Island about sixty-five miles northwest of the airfield.

This was a maximum-effort strike for the CAF at that time, with nine of the eleven Flight 300 pilots taking part, even though we no longer had many of our original SBDs. We caught more than a dozen loaded barges at sea and, with a combination of bombing and strafing, sank several of these small craft, with heavy loss of life. I almost felt sorry for the poor Japanese in the barges, who were loaded down with personal gear, had no defensive AA fire, and were limited by slow speed. Many of them jumped over the sides to escape the fire and, with their heavy equipment loads hanging from them, simply sank and drowned. Two days later we repeated the performance: We sank three more landing boats and damaged several others, killing large numbers of the troops being transported. From these two disastrous daytime attempts, the Japanese realized their mistake and went back to night Rat Patrol tactics, using barges only on a limited scale after dark.

VIII

About a week later, Barker and I were assigned the afternoon search up the slot. These searches were not difficult navigational problems, as there were numerous island landmarks to use as reference points. The main danger was the occasional Zero float-fighter that might be encountered at any time.

Out about one hundred miles, we intercepted a contact report by radio placing two destroyers and a light cruiser within range to the south of our position. We left the search and began a slow climb on a heading that would intercept the ships as they proceeded toward Guadalcanal. The ships were right where they should be, and we approached them from fourteen thousand feet without being detected. We dove on the cruiser from the west and out of the sun, with pullouts to the east and toward home. Both bombs near-missed, so close that the ship got a saltwater bath. Lots of twenty-millimeter stuff was shot at our rear ends as we left the scene on the deck. As we moved away several large splashes erupted on the water nearby—the cruiser was firing her big guns at us. We headed back to Cactus.

About halfway home, we saw a cruiser-type seaplane below us, flying low on the water headed in the general direction of the ship we had bombed. Barker and I both dove at him, but he saw us coming and started running away. As I swung in on him from behind and started firing, he did a climbing turn and came back toward me firing his cannon. At this critical moment my front fifties quit firing. Barker radioed that his guns were not firing so we broke off the short engagement and the Japanese left on the run toward his cruiser home. It is hard to say who was the happiest to leave—the Japanese pilot or ourselves!

The next day, 11 September 1942, we went out in the afternoon to attack reported enemy ships coming down but the weather was too bad to get to them, or to dive-bomb with any effectiveness. As for the noon raid, it was one of the biggest to date. From a foxhole outside our tent, we watched twenty-six Japanese bombers fly over the field without intercept. Their bombs missed and fell into the woods outside the field boundaries, doing little damage. But the whistle they made was something to hear; it put your hair on end. Later in the afternoon, twenty-four F4F fighters from VF-5 arrived, a Navy outfit loaded with many old friends, led by Lt. Comdr. L. C. Simpler and ops Lt. Howard Crews. This was a great fighter outfit arriving here in a time of need.

IX

The next night, 12 September, the Japanese really hit us with a monstrous shelling on a scale unlike any before. Many cruisers and destroyers began the show about 2100 and it lasted for three hours. We knew we were in for it when an overhead plane dropped a flare almost on top of our bivouac area. The first shell coming in got us out of our sacks on the double and into our slit trench (it was L-shaped, and several of us had dug it with loving care). All of the Flight 300 gang were in the trench together as the five- and eight-inch shells came crashing in. The shells were cutting trees off right over our heads, and the shrapnel was falling around us like hailstones. All of us in the trench survived, but the marines of VMSB-232 nearby were not so fortunate. A shell hit on top of their shelter, killing Lieutenants Rose and Baldinus and wounding two others. The whole thing was a nightmare.

After the shelling was over, artillery, mortar, and small-arms fire continued in the hills just south of Henderson Field. Maj. Gen. Kiyotake Kawaguchi was launching an attack with over two thousand of his Kawaguchi Butai; his objective was the airfield. Between his force and the runway was Lt. Col. "Red Mike" Edson and his Raiders and Chutes. The Japanese made a frontal attack and were slaughtered in large numbers—only a few made it as far as the airfield, where they also died.

I was scheduled to fly one of the dawn searches up the slot. Just before daylight, word came that the airfield was secure and it was safe for pilots to man planes for flights. Villarreal and I were dropped off at our assigned SBD in the parking area southwest of the runway.

As we approached the aircraft, I noted that a Raider was seated in the front cockpit, casually cleaning his automatic weapon. In the semi-darkness, I did not notice the dead Japanese soldier until I almost tripped over him. He was lying on the ground a few feet from the aircraft tail on the starboard side. A large bloody smear ran down the wing from the cockpit to the trailing edge of the flaps.

The Raider, a tall, thin youngster with a wispy beard and dressed in dirty fatigues, greeted me with a howdy as he climbed out of the cockpit. Red Mike had realized that some of the enemy might get through his lines to aircraft parked around the field. To prevent their destruction, he assigned one Raider to each aircraft with orders to protect them at all cost. The worn-out young man gave me this short and brutal account:

"I knew that any Jap that got this far would try to destroy the plane by putting a hand grenade into the cockpit. So I just sat in there waiting, and sure enough here came this gook right up onto the wing. I put my automatic piece against his chest and gave him a short burst—bastard never knew what hit him. Then I pulled him off the wing so you guys can fly this thing."

I thanked him for his courage and vigilance. Villarreal and I started the plane, taxied out, and took off. During the lonely single-plane search mission I had time to reflect on the bloody wing—a smear was all that was left of what had been a human being. Then I corrected myself: That had not been a man killed on the wing but a Japanese soldier—the enemy. My transformation to warrior was complete.

Kawaguchi made a second attempt to come through Edson's position that night, but the results were even worse for the Japanese than the previous try. After the battle was over, the marines named the place Bloody Ridge, a name that grassy knoll on Guadalcanal still bears.

X

The noon bombing raids continued on 13 September but, with reinforcements provided by VF-5's arrival, the Japanese airmen got a nasty surprise. Ten bombers and four Zeros were shot down, at the cost of Bill Wileman, a good friend from training days at Opa-Locka. He should have bailed out over the field, but decided to try a dead-stick landing to save the F4F and fell short of the runway and into the trees. Enemy bomber gunners had shot up the plane, knocking out the engine.

Apparently the Japanese also received reinforcements in the form of float-type Zeros, as two pulled a daring raid unexpectedly in the late afternoon. They arrived suddenly over the field, swung around, and shot down a marine dive-bomber who had just returned from a search and was in the landing pattern with wheels and flaps down. The whole thing happened practically over our heads as Fink and I were returning from the river bathing area.

This success brought four more Zeros on floats the next morning, but we had F4Fs airborne, and they shot all the Zeros down. Again the action was right over our heads. I saw one downed with a beautiful full-deflection shot. Then in the afternoon about fifteen more float-types attacked the field with nine shot down; Weasel Wesolowski got two of these. Tragedy hit the marine dive-bombers again, when 2nd Lt. Y. W. Kauffman and gunner Pvt. B. J. Arnold of VMSB-231 flew into the water after being attacked by float-Zeros while out on search. Wingman O'Keefe survived, but had to be evacuated.

On 16 September 1942 I flew what was to be my last combat mission with the Cactus Air Force. Led by "Bullet Lou" Kirn, CO of VS-3, a makeshift group of twelve dive-bombers left Cactus late in the afternoon to strike one enemy CA and two DDs located three hundred degrees, distance 140 miles, from the field. Encountering heavy AA fire both in the dive and during retirement, I placed a near-miss by the CA along with two others, while one hit and two near-misses were made on one DD. Ensign Newton with gunner Thornton failed to pull out of their dive and crashed into the sea, but all other planes returned to Guadalcanal safely.

Three days after that mission I was evacuated from Cactus by air in a DC-3. My last diary entry read:

16 September 1942. We had a couple of false alarms today—the Japs did not come with the usual noon raid. Fighting with enemy troops on our perimeter continues with the marines doing a good job up there in the hills overlooking the field. The nights are tough as we never know what to expect from these yellow bastards. No other news. As I write this I hear the P-400s of the Army strafing the Jap positions.

My time in hell was over.

XI

An epilogue: recently I ran into an old friend, Capt. Howard Crews, who was on the Canal flying with the Cactus Air Force in VF-5 at the same time as I was there with VS-5. He shot down a couple of planes and earned a Silver Star. We got to talking about those days and he made this observation:

"Hal, I don't know if anyone has ever figured it out, but most of the carrier-type squadrons that went to fly with the marines at the Canal in the fall of 1942 lasted approximately one month. During that time more missions were flown, aircraft and pilots lost, and real fighting accomplished than the same squadron would do in a regular six-month combat cruise aboard ship. The way it turned out, combatwise, was that we did a complete combat cruise in thirty days. When relieved the squadron was pretty much burned out—finished as a fighting unit—and had to be completely reorganized. It was rough duty!"

Howard, my friend, you have evaluated those days perfectly. There was no air combat in the Pacific war quite as unique, dangerous, and horrible yet satisfying to a naval aviator as a tour of duty with the Cactus Air Force.

8

VB-10

I LEFT Guadalcanal and service with the Cactus Air Force on 19 September 1942 in the company of Harry Liffner, Buck Manford, and Gil Guillory. We were airlifted by DC-3 transport plane to Noumea, New Caledonia, where the U.S. South Pacific Headquarters was located.

Emotions ran high that day of departure as the jungle hellhole faded from view beneath the wingtips. I had the elation of a survivor combined with the sorrow of leaving behind so many friends and fellow CAF pilots still engaged in the unequal struggle. Within a week all of Flight 300 were relieved of Guadalcanal duty and on their way back to Pearl.

Just how crucial the Cactus situation was became clear as we were debriefed by Rear Admiral McCain's staff at Noumea. Here we were regarded as men who had escaped from a Japanese trap —a second Bataan—where the issue was still so much in doubt that some high officials of government had already conceded defeat. Commander of the South Pacific forces (COMSOPAC) was Vice Adm. Robert L. Ghormley, with his headquarters in the *Argonne.* He had been against the Cactus operation from its conception and was certain that the area could not be held. I did everything that I could during debriefing to show the positive side of what we had been doing, but could see the concern and disbelief on the staff faces as we talked. After all, one only had to look at the physical condition of our group to get a feeling of defeat.

Fortunately, a few powerful U.S. leaders, including President Roosevelt himself, were determined to stop Japan's southward movement at the Canal. That miserable island, the seas around it, and the air above it would be a battleground as long as the Japanese cared to contest control. Unknown to any of us at the time was that both McCain's and Ghormley's days of leadership in the South Pacific were about over and a savior in the form of Vice Adm. Bull Halsey would, like the cavalry in an old western movie, arrive in the nick of time to save the day. Ghormley's departure was permanent; McCain would return.

We were a sorry-looking group, thin almost to emaciation, in faded, patched, but clean khaki uniforms, bearded, with a certain gleam in the eye that would not go away. All of us were suffering from malaria to varying degrees. I was lucky and had no lasting effects from this malady. Others were less fortunate—Harry Liffner was to have recurring attacks for the rest of the war, and many American servicemen never completely got rid of this common South Pacific disease.

The main cure for what ailed us was good food and rest. It was nice to have edible food again, with beer, French wines, cognac, and champagne. We could sleep without shell fire interruptions forcing us to take cover in bomb shelters. After all, we were back in Western civilization, albeit a French-oriented one, but Western nonetheless. As we walked the streets of Noumea we were proud of our unusual appearance. It was obvious to all that these skinny, bearded, and grim young pilots were not local officers on casual liberty, but combat vets who had just come from the fighting in the Solomons. We were different, with a defiant, haunted look about us that we wore like a badge.

II

One local resident was impressed but not frightened by what he saw. I was in a small shop looking for souvenirs when a well-dressed man in his early fifties approached me and started a conversation in French and broken English. He was M. August Maestracci, a local professional man, who insisted on taking me home for dinner and to meet his family.

It was a lovely family, two daughters and two sons, all younger than I, and an attractive, modest wife. The oldest daughter was eighteen and already a beautiful, mature woman. I was introduced to a genuine French-style gourmet dinner, complete with linens and candles. It was the first time I had eaten real French food, served one course at a time, each on a different plate, and a different wine for each course. The daughters assisted a maid in serving the food, and the entire operation went smooth as silk, taking us over two hours to complete.

By the time we got to the cognac and demitasse coffee I was feeling no pain, and clearly in no condition to get back to my quarters in the dock area downtown. I was escorted with considerable ceremony to the guest room, which had a big four-poster bed equipped with a feather mattress, something I had not seen since my childhood back in Iowa. It was completely draped with thin netting to keep out mosquitoes. My hosts bid me *bonne nuit*. When I awoke the next morning, I found all my clothes washed and pressed, my shoes shined, and I returned to duty a new man. Whenever I got back to Noumea later in 1942 I was welcomed to the Maestracci home as a son—God bless that wonderful French Caledonian family. I had one regret: I mentally kicked myself for having been so inattentive in my French classes back in Parsons College.

III

After a three-day sojourn in Noumea, we boarded a large Coronado for the flight to Hawaii. We were preferred passengers on Rear Adm. John McCain's personal plane, and that was nice, but the Navy usually has a reason to fly ensigns with an admiral and his staff back to a major base. When we arrived at Ford Island we were each greeted personally by Vice Adm. Bull Halsey, then processed through a brief physical and given four days of liberty in Honolulu.

After the liberty spent at the Moana Hotel catching up on booze and local girls, I reported to Ford Island command headquarters for orders. VS-5 was being disbanded, and most of the pilots had already returned to the United States for leaves and reassignments. They had departed for that world of gasoline rationing, food shortages, black market, and draft dodgers (known as 4Fs). But it wasn't all bad because there were no shortages of booze and beautiful women, and a returning Pacific combat pilot could find plenty of both.

So I said goodbye to Stinky Caldwell, Rog Woodhull, Goocher Downing, Red Austin, Elmer "Emool" Maul, Nick Nicholson, Yogi Jorgenson, Link Traynor, and my roommate Walt Coolbaugh. Some of these alohas were to be permanent ones: Red Austin, Elmer Maul, and Walt Coolbaugh were all killed in flying accidents within several months.

When I was not sent to the United States for reassignment with the others of VS-5, I knew my orders would be to another combat squadron in the area. Sure enough, orders were given me to report to Bombing Squadron Ten (VB-10) at Barbers Point field nearby. I couldn't help but notice that I was the only member of Flight 300 that did not go back to the States. I have been asked many times why this happened to me. I can only say that I was always lucky when it really counted! VB-10 in *Enterprise* became my home for the next six months: two major battles, Santa Cruz and the final battle of Guadalcanal, and a minor one, Rennell Island. Apparently I was needed there.

Arriving at Air Group Ten at Barbers Point, I found five former VS-5 pilots also assigned to the group in VS-10: Birney Strong, Skip Ervin, Redbird Burnett, Rastus Estes, and Rich Richey. Two pleasant surprises awaited me at VB-10. A former cadet buddy, whose friendship went back to E base days at Lambert Field, was in the squadron. Bob Gibson, also known as Hoot and Gibby, was in the ready room to introduce my new shipmates. I also found that an all-Navy dispatch (ALNAV) had just promoted me to lieutenant (jg).

Upon meeting the pilots of VB-10, I found another old friend present. Lt. (jg) Ralph Goddard had made the B-17 flight from Hickam to Suva with me just before Coral Sea—I had not seen him since leaving *Yorktown*. As we knew each other, we decided to cast our lot together as roommates on this new cruise. The CO was Lt. Comdr. J. A. Thomas, on his first war assignment; XO was Lt. V. W. Welch, who had seen combat with VB-6. These two were the only regular Navy pilots assigned to the squadron; all the rest of the group were naval reserves. Gibson, Goddard, and myself were combat-experienced—the rest were heading out for the first time, full of confidence and eager to get at the Japanese before the war ended without their getting a chance to contribute.

It was a good squadron in a good air group, but I never felt the same with this one as I had with VS-5, or would later with VB-2.

There was little time to get checked out with the squadron. The Big E had been in the yard at Pearl getting repaired from her wounds at Eastern Solomons and Air Group Ten was to go to sea as a new group with her. A night group grope gave me a chance to see the squadrons in action just a few days before going aboard for the war cruise and I was far from impressed.

I had flown a local checkout hop earlier in the day, and was surprised to see my name on the schedule for the night grope. I told Gibson that I was not ready to lead a section or division of new pilots I had never flown with in a group grope at night, so he put me on a night solo. I took off a little before the big event, climbed up to a safe place over the field, and watched the show. This group was at a stage of training that made a daytime grope difficult, let alone a night one. Staying well clear, I could see that many of the planes were getting lost or joining up in the wrong divisions as they flew over Barbers Point in the pitch black. After an hour or so of confusion, the planes began to land. I waited until things were safe, cautiously approached the field, and landed without incident, but what I had observed that night remained with me for the entire cruise.

IV

I flew aboard Big E with VB-10 on 16 October 1942 and sailed from Pearl Harbor on another war cruise. There was a sense of urgency in our sudden departure, as if those in high command places knew something was about to happen in the South Pacific that required the *Enterprise* and her newly acquired Air Group Ten. Running at flank speed, with the new battleship *South Dakota* alongside in formation, Task Force Sixteen rendezvoused with *Hornet* and her ships of Task Force Seventeen below the New Hebrides on 23 October. The fourth carrier-versus-carrier battle of 1942 was about to take place under command of Rear Adm. Thomas Kinkaid, who was flying his flag in *Enterprise*.

On the trip down, about the third day out, I was ordered to report to Comdr. John Crommelin's cabin. This famous naval aviator, one of five brothers who were Academy-graduate officers in the Navy, was air officer in *Enterprise* and was greatly admired by all of the air group pilots, especially the young ensigns and lieutenants (jg). Not without apprehension, I softly rapped on his door.

Commander John was a tall man, over six feet, whipcord lean, with sandy, thin light hair, a craggy face, and piercing blue eyes framed with the aviator's crow's-feet so typical of men who have spent their lives in the cockpits of carrier aircraft. His soft Alabama drawl put me immediately at ease.

"Hal, come in here, boy. I've been wanting to talk with you about your experiences at Guadalcanal. Get some coffee and pull up a chair."

Doffing my khaki overseas cap, I moved to the sideboard of the small cabin. Pouring a large mug of strong, hot coffee, I noted that we were not alone in the room. Seated at a round green-felt-covered dining table was a small man, dressed in the khaki uniform of a naval officer, but devoid of any insignia. About thirty years of age, he had a smooth, calm appearance that indicated a controlled intelligence, and his gaze was direct and straight in the eye. I had seen this man before in the wardroom at evening mess but had never met him. Crommelin spoke:

"Hal, I would like you to meet Eugene Burns. You may or may not know that he is an Associated Press correspondent assigned to our ship to provide combat news coverage to the folks back in the States. I wanted you two to meet as Gene is writing a book about this ship, and its men, and you can give him good solid information about the role of carrier aviation, especially *Enterprise* Flight 300, in controlling the air and helping the Marines hold Guadalcanal."

Eugene Burns acknowledged the introduction by rising from his chair and giving me a brief handshake. This meeting arranged by Crommelin was the beginning of a personal friendship that was to last until I left the Big E in late spring of 1943. In his book *Then There Was One*, released in 1944, Burns used materials from the countless conversations we were to have in the coming months, at sea and in port, between battles and near battles with the Japanese. He honored me by using a photograph of us, taken on the flight bridge of *Enterprise*, as the back dust cover of his book. Never without his pencil and notepad, this gentle, articulate man would survive the war, only to be torn to pieces by a mob of howling Iranians during a coup d'etat in Teheran in the midfifties.

After a short conversation between the three of us, Burns left Crommelin and me alone. I then answered questions, including several direct ones about what I thought of the leadership being provided naval air combat squadrons, when he looked at me with that penetrating gaze and asked:

"Hal, which medal would you rather receive for heroic combat action, the Navy Cross or the Silver Star?"

The suddenness of his question, and the fact that I realized he was serious, took me by surprise. However, it was not difficult for me to answer:

"Commander, the greatest honor that could ever be given me, other than a Medal of Honor, which can only be granted by the Congress, would be an award of the Navy Cross. It is the highest decoration that the Navy can give. I respect the Silver Star, but it is not to be compared to the Navy Cross."

He nodded his head in agreement. "Young man, I have heard good reports about your conduct during numerous attacks made upon enemy warships while flying from Henderson Field as a part of the Cactus Air Force. I know that you personally scored a hit upon a Japanese destroyer, which blew up and sank, and near-missed cruisers on two occasions. I understand that the Marines intend to decorate several of the carrier aviators who contributed so much to their mission and survival at Guadalcanal. That is why I asked you about the Silver Star—it is a favorite award of the Corps for heroic conduct against an enemy in the field. I am sure you will be receiving this award from them soon. I want you to know that I wish you were receiving the Navy Cross for your recent combat efforts on Guadalcanal as you richly deserve that decoration—more so than some who have already received it for earlier, lesser actions."

I expressed my sincere thanks for his praise, saluted smartly, and left his cabin. I was walking ten feet above the deck! To receive acclaim from John Crommelin, a man known throughout the fleet for his courage, integrity, and forthrightness, was better than getting a medal from some admiral who didn't even know you.

Commander John was to show his courage once too often. After the war, in 1949, as a captain about to be selected for rear admiral, he chose to fight the new Air Force leaders in the Pentagon by defending his beloved carriers in the public press. A shameful group of governmental high brass and others forced him into early retirement.

V

Search missions, while not as glamorous as strikes, were of great importance in providing accurate operational intelligence to a task force commander. Unlike the Japanese, who used cruiser floatplanes, our searches were flown by the dive-bomber squadrons in 1942. A typical search was laid out from the force, with sectors of ten to fifteen degrees, in the direction the enemy was believed to be. Two planes flew each sector approximately 200 to 250 miles out, then a cross-leg of 25 to 50 miles, and the return leg back to the carrier.

An aircraft carrier was not a stationary airfield, so there was relative motion to be considered in returning to a rendezvous point in the open sea. The place on the water where a carrier was to be when the scout planes returned was known as Point Option, and believe me it could be very optional! The preplanned location could change drastically if the carrier was attacked while the search teams were away. An attack could put the entire task force into wild gyrations at speeds of over thirty knots and any concern about maintaining a Point Option position under these circumstances became moot.

Each U.S. carrier had an electronic marvel on board to help the scout teams return safely. Known as the YE or ZB, it was a rotating radio signal–sending device mounted high on the carrier mainmast above the island. This device broadcast a different letter of the alphabet every thirty degrees as it rotated. These letters could be picked up by a receiver in a plane as it moved into the radio signal range of the carrier; from the letter heard the pilot could determine a bearing to the ship. In the corner of each pilot's board was a compass rose. When preparing flight data before starting a search, the pilot filled in each slice of the pie with letters designated for the YE that day. Limited to a range of about thirty-five miles, this device gave a returning pilot a reasonable margin of error. He could change his homebound heading to conform with that of the letter signal being received if he was off course. YE was especially helpful when normal visibility was reduced by clouds or weather and was sufficiently accurate to prevent a plane from missing the task force completely. If you were returning from a 250-mile search jaunt into enemy waters, or a long strike mission, the first faint Morse code dots and dashes in your earphones were as beautiful as a symphony.

I learned very early in my war search experience that the best way not to become lost while on a search was carefully to plan the flight before leaving the deck, and even more carefully fly that plan after takeoff. There were seldom landmarks to help you determine an exact location, so the only way to know where you were at a given time depended upon how well you flew headings for specific lengths of time over the bounding main relative to Point Option (the ship's location). These were the flight's legs.

All of the preplanned legs were carefully set up on a pilot's individual flight navigational chart board. This board, made of metal, was approximately eighteen inches square and fit into slots under the instrument panel of the airplane. It had a clear plasticlike top surface on which one could write with a soft grease pencil. Under the plastic surface was a lined compass disk, which could be rotated around a center pin; it was used to determine compass headings between points marked on the surface. The chart board's surface was boxed with lines forming squares properly labeled with existing latitude and longitude of the area. The board could handle flights of about three hundred miles in radius.

Each pilot also had a small metal computer consisting of two disks, mounted one above the other on a center pin. The lower disk (about four and one-half inches across) was marked in nautical miles (one to one hundred); the slightly smaller upper disk was marked in time of one to one hundred minutes. This small computer worked like an engineer's slide rule, when a pilot moved the disks, to give rates of speed and distances flown relative to time elapsed.

Point Option was usually located as near the center of the board as possible to simplify the determination of proper compass headings of flight legs between plots on the chart board's surface. The tricky part was that Point Option moved during the time the search planes were gone, although a good ship's captain and admiral tried to keep this point on the ocean surface as stable as possible by steaming within twenty-five to fifty miles of an established latitude and longitude.

So much for the search aspects of the two-plane scout team idea. Now we examine the attack phase. One of the most dangerous demands placed upon the two-plane scout team was that of climbing and attacking the enemy force after completing a contact report. Early in the war, scouts began attacking targets after contact, although only two planes, each with a five-hundred-pound bomb, was certainly a rather puny effort, especially if the force was composed of a large number of warships, including carriers, with defending fighters airborne. From all appearances, scouts should have had little chance for survival under these circumstances. But survive they did and creditably so.

I know of no incidents of a two-plane scout attack in either the Coral Sea or Midway battles. A favorite concept of Comdr. John Crommelin in *Enterprise,* it was part of the overall search schemes at Eastern Solomons, Santa Cruz, and the final defense of Guadalcanal. Lt. Ray Davis and Ens. R. C. Shaw's attack of *Shokaku* on 24 August (they both near-missed) was the first attack of a Japanese carrier by scouts. The numerous submarine attacks made by scout teams of VS-5 the day before, including one by Turner Caldwell and me, were among the first examples of the concept in action.

There are many examples of successful two-plane search and attack missions on record. Probably the most famous was the double hit of *Zuiho* by Lt. Birney Strong and Ens. Charles Irvine on 26 October at Santa Cruz. Lt. (jg) Robert Gibson and Ens. Buck Buchanan both hit the damaged cruiser *Kinugasa* on 14 November, which resulted in its sinking. Two VB-10ers, Ens. R. A. Hoogerwerf and Ens. P. M. Halloran, also attacked the cruiser force and claimed a hit, but Halloran was never seen after his dive. Lt. (jg) Martin Doan Carmody and Lt. (jg) Bill Johnson attacked the convoy of eleven transports and eleven destroyers they found west of Guadalcanal that same morning, as did Lt. (jg) J. L. Griffith and I, each team scoring a near-miss on a transport but losing Johnson to defending Zeros.

The two-plane search and attack concept was used extensively in the missions flown daily up the slot from Henderson Field. In fact it was during the period of August and September 1942 that the tactic proved to be both valuable and relatively safe to pilots of the Cactus Air Force, who had to use it because they had no choice. Any ships that we slowed down or turned back in the slot meant less enemy on the ground around the perimeter and less night shelling.

Why was the concept so successful? The major reason was the Japanese radar's inability to pick up the scouting Dauntlesses during either the search maneuvers or the climb to attack. It was possible to come in overhead at twelve thousand to fourteen thousand feet completely unobserved or detected, dive with only some AA fire to contend with, and leave the scene after the attack— just as Barker and I did on a cruiser in early September on routine search up the slot, as Gibson and Buchanan did on *Kinugasa,* and as Strong and Irvine did on *Zuiho.* Besides the AA, there was usually the danger of fighters, and there were a few losses to them. But unlike U.S. task forces, it was often possible to approach a Japanese force, report it, climb to attack altitude, and dive on it without detection until the bombs hit or near-missed the target. We seldom experienced this type of performance by Japanese scouts against our forces, because our radar would pick them up and the CAP would be vectored out to shoot the snoopers down. Japanese fighters were seldom vectored to us by radar.

Both searches and attacks changed later in the war. By 1944 most long searches from carriers were being done by TBFs, often accompanied by an F6F as escort. Dive-bombers were used for their main role—to attack and destroy enemy ships after they were found. But for a time in 1942 and 1943 those Dauntless Helldivers would search out, then attack, the enemy whenever and wherever they found him. It was an experience a scout never forgot.

VI

One of the great carrier searches of the Pacific War was flown from *Enterprise* on 26 October 1942 by the bombing and scouting squadrons of Air Group Ten, as a part of the fourth carrier-versus-carrier battle, known as the Battle of Santa Cruz.

This search had everything—two solid enemy fleet contacts and reports at separate locations; attacks by scouts on cruiser and carrier targets, including two hits on *Zuiho* putting her out of action; battles with intercepting Zeros, with several shot down by our scouts; and a highly hazardous return to the home carriers *Enterprise* and *Hornet* while these ships were being attacked by Japanese Val and Kate bomber and torpedo groups. All of these actions were conducted without the loss of a single scout dive-bomber.

As the sun was rising at 0610, *Enterprise* launched sixteen Dauntlesses on an eight-sector search covering from 235 to 360 degrees true. The first three sectors were assigned to VB-10, the remaining five to VS-10.

Hoogerwerf and I had Sector 2. We departed the Big E on a 250-degree heading. The weather was almost perfect for a search, with visibility clear as far as the eye could see. An occasional cumulus cloud did little to restrict the view, and gave some reassurance for cover if enemy ships or planes were sighted. As this was a maximum-distance search, with a good chance of enemy action, we ran at our most economical fuel settings to conserve precious aviation gas. I also observed my cardinal rule of flying sector headings carefully and with exact timing. All scouts carried a five-hundred-pound general-purpose (GP) bomb.

In many ways Santa Cruz was a carbon copy of Eastern Solomons insofar as the composition of the opposing carrier forces. The Japanese twins *Zuikaku* and *Shokaku* were back, with the *Zuiho* replacing the lost *Ryujo* (both CVLs.) A fourth carrier *Junyo* (another CVL) was nearby and would contribute planes to the fray. Opposing this four-carrier force were the U.S. *Enterprise* and *Hornet*. With the hitting of *Saratoga* on 30 August, and the sinking of *Wasp* on 15 September, both by submarines, these two ships represented the entire U.S. Navy carrier strength available in the South Pacific for this engagement.

Fate often plays strange tricks on men in combat. Sector 1 to the left and our Sector 2 contained no enemy activity either in the air or on the sea. Sector 3 to the right contained Japanese battleships and cruisers and Sectors 4 and 5 contained the enemy carriers. Hoogerwerf and I could have left our sector, like Strong and Irvine, and climbed to altitude toward the enemy contacts for possible individual attacks, *if we had known what was happening*. Because of unbelievably bad radio receptions, neither of our radiomen-gunners picked up a single transmission from the other scouts about their contacts as we flew our assigned sector headings. Lady Luck saw fit to give us a search sector that contained no enemy action, and we returned to Point Option only to find that carriers *Enterprise* and *Hornet* had been found and had come under attack from Japanese carrier planes.

When the search scouts began returning at about 1030, the enemy presence was evident. The Japanese carrier forces had already made one attack and *Hornet* was smoking from hits scored by Val bombers from *Shokaku,* but she was still operational. The Big E had escaped damage by hiding in a local squall.

With Hoogerwerf on my wing, I carefully performed recognition procedures as I approached the task force screen. Ships tend to fire at any plane they see after an attack, friend or foe. Once inside the screen circling the Big E, several other SBDs joined up until I was leading about a dozen aircraft in formation around the carrier.

Enterprise suddenly turned into the wind and signaled "Charley" (permission to land). I took my pickup group into a fast-break pattern to land aboard. When I landed first, the deck crew took my Dauntless forward to a spot just left of the center bow edge of the flight deck. These men were moving the landed scouts into tie-down spots as quickly as possible. The reason for this frenzied activity was announced over the bullhorn: radar showed a large number of bogeys, both dive-bombers and torpedo planes with escorts, approaching the force.

With enemy planes about to attack, the task force increased speed and the ship began defensive maneuvers. The LSO, Lt. Robin Lindsey, kept right on bringing planes aboard, many critically short of fuel. He gave cuts to planes that were high, fast, skidding, and off-line as the deck pitched and rolled with every change of the rudder. Miraculously there were no crashes during this landing period, and no bomb hits from attacking planes.

My gunner Eiswald and I had left our Dauntless quickly after tie-down as enemy aircraft at altitude were about to start their dives on the ship. I ran across the flight deck to the starboard side forward gun mount, which was located just outside and slightly above my stateroom. Here I had a ringside seat for the action as the Japanese pilots pressed home their attacks. All of the Big E's AA batteries were firing furiously, and several of the enemy planes were hit and were falling or exploding in the air. In addition to our fire, the *South Dakota* was also putting up an impressive mass of AA fire from her screening position about one thousand yards off our starboard bow. Japanese aircraft were being shot down at all

141

altitudes and points of the compass in a display of AA fire, superior both in volume and accuracy to any previous battle effort of a U.S. task force.

I asked the gunnery officer in the gun mount where I had taken refuge about the great shooting going on around me. He told me about a new proximity-fused shell that was being used for the first time. (As I recall, about every fifth or sixth shell fired had the fuse.) Marked with a painted projectile head, it would go off automatically as it passed a target if within twenty-five feet of it. These shells really made a difference, and were a well-kept secret until the end of the war.

The Japanese attacked in two groups, the first consisting of twelve Kates and twenty Vals, with sixteen Zeros as cover, coming from *Zuikaku* and *Shokaku*. A second eighteen Vals and twelve Zeros arrived from *Junyo*. These aircraft were manned with experienced men, led by combat veterans—the last survivors of previous carrier-versus-carrier battles. They bravely kept coming in spite of extremely heavy losses from our AA fire, and a few made the release point to fire bombs.

After several near misses we took a hit on the port bow, the bomb passing through the flight deck near my tied-down plane and exploding below at the waterline. The concussion of this bomb tossed my airplane over the side like it was a toy. The officer of the gun battery in the bow of the ship, Lt. Marshall Field IV, son of the famous Chicago millionaire industrialist of the same name, was blown into the air. He would have fallen overboard from the anchor chain area if one of his gun crew had not grabbed his legs and held him onto the forecastle deck.

Shortly after the port bow hit, a second 550-pound bomb struck midships near the island superstructure. It did not go off on contact but penetrated to below the hangar deck level before exploding. This was a serious hit; it killed forty *Enterprise* officers and men, and did extensive damage both on the hangar deck and in the officers' quarters below. It was a freak hit in that it hurt the ship at two deck levels, with most of the fatalities in officers' country, where both a repair party and a medical party were killed.

Almost as an anticlimax, part of the damage on the hangar deck included the office spaces of VB-10. By the time damage control parties finished putting out the fires, water damage had destroyed what was left of the files and records of the squadron. Personal losses were my original flight logbook that went back to my first flights in the Navy and my orders to VB-10 from VS-5. I ended up with a new flight log with a note inscribed in the flyleaf: "Old book lost due to operations of war on 26 October 1942 on USS *Enterprise.*" The orders were never replaced and represent the only gap in my personal file of all the naval orders I received during a twenty-one-year naval career.

One other vivid personal memory of this day is a humorous one. When I finally got to the squadron ready room from my temporary refuge in the starboard gun mount, I found a group of thoroughly frightened squadron pilots. The second hit had been close enough to shake up the entire ready room and the aftereffects were only starting to subside. As I walked around the space, I noticed the outline of a human form drawn in chalk on the steel deck near the blackboard at the front of the room. The drawing was labeled RESERVED FOR LT. DUFFICY. John Dufficy, a short, robust man, was a nonflying intelligence officer attached to the squadron. When the attack got to shaking everyone up, Duff hit the deck in earnest, spread-eagling himself on the ready-room floor. Someone with a sense of humor, and less regard for the accuracy of Japanese bombing, took that moment to draw an outline around the prostrate officer; it took some time for John to live the episode down.

VII

Let's look at how well the U.S. strike groups did in their attacks against the Japanese enemy carriers.

At almost the same time that Japanese scout aircraft found TF-16, U.S. scout SBDs were finding Nagumo's task force. Lt. Comdr. James "Bucky" Lee, CO of VS-10, and his wingman, Ens. William Johnson, got off a position report but were immediately hit by Zeros on CAP. They escaped in a running battle toward home, shooting down at least a pair of their tormentors. In addition to this report, Lieutenant Welch and Lieutenant (jg) McGraw of VB-10 radioed the sighting of a surface force of battleships and cruisers. The rival CVs were less than two hundred miles from each other.

Hornet was the assigned main strike carrier for 26 October and began launching as soon as the contact reports came in. First off was Lt. Comdr. Gus Widhelm with fifteen SBDs, six TBFs, and eight F4Fs as escort. The Big E also launched all planes left from the morning search—nine TBFs, eight F4Fs, and three SBDs under the leadership of CAG Comdr. Dick Gaines. A third strike group of the rest of *Hornet's* aircraft—nine Wildcats, nine Dauntlesses, and seven Avengers were also sent off for a grand total of seventy-four aircraft on their way toward the Japanese carrier force.

Each of these flights headed out on its own. First to get hurt were the nine *Enterprise* Avengers. About sixty miles from the ship, they were ambushed by Lt. Moriyasu Hidaka's nine Zeros from *Zuiho.* Three, including the squadron CO, Lt. Comdr. Jack Collett, were shot down and one had to turn back because of battle damage. Three of Lt. Comdr. Jimmy Flatley's escort F4Fs were also shot down in the melee. It was not a good beginning.

Next to get mauled by the many Zeros roaming about the sunlit skies was Gus Widhelm's mixed squadron of fifteen dive-bombers from VS-8 and VB-8. As they bored in to dive on the enemy carriers, Gus and three other SBDs were shot out of the formation. He made a water landing and with his gunner George Stokely was picked up three days later by a PBY; one crew got back to the Big E, although the pilot was wounded; two were never seen again.

As Widhelm went spiraling down with a dead engine, Lt. James "Moe" Vose took the lead of the eleven survivors and dove on the largest of the CVs below. In one of the best dive-bombing attacks of a Japanese carrier in the war, the *Hornet* dive-bombers pounded several hits into *Shokaku;* Vose proudly reported: "I claim four direct hits on this carrier."[1]

This report was, if anything, an underestimate. According to Japanese count, possibly as many as six one-hundredth-second fused thousand-pound bombs burst just under *Shokaku*'s flight deck after passing through it, blasting large sections of it into the air, starting fires, disrupting communications, and bringing all flight operations to a halt. As *Shokaku* had no planes aboard to burn and explode she survived.

This attack, and the two-plane scout attack of Strong and Irvine (described later), luckily knocked out two of the four Japanese carriers, or things might have gotten much worse for Kinkaid and the American forces. In a communications fiasco of unbelievable proportions, not another attack airplane from either *Hornet* or *Enterprise* made contact with the enemy flattops. Both bomber and torpedo planes attacked battleships and cruisers of the Japanese advance force with limited success (they were secondary targets). Of eleven Mark 13 torpedoes dropped, not a single hit was made; these mediocre weapons continued their miserable performance.

With both *Hornet* and *Enterprise* hit, the former seriously, we were fast losing the battle. A late-afternoon strike of nine Kates from *Junyo* attacked the injured *Hornet,* which was under tow of the cruiser *Northampton.* A single Long Lance hit on the starboard side led to uncontrollable flooding and the call to abandon ship.

Ironically, after removing all survivors, the U.S. destroyers *Mustin* and *Anderson* tried to dispatch the grievously hurt carrier with both shell fire and torpedoes, without success. In their haste to flee, the Americans left *Hornet* blazing fore and aft, but still afloat. In a shameful finale, the Japanese destroyers *Akigumo* and *Makigumo* came upon her adrift, tried to salvage her remains, then administered the coup de grace with four of their super Long Lance torpedoes at about 2300 that night.

The historians James and William Belote summarize Santa Cruz:

> The battle of Santa Cruz Islands had cost the Americans dear.
> *Hornet* was gone, along with 111 of her crew. Damaged
> *Enterprise,* with 44 killed and 75 wounded, was now the only
> American carrier operational in the Pacific. *Porter* had sunk and
> 74 planes had been lost, 20 or so in combat and 54 more in water
> landings or aboard sunken *Hornet.* Twenty-three pilots and ten air
> crew were missing. . . . Japanese planes shot down numbered
> 69, with few pilots recovered, a loss that took away a sizable
> proportion of Japan's remaining first-team pilots. Another 23
> planes had to ditch because of damage or loss of fuel. . . . Burned
> out *Shokaku,* much more severely damaged than in the Coral Sea
> battle, would require four months to repair, and *Zuiho* also was
> out of the Guadalcanal campaign. For Japan Santa Cruz was a
> victory won at nearly intolerable cost.[2]

Aboard the Big E, as we again buried the dead from another battle, the reality of our desperate situation was quite obvious. All one had to do was look around at the screening vessels moving swiftly away to the southeast—back to a semblance of safety and shelter—and try to find another carrier. There was none.

The *Enterprise*—and Air Group Ten—were alone.

VIII

One of the old VS-5 gang, and a personal friend who joined VS-10 to return to the South Pacific in *Enterprise* for Santa Cruz, was Lt. Stockton B. Strong. Known by his middle name, Birney, he had been one of the senior men in VS-5 and a survivor of the anti–torpedo plane patrol of 8 May 1942 at Coral Sea. Holder of a Navy Cross for his combat actions in that first carrier-versus-carrier battle, Birney was a Naval Academy class of 1937 graduate from an old Navy family, and had been a carrier dive-bomber pilot since finishing flight training in early 1940. As operations officer of VS-5 he had been my initial squadron boss when for my first nonflying assignment I was made assistant materials officer in his department.

Handsome, a Nordic blond type, about five feet ten inches in height, with a ruddy complexion, blue eyes, and deep dimples, he had the angelic appearance of a large cherub. Birney was a pleasant man whose easygoing personality covered an intensely ambitious sense of duty regarding his naval career. His recent marriage in Honolulu shortly after the Midway battle had been a squadron event of some magnitude.

Birney and Ens. John Richey comprised one of the search teams of SBDs that found *Ryujo* in the Battle of the Eastern Solomons on 24 August 1942. He made a contact report that led to the later sinking of this small carrier by an attack group from *Saratoga*. However, after reporting the position of the contact, Strong and Richey did not climb and make a two-plane attack upon this important enemy target; they returned to *Enterprise* still carrying their bombs.

This apparent lack of aggressive action was an affront to Comdr. John Crommelin, air officer of the Big E. In an impassioned talk with all pilots in the wardroom the night before Eastern Solomons, Commander John had stressed the point that each pilot had a duty to do everything in his power to engage the enemy and defeat him in the coming action. Strong's returning without complying with this indirect order rankled the air boss and he took action by putting Birney into hack (confining him to quarters).

This redress occurred on the afternoon of 24 August 1942 after Flight 300 had left the damaged *Enterprise* and ended up on Guadalcanal. As both the squadron CO Caldwell and XO Woodhull were with Flight 300, Strong, as third in rank, was acting CO of most of VS-5 still aboard the ship. There is no evidence of just what happened, and I was not there because I was flying wing on Caldwell with the attack group. In a discussion of the affair years later, Art Downing remembered that Birney had received some sort of brief disciplinary action after Eastern Solomons as the Big E was returning to Pearl Harbor for repairs of battle damage. He recalled that Strong was emotionally upset and spent a few days in hack. As Birney's roommate, he was close to the events.

Rear Adm. John Crommelin recently told me he had intended to court-martial Strong after the Eastern Solomons failure to attack *Ryujo*. Birney asked for a second chance and was *ordered* to return to immediate combat.

Strong ended up in VS-10 as a lieutenant third in rank to Lt. Comdr. Bucky Lee as his new CO. He was the only combat-experienced lieutenant in his new assignment and the only VS-5 lieutenant to go out again as a dive-bomber pilot. (Lts. Swede Vejtasa and Fritz Faulkner, previously of VS-5, were now fighter pilots in VF-10.) And as a new lieutenant (jg), I was the only veteran of Flight 300 and the fighting in August and September with the Cactus Air Force, to go back out with AG-10, so Birney and I had something in common.

We had been at sea in *Enterprise* for a few days, heading south for what was to be known as the Battle of Santa Cruz, when I dropped by Birney's stateroom after evening chow. It was my first talk with him since the squadron had split at Eastern Solomons. He was a man determined to attack and hit a Japanese carrier if the opportunity ever came his way again. We did not discuss what happened on 24 August, or anything about his relationship with Commander Crommelin. He did say that he intended to show Commander John that he was not afraid to attack the Japanese even by himself if necessary.

Birney Strong and Charles Irvine's spectacular two-plane attack of *Zuiho* on 26 October 1942, in which two five-hundred-pound bomb hits put the Japanese carrier out of action, was the finest example of this type of attack in the Pacific war. Fleet correspondent Eugene Burns wrote a stirring account of this attack at the time, and also covered it in his book. As a personal friend, he often gave me copies of his stories after he finished them. Using an original copy of his story, I want to tell Burns's amazing tale of how Birney Strong and Skinhead Irvine bagged a Japanese carrier, as told in their own words in interviews after their return to Big E.

IX

WITH A PACIFIC FLEET TASK FORCE OFF SANTA CRUZ ISLANDS, 26 OCTOBER 1942

Two grinning American pilots flying Dauntless dive bombers took on a piece of Tojo's fleet by themselves today, tore a large hole out of his newest carrier [*Zuiho*] and returned this afternoon without getting a scratch. Their action was the first blow in a battle which saw two Japanese carriers, a battleship and two cruisers heavily damaged and other warships hit.

Air Officer [of the *Enterprise*], Comdr. John G. Crommelin . . . commented: "Lt. Strong's and Ens. Irvine's feat was superb. The audacity of their attack and its skillful execution [combined with] their offensive-defensive tactics with the Jap fighter planes were in keeping with the best traditions of the Navy." He added: "Personally, I don't see how they got away with it."

Lt. Stockton B. Strong . . . said: "We were about 100 miles from the Japanese fleet when contact was made. My wingman Irvine—we call him Skinhead . . . and I [turned south and] climbed, and there they were like ducks on a millpond. Two nice flattops surrounded by cruisers and destroyers. Something you dream about. We came at them out of the sun and on the downwind, eh Skinhead?" Lt. Strong pulled off his helmet showing damp curly sandy hair; his eyes are blue as china.

Ens. Irvine, a rangy sharp-featured lad whose pants are always five inches too short for him, nodded. He said: "We split our wing flaps. It's no military secret, the Japs have flaps too. We pushed over into 80 degree dives, all the time expecting the fleet to start pitching up lead as we closed the distance."

"Yeh, I was looking for bumps from AA fire" put in Strong's Radioman 1/c Clarence H. Garlow, . . . "but nothing happened. I thought maybe we had gone nuts and belonged to the squirrels."

Lt. Strong, a veteran of the Coral Sea battle, went on with the story. "There was a nice red circle on the carrier's deck. My radioman Garlow tells me that there were about 20 planes parked on the forecastle. I released my bomb smack in the circle among the planes and then strafed the port side gun positions—they rim the ship—however, I was too anxious to get away to see much more."

Radioman Eligie Pearl Williams . . . said: "There was a big

cloud of black smoke belching out of her deck and a flash of flame as Mr. Irvine, my pilot, slipped his bomb into the same circle. Maybe we touched off their gasoline." He winked happily and continued: "But I didn't have much time to look either, because a dozen Jap [fighters] came shooting in from all sides. Honest to Joe, I'm telling you there weren't more than two or three bursts of [AA] gunfire from their entire fleet."

Radioman Williams, who operated two machine guns, added: "Mister Irvine didn't improve my hunting, bouncing me around the way he did dodging them Zeros and skimming the foam off the waves. But I'm glad he did. I reckon those Japanese followed us more than 50 miles while they made runs and passes at us but our [return] fire caused them to drop off one by one, excepting two or three who were pretty determined."

[When questioned he stated:] "Oh, sure, I got me a Zero. Before Mr. Irvine got us into a rain squall which was the prettiest sight I hope to see this side of heaven, I dropped him into the water burning. Then when we were through with the action, my pilot says: 'I feel like a smoke, what about you?' and we both smoked."

Garlow, Lt. Strong's gunner, got a Jap too. He said: "As these twelve Zeros were making alternating runs on us and then on Ens. Irvine's plane, they kept getting occasional hits with their two 20mm cannon and two machine guns. They hit our tail and knocked out the radio equipment. But one made a fatal error by turning his belly to me; right then I laced in a burst of fire, the gasoline started shooting out and he hit the water hard and burst into flames."

"I believe I could do better next time," concluded gunner Williams; "I was just a bit hasty in firing. I was on an empty stomach not having more than an orange [which] I ate just before we got into battle."

Rear Adm. John Crommelin was so impressed with the *Zuiho* attack that he told me recently: "Hal, I recommended Birney Strong for a Medal of Honor." Strong got a gold star to add to his Navy Cross. But more important than a medal to him was the respect and acclaim he received from fellow pilots. If there had indeed been any doubt as to the courage of this dive-bomber pilot, either in his own mind or the minds of others, it was erased forever in the few moments that it took for him to put his Dauntless into a dive—the maneuver that gave them both immortality.

X

As the smoke cleared away on the evening of 26 October 1942, a hurt but still defiant *Enterprise* sailed south for Noumea to assess her damages and bind up her wounds. The Battle of Santa Cruz was over and, with the loss of *Hornet,* the Big E was the last U.S. aircraft carrier facing the Japanese in the South Pacific. Her embarked Air Group Ten and the Cactus Air Force operating from Henderson Field were all that was left of the naval and marine air forces that had fought, and stopped, the Japanese Imperial Navy's expansion movements toward Australia.

When *Enterprise* arrived in the harbor at Noumea, the repair ship *Vulcan* was waiting to begin restoration of the big warship to battle readiness. No one aboard, from the lowest seaman to task force commander, had to be told how important the Big E was at this moment; she had to get back to top fighting condition as quickly as possible. Sixty officers and men from *Vulcan* and a battalion of Seabees worked around the clock to repair the new wounds received at Santa Cruz.

As usual, the air group went to the nearest airfield—in this case, grass-surfaced Tontouta—to conduct the never-ending flying requirements, including preparation of new aircraft replacements and repairs to the old. Living conditions were almost as bad as at the Canal, but without the bombing and shelling. We slept four men to a tent on cots rigged with mosquito netting to protect us from these malaria-bearing pests. On the bright side, there was swimming in a nearby river, cold Australian beer, and trips into Noumea for sightseeing; for me this included visits again with the wonderful Maestracci family.

It was to be a brief interlude. With repairs only half-done, and Seabees still working, the Big E received orders to go to sea. We flew the group aboard off the northeast coast of New Caledonia, amid the scuttlebutt that we were headed for Guadalcanal to stop another major Japanese thrust to retake that God-forsaken island's Henderson Field—what Vice Admiral Halsey called his unsinkable aircraft carrier. The date was 11 November 1942.

A somewhat fearful Task Force Sixteen, under Rear Adm. Thomas Kincaid, headed for a point southwest of Guadalcanal to be in position to attack enemy ships coming down the slot and also to support air and surface operations at Cactus. Not even the presence of Task Force Sixty-Four with the new battleships

Washington and *South Dakota* and supporting destroyers, under the command of Rear Adm. Willis A. Lee, could allay the deep misgivings that we in *Enterprise* felt at that moment. Here we were, the only U.S. aircraft carrier left in the South Pacific, battered and defiant, going out to take on the entire Japanese fleet which included at least two or three operational carriers still capable of action. It looked like Santa Cruz all over again, this time without the *Hornet.*

But there was one big difference in how the coming decisive battle was to be directed as opposed to those of the recent past: A new South Pacific commander, Vice Adm. William "Bull" Halsey, had replaced the reticent Vice Adm. Robert Ghormley in mid-October. Unlike his predecessor, Halsey was determined to hold Guadalcanal and would use every ship and airplane at his disposal to do so. However, even with this dedication, the odds in the coming battle were heavily pro-Japanese.

All intelligence sources available indicated that the Japanese were going to make a major effort to retake the American position on the beleaguered isle. This effort would include reinforcement of existing forces, supplies for a maximum attack effort, and support from whatever surface warships and air forces were needed to get the job done. It was logical to assume that the air effort would include at least two aircraft carriers in direct support.

As the Big E and Task Force Sixteen sped northwestward, searches were fanned out ahead for two hundred miles on the morning of the twelfth. These searches were divided between VB-10 and VS-10 and included both single- and two-plane efforts. In spite of squally weather, with limited visibility and restless seas, my fellow scouts and I found no evidence of Japanese ships at sea.

On the morning of 13 November 1942, TF-16 was on station at a position 280 miles southwest of Guadalcanal. With no contacts or reports of Japanese carriers at sea from the morning search, it was decided to send nine of VT-10's TBFs into Henderson Field to augment the existing Cactus Air Force, which was sorely short of torpedo planes. Eight were loaded with torpedoes and one with four five-hundred-pound bombs. Under the command of Lt. Albert "Scoofer" Coffin, CO of VT-10 since the tragic loss of Lt. Comdr. John Collett at Santa Cruz, the flight was escorted by six VF-10 fighters.

Unknown to the leadership in *Enterprise,* a bloody surface ship engagement had occurred east of Savo Island shortly after midnight. In Sealark Channel, also known as Ironbottom Sound, a Japanese surface force of two battleships, light cruiser, and eleven destroyers, intent upon shelling Henderson Field and destroying the Cactus Air Force on the ground, collided head on with a U.S. surface force composed of two attack cruisers, three light cruisers, and eight destroyers. In the ensuing melee, the U.S. force was badly mauled, losing four destroyers, *Cushing, Laffey, Barton,* and *Monssen,* and two light cruisers, *Atlanta* and *Juneau,* with the cruisers *San Francisco* and *Portland* badly damaged. Among the many American casualties were Rear Adm. Daniel J. Callaghan in *San Francisco* and Rear Adm. Norman Scott in *Atlanta.* The Japanese force lost the destroyers *Akatsuki* and *Yudachi,* and the battleship *Hiei* was seriously damaged.

Although the surface exchange had been a disaster to the U.S. force, one important result was favorable: the Japanese had not shelled Henderson Field and the Cactus Air Force was still a force-in-being. At dawn both fighters and dive-bombers took off to sweep the area and found the badly damaged *Hiei* slowly moving away near Savo Island. She had taken over eighty-five shell hits in the night action and was in dire straits.

Like a disturbed fire anthill, SBDs came streaming out from Henderson Field to finish off the wounded battleship. Maj. Joe Sailer, XO VMSB-132, and Maj. Bob Richard, CO VMSB-142, with their dive-bombers, began attacks that were to continue throughout the day. Marine squadron VMSB-131, equipped with TBFs and torpedoes, made the first Marine torpedo attack from Cactus; *Hiei* was in serious trouble, with more on the horizon.

A little after 1000 saw the appearance upon the scene of VT-10's nine TBFs, which had been launched from Big E. Lt. Scoofer Coffin, rounding Cape Esperance en route to the Canal, spotted the Japanese battleship. Splitting his eight torpedo-bearing aircraft into two sections of four planes each, he led the Buzzard Brigade with their torpedoes in an anvil attack from both bow bearings. Frenchy Boudreaux brought up the rear with a load of bombs. They left *Hiei* claiming three new hits, and sinking became almost a certainty. At sundown, after more hits from additional attacks, the first Japanese battleship to be finished off by air power in the Pacific war slipped beneath the waves near Savo.

That night, Japanese surface forces consisting of cruisers and destroyers came in to shell U.S. positions on Guadalcanal, but did not put Henderson Field out of commission. In the early morning of the fourteenth, the Big E again sent out her standard morning search.

From a launch position about two hundred miles southwest of Guadalcanal, the scouts would be flying up to Russell, Rendova, and New Georgia islands—the southern boundary of the slot. This time, the third day of morning searches, they found the Japanese for what was to become a major confrontation.

Shortly after 0700, the first word of a contact came from Lt. Bill Martin, XO of VS-10, who reported ten aircraft inbound about 140 miles north of the task force. Assuming these aircraft to be Japanese (they weren't), it was hastily decided to launch the ready strike group immediately, to clear the deck in case of an air attack. Seventeen SBDs loaded with thousand-pound bombs, under the leadership of Lt. Comdr. Bucky Lee, CO of VS-10 and acting CAG for this mission, departed northward with an escort of ten F4Fs of VF-10. Overhead CAP was increased and all hands went to general quarters to await further developments.

Rear Admiral Kinkaid was gambling when he launched everything he had on the sketchy information received from Martin. But luck was with the Americans, when at 0805 Lt. (jg) Robert D. Gibson reported that he was sighting many Japanese ships just south of Rendova Island, including "two BBs and one possible CVE." While the report was in error in ship types (there were no battleships or carriers), it was completely accurate in numbers and position. He had found the Japanese Eighth Fleet under command of Vice Admiral Mikawa, which consisted of four heavy cruisers, two light cruisers, and six destroyers. Part of this group had conducted the Cactus bombardment of the night before.

After making his report, Bob Gibson and his wingman Buck Buchanan climbed slowly to seventeen thousand feet and placed themselves in a position to dive on one of the heavy cruisers. They picked already damaged *Kinugasa* and dove in unison.

Like Strong and Irvine of VS-10 had done on *Zuiho* at Santa Cruz, Gibson and Buchanan of VB-10 conducted a perfect dive-bombing attack on the *Kinugasa,* reporting two direct five-hundred-pound bomb hits that reopened wounds made a short time before by Marine dive- and torpedo bombers from Cactus. They then headed their planes for Henderson Field.

153

Ensigns Hoogerwerf and Halloran, in their sector next to Gibson's, heard his contact report. They immediately began climbing toward the scene, arriving shortly after the Gibson-Buchanan attack. Picking an undamaged heavy cruiser, they attacked from sixteen thousand feet. Hoogerwerf missed, but saw an explosion on the target cruiser, which he believed to be a hit by his wingman Halloran. As Halloran and his gunner were never seen again, it is probable the explosion witnessed was their Dauntless crashing on the deck of the Japanese cruiser target; such a crash was reported by that ship when it returned to its home port in Japan. Hoogerwerf returned to the Big E.

Lee also heard Gibson's contact report and, after some confusion about proper headings to the scene, proceeded to the Mikawa force. Attacks by the combined VS-10 and VB-10 dive-bombers resulted in heavy damage to the light cruiser *Isuzu* and a near miss of *Chokai*, the flagship. While leaving the scene, several pilots of this group observed the heavy cruiser *Kinugasa*, hit a short time before by Gibson and Buchanan, roll over and sink. All aircraft of this attack group survived and headed for Henderson Field.

While the sighting and attack of the Japanese cruiser bombardment force near Rendova Island were going on, probably the most important discovery of the battle was taking place to the northwest above New Georgia Island in the slot. Here Lt. (jg) Martin Doan Carmody and his wingman, Lt. (jg) W. E. Johnson, in Sector 2 had found a huge Japanese convoy of eleven transports screened by eleven destroyers, on course 140 degrees. Like a giant spear heading for Cape Esperance, the western tip of Guadalcanal, these were the reinforcements that everyone had heard were coming to beef up existing Japanese troops already surrounding U.S. Marine and Army defenders—the additional punch to overwhelm our beachhead and put an end forever to Cactus Air Force operations.

Carmody, a big, good-natured Irishman with a grin a yard wide, had reddish hair and a personality that made him one of the best-liked men in Air Group Ten. He was a fighter who came from pugnacious stock. Known as "Big Red" or simply "Red" to his friends, he loved his Irish ancestry. He once related to me a favorite story about his grandfather. In a conversation with another Irishman, Grandpa Carmody was asked where in Ireland the clan "sprang from." Big Red's grandparent spoke for all the Carmodys when he replied: "We don't spring from, we spring at."

After making a detailed report of the twenty-two-ship enemy force, Red and his wingman Johnson climbed to altitude and dove on one of the largest transports. Both scored near misses, one so close that it did extensive hull damage. A threat awaited them when they pulled away, however, because several Zeros were present and began attacks. Carmody, with gunner A2/c. John Liska shooting down one of their tormentors, made it to nearby clouds and escaped. Unfortunately, Johnson and gunner A3c. H. P. Hughes, Jr., were shot down—both Carmody and Liska saw the Dauntless land in the water only to be strafed by two of the Zeros. The victims were never seen again. The survivors returned to the Big E with a cupful of gasoline left.

Hearing Carmody's contact report, I turned starboard to a northeast heading and started a slow climb to altitude. I knew about where the convoy was as I was familiar with the slot from numerous flights into the area during my weeks on the Canal two months before. Sure enough, Griff and I found them where they should be—of course, a force of twenty-two ships was not too hard to spot!

I wanted to conserve as much fuel as possible, so I headed straight on in for an attack. Coming from the west at fourteen thousand feet, we went down on a large transport—one in a line of three on the southernmost part of the formation. This approach allowed us to drop, then pull out to the southeast on a heading back to *Enterprise*. I had already made up my mind to return to the ship if possible, going to that God-forsaken strip at Cactus only if necessary. Both of our bombs were near misses, damaging the target and slowing it down as we left the area on the deck at maximum speed. Except for some AA fire, mostly from the screening destroyers, we had no opposition as we sped away. With enough fuel, we arrived back at the ship without incident.

Thus, by 1100, both Rear Admiral Kinkaid in *Enterprise* and Maj. Gen. Frank Woods at Henderson Field realized the Japanese threat that had to be stopped was the eleven transports carrying approximately thirteen thousand troops with all their gear. With the main part of Air Group Ten already at Henderson Field, the remaining eight SBDs and twelve F4Fs—every plane that could carry a bomb or fire a gun—were readied to join the battle in conjunction with the Cactus Air Force.

Skipper Thomas and XO Welch had already gone with the first

VB-10 attack group in the morning, so Lieutenant (jg) Goddard, as senior man aboard, set up a flight of the remaining VB-10 aircraft available for this final launch. It turned out that there were more than enough fresh pilots to man the five squadron aircraft up for the strike. At 1310, eight SBDs with twelve F4Fs of VF-10 as escorts under CO Flatley, departed to attack the convoy of ships in the slot and then go on to Henderson Field and continue the effort from there. Watching them go, I was thankful I was not returning to that Cactus hellhole, still so fresh in my memory.

The seven hours of daylight, from 1100 to 1800 on 14 November 1942—the time the Cactus Air Force and AG-10 had to destroy the Japanese reinforcement fleet—was possibly the most hectic, frantic period of many that took place at Henderson Field. A coordinated effort between the Navy carrier pilots and their Marine brothers-in-arms, combined with a superhuman effort from the aviation ground support personnel, kept a steady stream of SBDs and TBFs carrying bombs and torpedoes shuttling back and forth from the field to the convoy targets. All available F4Fs were also airborne in an attempt to keep enemy Zeros and float-fighters off the bombers; they were not always successful and some of both attackers and defenders were lost.

Many Marine and Navy pilot heroes were involved: Maj. Joe Foss flew almost continuously, shooting down several enemy planes. Lt. Col. Joe Bauer, Cactus fighter squadrons commander, was lost late in the day when his shot-up F4F landed safely in the water, but he was never found. Maj. Joe Sailer led strike after strike of dive-bombers, both Navy and Marine, out to the fray. Mixed sections and divisions of Navy and Marine pilots flew together, depending upon what aircraft were available, armed, and ready to go. Ens. Chuck Irvine of VS-10 flew out to the scene and made a solo attack after his SBD became armed and ready and everyone else had already left for the targets. Most pilots flew at least two missions and some, like Hoot Gibson, got in three.

The victory was not without cost, especially to VB-10. The trials of the squadron are exemplified by the hero of the following story.

NAVAL AVIATOR CADET BUELL
SUMMER - 1941

Yearbook photograph of me when I was
an aviation cadet at Pensacola, Florida,
May 1941 (age 21).

In this photograph I am standing beside
an N3N trainer after my first Navy solo
flight from Lambert Field, January 1941.

DEPARTMENT OF THE NAVY

Date. Dec. 10. 1941.

NAVAL AVIATOR No. 9095

This Certifies that

Harold L. BUELL

Ensign, A-V(N), USNR

born 4 *day of* Nov. 1919
*having fulfilled the conditions pre-
scribed by the United States Navy
Department, was appointed a*

NAVAL AVIATOR

on October 1, 1941

Chief of Bureau of Navigation.

U. S. GOVERNMENT PRINTING OFFICE 16—28322

Aer. 4120 **3048**

U.S. NAVAL AIR STATION
Pensacola, Florida
STATION

27 Aug. 1941
DATE ISSUED

This is to certify that

HAROLD L. BUELL
NAME

Ens., A-V(N) USNR
RANK

has passed the test in INSTRUMENT FLYING
prescribed for pilots of

THE UNITED STATES NAVY

and is qualified to proceed on Instruments in

Single engine
TYPE OF PLANE

TYPE OF PLANE

A. C. READ,
Capt., U. S. Navy,
COMMANDING.

Also qualified for let-down instruments

Above: Copy of my original naval aviator's license
and instrument rating, awarded 1 November 1941.
These cards are shown in their original leather folder
as issued to each graduating cadet.

Above: Pen-and-ink copy of Bombing Squadron Ten
(VB-10) insignia. I created the original design in November 1942.

Right: My pen-and-ink copy of early war insignia of
Scouting Squadron Five (VS-5).

Left: Seamen Hank Hartman, Bob Gibson, and me in
front of a Navy SBC-4, Lambert Field, Naval Reserve
Air Station, Robertson, Missouri, January 1941.

"Scratch one flattop," the death of the Japanese carrier *Shoho* at Coral Sea, 8 May 1942. *U.S. Navy.*

Left, top: Enterprise under way before World War II, probably about 1939. Note biplane fighters on flight deck. *U.S. Navy.*

Left, bottom: Pilots of Bombing Squadron Ten on the flight deck of *Enterprise,* October 1942, just before the Battle of Santa Cruz. Left to right are (first row) Wiggins, me, Frissel, Robinson, Stevens, Dufficy, Leonard, Welch, McGraw, and Thomas (CO); (back row) Wakeham, Griffith, Hoogerwerf, Goddard, Gibson, Halloran, Buchanan, Nelson, Allen, West, and Carroum. *U.S. Navy.*

Henderson Field, Guadalcanal, in August 1942. Photograph taken by a Dauntless pilot from *Saratoga*. *National Archives*.

An SB2C Helldiver at the cut position for landing aboard the carrier and a second plane in good interval position following. *U.S. Navy*.

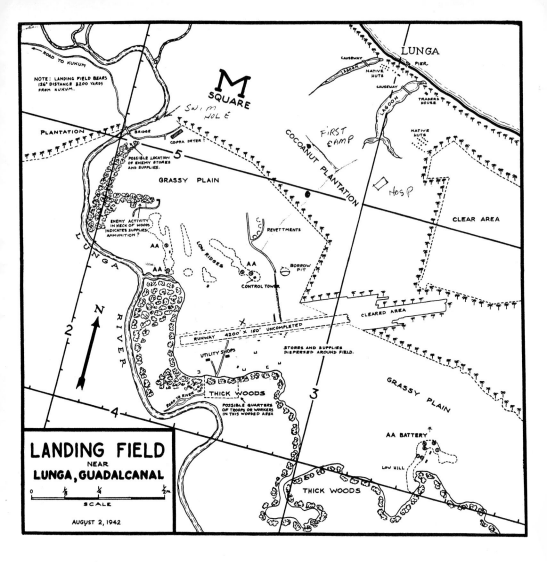

These are copies of three charts issued to me for use in the 7 August 1942 invasion of Guadalcanal. I carried these charts on all flights and strikes from both *Enterprise* and Henderson Field during August and September 1942. Numbers written on charts show where I dropped bombs during the 7–9 August invasion support period. Charts were made on *Enterprise* from intelligence reports and used by pilots for target identification and close air support of invasion troops. The original three charts are on permanent display in the Admiral Nimitz State Historical Park and Museum, Fredericksburg, Texas. *U.S. Navy.*

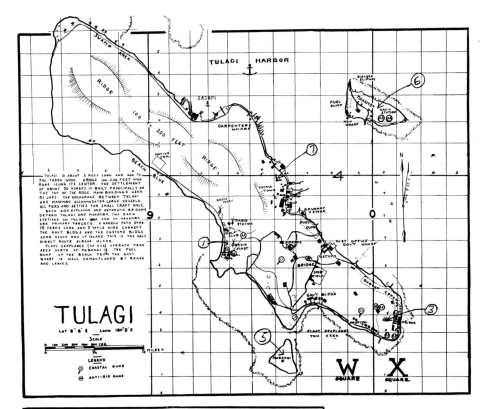

TULAGI

TULAGI HARBOR

SWAMP AREA

RIDGE 100 200 FEET

BEACH BLUE RIDGE

SASAPI

CARPENTER'S WHARF

CHINA TOWN

NATIVE CEM

RADIO MAST

RADIO STATION

B. WHARF & STORE

FUEL DUMP

POST OFFICE GOVT WHARF

RESIDENCE

CUSTOMS

BRIDGE

SPORT FIELD

GOV'T BLDG'S

PRISON

FLOAT SEAPLANES THIS AREA

MAKAMBO

FUEL DUMP

MAIN WHARF

RADIO STATION

MABANGI I.

TULAGI IS ABOUT 2 MILES LONG AND 200 TO
300 YARDS WIDE. A RIDGE 100-200 FEET HIGH
RUNS ALONG ITS CENTER. THE SETTLEMENT
OF ABOUT 50 HOUSES IS BUILT PRINCIPALLY ON
THE TOP OF THE RIDGE. MAIN BUILDINGS USED
BY JAPS. THE ANCHORAGE BETWEEN TULAGI
AND MAKAMBO ACCOMODATES LARGE VESSELS.
ALL PIERS AND JETTIES FOR SMALL CRAFT ONLY.
BOTH HIGH EXPLOSIVE AND AUTOMATIC AA GUNS
DEFEND TULAGI AND MAKAMBO. TWO RADIO
STATIONS ON TULAGI AND ONE IN MAKAMBO
ARE PRIMARY TARGETS. A NARROW PATH SOME
75 YARDS LONG AND 5 YARDS WIDE CONNECT
THE GOV'T BLDGS AND THE CUSTOMS BLDGS
NEAR SOUTH END OF ISLAND. THIS IS THE ONLY
DIRECT ROUTE ACROSS ISLAND.
FLOAT SEAPLANES (VF 475) OPERATE FROM
AREA NORTH OF MABANGI I. THE FUEL
DUMP UP THE BEACH FROM THE GOVT.
WHARF IS WELL CAMOUFLAGED BY BRUSH
AND LEAVES.

LAT 9° 6' S   LONG 160° 9' E

SCALE
0 100 200 300 400 500 YDS.
0 ½ MILES 1

LEGEND
⊙ COASTAL GUNS
⊕ ANTI-AIR GUNS

W SQUARE   X SQUARE

GAVUTU ISLAND

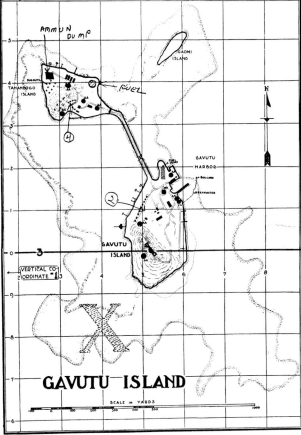

AMMUN DUMP

GAOMI ISLAND

TANAMBOGO ISLAND

FUEL

GAVUTU HARBOR

BREAKWATER

GAVUTU ISLAND

VERTICAL CO-ORDINATE "1"

SCALE IN YARDS
0 100 200 300 400 500 1000

Above: U.S. carrier *Wasp* afire from submarine torpedo hits before sinking, in September 1942. *National Archives*

Left: Eugene Burns, Associated Press correspondent, talks with me on the bridge of *Enterprise,* January 1943. *U.S. Navy.*

Right, top: Copy of the original Palau Island chart issued to me before the 30 March 1944 strikes and carried on those attacks. *U.S. Navy.*

Right, bottom: Strike chart that I carried while leading the attack and sinking the ship off Sarmi, New Guinea, on 21 April 1944. Notes describing the attack were drawn on it at the debriefing. *U.S. Navy.*

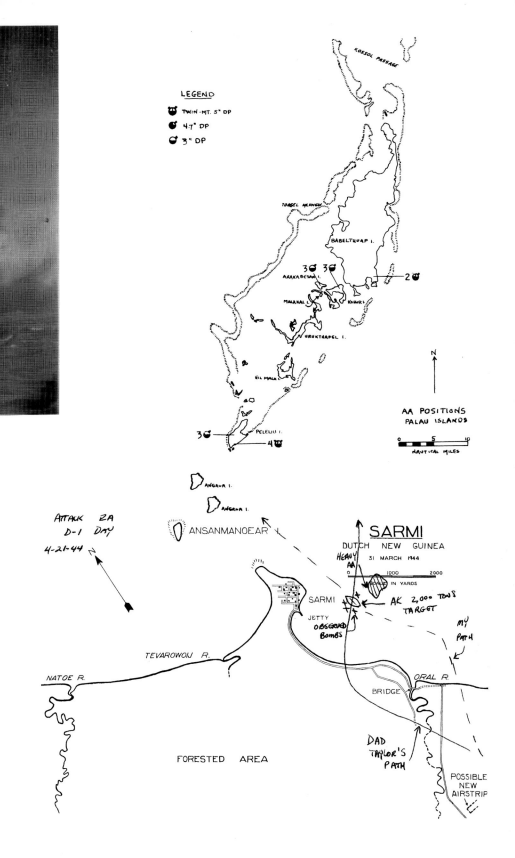

LEGEND

⬤ TWIN-MT. 5" DP
⬤ 4.7" DP
⬤ 3" DP

KOSSOL PASSAGE

TOAGEL MLUNGUI

BABELTHUAP I.

3⬤ 3⬤   2⬤

ARAKABESAN I.

MALAKAL I.   KOROR I.

URUKTHAPEL I.

EIL MALK

PELELIU I.

3⬤
    4⬤

N

AA POSITIONS
PALAU ISLANDS

0   5   10
NAUTICAL MILES

ANGAUR I.

ANGAUR I.

ATTACK 2A
D-1 DAY

4-21-44   N

ANSANMANOEAR I.

SARMI
DUTCH NEW GUINEA
31 MARCH 1944

HEAVY
AA

0   1000   2000
IN YARDS

SARMI

JETTY

OBSERVED
BOMBS

AK 2,000 TONS
TARGET

MY
PATH

TEVAROWOIJ R.

NATOE R.

ORAL R.

BRIDGE

DAD
TAYLOR'S
PATH

FORESTED   AREA

POSSIBLE
NEW
AIRSTRIP

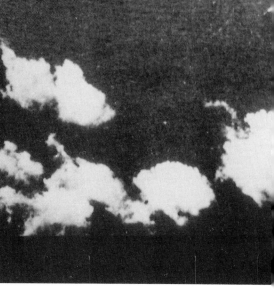

Above: Epic picture taken just after my division of six planes had finished the attack on *Zuikaku* at Philippine Sea, 20 June 1944. *National Archives ·*

Left: Picture of Lt. Jack "Dad" Taylor and me, taken in the VF-2 Ready Room, *Hornet,* after First Battle of Philippine Sea.

Vice Adm. Marc A. Mitscher presenting the Navy Cross to me, August 1944: Capt. A. K. Doyle and Rear Adm. J. J. Clark are in the background. *U.S. Navy.*

Air Group Two and ship commanders pose in front of a scoreboard painted upon *Hornet's* island, September 1944. Left to right are Ford (CO, VT-2), Campbell (CO, VB-2), Doyle (CO, *Hornet),* Dean (CO, VF-2), and Johnson (Air Boss). The scoreboard had flags showing planes shot down and ships sunk; bombs indicated number of strikes on targets. A second version of the scoreboard, painted upon a board panel, was kept on the hangar deck; this panel now resides in the National Naval Aviation Museum, Pensacola. *U.S. Navy.*

Above: Death of a ship in Manila Bay, Philippines, 21 September 1944. *Official photograph, U.S. Navy.*

Below: Copy of my Jocko Jima Development Corp. share certificate number 20.

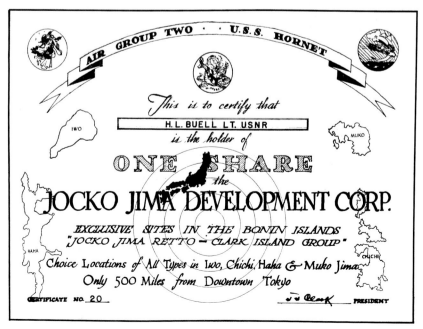

Above: Lt. Edwin "Big Ed" Wilson and I at the Copacabana night club, New York City, on 13 August 1945, the night before VJ Day. *Courtesy of Edwin Wilson.*

Left: Aboard *Hornet* in May 1944, I am standing in flight gear next to my SP2C Helldiver. *U.S. Navy.*

XI

Physical requirements for naval aviators are, and always have been, exacting. In addition to perfect health, excellent vision, and a spotless medical history pilots could not be too large or too small. The reason for a size requirement was logical: Many aircraft cockpits, especially those of carrier VF and VA, were a standard size. If a pilot was too big he would not be able to fit into the space allowed; too small and he would be unable to reach all of the controls. Careful screening at the time of original induction into flight training kept both extremes—large and small—out of CV combat aircraft.

Among the pilots in VB-10 was Ens. Jefferson H. Carroum from Smackover, Arkansas. "Tiny," as he was known to his fellow pilots in the squadron, if not the smallest aviator in the Navy, certainly had to be among that group at five feet four inches tall and 125 pounds. But though he was small, he was in perfect physical condition, strong, and tough.

Late afternoon of 14 November found Carroum flying wing on Lieutenant Welch in a VB-10 formation of seven SBDs approaching the Japanese troop ships northwest of Guadalcanal. This flight was the last of many that had been pounding the oncoming Japanese transports since their discovery in the morning. Of twenty-two ships in the original convoy, only five transports and five destroyers remained; five transports had been sunk and one had turned back, each with a destroyer to assist it. There had been some Zero opposition, but few losses. With a shortage of F4Fs, this flight was attacking without fighter cover.

The flight leader was Lt. Comdr. J. A. Thomas, CO of VB-10. For some reason he delayed his climb so that the formation reached the target area without sufficient altitude to make an immediate attack. After taking about twenty minutes to climb to twelve thousand feet in this dangerous area, Thomas headed over the ships to dive. By this time Zeros had spotted them and were rushing to intercept.

With seven planes, the dive-bombers were not flying a standard six-plane division formation. The first three aircraft, Thomas, Gibson, and Stevens, were in a regular three-plane section followed by a second section of four planes in a loose double-pair of two planes each. At a vulnerable time, just before breaking formation to dive, the seven were set upon by twelve Zero fighters.

Gibson was the first victim, falling out of the first section after being hit several times by both 7.7- and 20-mm shells. Using excellent evasive tactics, he outflew an enemy protagonist and landed his damaged Dauntless back at Henderson Field. Both Thomas and Stevens were able to dive on the transports and escaped further fighter attacks on their return to base.

The loose four-plane second section of Welch, Carroum, Wakeham, and Robinson received the main fury of the Zeros' attacks. Welch and Wakeham were shot down and lost. Robinson, like Gibson, fell out of his group after taking several hits, and survived repeated runs from a persistent Zero pilot who followed him across the nearby Russell Islands. Teyshak, Robby's gunner in 10-B-11, counted sixty-eight holes in their airplane when they landed back at Cactus. Jeff Carroum crash-landed his shot-up SBD into the water after diving on a transport, and with gunner Hynson began an incredible swim for survival.

The magnificent fight for life made by Tiny Carroum after ditching his plane is one of the great survival stories of the Pacific War. Briefly knocked unconscious when he struck his head as the aircraft crashed, he revived as water came into the cockpit and was able to crawl out onto the wing. Gunner Hynson got the raft free of the plane, but fear of strafing kept them from inflating it immediately. As the plane sank, the tail caught the raft, taking it down, and they were left in life jackets twenty-five miles north of the Russell Islands.

They removed their shoes, and Hynson also removed his pants and shorts. They began swimming south as darkness fell, using the Southern Cross to set a course. In the distance they saw fires burning from the sinking transports attacked earlier. Their goal was to swim to the Russells; their greatest fear was the possibility of shark attacks.

By 1000 the next morning, 15 November, Hynson was beginning to weaken. Carroum was a powerful swimmer so he dropped back to encourage his crewman to keep going. Finally Hynson asked Tiny to go on ahead, get to land, and return with help. The little man kept swimming strongly toward the distant island.

The sixteenth, his second day without food or water, found him sunburned, with eyes swollen shut and strength ebbing. But he kept swimming, always in the direction of the island, until finally he reached a lagoon. He could see huts and tried with his last strength to make shore. The currents were against him, and when night came he again passed out, sleeping the entire night.

When he awoke on the morning of the seventeenth, Tiny was still near the lagoon. He realized that he must make it during the daylight—he would not survive another night in the water. Late in the afternoon he felt bottom under his feet. So exhausted that he could not walk, he crawled, thrashed, staggered, and reeled the last few yards to shore, cutting his unfeeling feet on the glass-sharp coral. At approximately 1800 he dragged himself onto dry sand; he had been in the ocean seventy-three hours. No trace of Hynson was ever found.

Carroum had his first drink from a muddy pool of rainwater by the ocean's edge, then passed out from exhaustion and slept until morning. Local natives found him, fed him, and bathed his wounds. After a few days of care, the native chief contacted a nearby coastwatcher, and ten days later a PBY landed in the lagoon. Tiny was loaded aboard from a log canoe, returned via Tulagi to Espiritu Santo and VB-10, told us his story, then returned to the States.

Ens. Jefferson "Tiny" Carroum's survival was an inspiration to me for the remainder of my time in combat. He had shown that one could get through almost any trial with courage, determination, and perseverance against all odds.

XII

When night fell on the fourteenth and the last of the Cactus Air Force fighters and dive-bombers were gone, Rear Admiral Tanaka had only four transports and his flagship, the destroyer *Hayashio,* left in his reinforcement group. He decided that he was whipped and was about to turn the pitiful remnants back to his Shortland Islands base; he describes his memory of the event:

> The impression is indelible in my mind of bombs wobbling down
> . . . of carrier bombers roaring toward targets as though to
> plunge full into the water, releasing bombs and pulling out barely
> in time, each miss sending up towering columns of mist and
> spray, every hit raising clouds of smoke and fire as transports
> burst into flame and [took] the sickening list that spelled their
> doom . . . [As the smoke rose] the tragic scene of men jumping
> overboard from burning, sinking ships was revealed.[3]

At this late moment, Tanaka received the order to continue on to Doma Cove and land what was left of his charges. He was informed that help was on the way in the form of a battle force of one BB, two CAs, two CLs, and nine DDs that would cover his landings, fend off any American surface ships that came around, and shell Henderson Field on the way out.

Anticipating this very kind of move, Halsey had ordered Task Force sixty-four, composed of the battleships *Washington* and *South Dakota* with four destroyers, to head for Sealark Channel to challenge any Japanese force that might try to shell Henderson Field, and to sink any remaining transports found.

The two forces clashed about midnight in another bloody night battle. American forces lost three destroyers and *South Dakota* was damaged, while sinking the Japanese battleship *Kirishima* and one destroyer. More important than the losses was that Henderson Field escaped shelling, and the Cactus Air Force was out again at the crack of dawn on 15 November 1942.

All dive-bomber and torpedo squadron aircraft flyable began hitting the remaining Japanese transports, which had been beached by Tanaka at Tassafaronga Point. The CAF found them only twenty miles from Henderson Field, and began to pound to pieces this last vestige of the once proud Japanese twenty-two-ship reinforcement convoy. Following the motto of Scoofer Coffin's Buzzard Brigade, Marine and Navy attack planes proceeded to "mop 'em up."

When my roommate Lt. (jg) Ralph Goddard arrived at the scene he looked about for something better than the battered ships to hit with his thousand-pound bomb. Using his prewar forest ranger training, he spotted paths leading from the beached ships into trees nearby. Picking a spot among a large grove of palms, he dropped his bomb. He hit the jackpot, setting off a secondary explosion and fire that Marine veterans said was the largest ever seen on the island. The explosions continued along a quarter-mile chain as burning fuel and ammunition sent smoke and flames hundreds of feet into the air. The Indian had made his major contribution to the war.

How large was the attack-type Cactus Air Force that wrought such destruction in this three-day final battle of Guadalcanal? Four dive-bombing squadrons took part: VMSB-132, VMSB-142, VS-10, and VB-10, averaging fifteen flyable aircraft for each squadron for a total of about sixty Dauntless SBDs. VMSB-131, VT-8, and VT-10 were flying TBFs; VT-10 had nine and VT-8 was down to their last four, so a fair estimate of these aircraft would be twenty-five. Thus about eighty-five planes, carrying bombs and torpedoes in repeated attacks, stopped the Tokyo Express for the final time.

But what a price was paid! As a flyer I had never realized what terrible losses our surface Navy suffered at the time. Not until I read Eric Hammel's *Guadalcanal: Decision at Sea* did it sink in how horrible were the casualties in the two bloody nights of 13 and 15 November. By risking everything, two gallant U.S. battle forces drove off superior Japanese forces that would otherwise have shelled Henderson Field. It is logical to assume that heavy cruiser and battleship shells ranging from eight to fourteen inches in size would most likely have knocked out the very planes that were to save the day, especially on the fourteenth. That date will be long remembered by every Marine and Navy man—both flyer and ground support—who hacked away at what looked like a tidal wave rushing to engulf them.

The final battle of Guadalcanal (I like that name) was of much greater importance than history has credited it. Part of the reason for this oversight may be because it was not a classic carrier-versus-carrier duel like Eastern Solomons and Santa Cruz. Careful examination of this fight shows results for the United States certainly equal, and perhaps superior, to previous defensive battles. Here are some conclusions:

1. The Japanese finally realized they were beaten at Guadalcanal, and would shortly withdraw their troops from the area.

2. For the first time in the war the Japanese Navy lost two battle-ships in a period of three days.

3. The destruction of the reinforcement convoy ended the last major landing operation the Japanese were to attempt in the Pacific war.

4. For the first time in 1942 the Japanese did not support a major operation with aircraft carriers. Many historians wonder why Yamamoto did not use the two or three carriers he had at the time. The answer almost has to be that these ships did not have the necessary aircrews available to make them opera-

tional. The battles of Coral Sea, Midway, Eastern Solomons, and Santa Cruz had drained the pilot's blood from the air groups to the point where they were no longer capable of combat action.

5. The willingness of the Americans to commit every surface ship, and the only operational aircraft carrier they had, under the new leadership of Vice Admiral Halsey, showed the determination and confidence that was growing in the U.S. Navy about holding Guadalcanal.

6. The decision to use the air group from the only aircraft carrier to augment the Cactus Air Force and fight the action from Henderson Field, after the Japanese carriers did not come out, was a brilliant tactical decision that probably won the battle.

7. The final battle of Guadalcanal was Japan's last hurrah.

Enterprise had headed southeast after launching everything at approximately 1300 on 14 November. She returned to Noumea, where workmen continued repairing her Santa Cruz wounds. It would take several days for the victorious air group to get back to the ship, either in their own planes or by military air transport. Meanwhile the air boss, Comdr. John Crommelin, was busy arranging for new SBDs and F4Fs to be brought in to replace those lost or transferred to the Marines.

When there was time for the air group to count losses from the 13–15 November adventure with the Cactus Air Force, it was a sobering moment for VB-10. Overall losses had been amazingly low considering the ferocity of the fighting. The Marines had lost the famous Lt. Col. Indian Joe Bauer and two other fighter pilots. One of these was rescued with Tiny Carroum. VF-10, the Marine dive-bombers, and all torpedo outfits had no personnel losses. VS-10 lost one scout bomber crew. Thus VB-10 was the only big loser, with four pilots and four gunners shot down. The return of Tiny Carroum reduced the final total to seven men gone.

Replacement pilots arrived almost immediately, bringing the squadron to a total strength of twenty-one pilots, two more than we had entering Santa Cruz. The lost XO, Lt. V. W. Welch, was not replaced; for the next three months VB-10 had as XO nonflying Lt. John Dufficy, one of two AV(S)s (aviation specialists) assigned, an unusual arrangement I never encountered again during my flying career in the Navy. One of the replacements was a Norfolk Deck Dodger named Roger Scudder; another was Walt Finger, a fellow midwesterner from Illinois, who became a close friend.

On 3 December we went briefly to sea to qualify the new men and check out the now-repaired Big E. We left Noumea, and our home port became Espiritu Santo, where we would be closer to action if needed.

XIII

Wartime naval aviators gave nicknames to almost anything. This included cars, airplanes, best girls, friends, or any possession of importance to them. Rarely did one answer to a given name but rather to a nickname that often had a story behind it. Sometimes a title was humorous, and usually tied into the background or experience of the person involved.

Among my named possessions was a government-issue Colt .45 automatic checked out to me as a personal sidearm. It was common practice for pilots to carry either a .38 or .45 on all strike missions, and when ashore anywhere in the war zone. The preferred way to wear a hand weapon was in a shoulder holster fitted under the armpit opposite the gun hand; as I was right-handed, my shoulder holster was under my left arm. The holster hung down from a strap that looped over the top of the shoulder with a second strap around the chest under the other arm, snapping or buckling in front.

The Navy did not issue shoulder holsters, so we made our own. Mine was of soft brown leather, which folded around the gun and then laced together with a thin thong. It had a small snap tab that fitted over the top for security of the weapon. When I had completed this bit of leatherwork I carefully engraved a nickname into the shoulder holster surface: Pua-ena.

Pua-ena means "hot flower" in Hawaiian—hot in the sense of both color (red) and beauty (passion). It was the nickname of a lovely Irish-Hawaiian girl who lived on Oahu. She possessed the characteristics of her Hawaiian name in abundance and the name seemed appropriate for my sidearm.

Pua-ena played a vital part in an incident that happened to me on New Caledonia right after the final battle of Guadalcanal. The Big E had returned to Noumea to finish repairs of battle damage and the squadron followed the usual procedure of operating from the primitive Tontouta airfield.

The only way one could get a hot bath, clean clothes, and a good meal was on *Enterprise* in the harbor. All pilots were divided into four groups, with three days on duty and one day off, back at the ship, if desired. This provided a break in camping-out at the field for a night of civilized living aboard ship every fourth day—a nice arrangement.

I had spent a night aboard with a good meal, a bath, a movie, and sleep on clean sheets in my cabin. After an early breakfast, I caught a boat from Big E to the dock to return to the drab conditions at Tontouta. I was wearing clean khakis and carried a small, green flight bag with personal belongings. Pua-ena was nestled in her holster under my left arm.

Upon arrival at the bustling dock, I looked up the debarkation chief to arrange transportation out to the airfield, which was about fifteen miles away on a winding road over a low mountain range. An early-morning rain shower had passed, traces of fog were already burning off, and a beautiful day lay ahead.

My ride turned out to be in a large truck loaded with aviation spare parts, including a couple of SBD engines in crates. It was a heavy-duty vehicle with double-pairs of four wheels on each side under the bed and dual ones on the cab—a fourteen-wheeler counting the two for front steering. The driver of this behemoth was a burly, muscular Seabee, with a New York accent so thick I could hardly communicate with him. I swung myself up into the cab, placed my green bag on the wide seat between us, and we got underway down a coral-surfaced, single-laned highway.

The driver wanted to talk, and started relating his life story to me in Brooklynese as we made our way up the mountainside. It was early and few others were on the road, so the big Seabee kept increasing our speed as we climbed. The road surface had not dried out completely from the earlier rain, and thus was quite slippery; the higher we got the more uneasy I felt. By this time the road had become just a ledge cut out of the mountain, with a drop-off on my side of more than a hundred feet and no guardrail between us and eternity.

The Seabee had reached a point in his story about being drafted out of a high-paying job driving for a trucking firm, and the emotion he was feeling affected his judgment. We were moving much too fast for road conditions and I was about to ask him to slow down when a near-calamity occurred.

Approaching a slight bend in the road and still climbing, a jeep suddenly appeared coming from the opposite direction. We were in the middle of the road, and the Seabee slammed on the brakes while moving to the right to clear the oncoming vehicle. The other driver went as far to his right as he could until he was scraping against the mountain; it was enough and we missed each other by inches. The jeep continued down the road while our truck went into a violent skid toward the unguarded precipice. Out of control, its brakes locked, the rig slid broadside, finally stopping on the shoulder of the road, and teetering on the rim of a cliff.

The whole episode happened so suddenly it took a moment for me to realize that I was staring death in the face. As I looked out the cab window on my side, there was nothing but open space with tree tops sticking up from below. The truck was hanging on the edge of at least a one-hundred-foot sheer drop, held there by the gripping action of the brakes in the twelve wheels under the loaded bed. I was frozen in my seat, fearing that the slightest shift of weight might be enough to tumble us into the ravine.

My companion in this misadventure had not spoken a word except a profane obscenity at the start of the skid. His foot was rigid on the brake pedal and his muscular arms bulged as he gripped the steering wheel so hard his knuckles were white. Sweat poured down his face from the strain, and he began making small gasping noises as the enormity of our plight began to register in his mind. I spoke as calmly as possible:

"Hold everything just as it is. Do not move your clutch or brake feet. Let the engine idle. Someone will come along in a few minutes to help us. We are okay."

The man did not reply but kept gasping for air in a hyperventilative manner, and his eyes darted about looking for a way to escape. After a few moments, I saw his left hand loosen from the steering wheel and start to move toward the door handle. The thought hit me: This bastard is getting ready to open his door and jump out, letting me go over the precipice with the rig!

The survival instinct and my guardian angel must have acted in my subconscious, as there was no planned thought in what I did next. In a movement secretly practiced for months, my right hand moved to the shoulder holster. Smoothly my right thumb flipped up the security tab and, in one swift motion, I drew Pua-ena from the sheath; my left hand grasped the top of the barrel and charged a shell from the clip into the chamber, moving back the firing hammer. I pointed the gun at the Seabee and said:

"Go ahead. Open the door and jump. But if you do, you'll be dead when your feet hit the ground as I will blow your head off as you leave."

There is nothing quite as striking as the business end of a Colt .45 automatic pistol pointed at you at close range. The hole in the barrel takes on the dimensions of a shotgun. My companion looked, heeded my words, and did not move again. The next few minutes dragged by like hours as the truck seemed to rock on the lip of the cliff.

Assistance arrived in the form of a truck with two marines coming down the road en route to the dock area. A sergeant came running up and I suggested that he anchor his vehicle against the mountainside and run the cable from his front-mounted winch around our truck frame by the left front wheel. Another truck arrived from the other direction during these preparations; its driver ran a cable to the rear axle. Then both drivers tightened their winches in unison and pulled our wayward vehicle back from the brink of destruction onto the main roadbed. In a subdued manner we continued on to Tontouta field.

I had closed the hammer and returned Pua-ena to her holster when the first rescue marine came up to the cab, so no one but the Seabee and I knew what had transpired earlier during those horrible moments when two lives hung in the balance. The man figured that I would report him to higher authority at our destination, but I never even asked his name. I took my green flight bag from the cab, got into the squadron transportation van, and left for VB-10 operations. I wanted to put the incident out of my mind as if it hadn't happened; this one I kept to myself.

XIV

There is something about sitting around in wartime, waiting for the next mission, that can get to people and bring all kinds of demons out of the closet. Each time the Big E returned to her anchorage at Espiritu Santo, the air group went ashore. For the officers and men of the ship it was a time for repair of battle damage, routine ship maintenance, re-supply, and some rest before going out again to face numerically superior Japanese air and surface forces.

For the officers and men of the squadrons it meant receiving new airplanes to replace losses, repair and maintenance of existing aircraft, and training of pilots, especially replacement ones. But it also meant living in rat-infested Quonset huts or tents, bad food, heat, bugs, no hot-water showers, outdoor toilets, and boredom while waiting for another call to face the Japanese alone. For the *Enterprise* and her air group, as the new year approached, "and then there was one" was reality.

In fairness, it wasn't all bad. Everyone got mail and sent some out. We often found a little booze from somewhere and would have a party. The poker games never ended, there were outdoor movies at night, and numerous spare-time activities to keep boredom at acceptable levels.

Sometimes the air group and squadron commanders would come up with training ideas that would invoke little enthusiasm from their charges. There was a small part of the AG-10 leadership that wanted to prepare all pilots to do night combat strikes from the carrier. I had seen, and taken part in, night combat efforts at Guadalcanal and knew how futile these efforts could be from land, much less from a carrier deck. The levels of aircraft instrument technology and pilot-training techniques in 1942 were not good enough to make night work from carriers possible with an acceptable degree of operational safety, especially with large numbers of aircraft flying around in formation together. Every predawn launch and rendezvous before a major combat strike had proven this point over and over, with accidents (some fatal) and loss of tactical organization within sections and division. The British had learned this lesson and did night strikes and intercepts with individual planes, in pairs, or very small strike units of specially trained night pilots and crews. The group grope concept of large numbers of different types of aircraft operating together from a deck at night had proven ludicrous at this stage of carrier warfare development.

However, this truth did not mean that there would be no more air group gropes at night in AG-10. After a few night solo fams (checkouts), then sections and divisions, a graduation exercise of a thirty-two-plane night group grope was planned. This flight would simulate a deck combat launch of twelve fighters, twelve dive-bombers, and eight torpeckers from the field at Espiritu Santo. Planes would get together by type, then rendezvous as a group, fly out to sea together a short distance, and return to the field, break up, and land. The date set for this extravaganza was the night of 13 January 1943.

As air officer of VB-10, I often did the test hops for squadron aircraft after checks, new engines, and other flight necessities. The afternoon of the thirteenth found me performing a flight test and, after hanging around the airfield to check things out, I headed north out to sea for a brief engine run-in. Local weather was good, with scattered clouds and normal prevailing winds.

I did not get more than a few miles away from Espiritu Santo Island when I noticed a huge storm front stretching from the north around to the southwest, covering better than 150 degrees and towering up thirty thousand to forty thousand feet in altitude. This was no small storm but a vast frontal buildup already in solid form and moving in a general direction toward the island. As visibility was excellent, I judged the storm to be sixty miles away. I turned about and returned to the field.

Because of the size and intensity of the approaching storm, I went to operations and reported what I had seen. I suggested that serious consideration should be given to canceling the planned night grope, as the storm might arrive in the middle of the operation and cause some problems with over thirty planes in the air. I tried to make the point that this was no ordinary storm coming—in fact it looked like a real bear. I was told that everything was okay and due consideration would be given my report by the CAG and squadron COs. Apparently no other reports about the storm had come in from ships at sea or other aircraft, so the group brass may have thought I was overreacting to local thunderstorms—an almost daily occurrence that time of year.

The flight was not cancelled, and we prepared to man aircraft shortly after sunset. VB-10 was to fly six SBDs and VS-10 six. I was to lead my three-plane section, and my roommate Ralph Goddard the other three. I got the group together at our aircraft revetment and carefully went over the flight plan one last time, stressing to the wingmen to fly position like they never had before, because I was sure we were in for a rough time.

As we taxied from the aircraft parking spots, the wind was already beginning to pick up and a light rain was falling. I looked to my left and Ralph gave me a farewell wave of his hand; I returned the salute and hurried to the end of the runway.

The six of us from VB-10 were experienced pilots with highly developed air discipline. I had my section together, and was turning back toward the field when the storm struck in force. I don't know what aerologists call that type of weather in the South Pacific but around Florida it is called a tropical storm just short of a hurricane, with winds up to fifty to sixty knots and rain so heavy that visibility is reduced to zero. With no field lights except those outlining the runway, we had nothing to use as a reference point to keep from being blown away from the island. I was also afraid of hitting some rocky clouds, as the mountains went up to six thousand feet on the western side of Espiritu Santo.

My section was among the last of the scheduled planes to take off. With more than thirty aircraft milling around in the storm, several began to try to get back down on the airfield immediately. Radio discipline quickly disappeared, with everyone calling for landing clearance at once. I switched my radio to the Big E's emergency channel, praying that someone would be on duty at the ship's ops room, and gave them a call. My guardian angel was on emergency duty, and an immediate answer came crackling back.

I had a plan, but because of blackout regulations on the ships it was in a sense an illegal one. I stated in as calm a voice as possible that my flight was in an emergency due to the storm and that we needed a visual reference point immediately. I then suggested that one or more searchlights be turned on and shined straight up over the ship from its anchorage in the harbor. Quickly two lights came beaming up through the darkness and driving rain, to be followed shortly by more from other ships, until the sky over the harbor was glowing with rays of light shining up through the storm. In spite of the torrential rains, enough light was visible to enable me to set up a racetrack flight pattern over the harbor. Other aircraft began joining up until I was leading over a dozen SBDs and TBFs in formation at two thousand feet above the bay through buffeting winds and sheets of rain.

At Bomber One, the main field, things began going wrong as aircraft tried in desperation to get back to earth. Almost immediately after the storm hit, a major crash occurred on the field. An F4F landed on top of a TBF, creating a huge pile of scrap metal in the center of the runway, effectively closing it to further landings until the rubble could be removed. But there was no crash crane available to do the job quickly, so men began to work frantically with tractors to clear the wreckage, while the storm increased in fury and aircraft continued to mill around in the darkness.

In addition to Bomber One, there was a second smaller field nearby used by fighters only. It did not take long to close this field too when an F4F landed with wheels up and was promptly hit by another landing fighter, forming a barrier of tangled debris. Thus both fields were blocked, with inadequate crash equipment available to clear them efficiently.

Grimly my flight clung together and continued to circle the spotlight beams of the ships in the harbor. We could hear reports coming in from the airfields and realized that both were closed. There was nothing to do except circle and wait out the storm, hoping that ground personnel would clear the runways for landings before our gasoline ran out, or the storm killed us.

It was one of the toughest flights of survival I ever flew—worse in some ways than combat. My flight logbook indicates that we flew around fighting vertigo, rough winds, and driving rains for three hours. Finally the runways were reported clear, landings resumed, and the storm abated a little as it moved on. I waited until the rush was over and went in last. When I taxied to my parking spot I noticed that Goddard's spot next to mine was empty —the tall, dark Indian was missing.

Leaving the plane in a cold rage, I hurried to the operations shack. I knew that some planes, and possibly personnel, had been lost, but had no idea that it was as bad as it turned out to be. The night's fiasco cost Air Group Ten two experienced dive-bomber crews, a couple of fighter pilots, and six aircraft. An old friend and fellow Norfolk Deck Dodger, Lt. (jg) Henry "Skip" Ervin and his gunner, of VS-10, simply disappeared; no trace of them or their SBD was ever found. My roommate and close friend Lt. (jg) Ralph Goddard and his gunner had crashed in the harbor; the SBD containing their bodies was found the next morning and we buried them on a nearby hill overlooking the spot where they died so needlessly. As I recall, one or two of the fighter pilots involved in the ground crashes were killed or seriously injured.

I will never know how I escaped a court-martial that night. At the operations shack I encountered several of the ranking officers, including my CO, and, in my anger and frustration, told them all off using language liberally sprinkled with four-letter words. To me it was a disgrace—a breach of honor—to lose fine young men in this manner. There had been ample warning of the approaching storm and, after all, the whole mission was only a training one that could have been scrubbed and never missed. Unfortunately, this kind of imprudent leadership was all too common, especially in that first year of war, and good men paid for rash mistakes with their lives.

Of course there also was bad luck to contend with. In April 1943, just before the air group and *Enterprise* headed for the United States and a much-needed rest, an incident occurred at Espiritu Santo that vividly illustrates this point. A small hundred-pound bomb, being used as a seat by two ordnancemen at an outdoor movie, exploded, killing sixteen men and wounding more than thirty others. Most were air group personnel, including pilots, aircrew, and other aviation rates (classifications). I had just left the island for the United States, so I missed this grievous event.

It is hard to blame such a tragedy on anyone, or to understand how it even happens, so the element of luck enters the picture as a real factor in survival. However, the storm losses were caused by decisions made by men in positions of power, authority, and leadership who were responsible for the lives and property entrusted to their care. While you expected they would make mistakes, it was not good for morale if these mistakes were based upon indifference and repeated over and over.

Approximately two months after the storm, still striving to night-qualify pilots, VS-10 lost six Dauntlesses when they could not penetrate a severe storm over Espiritu Santo upon returning to the field from the Big E operating at sea. Fortunately no one was killed in a mass ditching off Malekula just south of Bomber One, but six more valuable aircraft were gone without firing a shot at the enemy. In fact, the dive-bomber squadrons of AG-10 lost more aircraft in these two operational debacles than they did in combat with the Japanese at both Santa Cruz and the final battle of Guadalcanal combined. I rest my case.

XV

On 28 January 1943, *Enterprise* sailed from Segond Channel, Espiritu Santo, in company with *San Diego* and five destroyers, as Task Force Sixteen. Commanding this force was Rear Adm. Frederick C. Sherman, former CO of the *Lexington* when she was lost at Coral Sea, and now our new task force commander. We were operating under orders from Vice Admiral Halsey and they were simple ones: Assure the safe passage and arrival at Guadalcanal of four transports full of troops and equipment—if any Japanese forces appear they are to be destroyed. After unloading, pick up the last of the marines who have been on the Canal since the landings back in August, and return them to bases south for a well-earned rest.

By noon all seventy-four aircraft of Air Group Ten were aboard and course was set for the Coral Sea. A second task force built around *Saratoga* was in the area, and joint operations were planned. "Torpedo Junction," as the *Saratoga* was known to Big E sailors, was finally back on station, fully repaired from her latest torpedo hit of five months before.

The next day was a peaceful one, with routine flight operations, normal ASP and CAP flights, refresher landings, and dive-bomber attacks upon a towed sled. When I landed back aboard in midmorning I was directed to the admiral's area on the bridge. Here I found Eugene Burns, newly assigned *Enterprise* executive officer, Comdr. John Crommelin, and Big E skipper, Capt. O. B. Hardison with the admiral. After routine greetings were completed, Crommelin spoke:

"Admiral Sherman, we are gathered this morning to ask a favor of you. Gene Burns is about to complete a book about the first year's actions of *Enterprise*. He is calling it *Then There Was One*, and it will be coming out from Harcourt, Brace and Company. It is a good book and tells the Big E story very well. Gene wants a picture or two for his book and for the dust cover. After some discussion, we have picked a pilot we would like to have pictured with you and Gene for the book. We have picked Lt. (jg) Hal Buell because we feel he represents the spirit of all the pilots who fly from *Enterprise* against the enemy. Hal is only a lieutenant (jg), but he is one of the most senior combat pilots now aboard, having served with VS-5 in this ship before coming on this cruise with VB-10. He was with Flight 300 for a month, flying from Henderson

Field, Guadalcanal, and has helped Gene in his coverage of this important part of *Enterprise* squadron's effort in the book. He was also at Coral Sea in the *Yorktown,* so you and Hal are fellow survivors of our first carrier-versus-carrier battle. We have a photographer here now if you will grant us this favor."

The admiral, a gracious and modest man, consented to the intrusion and several pictures were taken. I was speechless, as I had no prior warning of this honor being given me. And sure enough, when the book came out in early 1944, there was my picture with Burns on the dust cover. I have kept these photographs of what, to me, was a momentous day in my life.

Of course my pilot-shipmates had to give me a bit of good-natured ribbing about my new status in high places. There were several conversations in the ready room as to just what the admiral and I found to talk about during the picture session. The admiral had a black and white cocker spaniel that he took to sea with him —in fact, Wags (the dog's name) was a survivor of the *Lexington* sinking. One of my squadron friends insisted that the admiral had called me up to his bridge because he had heard that I was good at handling waste materials and wanted sound advice about how best to take care of Wag's daily excretions. I denied knowing anything about such matters, and refused the dubious honor of being an expert in this field, stating that I probably should be, however, considering what I had to put up with as air officer of VB-10! I admit that the discussion did bring up a very interesting question: How were Wags's calling cards handled? I never found out the answer.

That night the admiral received information that changed any plans previously made and brought out Operation Order 2-43. The word was that the heavy cruiser *Chicago* had just been seriously damaged by air attacks near Guadalcanal and was under tow by *Louisville* seeking to escape from the area. We were to find them and provide air cover for their withdrawal to more friendly waters. As we were southwest of their reported position by at least 350 miles, our task force turned to an intercept course at twenty-eight knots.

At 0545, just before dawn on 30 January 1943, four SBDs of VB-10 took off on two search sectors to locate Task Force Eighteen and the crippled *Chicago.* Lt. (jg) Bob Gibson and Ens. Red Hoogerwerf flew the left sector and Ens. Dan Frissel and I the right one, running out on a line of last known position of the force. We all found the cruiser, still being towed by *Louisville,* just off the eastern tip of Rennell Island, about 120 miles from *Enterprise. Chicago* was low in the water aft, had no engine power, and was leaving a broad trail of oil that looked like Route 66 running back toward Guadalcanal—the scene of the original attack the evening before. The two ships were making a slow four knots way, with the rest of Task Force Eighteen, consisting of three heavy and three light cruisers and eight destroyers, weaving about in a protective formation. The general movement was in a southeastward direction toward Espiritu Santo.

We reported the position of TF-18, made several assigned message drops, and by 0800 the first four-plane CAP of Grim Reapers from the Big E began a defensive vigil over *Chicago.* Soon thereafter the seagoing tug *Navajo* arrived and took over towing duties from *Louisville.* Our mission completed, we flew back and landed. In midafternoon the undamaged cruisers were ordered to Efate; they departed leaving six destroyers and the hard-pressed tug plugging away at a four-knot tow speed. With agonizing slowness some distance was being made away from the danger of another air attack from the north, but the wide trail of oil still stretched to the horizon—an arrow pointing to the wounded warship.

Throughout the day the *Enterprise* maintained CAPs over both *Chicago* and Task Force Sixteen, staying thirty to forty miles south of the cripple yet within easy range for either CAP to assist the other. As the day wore on, everyone began to breathe a little easier. But at about 1545 a message finally came over the air from Guadalcanal: An estimated eleven enemy twin-engine Betty bombers were headed our way, course 150 degrees, distance 130 miles. This would bring them into our area in approximately forty-five minutes.

This early warning gave the Grim Reapers of VF-10 some extra time to prepare a welcoming committee for the incoming Japanese raid—time sorely needed when using the rugged but relatively slow F4F as interceptor. As the CAPs prepared to intercept based upon instructions coming from a fighter director officer (FDO) in the radar room of the Big E, a lone Mitsubishi Type 1 was spotted inbound toward *Chicago* from Rennell Island. Lt. Comdr. William "Killer" Kane, XO of the Reapers, dispatched four of his flight to deal with this snooper. The Wildcats caught the loner and shot it down, but not before the crew got off a message verifying the damaged *Chicago's* position, and possibly that an aircraft carrier was also nearby.

Enterprise went to general quarters, with radar tracking a flight of twelve Betties coming toward the two task forces. These planes were carrying torpedoes—the terribly efficient Long Lances that had been sinking U.S. warships at sea and in port since being so effectively used at Pearl Harbor on 7 December 1941. It was a particularly dangerous weapon when used with the Betty bomber as this type of aircraft could use altitude for a high-speed approach and was fast enough to make interception tough in a maximum speed, let-down type attack.

Approximately 1630, the FDO vectored Lt. Mac Kilpatrick's six F4Fs, on station over *Chicago,* to intercept the incoming bogeys. The Japanese Bettys were spread out, line abreast, using their altitude to increase speed in a long power glide attack toward both *Chicago* and *Enterprise.* They were following the path of oil on the sea that ran back past Rennell as far as eye could see.

When the Japanese flight leader saw Kilpatrick's six fighters swinging into an attack position between them and the Big E, which was twenty miles away, he made a decision that assured *Enterprise's* safety but doomed *Chicago:* he turned his flight straight for the cripple. At four knots tow speed, the cruiser was a sitting duck much nearer to the bombers.

The next few minutes saw an aerial firefight as violent as any one small action in the war. Like an angry swarm of hornets defending their nest, the Grim Reapers of VF-10 tore into the twelve Bettys. Both task forces' CAPs came into the fight, with Kilpatrick getting first blood, followed by CO Jimmy Flatley and XO Killer Kane and their flights. The olive-colored planes with the bright red meatball insignia began falling in and around TF-18—a kaleidoscope of flames, explosions, and billowing black smoke amid the clatter of both aircraft and AA guns.

The Japanese pilots were brave men, pressing home their attacks in the face of almost certain death. But they had met their match in bravery this day—the Grim Reapers were not to be denied. The slashing F4Fs followed the Bettys right into the screening ships' AA fire in their determination to shoot down all of the enemy. The efforts were magnificent, but to no avail. At least eight of the bombers launched torpedoes before falling to flaming deaths; the Long Lances sped on their paths and four of them hit the unfortunate *Chicago*—one hit an escorting destroyer. Within twenty minutes of the first hit, the cruiser rolled over and sank. Over one thousand officers and men were recovered from the water. The damaged destroyer was able to contain its wound and escape.

Only one of the attacking planes survived—it was last seen leaving the action area headed north. The Reapers, who lost no aircraft, claimed that one of the enemy was allowed to escape and return to tell his squadron mates what happens to planes that invade the *Enterprise* and Air Group Ten turf. Yet we were all a bit sad; in spite of finding our injured shipmates and protecting them as well as possible, the effort had not been sufficient. A cold fact remained that *Chicago* now resided in the South Pacific depths, and another major warship had been lost to Japanese airmen and their Long Lance torpedoes.

Task Force Sixteen returned to Espiritu Santo and we went back to the boring grind of waiting and training for further action if called upon. It turned out that this small battle was the last one for all of us, VB-10, the air group, and the Big E, on this war cruise. During the next few months we would head to the States for rest, reassignments, and repairs. Some, including *Enterprise,* soon returned to the fight and its ultimate conclusion aboard *Missouri* in Tokyo Bay. One of those destined to return was me.

XVI

I do not recall just how the two shrunken heads came into Air Group Ten's bivouac area on Espiritu Santo, or who specifically claimed them as property. Probably they were part of the loot that Lt. Tom Ramsey, Lt. (jg) Rastus Estes, and the others brought back with them after a mass ditching off Malekula Island just south of Espiritu Santo. Six SBDs of VS-10 became lost in a severe storm when returning to Bomber One from the *Enterprise* on 17 March 1943. One pilot landed beside the DD *Coney;* the other five splashed down in two groups with Estes, Lucier, and Bloch landing together at Hambi, a small isle off the coast of Malekula; Ramsey and his wingman landed a little farther down. Rumors persisted at the time that the lost pilots were looking for a French hospital area, with its female nurses, as a ditching site. As they never found it, the participants denied the rumor.

The six pilots returned to the AG-10 bivouac area as heroes because they had survived an emergency. They were loaded with stuff traded from the local natives, who had not had much contact with white men. Shortly after the return, two grotesque dark brown objects each about the size of a softball appeared suspended from a tent rafter, hanging by jet black hair at least two feet long. The weird forms were a pair of shrunken human heads.

The area containing Espiritu Santo was called the New Hebrides. Southeast of the Solomons and thirteen hundred miles east of Australia, this island group included Pentecost Island to the east and Malekula to the south, with other smaller islands both north and south of Pentecost. The natives were Bunlaps, who were known for both cannibalism and head-hunting. Human flesh was called "long pig" in pidgin English. A favorite native joke was to pinch your arm or stomach and state solemnly: "You makeum fine long pig." They would then grin broadly showing their front teeth. If their upper canine teeth and the incisors between were filed to points it was supposed to indicate that the possessor had participated in a meal of human flesh. Fortunately the practice had been mostly eradicated by the British, French, Australians, and missionaries of various religious sects during the years prior to World War II, especially the killing and eating of "white meat." However, killing and dining on each other by hostile tribes still continued in the deep jungle areas.

Decapitation of an enemy and keeping the head as a trophy was a tradition of long standing in this part of the world. I'll never forget the horror that I felt when I approached the jungle abode of a local warrior-chief. On each side of the entranceway were several human heads, mounted on short posts, in varied stages of decomposition from shreds of dried flesh and hair to bare skulls. The effect was a bit like a bizarre picket fence fronting an Iowa farmhouse.

The shrinking of heads for trophies was a special operation performed by witch doctors of the tribe or clan. The process involved treating the head by soaking it, breaking it, and taking out pieces of the skull, teeth, and other bones, thus reducing the basic structure without changing the main features of the face. Eyelids and lips were stitched together and all hair was kept in its natural state at full length. Correctly done, a shrunken head could retain in miniature the general appearance of the original person.

Fortunately for U.S. pilots, natives throughout the South Pacific often exposed themselves to great danger while saving and returning airmen to safety, even in the midst of Japanese-held territory. There were diverse reasons for this assistance. Foremost was that the natives were used to working for and with the English, Australian, and French government officials, settlers, and missionaries who were living throughout the islands when the war started. Many of these white men remained in hiding as coastwatchers on Pacific islands invaded by the Japanese, and the natives, for the most part, remained loyal to them. The Japanese, on the other hand, were often cruel and oppressive in their conduct with natives. They would kill for little reason, confiscate food supplies the natives needed to survive, and often enslave the able-bodied men in labor groups to build airfields and military positions. Americans would reward natives for helping them work on facilities, for scouting with troops, and for bringing in missing flyers who had been shot down in combat.

I personally noted that many of the natives throughout the islands were in awe of U.S. pilots, almost to the point of considering them gods. After all, aviators controlled huge iron birds that flew away from airfields and returned—birds that could spit death and lay eggs that made huge craters in the earth, while destroying buildings and starting fires. Men who could control these birds could not possibly be ordinary humans, so they must be gods.

The natives were fascinated with airplanes and wanted to get near to and touch them. They could not understand how the engine of a parked plane could be cold when you felt it (bird asleep?) then be hot when it came back from a flight. Many believed that the pilot woke the bird up (started the engine), directed its activities up into the sky, and the bird went back to sleep when the pilot shut down the engine. They were impressed by the big cargo birds that brought all the wonderful things that were part of our civilization—things that they came to like and want for themselves. Above all, they admired and respected the pilot-gods who controlled the iron birds and bravely flew with them into the sky.

Back to the shrunken heads. The two grim objects, swinging gently in the island breezes, were a novelty to the pilots of the air group. Word spread about them, and everyone dropped by to see the unusual display. The heads appeared to be quite old, but they still retained a certain rank odor, and their stark appearance had a shock effect on even the coolest observer.

Some time later, we had a big party one afternoon and a few of the revelers returned to the bivouac area feeling no pain. As we all carried sidearms, either .38s or .45s, usually in shoulder holsters, and no one checked these weapons at the door, the potential for lethal horseplay after drinking was present.

No one ever admitted starting the action that followed. A particularly tipsy pilot living in the "head" tent drew his .45 and, shouting something about Japanese snipers, started blasting away at the hanging heads. He was immediately joined by several others and the air was filled with .38 and .45 slugs winging their way toward the hapless objects. Most of the fusillade missed, but a few bullets found their mark, and shattered the heads into fragments of dried skin and hair. Additional damage was done to the tent roof as the bullets exited into the sky. Fortunately no live human was hurt.

The noise of the barrage brought jeeploads of military police to the area, as well as everyone living in the vicinity. The MPs didn't think it was very funny and would have made some arrests among the smoking gun owners if squadron COs had not taken over and calmed everything down. Nothing happened to the shooters and CAG put out a new directive setting up a bunch of regulations regarding the wearing and firing of sidearms by pilots.

There was one punishment for the residents of the tent. The next rain storm wet down both men and gear when water poured through the bullet holes. The remnants of the two shrunken heads were buried without ceremony.

I acquired one trophy while at Espiritu Santo and had it made into a beautiful piece of jewelry for my wife. It is a circular boar tusk pendant like those worn by the chief and other dominant males of the Bunlaps. It is made by removing a boar's upper tusks, which allows the bottom ones to grow into a circle. The boar must be kept in a pen like a pet while the tusks develop. One of the ruling family gave me a perfect one as a gift; I returned the favor by giving him a Case hunting knife and white dress shirt. He wore the shirt to church on Sunday, with the tail hanging out over his loincloth.

9

PREPARATION TWO

I

IN FEBRUARY 1943 the first in a series of orders transferring
Big E pilots back to the United States for reassignment arrived
with the detachment of Comdr. Jimmy Flatley, CO of VF-10, who
turned his command over to Lt. Comdr. W. R. "Killer" Kane.
About mid-March Lt. Comdr. James R. "Bucky" Lee was ordered
home and turned VS-10 over to Bill Martin. At the end of the
month it became my turn.

●

UNITED STATES PACIFIC FLEET
AIR FORCE
FLEET AIR COMMAND, NOUMEA

29 March 1943

From: The Commander Fleet Air, Noumea
To: Lieutenant (junior grade)

        Harold L. BUELL, A-V (N), USNR
        USS ENTERPRISE

Subject: Change of duty.

     1.   You are hereby detached from your present duty and
from such other duty as may have been assigned you; will

proceed and report to Commander Naval Base EBON, for first available government transportation to a port in the United States, and upon arrival you will proceed and report to the Commander Fleet Air, West Coast, to duty involving flying.

2.   Upon completion of any travel in compliance with these orders for which you are entitled to reimbursement, you are hereby directed to forward the original and one certified copy of these orders with all endorsements thereto, to the Bureau of Naval Personnel for approval.

M. A. MITSCHER

There had been considerable scuttlebutt in *Enterprise* for some time that orders would be coming for carrier combat pilots, regardless of rank, because of the demand for this experience in the new air groups being formed. As I was on a second squadron war cruise, and had been in continuous action for a year, including a Guadalcanal hitch, my name was near the top of a list sent back to the Bureau of Personnel in answer to a dispatch from the Commander of South Pacific air forces via the Commander of air forces in the Pacific for such pilots. It turned out that these orders got me back to the States about five weeks ahead of the rest of the squadron and Air Group Ten. They left the ship when it arrived back at Pearl Harbor on 8 May 1943. The group was broken up, with pilots and aircrewmen who had completed an entire cruise with *Enterprise* receiving orders to training commands, staffs, or new squadrons and air groups being formed on both the East and West coasts. Pilots who had come to the ship as replacements during the cruise went to Sand Point Naval Air Station at Seattle as the nucleus for a new Air Group Ten. A few Academy-trained regular veteran leaders, such as Ramage, Kane, and Martin, also remained with the new group as squadron commanders.

In the midst of this important change of my personal fortunes, two significant events occurred in the squadron. On 26 March 1943, a replacement for our XO, lost back in November, arrived at Espiritu Santo to fill this important billet. Lt. James D. "Jig Dog" Ramage, USN, was the man, and a finer one could not have been found. He was just what the squadron needed to compensate for the often vacillating qualities of leadership being provided by the CO, Thomas. I only got to spend a short time around Jig Dog before leaving VB-10, but I liked him from the start; he went on to great achievements in both Air Group Ten and *Enterprise.*

As if getting Ramage as XO wasn't enough good luck for the "Head-hunters," a second change added further to an improved situation. The CO, Lt. Comdr. J. A. Thomas, was promoted up to CAG, replacing Comdr. Dick Gaines. New CO for VB-10 was my old friend and shipmate from VS-5 and VS-10, Lt. Stockton Birney Strong. These two changes were almost enough to make me tear up my new orders home—but not quite!

So I left the Big E with mixed emotions. It had been my home for a year with two squadrons and I had developed many friendships among ship's officers and crew. There had been moments of terror and agony as well as thrills of victories jointly shared. Of four aircraft carriers flown from in the Pacific war, this one was, and still is, nearest to my heart.

First available government transportation from Ebon, Marshall Islands, was to be the cruiser *San Francisco.* Leaving port on 7 April, she took me to Pearl Harbor in eight days. Upon arrival, I hit the beach for my first liberty in about six months. For three days I saw old friends in the Honolulu area, then went aboard AP62 *Kenmore* the morning of 18 April 1943 for the final sea leg home.

Unlike my trip out to Hawaii in 1942 in *Castor,* the trip back found me with no duties other than eating, sleeping, and utilizing my spare time reading, walking, or playing cards. The inevitable poker games were in progress and I found myself profitably engaged for hours on end. Everyone had a good bit of money saved up for stateside use on leave, so these games were paradise for a reasonably proficient poker player with emotional control of his game. I was a steady player inclined to conservative betting within the known odds of the cards, seldom indulging in wild chance-taking in violation of sound principles of the game. My winnings grew slowly but steadily and by the time *Kenmore* passed under the Golden Gate Bridge on the morning of 26 April 1943 I had won more than five hundred dollars. This windfall, combined with over twelve hundred dollars accumulated during my more than one year away, gave me a tidy sum for a leave period in Iowa before reporting to a new duty station. I carried this fortune in cash in a money belt under my clothing next to my skin, removing it only to bathe.

Departing AP62 from the dock area with my gear, I reported to the office of Commander Fleet Air, US Naval Station, Alameda, California. The staff there told me to take two days liberty (a weekend) and report on Monday for an evaluation and a new set of orders. Leaving my stuff at the transit BOQ, I headed for the St. Francis Hotel, a room, and a real shore leave weekend.

I had a great weekend and presented myself, with hangover, to Fleet Air Alameda offices as I had been directed the preceding Friday. Officers of all ranks were roaming about in the onerous process of getting new assignments. Most veteran pilots were interested in stateside orders only, preferably to the Training Command. The last thing most wanted, or expected, was assignment to a new air group forming to go west. With so much going on, I figured it would be a long morning. To my surprise I was summoned by loudspeaker and told that a Capt. C. Wade Mc-Clusky wanted to see me in his office.

II

I knew Wade McClusky by reputation only—we had never met personally. A native of Buffalo, New York, he was a graduate of the Naval Academy, class of 1926, had been in naval aviation since 1930, and was a veteran pilot in *Enterprise* when the war began at Pearl Harbor. As Commander of Air Group Six flying from Big E at the Battle of Midway, McClusky made the fateful decision to turn in the direction of a speeding enemy destroyer's course and thus, with his group of dive-bombers, found the Japanese carriers at maximum range. He quickly led an attack that sank three of the carriers in six minutes, losing many of the dive-bombers in his group. Wounded in the arm and shoulder by Japanese Zero fighters, he survived to fly his badly damaged SBD back to *Enterprise*. A fourth Japanese carrier was sunk later in the day. In leading this strike, McClusky earned the distinction of conducting the single most successful dive-bombing mission against Japanese naval carriers ever made.

Forty-two years of age, Wade McClusky was a striking figure in his naval uniform that morning in May 1943. About five feet eight inches tall, with a well-conditioned athletic figure, he had a craggy, handsome face with aviator's crow's-feet around his china-blue eyes. Circling from behind his desk, he moved to meet me with hand outstretched in greeting: "Hal, I'm Wade McClusky. I have been looking forward to meeting you."

We shook hands. A secretary poured two cups of coffee on the side table. I saw a platter of doughnuts and took one; with hot coffee and a doughnut, my hangover began to get better. As we sipped, the captain spoke:

"I'm going to get right to the point, Hal. My boss, Capt. Murr Arnold, saw your name on the incoming list of officers for assignment. He remembers you from VS-5 and the old *Yorktown* days. He asked me to talk with you about something of great importance to our carrier Navy at this significant time as he is not here to see you himself today. Quite simply, we need you to go to a new air group forming up to provide combat experience so badly needed in these squadrons."

Frankly I was caught out of position. I must admit that I had not given much thought to the possibility of any other orders than to the Advanced Training Command, where new pilots were given final smoothing up before orders to a fleet squadron. It was the type of orders most of my squadron buddies of 1942 had received when they came back. McClusky continued:

"It may seem hard to believe, Hal, after what you have been through the past year, but there is no shortage of naval aviators —only aircraft carrier air groups. With the new Essex-class CVs coming into the fleet, the big job now is to get good groups aboard them. The training commands have done a hell of a piece of work preparing basic naval aviators for commissions and wings of gold. Our standards are still high, and we are not only getting the best young men, we are still turning out the finest naval aviators in the world." He paused, took a sip of coffee, then continued:

"Our big problem now is providing some combat-experienced pilots as leaders for the new air groups being formed. Most of the older pilots, like myself, cannot go back to combat-flying assignments because we are too old and too senior. Hell, most of us were too old for fighting when the war started and we were caught aboard as squadron commanders and CAGs. We found out in a hurry that carrier air warfare, for the most part, is a young man's game. And with the tremendous growth now taking place in our carrier forces, there are personnel demands that can only be met from my age group. With rare exceptions, the older combat veterans will not fly in action again.

"Moving down to the next level of seniority, we find the combat shortage problem is combined with career demands for numbers of regular Navy flying officers. Other requirements for naval experience take many of this group—there are also officers in the group that want a combat flying command assignment immediately. Men like Killer Kane and Bill Martin, both friends of yours from *Enterprise*, and a few others, will stay in a flying status as squadron COs and occasionally as a CAG. But most new squadron and air group leaders will come from their peer group of regular navy officers and, while these men are experienced naval aviators, they do not have war experience."

While giving me this briefing, Captain McClusky had been pacing back and forth with an occasional gesture for emphasis of a point he was making. He stopped, faced me, looked directly into my eyes, and said:

"We finally arrive at your level of seniority—probably the most important group of the three. Made up of a few ensigns, mostly lieutenants (junior grade), and some lieutenants, this group of combat-experienced pilots are survivors of the first eighteen months of the Pacific war. For the most part they are naval reserves, trained in the prewar AVCAD program, with a few Academy regulars and enlisted pilots who have been commissioned. When these officers first began coming back from the Pacific, there was a priority requirement for them in the Advanced Training Command, especially fighter and dive-bomber types with the latest tactical know-how to pass on to the graduating aviators who were heading straight into combat as replacements. They did a great job filling this gap, and I think that this training concept has been one of the factors in keeping our losses down since Midway. As you know, our losses there were frightening.

"What we are facing now is the preparation of quality air groups to go aboard the new carriers. Most of the rest of this year will be given to this task, with only occasional operations against the Japanese with existing forces. By early 1944, with the new Essex-class carriers and air groups joining existing forces, we will begin the campaigns that will wipe the Japanese fleet, and island land forces, off the face of the earth."

He resumed his pacing, and continued:

"Murr Arnold and I, with others, strongly believe that these new air groups will only be as good as the combat know-how they take with them to the Pacific. Heaven knows that we don't want to repeat over and over the mistakes that have been learned at considerable cost in lives and aircraft in the past. As we see it, Hal, the answer to this problem is assignment of the best pilots in your age group to key positions within these squadron organizations; the bad part of this solution is that it requires returning for another war cruise the very men who have already given so much.

"So you can see that I do not have an enviable job trying to explain this problem to you. And there are many angles to consider with no easy answers. For example, there are returning pilots in your group that we do not want to reassign to combat. Some are burned out and have no fight left in them. Others were not aggressive and performed below the minimum level of standards desired of naval combat pilots. A few flatly refuse to go out again. What we have left are somewhat like the nuggets of gold in a placer miner's pan—they are few and very valuable. You are one of those nuggets."

Captain McClusky's face was grim and his voice was forceful as he said: "Lt. (jg) Harold Buell, I would like to assign you to a dive-bombing squadron now forming up that badly needs your battle experience. How do you feel about a set of orders continuing you in a combat status?"

It was plain that Captain McClusky was giving me a chance to offer any serious objection I might have against his proposal. Perhaps he wanted me to volunteer for the assignment after hearing the briefing on the seriousness of the overall picture. Clearly the ball was now in my court, and a reply to his question was expected. After a brief pause, I said:

"Captain, I'm sure you know the old Navy and Marine Corps saying about keeping one's eyes and ears open and never volunteering for anything. I am here to receive a new assignment for duty involving flying, and am prepared to accept any orders that you see fit to give me. I would like to know about how long I will have before heading back, if that is your assignment to me."

"Hal, I intend to send you to ComAirLant at Norfolk, Virginia, for assignment to a squadron forming on the East Coast, rather than one here. By the time you finish your leave and travel, get to your assignment somewhere on the East Coast, train and equip with a squadron, and arrive back out here for carrier assignment, it will take at least six months. How does that sound?"

After what I had been through on a double-war cruise just completed it sounded okay and I told him so. I would be going back to war much sooner than expected, but a six-month break was better than nothing. Deep inside I felt a sense of satisfaction in remaining on sea duty in a squadron preparing for a combat cruise—a place where I was needed and, strangely, where I wanted to be until the Japanese were beaten.

The good captain made his estimate on the short side; it would be more than seven months before I sailed west under the Golden Gate.

III

I left San Francisco on 2 May 1943 via Union Pacific Railroad for my hometown in Iowa. My orders provided for fifteen days leave and travel time before reporting at Norfolk. I had been gone approximately fifteen months.

First stop was Newton to pick up my Ford convertible coupe, which I had left in the care of a girlfriend. After a brief visit at her home, I left in the car for Ottumwa and a joyful reunion with my three sisters and foster parents, the McElderrys.

A major change in the character of my hometown had taken place during my absence: it had become a Navy community with a new naval air station. Several hundred acres of farmland north of the city were now covered with concrete runways, hangars, and other support buildings, and basic training of naval aviation cadets was in full swing. The streets were filled with both cadets and pilots wearing aviation greens—a far cry from the days just prior to the war when returning home on leave wearing my greens, I had been mistaken for a member of the Royal Canadian Air Force!

It was nice to have a naval air facility, although small, right in my home area, and I began enjoying its welcoming atmosphere at once. The commanding officer was Capt. B. E. Grow, USN, who had been a senior officer in *Wasp* when she was sunk in 1942. He included me in several station activities, and had me speak to his staff of officers engaged in cadet training. I also helped in a big bond-selling campaign then in progress, and spoke at the Kiwanis Club as an official guest of the Navy. It took me some time to get used to being treated as a hero by friends and acquaintances.

I had a fear of speaking in public, or to reporters, because of ALNAV 250, a policy statement from Secretary of the Navy Frank Knox relative to the conduct of naval personnel while on leave or liberty:

RESTRICTED MAILGRAM: ALNAV #250

ALL OFFICERS AND MEN ARE REMINDED OF THE
VITAL NECESSITY OF RESTRICTING TO THOSE WHO
NEED TO KNOW THE NATURE OF THE SOURCES OF
OUR INTELLIGENCE INFORMATION OF THE ENEMY
X PARA EXCEPT AS REQUIRED BY OFFICIAL
BUSINESS NO REFERENCE SHOULD BE MADE TO
INTERROGATION OF PRISONERS OF WAR COMMA
CAPTURED DOCUMENTS COMMA COUNTER
ESPIONAGE OR ANY OTHER SOURCES X PARA
BEFORE ARRIVAL IN PORT FOLLOWING A PERIOD OF
COMBAT OPERATIONS PERSONNEL GOING ON SHORE
LEAVE SHALL BE SPECIALLY CAUTIONED
CONCERNING THESE SECURITY MEASURES.

I decided that the best way to be sure of not violating the intent of ALNAV 250 was to include the local base intelligence officer in any speaking engagements or interviews I was called upon to give. I would clear with him the basic speech planned—that was the easy part. It got a bit tougher during the question-and-answer period after the formal speech was over. You found out quickly that people in the audience might ask you anything, not being aware that a question might have sensitive overtones. I would repeat the question, then look over to the intelligence officer sitting nearby. If he nodded his head, I answered the question; a side-to-side shake told me to state that the question could not be answered because of security restrictions. It was a foolproof system and I was often surprised at what the intelligence officer would let me answer. If required to make the decision, I would not have had much to say. A newspaper story from the *Ottumwa Courier* gives an example of information that was allowed:

DON'T EXPECT JAPS TO SURRENDER LIKE GERMANS

—Lieutenant Buell

In the opinion of Lt. (jg) Harold Buell, navy dive bomber pilot who has seen considerable warfare in the South Pacific, "The Japs would not have surrendered the way the Germans did in Tunisia had they been cornered in such a manner by our troops."

Speaking before a meeting of the Kiwanis Club at Hotel Ottumwa Monday night, Buell declared: "I have seen them in action and they simply do not surrender. We've taken but very few prisoners among the enlisted men and it is almost impossible to take a Jap officer prisoner. They are brave fighters and face death in the belief they are dying for their country and emperor."

Asked whether the Jap pilots are as capable as the American flyers they face, the LTJG replied: "They are not. It is the replacement pilots who will win the war, not the original ones. The original pilots will mostly be gone by the time the war is won. In my own original squadron, for illustration, only five out of 22 of us remain in combat. Our replacement pilots and machines are much better than anything the Japs have."

Buell has taken part in eight officially recognized engagements with the enemy and has been cited for sinking a Jap destroyer. His sisters, Mrs. Edith Newell and Mrs. Elsie Bryant were guests at the meeting.

Considering that this story appeared in May 1943, it revealed two very important facts concerning the Pacific war long before events would prove them to be true. I correctly predicted that the Japanese would not surrender, even when cornered, and the bloody battles in the Marianas, Peleliu, Tarawa, Iwo Jima, Okinawa, and the Philippines that were still ahead would prove this assumption valid. Only the atomic bomb and its horrible consequences would bring the Japanese military leaders to the surrender table. As for old combat pilots, few individuals survived two war tours, and when the war ended in August 1945, most aviators from the first carrier-versus-carrier battles of 1942, Japanese and American, were either dead or serving in noncombat billets.

Before I knew it, my fifteen-day leave period was about over. With only a few days left I received a call from the Navy public relations officer for the Iowa-Nebraska area located in Des Moines. He had heard about my efforts as a speaker in local bond-selling rallies. Would I come up to Iowa's capital to speak at fund-raisers there for a couple of days? My answer was a short and direct no—my leave was about over and I already had spent too much of my brief time helping the Navy and federal government with charitable efforts. Much to my surprise the PR officer was sympathetic to my plight and proposed an alternative: Would I come up if he could get me a fifteen-day extension to my leave?

Scarcely believing my ears, the answer was an enthusiastic affirmative! He told me to stand by for a message within twenty-

189

four hours. The next morning the following cable arrived at the local naval air station:

```
FROM:  NAVCOM GREATLAKES ILL
TO:    NAS OTTUMWA IOWA

FOLLOWING FROM NAVCOM WASHINGTON ONE TWO
ZERO TWO ZERO NINE X FOR LIEUT JG HAROLD
LOVE BUELL X ABLE VICTOR NAN UNCLE SUGAR
NAN ROGER AUTHORIZED FIFTEEN DAYS
ADDITIONAL DELAY REPORTING COMAIRLANT IN
OBEDIENCE DESP ORDERS MAY ONE X FROM
BUPERS X DELAY COUNTS AS LEAVE X KEEP
BUPERS ADVISED ADDRESS
```

I was impressed by this efficiency of the Navy's Public Relations Office, and a few days later headed for Des Moines to keep the promise to sell bonds, driving what, for me, was a new car—a cream-colored 1941 Chevrolet convertible coupe with less than ten thousand miles on the odometer. My guardian, Dr. Donald McElderry, had a friend who ran the local Chevrolet dealership. Due to wartime restrictions there were no new cars, and good used cars were at a premium. The friend wanted to do something for "that orphan boy you raised who has been out there fighting for all of us back here," and told him to tell me to come down to the showroom. There stood a Chevy convertible in mint condition —a car that had cost $1,050 new. He wanted $850 for it and "doing something" for me was letting me have the first chance to purchase it.

I really liked my little robin's-egg blue Ford roadster and told the dealer so, but did need more room than the single-seated Ford gave me. The Chevy had a small second seat behind the front one and this area would provide space for passengers, although crowded, and all my gear when I moved from one air station to another. I offered him four hundred dollars and my car, saying that if he really wanted to do something for me he would take the offer. He liked my Ford and my offer, so we had a deal. His eyes popped out when I opened my shirt, took off my money belt, and counted out the four hundred dollars in cash from my gambling profits.

I then made my first trip in the new car to the Union Bank & Trust Company nearby and opened an account with the remaining

190

funds in the money belt. My oldest sister, Edith Newell, worked as a teller in this bank. After setting up a new account, she introduced me to the teller working next to her, Pat Nixon. Her husband was a Lt. (jg) Richard Nixon from the local air station. As he had just received orders to go to sea and had already left for the West Coast, she was tying up loose ends before leaving to join him in California.

Dick Nixon had reported to the Ottumwa Naval Air Station in the late fall of 1942 as aide to the executive officer. It was his first assignment as a new naval officer after finishing a two-month training course leading to a commission at Quonset Point, Rhode Island. He was one of those "ninety-day wonders" of World War II naval necessity, and a good one. He was to serve for four years, leaving active duty a lieutenant at the end of the war. Later, as President Nixon, he would say of his naval service: "I grew up in the Navy."[1]

So there I was, dressed in my best blues, headed for Des Moines and a speaking engagement at noon in return for the leave extension that the Navy PR officer had gotten for me. It was a beautiful spring day in May, so I put down the convertible top to enjoy the ride. With plenty of gasoline for the car, thanks to the local OPA (Office of Price Administration) Board's generosity of ration tickets to the cause of war bond–selling activities, I was a long way physically and mentally from the previous May and the Coral Sea fighting. It was good to be alive.

I was to check into the Fort Des Moines Hotel, one of the city's best, located in the heart of everything, where a room was being held for me. Entering the city I noticed that the streets and sidewalks were crowded with women in uniform—short, tall, plump, thin, beautiful, and plain. Some were officers and there were sergeants and privates galore. What was going on? Then it hit me: All this activity was WACs on liberty from the women's army training center, Fort Des Moines, one of the largest in the country.

As a naval officer, I was used to seeing numbers of military personnel on leave in port cities—men, that is. The people in uniform here were mostly women, and this was a new experience for me. As I drove down the street in the open convertible, I realized that I was creating quite a stir among these troops. Calls and whistled greetings were directed my way, including a few not-so-discreet propositions. The male macho sex role had been reversed!

Things went okay as long as my car kept moving, but finally I had to stop for a traffic light. At that point my vehicle and I were inundated with women in uniform. Someone opened the car door and simply got into the convertible, and in an instant the car was filled to overflowing with happy, laughing WACs. There wasn't much I could do about the situation except to keep moving to the hotel. It was quite a sight to the doorman when I pulled up with my noisy load of voluptuous, uniformed female riders!

It took me some time to convince them that the fun was over and that I had to check in to prepare for duties expected of me immediately. A couple of them were so persistent that I took their names and telephone numbers, promising to call later during the weekend for some serious revelry. The hotel registration clerk, a man, explained to me that I was witnessing the way things had been every weekend since the WAC program had opened out at the fort. He said that it was almost impossible to get a hotel room on a weekend as the women took the city over, with liberty parties planned in great detail weeks or even months ahead of time. There was such a shortage of men because of the war that the remaining local males could have their pick of dates, and as many as they wanted or could afford. A serviceman back on leave like myself was fair game and he would be approached not only by the WACs but by large numbers of local girls who were unattached and looking for male companionship.

I gave a speech that noon and one on Saturday, both to big crowds that bought lots of bonds. The *Des Moines Register* ran a feature story on me (with photograph) in the Sunday edition and a couple of short ones on both Friday and Saturday. Everyone gave me the hero treatment—it was a weekend in Valhalla. Iowans are honest, forthright, and generous people, and, as I was one of their own who had returned victorious from the war, they threw a party for me.

As for Des Moines, the proud capital of Iowa, there are probably few left who still remember when it was invaded and conquered by the WACs during World War II without firing a shot. In fact, there are some who may deny that the take-over even occurred. Don't believe them: it happened because I went there and saw it with my own eyes—those amazons were real!

The additional leave gave me time to make an important visit to old friends some distance from Ottumwa. Located over two hundred miles north, near Mason City, Iowa, was the small town of Plymouth. You knew you were in the town when you came to a flagpole flying the stars and stripes that sat squarely in the middle of an intersection of two graveled roads. Drive four blocks in any direction from the flagpole you were out of town. In those days Plymouth was small—today it barely exists.

Plymouth was the home of the Dixson family. Ray and Sylvia Dixson were like foster parents to me because I had lived with them for brief periods during my orphaned formative years. Since their daughters Grayce and Dorothy were married and gone from home, they now lived in the white-frame, two-story house with a school teacher, Hazel Moody. Uncle Ray, as I called him, had a farm implement business of some magnitude in nearby Mason City, ten miles away.

My return to Plymouth from the war was an event worthy of a celebration. A favorite way to honor someone in this small rural community was to have a co-op dinner in the Methodist church hall or high school gym. Each friend would bring a dish or two of food, and there was usually a musical combo, with a few short remarks from a couple of speakers and the guest of honor. The meal would start at six in the evening, with all participants back home by ten in order to get a good night's sleep before the next day's work.

My tribute dinner was held the night of 22 May 1943. With more than 150 turning out, the high school gym was used. Farmers and their families who had known me in years gone by came from miles around. Most of them had sons away in the armed forces—young men who had been my childhood companions, teammates, and hunting pals. I was surprised how many people could hear about a simple dinner and manage to take part on short notice.

It was an emotional occasion. I stood at the main entrance in my navy blue uniform with gold stripes and wings and greeted each man, woman, and child who entered. Clasping the rough calloused palms of these strong farm men, I remembered my days of toil in the fields during the depression.

It is hard to describe an Iowa co-op dinner and do it justice; one has to take part to appreciate the sheer grandeur of simple farm foods prepared by skilled hands from old family recipes going back for generations. Because of the diversity of population in the area, many different ethnic dishes were on the menu, including French, German, Swedish, Bohemian, Italian, and English. The variety and generous amounts available, combined with skillful preparation, made an Iowa co-op dinner a gourmet affair.

After a blessing and main part of the meal, the program began during dessert and coffee. There were songs and musical numbers, and the mayor welcomed me back to the town. A state representative gave a few remarks. Then a local bard by the name of Arthur Holroyd manned the podium. Noted for his Longfellow-like odes, Holroyd recited his "Tribute to Harold Buell," a work that he had created especially for me and the occasion. I must admit that the tribute and applause that followed it moved me almost to tears. After Arthur's presentation I spoke briefly, thanking everyone for honoring me, and we went home.

Before leaving Plymouth the next day I stopped my car in front of the town hall. A permanent honor roll had been erected beside the hall, with names of every man, and one woman, who had left the area to fight America's enemies, inscribed on its face. There were eighty-two names in all, representing the life's blood of Plymouth and the surrounding countryside.

A few names had gold stars next to them; one of the starred names was Leland Faktor. I remembered him as a small, thin, very quiet boy when we had been fellow students in Plymouth High School in 1936. He joined the Army Air Corps after graduation in 1938. He had died as an engineer-gunner in B-25 number 40-2270, one of the sixteen such bombers led by Lt. Col. James H. Doolittle on the Tokyo Raid, 18 April 1942, flying from the *Hornet*. The third plane to take off on this historic mission, piloted by Lt. Robert M. Gray, they hit assigned targets in Tokyo, then flew on to China, bailing out near Chü-hsien from fuel exhaustion. Corporal Faktor was unlucky; his parachute either did not open completely or he hit the aircraft when leaving. His body was found the next day by Chinese peasants and interred in a small cemetery southeast of the village of Wan Tsuen, far from the rolling Iowa prairies of his homeland.[2]

There among the names—Chehock, Woodhouse, Helm, Lyke, Heinselman, Reynolds, Rezab, Snell, Bernhardt, Sponheim, Will-ford, Davis, Halbrook, Kenny, and many more was mine—Buell. Although Plymouth was no longer my home, I was listed among these old friends and schoolmates. A feeling of pride and comfort in being thus remembered moved through me: How could I lose on my forthcoming third squadron war cruise with this band of brothers?

IV

It was finally time to move on to the East Coast assignment at Norfolk. I had been staying with my second older sister, Elsie Bryant, in Ottumwa and, with optimistic sadness, my three sisters bid me goodbye. The youngest, Jinny Van Alst, came from nearby Pella to see me off. All had hoped that their brother would be assigned to shore duty at the local naval air station.

I had saved a couple of days leave, and my travel time, to have a fling in my favorite city—Chicago. My plans were to drive to Geneseo, Illinois, pay my respects to the family of Johnny Lough, then go to the Windy City, get a room at the Sherman Hotel in the Loop, and do the town. I had promised a Big E shipmate, Lt. Hubert Howard from Winnetka (just north of Chicago) to get in touch with his parents and tell them he would be coming home on leave in June or July when the ship arrived at Seattle for a major overhaul. The censors would cut any information about this event from his letters to them. He also had suggested that I might enjoy doing the nightspots with his lovely cousin Merikay Howard, who lived just down the street from his home.

After visiting the Loughs, I checked into the Sherman, then called the residence of Hubert Howard, Sr., as promised. What was to be a simple message, and a possible date with a pretty girl, fast turned into a real liberty adventure. It seems that Hubie had written quite glowing accounts to his family about a young Iowa flyer he had become friends with on the ship, so both his and Uncle Eugene "Tex" Howard's families wanted to meet and talk with me. I was told to check out of the hotel and drive north to Winnetka, where everyone would be waiting.

Following their directions, I arrived at the Eugene Howard home, to be a guest for as long as I could stay. The festivities started with a huge cocktail party that afternoon and evening, with dozens of guests coming in to meet the pilot friend of Hubie Howard who had just arrived back from the Big E and the Pacific carrier battles. I was the first live survivor of those sea battles who had returned, and nothing was too good for me.

An old established family in Illinois, the Howard clan had large holdings in coal mines in the lower part of the state, as well as other real estate and business interests. Hubie had told me that his father, when a young man, had attended the same Parsons College that I had gone to before leaving for the Navy and war. Hubert, Sr., was now a trustee of Parsons and a generous financial benefactor to his old alma mater.

Like my friend Hubie, the gray-haired Howard brothers were tall, handsome men with a pleasant, easygoing manner. Their wives were gracious well-groomed ladies dressed in the latest fashions. The cream of Winnetka society was at that first party, with me the guest of honor. By the time the evening was over, a social calendar was set up for me that was to take every waking moment of the next four days. Directing me through these activities were the two lovely women of the family of my host Tex Howard: The efforts of Mrs. Howard, called L. B., and daughter Merikay made me an instant celebrity.

Just as in Iowa, these people were hungry for information about what was happening in the Pacific war. I once again had to be careful about what I said, even in casual conversation, lest I violate the rigid security regulations of the Navy. Looking back, I was perhaps overcautious, but at the time the worry was real. I fell back on my previous routine of having a naval public relations or intelligence officer from nearby Glenview Naval Air Station present for any speeches before crowds of any size. News reporters for the *Chicago Tribune* and *Sun* started showing up at public functions and other recreational spots, trying to get exclusive interviews, but I ran everything through naval public relations. The following is a typical news story that appeared in the Chicago papers at the time, Navy approved:

PACIFIC VICTORY CHANCE LOST BY JAPS, SAYS PILOT

Guadalcanal Marines Were Vulnerable

The Japs lost their big opportunity for victory in the Pacific when they failed to counter-attack at Guadalcanal within the next 30 days after American marines landed, Lt. (jg) Gerald Buel [*sic*], navy dive bomber pilot, said here yesterday.

Lt. Buel, who is visiting at the home of Mr. and Mrs. Eugene Howard, 1015 Pine Street, Winnetka, parents of Lt. Hugh Howard, who served with Buel on the carrier *Enterprise,* said a determined attack by 10,000 Japs within the next month after the marines landed would have changed the course of the war in the Pacific.

Beaches Lightly Defended

The beaches were only lightly defended with machine guns, Buel said, and there was a shortage of supplies of all kinds. Submarines landed gasoline at night and runways of Henderson Field were so short the planes could not take off with 1,000 pound bombs without sacrificing part of their gasoline supply.

Buel was part of the squadron of 11 dive-bombers who were stranded on Guadalcanal for 30 days in August and September 1942, when the *Enterprise* was forced out to sea under Jap attack. The navy pilots joined the marine flyers, losing all but one of their 11 planes during the 30 days they helped defend the island.

Buel is en route to the east coast for reassignment to another dive bomber squadron after 15 months in the South Pacific area, most of the time being spent aboard the *Enterprise.* He and other navy pilots helped defend *Lexington* in the Coral Sea battle. Buel missed the [main] Midway battle by two days, his squadron being detached from *Yorktown* just before that carrier left Honolulu because of planes [and pilot shortages from losses] in the Coral Sea.

Win Despite Jap numbers

He pointed out that every American naval victory in the Pacific so far has been gained in the face of Jap superiority in planes and carriers. Now that this superiority has been reversed, Buel predicted the next big naval battle with the Japs will bring a loss of Japanese ships and men far greater than any battle of the past.

The Japs, he said, have their "fortress of the Pacific" just as

Hitler has his "fortress of Europe" and it will be up to allied air and sea forces to invade this "fortress" but with more carriers and with a greatly increased air force in the Pacific. He said American naval officers are confident the job can be done.

Buel's greatest moment in his 15 months of service, he said, was when he pulled his plane out of a dive to watch the bomb he had just released plunge into the magazine of a Jap warship crowded with soldiers, sending sheets of flame and debris of the ship 500 feet into the air.

In reviewing the newspaper stories of that time I am still surprised at some of the things that the Navy allowed a young lieutenant (jg) combat aviator to say in public gatherings, usually war bond connected, without censorship. And I am quite proud of my predictions, usually made in answer to questions directed to me from those audiences. The next big carrier-versus-carrier sea battle was to be the Marianas Turkey Shoot in June 1944, where Japanese losses in planes, ships, and men would exceed those of any previous battle. The landings on Japanese-held islands, begun in late 1943, started the invasion of "fortress Pacific." Thus two more of a young naval pilot's predictions of the war's future operations would come true a year later.

V

The caper would not be complete without relating the interesting mistaken identity that occurred several times to me during the visit to Chicago and its environs.

Robert Taylor, the famous movie actor, was serving as a naval aviator lieutenant under his real name, Spangler Arlington Brugh, and was stationed at the local Glenview Naval Air Station. His wife, Barbara Stanwyck, was with him at times—a well-known actress in her own right. As there had been much publicity in the local newspapers and popular movie magazines about his assignment, Chicagoans had seen pictures of him in uniform and knew he was in the area on duty.

Apparently there was a resemblance between Taylor and myself when in our naval aviation uniforms. I noticed people acting strangely around me when I first arrived in Chicago and checked into the Hotel Sherman. Two young girls had come up to me in the lobby and one asked for my autograph. I was taken aback, but took her pen and wrote my name in the book she was carrying. When she saw my name she said: "Mr. Taylor, I wanted your movie name not your real one." Apparently my scrawled Buell was enough like Brugh to confuse her. I took the pen again, wrote Robert Taylor, and walked away. She was certain she had a genuine Taylor autograph while my ego was properly inflated. Later at the Howards' and a carrier qualification training unit (CQTU) party several people asked me if I realized that in my uniform I looked just like Robert Taylor; it was pretty heady stuff!

The whole crazy thing came to a climax when Merikay and her mother got tickets to a play in downtown Chicago called *Voice of the Turtle*. We all went, with me dressed up in my best set of blues. The people around us in the theatre did an unusual amount of staring and whispering—apparently the audience was convinced, by suggestion and gossip, that Robert Taylor was attending the play. But, except for smiles and nods, everyone respected my privacy and no one came up for autographs or conversation.

After the play, L. B. went home in the family car while Merikay and I decided to do the town. We entered the Sherman Hotel intending to take in the nightclub entertainment, which was about to start. Several people were waiting to get into the place, so I approached the maître d', impressive in his black formal attire behind a velvet rope, and asked about getting a table for the next show. He gave me a big smile, took down the rope, and told me my usual table was waiting! We were taken to the best ringside table in the place and surrounded with hired help—VIP treatment, obviously.

Merikay thought it all very amusing, and I was in a daze. It also crossed my mind that there was probably an astronomical price tag attached to this kind of service. I was about to get back together with the head man to clear up any mistaken ideas when a lovely voice said: "Hello there lieutenant, you must be the young man I have been hearing about."

I looked up, and then rose unsteadily to my feet. Standing there in all her fame and beauty was Barbara Stanwyck!

I asked her to join us and she did. It turned out that her husband was out of town for a few days on Navy business and she was visiting friends in the hotel. People had been telling her that there was a young navy flyer in town who looked like her husband. When a friend in the Sherman lobby told her she had seen her husband go into the ballroom with a woman, she decided to investigate for herself.

It was a delightful evening. Mrs. Taylor (or Brugh if you prefer) had some champagne, watched the show, and was very charming. Then she gave me the compliment of my life when she said: "Hal, you really do look just like my Bob!" This flattery brought out one of my youthful characteristics—I blushed!

After the floor show, Barbara Stanwyck Taylor Brugh bid us goodnight and departed. By this time Merikay and I were drinking champagne flips and the night was still a pup. We continued dancing and enjoying the attention that my brief notoriety had brought us. I even quit thinking about the enormous amount of money all the festivities and services were going to cost me. But all good things must end and I finally asked for the tab.

The headwaiter, still smiling, informed me that the evening was on the house. To this day I don't know if this generous act was the hotel's own or if Mrs. Taylor took care of it. I do know one thing: To a young lieutenant (jg) with a limited income, who was beginning to run low on cash without having had a payday for over a month, it was a gift from heaven.

A tired but happy naval pilot departed the next morning for Norfolk and further orders. Driving the "Gray Gremlin" (Merikay Howard's nickname for my car) I headed east on the same highway that Johnny Lough, Yogi Jorgenson, and I had traveled that November in 1941 en route to our first assignments.

Although almost half a century has come and gone, I still remember the Howards and my fantastic Chicago liberty that their kindness made possible for me before returning to combat in the Pacific. Hubie Howard and his wife are now retired in Naples, Florida. All the other Howards are gone—his dad, Uncle Tex, their wives, and Merikay—gone but not forgotten.

VI

Arriving at the Norfolk Naval Base, I went immediately to the Naval Air Station and the offices of ComAirLant (Commander, Air Forces, Atlantic). After a physical, I got my orders to Bombing Squadron Fourteen, located somewhere near Cape May, New Jersey, Naval Air Station, for immediate compliance. Driving up to Cape May, I found that VB-14 was stationed at a small field southwest of Wildwood, which in turn was just below Atlantic City, both well-known seaside resort communities. With the summer beach season starting, it was exactly the right time for both good flying and good off-hours liberty. So far, every promise made to me by Wade McClusky in Alameda was coming true.

There were two dive-bombing squadrons at Wildwood Naval Air Station, my new assignment VB-14 and a sister squadron VB-15. Both outfits were flying the latest SBD-5 Douglas Dauntless aircraft fresh from the El Segundo Plant. The squadrons had been commissioned, along with VF-2 and VT-2, on 1 June 1943 at Quonset Point, Rhode Island; the group was to be Air Group Two. An influx of pilots of all ranks had been arriving since the commissioning, including the two commanding officers, Lt. Comdr. G. B. Campbell for VB-14 and Lt. Comdr. Jim Mini for VB-15. While the fighters went to Atlantic City and the torpeckers remained at Quonset Point, the dive-bomber squadrons were assigned to Wildwood for further training. Around 1 August 1943 the two squadrons were combined into one thirty-six-plane outfit and designated Bombing Squadron Two. As Campbell was senior to Mini, he became commanding officer of the integrated squadron.

It did not take me long to analyze the current situation with a bit of concern. Some of what McClusky had said back in Alameda about combat experience began to emerge crystal clear, and the facts were disturbing. The lack of this experience among my new shipmates was disconcerting. There was only one other combat pilot in the entire combined squadron, Lt. (jg) Vernon Micheel, a fellow Iowan from Davenport. Known as Mike, he was a survivor of Midway with a Navy Cross—a sharp little guy with blond hair and striking pale blue eyes. Like me, he also was disturbed by the lack of war experience around us, especially at the command level. None of the top three senior officers—CO, XO, and flight officer —had either combat or carrier experience.

Mike and I agreed that we were faced with a survival situation. We were senior enough to be division flight leaders and thus had a good bit to say about who would fly with us. The first rule of survival we had both learned in our war cruises was the importance of good wingmen and second-section leaders to make up our six-plane divisions. I began a screening process, carefully observing the flying abilities of the numerous ensigns and lieutenant (jg)s who made up the squadron roster. I was looking for the magical combination of good flying skills and a desire to learn how to survive. Not wanted were the smartasses and hotshots who thought they already knew all there was to learn about flying, and considered themselves ready for combat immediately.

Along with looking at the flying talents of my new shipmates, I got to know some of them personally and in a social setting. I had a set of wheels, so there were always requests for rides into Wildwood for liberty. As these contacts developed, certain of the young pilots began to emerge from the mass as potential future members of my division. Among this group were Dave Stear and Ralph Scheurer, who would become my wingmen, and Jack Taylor, Ralph Yaussi, Glen LaMoyne, and Don Ransom, who would make up the second section and standby pilots of my division—a group that would remain together for the entire war cruise without a loss. To me, and later to Rear Adm. Jocko Clark, this courageous collection of dive-bomber pilots became known as "Buell & Company."

VII

After a week of observations, I made a proposal to this group about setting up a permanent base of operations ashore for liberty use. My idea was to get a house in town where we could go, after flying all day, for boozing, entertaining women, and generally having a good time away from the Navy base and rigid routine. We would all keep our regular BOQ rooms, using the rented place for the sole purpose of entertainment and temporary quarters. It ended up with six ensigns and myself splitting costs for a furnished house, and a steady supply of booze, mixers, and snacks. The place had a large living room with a fireplace, a dining room, a kitchen, three bedrooms, and two baths on two floors; the landlady lived in a basement apartment with its own entrance and facilities.

We were lucky to find such a neat arrangement right at the start of the summer vacation season in the area. I don't recall who provided the lady's name and address but I do remember going to her place in the southwest part of Wildwood to make my pitch. She was an attractive young widow with a little boy who thought that pilots, especially Navy ones, were better than firemen, policemen, and cowboys. With him on my side (after giving him a couple of Japanese yen notes from my Guadalcanal booty) his mother finally listened to my story. I made no excuses for the fact that we wanted her house to have fun in for the next three months while we trained to go to the Pacific. I assured her that my friends and I were gentlemen; we would not break things or damage the property; we would bring in a maid at least once a week to clean everything thoroughly. She would be right there and could look in on things whenever she wanted, and I, as the senior officer of the lot, would be responsible to her at all times. With the first month's rent in cash and a three hundred dollar deposit check she could hold to cover her possessions, it was a good offer. Almost reluctantly she agreed to the deal because, she said, she needed the money and all that room was just going to waste.

We christened the establishment the "Snake Ranch."

After we got the ranch in operation, we gave each other snake names. As leader I was called King Cobra; Kish, a large, muscular man, became Python; Stear became Diamondback; Dad Taylor, a sandy-haired giant, was Copperhead; LaMoyne, a cajun from Louisiana, was Cottonmouth; Ransom ended up as Water Moccasin; and Ralph Yaussi as Garter Snake.

The main purpose of the Snake Ranch was recreational—to have a place to bring girls we met on the boardwalk or in the bars of Wildwood for a party or to spend the night. A supply of food and drink was available and activities often ran throughout the night, especially on the weekends.

Sometimes on a Saturday or Sunday afternoon we would find ourselves sitting around, drinks in hand, shooting the bull. Then someone would ask me to tell a sea story—give the real word about how it was going to be out there when we left this Garden of Eden and headed west from the Golden Gate. I used these magic moments to talk seriously about our military specialty of dive-bombing—to get across important tactics being practiced in our planes each day in order to stay alive in the near future. It went like this:

"Let's talk about the correct way to make a dive-bombing attack upon an enemy target. A good dive-bombing run is a carefully planned and executed maneuver that requires coordination, timing, and guts. It consists of seven distinct parts: the approach, the break, the dive, the shot, the pullout, the retirement, and the rendezvous. All parts are important, with the first four essential to consistency in getting a hit, while the pullout, retirement, and rendezvous may determine whether you live to make a run another day.

"After the takeoff launch and initial rendezvous near the task force, our bombing flight will begin a slow climb in formation to altitude. I like to use fourteen thousand to sixteen thousand feet, which is just below required-oxygen level, yet adequate to avoid most AA fire in the approach. This gradual climb to altitude is on a course heading toward the target, using as little fuel as possible.

"A dive-bombing flight is normally twelve planes—two divisions of six each. A division is made up of two three-plane sections. We use the three-plane section, rather than the standard two-plane fighter section, because the third aircraft with its set of twin rear-seat .30-caliber guns and front .50s is essential for sufficient defensive firepower against fighter interception runs. Remember, a three-plane section of dive-bombers flying a tight formation is a solid defensive unit against fighter attacks; a six-plane division is almost impregnable; a twelve-plane flight group has so much firepower that Japanese fighter pilots seldom attack a solid formation of that size. This flight formation is maintained after initial rendezvous until the break for the dive, and returns together as soon as possible after an attack. A typical carrier deck load strike consists of twelve fighters, twelve dive-bombers, and eight torpeckers—a total of thirty-two aircraft.

"As we approach our target, a dive-bomber flight maintains its formation, the tightness depending upon whether enemy fighters are around or if high-level flak is coming into the formation. The approach begins while we are still several miles from the target by both a slight loosening up of the formation and a gradual loss of altitude. The altitude reduction is exploited to build up speed and, combined with slight changes in the group's headings, to give the enemy ship or ground gunners a firing problem in three dimensions —altitude, direction, and speed. All are constantly changing during the brief run-in time our aircraft are within high-altitude AA range before diving. If bursts appear ahead of the formation, we turn toward and fly into them and continue the approach, as high flak rarely bursts in exactly the same place twice, especially from moving ships. The use of any cloud cover available and, when possible, going into the dive from out of the sun gives enemy AA gunners a multitude of tracking and aiming problems to solve at one time. All of these elements are effective in avoiding AA fire when attacking Japanese targets as they have not developed, to date, a radar-controlled gunfire system that works consistently or efficiently. They rely upon standard optical sights, with shell fuse settings preset at diverse altitudes, and mass firing in areas where each shell is labeled 'to whom it may concern.' Consequently, we can attack a well-defended Japanese target such as an aircraft carrier within a task force and lose relatively few planes to AA fire. When Japanese pilots attack our forces, the combination of radar fire control and proximity-fused shells takes a heavy toll of those planes which make it to the dive point.

"The approach, when done correctly by a competent leader, brings the flight into a target so that each individual pilot following will have a chance for a good dive, yet maintains maximum protection against fighter attack right up to the break point. This type of coordination requires a team effort involving careful timing, and is attained by hours of practice runs in formation to the break point, as well as individual practice in diving accurately after the break. This movement is sometimes called a 'high-speed approach' due to the pick-up in speed before diving while descending from maximum cruise altitude to a final push over at ten thousand to twelve thousand feet. At the break each pilot becomes responsible for his individual plane and dive—throttle setting, prop pitch, dive brakes, canopy open—all the details that can influence his dive.

"We are now at what is probably the most interesting and unique part of a good dive-bombing attack—the dive itself. The idea of destroying a target, especially a moving ship, by diving and striking it with a bomb was developed by our Navy along with carrier aviation itself. The famous Stuka dive-bomber of the German Luftwaffe, which has been a devastating weapon when used with the Blitzkrieg in Europe, is an adaptation from early American naval dive-bomber concepts that German air leaders observed at U.S. air shows in the twenties and thirties. After seeing Navy pilot demonstrations of the technique, they bought two planes from Curtiss and copied both the plane and the idea.

"I have a basic hypothesis concerning the art of dive-bombing, which is my own and you probably have not heard before: When you dive-bomb a target you do not drop a bomb—you fire it. Horizontal bombers drop bombs; glide bombers 'chuck' or 'toss' bombs; low-level bombers 'skip' bombs; all of these methods involve dropping a bomb. We are distinctive pilots flying specifically designed dive-bombing aircraft and, in our seventy-degree dives, we are a flying weapon aimed at a target below. Our dive speed is the velocity of the projectile, which is fired at point-blank range at the target. Thus we do not drop a bomb at all—we fire a shell from a weapon.

"The perfect dive angle, as far as I am concerned, is seventy degrees plus one or two degrees. Over seventy-five degrees puts you 'on your back' and makes smooth control in the dive difficult to impossible. Less than seventy degrees can find you too shallow for accurate aiming and firing of your bomb; it also makes you more vulnerable to AA fire, the most dangerous detractor at this point of an attack. By setting up a standard seventy-degree dive each time, you also eliminate some aiming error because you know where your bomb will hit relative to a point of aim, just as a sniper rifleman knows where his bullet will strike when fired.

"Once in the dive, the most important factor remaining is to control the dive flight path so as to reach the release point (I like to call it the firing point) with your aircraft in stable flight and not skidding. The slightest skid when you fire your bomb means that your hit will be off target in the direction of the skid. This one mistake is a major reason why so many bombs are near misses instead of hits. Your point of aim is correct, but the bomb follows the line of the skid and you have a miss. This truth is the same with any plane and any bullet, rocket, or bomb: If you are not flying your aircraft in trim, your shot does not strike where you aim it. To control this type of error you must fly your airplane instead of letting it fly you. Smoothness on the controls and judicious use of tabs and rudder will eliminate a skid. It all sounds rather simple, but consistently smooth flying is not common in the excitement of getting shot at and exposing yourself to death. That is why we keep practicing, and I keep yelling at you for improvement—I want us to become so good as a team that we will put our bombs on target automatically no matter what the opposition.

"Standard pullout procedure after firing a bomb is to bring the control stick back in a smooth yet positive manner, being careful not to jerk the controls in the process. Jerking can cause you to toss the bomb off course and, more seriously, can cause structural failure, or blackout, from excessive g forces on both you and the plane. Thus the pullout becomes a sweeping maneuver using the remaining altitude to the deck, putting the aircraft in level flight just above the ground or water, and going away from the target at maximum speed. To attain this utmost escape velocity, cleaning up the airplane during the pullout sweep is essential as soon as safely possible. The leader will use a lesser throttle setting, leaving a margin of power for wingmen and second-section planes to have something extra to catch up and rejoin the formation.

"Retirement from the target is a particularly dangerous time for all of us because single dive-bomber aircraft are good targets for enemy fighters. Also, departing aircraft are within range of smaller AA guns, including twenty- and forty-mm mounts for a brief time. Thus the retirement course should avoid any ship or AA positions insofar as possible. A weaving, twisting flight pattern is flown by each aircraft as it heads for the rendezvous point. You will be changing course, altitude, and speed simultaneously, just as you did in the high-speed approach before the dive. Your bobbing and weaving departure gives the defending gunners the same sighting problems as before. We are all moving toward a previously picked point with the intention of getting all aircraft together in formation as quickly as possible. Any additional attacks made by dive-bombers during this crucial retirement and rendezvous must be considered targets of opportunity, and secondary to the absolute necessity of getting the formation back together to defend itself against enemy fighter attacks.

"As we head back for the ship, secure in our defensive formation's strength and proud of a successful dive-bombing attack without a loss, a feeling of pride and achievement will fill each of you that is like no other emotion you have ever experienced. This postattack feeling of exhilaration is what Gen. Robert E. Lee was talking about as he watched his army moving to victory on a battle-field, when he said: 'It is well that war is so horrible, otherwise we might grow too fond of it.' "

VIII

All good things have to end sometime, and the Navy showed excellent timing when ordering VB-2 to close up shop at Wildwood and move to Quonset Point, bringing the squadrons of Air Group Two together for the first time since commissioning in June. Leaving right after Labor Day, our departure coincided with the end of the beach vacation season at Wildwood. Thus we would not miss the suntanned beauties frolicking in the sand, as these activities were over for the summer anyhow. It was time to move our flying into cooler climes, and our liberty pursuits to big-city settings—Providence, Boston, Philadelphia, and New York. We threw a final party and closed the Snake Ranch forever; it had been a good summer for both work and play.

Quonset Point Naval Air Station was to be our home for the next two months. With the three air group squadrons finally together, practice group flights were initiated. We made numerous simulated attacks against targets of opportunity in the area—ship convoys, both surface- and air-towed targets, Army troop maneuvers on Cape Cod, and any Army Air Corps intercepts we could find.

During these practice strikes the first evidence of lack of experience and leadership from the top officers of VB-2, so vital to a combat squadron, began to show. As for my division of six planes, hard work of the past summer was paying off and, while we were still making mistakes, we were working together in a superior fashion. I kept pounding away at basics—quick joinups, good formation flying, smooth breakups, and fast rendezvous after dives. I wanted these men to be the best and they were responding.

CAG of AG-2 was Comdr. Roy Johnson. Of medium height and stature, he was a quiet, calm leader with many of the same personal characteristics I had seen before in regular-Navy men like Crommelin, Thach, Lee, and Flatley. We first met as Commander Roy was dismounting from an F6F on the flight line after a group grope. An excellent aviator, he had to be concerned with what he was seeing relative to the dive-bomber squadron of his group. From our first conversation, I felt a tremendous respect for him and sensed that he returned it.

During an eighteen-month assignment to VB-2, Roy Johnson was first my CAG and then air boss and XO in *Hornet*. We were friends; he often asked my opinion and advice about combat activities when we got to the Pacific in 1944, and listened carefully to both. He was the most intelligent senior naval officer I served with during my twenty-one-year naval career.

An event of some significance to the squadron took place during the Quonset stay—the official insignia was chosen. Many ideas had been suggested, but one from George Garbe—Vertigo, the Sea Wolf—became the winner. It consisted of Walt Disney's big, bad wolf, complete with aviator's scarf, helmet, and goggles holding a bomb in his teeth. Lt. Bill Pattee, one of our officers who was from San Francisco, used his California influence to get the Disney Studios to make the official drawing of Vertigo, and VB-2 became known as the "Sea Wolves." One of the most original and colorful squadron insignia of the times, we wore it on our flight jackets, put it on the aircraft, and there were some who might even have put it on their skivvies.

IX

About the first week of October, VF-2 fighters received orders to leave immediately for the West Coast and then Hawaii. This started top brass to worrying that the air group was being broken up and the squadrons would end up as individual replacements on carriers instead of as a group. In the middle of October we were informed that the entire squadron of dive-bombers would fly across the country starting on 31 October, to be based temporarily at Santa Rosa Naval Air Station until transportation could be set up for further movement to Hilo, Hawaii. VT-2 received similar orders.

Flying the entire squadron across the United States, with support personnel and gear moving by train, was no small project. We flew in six-plane divisions, each one pretty much on its own, and followed a preplanned flight track across the country, with RON (remain overnight) stops at certain bases. The first day, 31 October 1943, we departed Quonset Point and flew to Norfolk, refueled, and continued on to Atlanta, for the night. The second day took us to Barksdale Army Air Corps base outside Shreveport, Louisiana, where we had to stay an extra day because of bad weather. On 3 November we moved on to Midland, Texas, where one plane in another division was damaged in a wheels-up landing. The next day, 4 November (my twenty-fourth birthday) found us at Tucson for the night.

Up to this point my six-plane division had flown a perfect cross-country hop. Unlike some of our comrades, no one had experienced a bad airplane, gotten lost, or even come close to a problem. Things were going so well we decided to fly the next leg to Los Angeles rather than San Diego, as liberty would surely be better at the former destination.

The flight northwest across the lower Rockies was beautiful, without a cloud in the sky. With clear weather, I was not expecting serious trouble getting into Los Alamitos Naval Air Station just northeast of San Pedro Bay. However I had not considered that insidious weather phenomenon around Los Angeles called smog, which had a way of forming in the afternoon quite suddenly, reducing visibility to instrument limits in a matter of minutes.

Sweeping down from the Santa Ana mountains toward the sea, I found that smog was forming so fast I could not see Los Angeles, Long Beach, or even the coastline. Calling the tower at Los Alamitos, I was told that the field was open, with a couple of planes making touch-and-go landings, but visibility was dropping to limits that would require closing any moment.

Without declaring an emergency, and keeping the panic out of my voice, I told the tower operator that I was overhead at ten thousand feet with six planes that had burned most of their fuel coming from Tucson. Using the Navy homing beacon as a fix, I was going to spiral down to the field—would he please keep the duty runway open for about five more minutes? He said that he would.

After getting the altimeter setting and moving the planes into a tight formation, I began a gentle spiral down around the homer. In those days of loose instrument rules, much of what we did in formation letdowns was whatever we put together at the moment. Descending in a military air-space, we were not breaking any Federal Aviation regulations—only some Navy ones. Make no mistake about it—the maneuver was dangerous.

We entered the smog completely on instruments. With six planes flying as one, we kept going down. Passing through one thousand feet I began to get nervous; at less than five hundred feet I was about to wave the landing off, when I saw the ground below and we had contact.

To my left was a Navy TBF with its wheels and flaps down in the landing pattern. I eased along outside him, and the field lay dead ahead in the mist. I called the tower for a carrier break, and at about two hundred feet we did a tight pattern around the field to perfect landings. As the last SBD hit the runway, the tower closed the field. By the time we got to the parking apron, visibility was so limited it was getting dangerous to taxi.

With a sigh of relief, and giving thanks to my guardian angel, I climbed down from the cockpit. Due mainly to my stupidity I had endangered all of us by getting caught in bad weather. The good part of the affair was that we had saved our hides with some excellent flying and had not panicked; it was a good omen of things to come for Buell & Company.

Inside operations I was greeted by a lieutenant commander duty officer. I fully expected to get chewed out, but instead he congratulated me for a great piece of division flying, saying that we had set a new record for successful penetration to landing of a formation in below minimum weather conditions. I thanked him and acted like what he had just seen was standard procedure for our squadron.

Later I apologized to the flight for not using better judgment in going to San Diego, as originally planned, instead of smog-ridden Los Angeles. To a man they were happy that we had been tested and found worthy. We agreed not to relate the experience to anyone who might pass the story on to our CO, G. B. Campbell. The flight diversion was not brought up again.

The next day we continued north to Alameda, then northwest to Santa Rosa. A new field had just opened in a small town located sixty miles north of San Francisco. We continued flying daily in preparation for leaving the country, with lots of liberty in the "City by the Bay." The weather was getting colder, Christmas was coming, and our tempers were getting shorter as we waited for those final orders. With departure to combat so near, everyone's patience was wearing a little thin.

Four days before Christmas the waiting ended. We flew our SBDs to Alameda for loading aboard a new CV, *Coral Sea*. With all gear we passed under the Golden Gate at 1625 on 22 December 1943 headed for Hawaii. At sea Christmas wasn't real and brought home the finality of the situation—each turn of the ship's screws was separating us from our loved ones, perhaps forever. I had done it before, but that did not soften the emotions I felt at Christmas time far from hearth and home.

The new year found us at a naval air station outside Hilo on the Big Island. We welcomed in 1944 by drinking too much at the officers' club. It was a place without, for the most part, female companionship. Lt. Comdr. Russ Lord, XO since commissioning of VB-2, left because of physical problems, and Lt. J. R. Smith replaced him. Big George Kish, a close friend, left to go to VB-17; they got a good man and we lost one.

And we were about to meet the Beast.

X

I regret to say that I learned too late that it was not what a person did, but what he got the credit of doing that gave him a reputation.

—MAJ. GEN. GEORGE CROOK, 1864

In January 1944, there was no combat-experienced naval aviator alive who felt the stigma of a lack of decorations on his left breast more than myself. A veteran of eight major engagements, four carrier-versus-carrier battles, and a month of intensive combat at Guadalcanal in the early, tough days, I did not wear a single decoration with my campaign ribbons and stars. While some had been earned or promised, none had actually been awarded.

Like many others in the same situation, I found it was easy enough to act like this recognition did not mean anything, and in truth it didn't. It was reward enough to be alive—to have survived. I had seen high decorations go to men who did not merit them, while others who should have been decorated received nothing. The most total lack of awards to aircrewmen who flew with the pilots was a disgrace through most of the war. Fine pilots received no recognition while their leaders got high awards; some were decorated accidentally, and a few were credited with acts actually performed by others. But none of this changed my own feelings of inadequacy in this vital area of respect.

So it was with a small feeling of solace that I received my first official recognition from the Navy, at Hilo Naval Air Station, in the form of a Presidential Unit Citation awarded to *Enterprise* and her air groups. In my case it was a double award—one for service with VS-5 and the other for VB-10. The chief of naval personnel thought this unusual enough to send his congratulations by letter, with his personal signature, rather than the usual mechanical-pen one. After a brief ceremony at a squadron inspection, I told my flight that we would get our share of medals in the coming actions because we were getting good at dive-bombing, and we would bring back pictures of our claims whenever possible. I didn't have to tell my charges that I coveted a major decoration in the worst way as we finished preparations to go out on what was to be my third war cruise. As it would turn out, Buell & Company were destined to do well and be recognized for their deeds.

I cannot leave this subject without telling about my wayward Silver Star. I did not hear anything more about an award of this medal, based upon my Cactus Air Force fighting, during the war, and I had almost forgotten my conversation with Crommelin about it back on the Big E in 1942. Then one day in the spring of 1947 I ran into Maj. Gen. Richard C. Mangrum, USMC, in the Pentagon where I was doing staff duty with the Directorate of Intelligence.

Dick Mangrum had been the CO of VMSB-232 on Guadalcanal —the outfit Flight 300 had flown with in the Cactus Air Force. During lunch together, he asked me why a ribbon for the Silver Star, which had been recommended for me by the Corps, was not on my chest with my other decorations. I replied that I had not received the award, only heard about being recommended for it. Mangrum was quite upset by my answer and said that he would look into it, but nothing happened.

In the fall of 1950, with Korea on the horizon, the Navy decreed that regular officers would be required to wear large medals on dress uniforms for designated ceremonies, as prescribed by uniform regulations. Officers were directed to get all awards and prepare them for wearing when required. Any medal missing would be granted or replaced by producing evidence of its award to a command headquarters.

As a regular lieutenant commander, I was a student in the Marine Corps Schools at Quantico, Virginia, at the time. Washington, D.C., with its myriad record-keeping bureaus, was close by, so I made a trip to the awards section and asked to see my file. To my surprise I found a citation for a Silver Star to an Ens. Harold Lloyd Buell, signed by Vice Adm. W. F. Halsey, in my records with my other awards. I asked the person in charge if the citation was my property; his answer was yes. I then requested the original signed Halsey citation and it was given to me.

With this citation in hand, I went to see Col. A. D. Cooley, USMC, who was director of the Junior Course, Marine Corps Schools. We knew each other from combat days on the Canal in 1942. He looked it over and stated that as far as he and the commandant of the Marine Corps Schools were concerned I was due a Silver Star that had never been awarded and proceeded to hand one to me. I protested that perhaps the whole thing was not official; his reply was that the Schools Command was rectifying an error that someone had made back in World War II, as ordered in the recent directive, and now the matter was closed.

Today I have an old citation from Halsey and the brilliant Silver Star framed among my treasured awards from those days long ago. But I have never worn this award officially on my uniform, and I don't think that I ever shall. Too much time has passed to try to straighten out why a decoration, meaning so much to me in 1942, was sidetracked and filed in a dead-end folder in a Washington bureau. No wonder Adm. Ernie King was appalled by Halsey's paperwork, as handled by a staff under the supervision of Miles Browning, back there in 1942 and 1943!

But when I start getting myself a little too worked up on this subject, I recall the verses of a song that was composed back on the Canal during those dark days in the fall of 1942. We weren't thinking about medals then—only how to survive for the next twenty-four hours. I'm not sure this tune had any one author, but rather believe it was a joint effort. It goes like this:

I Wanted Wings

I wanted wings 'til I got the God-damned things,
  Now I don't want them anymore.
They taught me how to fly, then sent me here to die,
  I've got a bellyful of war.
You can give all the Zeros to the dashing heroes,
  Distinguished Flying Crosses do not compensate for losses,
Buster. I wanted wings 'til I got the God-damned things,
  Now I don't want them anymore.

10

ISLAND RAIDS

I

Oh Mother, dear Mother, take down that blue star;
   Replace it with one that is gold.
Your son is a Helldiver pilot,
   He'll never be thirty years old.

(AUTHOR UNKNOWN)

THINGS WERE rolling along in a routine fashion for VB-2 at Hilo when we were notified that our SBDs were to be replaced with SB2Cs immediately. A few of the Helldivers were brought in by VB-8 pilots and I made a checkout flight on 6 February 1944. My first reaction was that the Beast, as this Curtiss monster was called, would be trouble for the squadron. Compared to the steady, forgiving SBD, this aircraft required much more pilot ability to fly both operationally and as a dive-bombing weapon.

From a personal viewpoint, there were features about the SB2C that appealed to me from the start. It had four twenty-millimeter cannons firing forward from the wings—a lot more firepower than the SBD's two .50 calibers, which were timed to fire through the prop. It could carry a larger bomb load, with the main load in a bomb bay and wing racks for still more bombs. The Helldiver was a lot faster, both in a dive and cruising, and could stay in the air almost as long as a Dauntless. It turned out that it could really take punishment and still get home—a valuable asset. The gunner's twin mounts were also improved.

The disadvantages of the Helldiver far outweighed the pluses for most of the squadron pilots, especially the least-experienced ones, who were already having trouble in an SBD. It is one thing to fly around operationally without killing oneself on routine assignments—it is quite another to handle a plane on a combat mission, fully loaded with bombs and ammo, while getting shot at. To take the majority of VB-2 pilots out of the only combat aircraft they had flown, and were just starting to be able to use as a weapon, put them into the Beast, and then launch them on a combat mission was imprudent. Yet this was to be the fate of VB-2; we would have only four weeks in the new planes before deployment. We would pay a heavy price at sea for this rash decision made high up by someone who apparently had been forced into a very unpleasant choice due to other factors.

In early March the USS *Hornet* (CV-12), one of the new Essex-class aircraft carriers coming to the Pacific fleet in a steady stream, arrived at Pearl Harbor. To the pilots of Air Group Two, training throughout the islands, came the exciting news—we were going aboard *Hornet* to replace Air Group Fifteen. The fact that we were replacing another air group at the request of the ship's commanding officer was of no concern at the time—the orphans had a home.

Commanding *Hornet* was Capt. Miles R. Browning, well-known as Vice Adm. Bull Halsey's chief of staff in the first year of the war. When Halsey became ill in May 1942, just before the Battle of Midway, Browning went to sea with Rear Adm. Ray Spruance, commander of Task Force Sixteen, with the Halsey staff for that battle. Browning's short temper made him widely disliked in the Navy, but despite his shortcomings, the victory at Midway had made Browning a hero. He emerged from Midway at the top of his career.

Because of the impact that this ship and its commanding officer was to have upon VB-2, a brief sketch of Browning's personality is essential. Naval historian Samuel Eliot Morison called him "one of the most irascible and unstable officers ever to earn a fourth stripe, but a man with a slide-rule brain." Retired Commander

Thomas B. Buell, in a biography of Spruance entitled *The Quiet Warrior,* describes Browning:

> A lean, hawklike man, he was emotionally unstable and evil-tempered, becoming angry, excited, and irrational with little provocation. He drank too much, too often, and had a capacity for insulting behavior, especially when drunk.[1]

I remember Captain Browning as a scowling, chain-smoking martinet who prowled the bridge of *Hornet* like a caged animal. Every order was a snarl, and his subordinates reacted to him with fear and hatred. His use of profanity was well-known, and he was not above dressing down an officer or enlisted man on the flight deck from the bridge, without using, or needing, a bullhorn. Pilots kept a discreet distance from the captain at all times.

Hornet was also a flagship, with newly promoted Rear Adm. J. J. "Jocko" Clark coming aboard at the same time as AG-2. Clark knew Browning well and described this arrival to board *Hornet* in his autobiography:

> Capt. Miles R. Browning, a former classmate, met me at the gangway. In previous years we had experienced personal difficulties, mainly because of his testy temperament, and I could see a look of consternation cross his face as I stepped on board. Immediately I reassured him that my sole purpose was to win the war and that, regardless of our former differences. I would recommend him for promotion if he did a good job.[2]

At that time Clark was willing to give Browning a fair chance to prove himself.

Meanwhile, it did not take long for pilots of AG-2 to learn that their new home was an unhappy ship. They were replacing AG-15 in *Hornet* because Browning had evaluated that group over a period of several weeks and declared it not ready for combat operations. He was particularly dissatisfied with dive-bomber squadron VB-15, led by Lt. Comdr. Jim Mini. As this squadron had formed up in Wildwood at the same time as we had (summer of 1943), many friendships existed between the officers and men of both groups. After a few joint happy hours in the island clubs, and the ensuing "hangar flying" between pilots, our group had the word on Captain Browning.

The picture was not a pretty one. Everyone knew Browning's reputation for running a taut command. But he had some other characteristics, fostered by frustrated career expectations, that made him a man practically without a friend. To go along with his dogmatic attitude and vicious personal manner, Browning had a fatal character flaw: he would not delegate authority to his subordinates.

A cooperative relationship between a carrier's captain and the air group personnel operating from that carrier is vital for both members of the partnership. There are two accepted ways to achieve this. One is for the captain to regard the airmen as a group apart, and allow them their own commands and discipline. In this case, the air group commander retains responsibility for his pilots and their actions, dealing with the captain through the carrier's air department head. The other way places the carrier captain directly in charge of the air group while on board—the air group becomes just another ship's department. The first way makes for a happy air group; the second almost never works. Browning had used the second way with AG-15.

When AG-2 flew on board *Hornet* on 8 March 1944, I had a special passenger in the rear seat of my Helldiver instead of my gunner Lakey. Naval reserve lieutenant Herman Rosenblatt, flag secretary on the admiral's staff, was assigned to ride with me. From him I received the news that we were headed for a task group rendezvous at Majuro in the Marshall Islands. From there, Task Force Fifty-eight would launch a combined attack on a Japanese base in the Palau Islands. We would be striking a sizeable Japanese harbor-airfield complex to support Army General Douglas MacArthur's next move along the coast of New Guinea.

Heading AG-2 was Comdr. Roy Johnson, who was highly regarded by Rear Admiral Clark. This put the group in a more favorable position with Browning than our predecessor. More important, Clark was on board his first flagship as a rear admiral. He was determined that both this flagship and the air group flying from it would perform their duties in a manner favorable to his professional image and reputation as a new task group commander. Browning now had someone watching his every move

218

and the time for him to produce solid results as a carrier captain had arrived.

Captain Browning, however, did not rise to the challenge. The first in a series of mistakes occurred as the *Hornet* entered Majuro Lagoon. Browning carelessly turned to port at the wrong time, threatening to run the ship aground. Fortunately, Rear Admiral Clark knew the harbor from recent experience as captain of *Yorktown* and recognized the danger.

Clark ran to the bridge shouting, "Captain, you are going aground!"

"Oh, no, I'm all right," Browning replied.

About that moment a destroyed on his port side began frantically blowing her whistle as a danger signal, finally convincing Browning to correct his error with haste.

At Majuro, Clark met with Vice Adm. M. A. Mitscher, commander, TF-58, and was promised his own task group as soon as possible. Meanwhile he was to function in a training status under Rear Adm. A. E. Montgomery's Task Group 58.2 for the Palau operation. This led to a second confrontation with Browning over an outgoing message. Clark later recalled:

> Browning wrote out a message insubordinate in substance to
> Montgomery. As soon as it was brought to me for release, I went
> to Browning's bridge and appealed to him not to send it. Had
> Montgomery received that message, I am sure he would have
> demanded Browning's immediate detachment.[3]

So, in an unhappy ship under command of a tyrannical captain, VB-2 headed for combat flying an aircraft appropriately named the Beast.

The vast armada, known to history as Task Force Fifty-eight, was a power to behold. As I flew preparatory flights with my own division of six Helldivers I could not look over the huge fleet, stretching as far as eye could see, without a shiver going up my spine. What a difference this was from when we had sortied from Espiritu Santo with *Enterprise* in the fall of 1942 to face the Japanese fleet with a puny single-carrier force! Now there were three or four carriers in just Task Group 58.1. Multiply this by four and you got anywhere from twelve to sixteen carriers in the complete

TF-58. I began to feel the confidence this powerful force radiated as it cruised through South Pacific waters.

Just as my passenger Lieutenant Rosenblatt had told me, when we sortied from Majuro our target was the Palau group in the western Caroline Islands, 575 miles east of the lower Philippines. Because of its position flanking MacArthur's coming army invasion of Hollandia, the area needed to be knocked out. Just what would be found we didn't know. There was a large harbor and a major airfield at nearby Peleliu. My diary notes of the period follow:

USS Hornet, *at sea, 1 April 1944.* First combat for VB-2 is over. We have completed our first assignment aboard *Hornet.* The force was sighted several times on 29 March by Japanese scouts as it approached the target area, with several being shot down by our force fighter cover.

My division was on the first hop, a predawn takeoff strike on 30 March, which was designated K-day. We manned our planes at 0620 but did not get off the deck until about 0710. No explanation for this delay was ever given and inhibited launches seldom go well. Two TBFs crashed during this takeoff, dropping into the drink; I saw the tail sections go drifting by the ship. One pilot known as the Greek drowned.

After takeoff and joinup, I noticed one plane of my division was missing. This turned out to be Reefer Ransom who also hit the brine on launch. (He survived.) We were loaded with two thousand-pound AP bombs, the largest load we could carry. After the rendezvous I had eight planes joined on me plus six more from the carrier *Bunker Hill* with the Skipper and his wingmen nowhere in sight. The escort fighters were with us so we departed for the target with me leading the collection. The Skipper with his section finally showed up and he moved himself into the lead as the target was coming into view.

Our objective was shipping in Palau Harbor. As we approached I could see several fires burning on the airfield at Peleliu to the south of the harbor. There were many transports, tankers, and support ships both at anchor and at piers as well as a cruiser and four DDs present. [Rear Admiral Clark reported seventy ships in the harbor; thirty aircraft were shot down with another thirty-six destroyed on the ground; and forty more aircraft were shot down the next day after a night replacement effort by the Japanese, in his report of this operation to Mitscher.]

My division spread out a bit as we made an approach from the east with the sun at our backs. I initially planned to attack a ship in the western lagoon and pull out toward the west. However, as I approached I saw what I thought was a small CVE tied up at the main pier. I did a ninety-degree turn to port at high speed and started down on this target. As I dove it took shape into a large transport ship. The high AA fire had been fairly intense but not accurate and no one was hit by it. Our dives started at about eleven thousand feet and I released around twenty-two hundred feet with a good dive and target well in the sight. Dave Stear and Ralph Scheurer, my wingmen, were with me all the way down and also released on the transport ship target. Jack Taylor and LaMoyne dove on another ship, possibly a light cruiser. Upon release of bombs all aircraft retired to the south and east. Not much small stuff was fired at us and we got clear of the harbor in good shape.

As we were leaving the area, heading east, I spotted a small coastal freighter under way offshore, being led into the harbor by a sampan. Using my cannons for the first time, I made a run on the freighter, getting many hits. Stear followed me, giving them the same treatment. The ship stopped dead in the water and started smoking. I did a wingover and returned on a second run. This time I really got hits until my left cannons jammed; explosions took place inside the ship and Dave poured still more into it. We left the freighter on fire, dead in the water and sinking. We then joined up and returned to the ship with two *Bunker Hill* planes still in the formation.

Upon return to the ship and counting noses one of the Skipper's wingmen was missing. It was Tex Hardin, a good friend and one of the finest guys in the squadron. He was last seen pulling out of his dive over the harbor; no one saw Tex get hit or a plane go down. Nothing was heard over the radio—he just disappeared along with his gunner Hills. This was VB-2's first combat loss and it was felt deeply by everyone.

I had seen a large fire burning where we had dropped our initial bombs but because of a fast departure and the freighter affair, none of us were sure about target hits. Later observations [and pictures] proved that a large AP (transport ship) was sunk in the location of our attack and we were credited with a kill. [Months later I received a special award of an Air Medal, signed by Admiral Nimitz, for this attack. Due to his stature as commander-in-chief of Pacific forces, this simple award on his official headquarters' stationery, and bearing his signature, is one of my most treasured.]

Immediately after return, debriefing, and a sandwich, we prepared to go out again. The target this time was Peleliu Airfield. My division went in behind Mike Micheel and his group [a twelve-plane attack]. We were each carrying one 1,000-pound GP bomb in the bays and a 250-pounder on each wing. All planes approached the field from the northeast, boring right in from 10,500 feet altitude. I released a bit higher than on the ship, letting bombs go at three thousand feet and using my remaining altitude for high-speed retirement. Leaving to the south, Dave was hit by a forty-millimeter shell in his left wing, but he was able to stay in formation. I then discovered that I still had my thousand-pounder aboard. I headed across Angur Island and dropped it from twelve hundred feet horizontally, hitting nothing but beach and water. Some fires were set in the target area as all bombs but mine were released on runways and dispersal areas of the airfield.

Going away from Angur Island southward in a running rendezvous, Mike called me on VHF. He reported that he had been badly hit in the starboard wing, his gunner had been wounded, but he was still flying and would follow me home. By this time we were all together and headed back to *Hornet*. Both Mike and Dave landed aboard safely without flaps. Mike's wing had taken a bad hit and burned, with his control cables exposed and almost severed. His gunner, Hart, lost a forefinger of one hand from a piece of the shell that came through his cockpit. Dave had a bad hole in his wing flaps but no fire. [Hart was back flying in a couple of weeks, minus his left index finger—a typical example of the courage possessed by navy aircrewmen.]

Upon return, we learned that Lt. (jg) John Houston, and gunner Freeman, of Mike's division, had been hit in their dive and burst into flames as they were pulling out. Both were seen to bail out of the plane and land in their chutes about one hundred yards offshore. As the rescue submarine did not pick them up, they may have been taken prisoners by the Japs—hope is slim.

Leaving the Palau area the next day, a diversionary raid was sent in to hit Woleai Airfield as we headed back to Majuro. I led a ten-plane strike to the atoll, dropped bombs on runways and dispersal areas, and returned safely. However, another plane went into the drink on takeoff; both Ensign Sills and his rearseatman McDonald were lost. Thus VB-2, in its first routine combat, lost four aircraft: two shot down over the target and two operationally off the carrier. Three pilots and gunners were gone and one crew survived. Additionally, several aircraft had been damaged by the intense AA fire encountered. A total of twenty-five aircraft were lost by Task Group 58.1 in this operation.

It had been an educational experience of how much combat had changed, yet remained the same, since I had left a year before. One new innovation of great worth was the first use of a lifeguard submarine. Having as sanctuary a U.S. submarine near the target, at sea, where pilots could land damaged aircraft or bail out and be picked up by Navy shipmates (and thus live to fight again) was both a morale booster and a saving of valuable personnel. The use of dawn fighter sweeps to catch enemy aircraft on the ground, made possible by the greater numbers of fighters we had aboard, and a more efficient Grumman product called the F6F Hellcat, was reducing the dangers both of Japanese fighter interceptions of dive-bombers and torpeckers at the targets, and of successful enemy aerial attacks on the fleet. Improved weapons, such as the new twenty-millimeter cannons on the Helldivers and better .50-caliber guns on the fighters, SB2Cs, and TBFs, were making an impact on the efficiency of both aerial gunnery and strafing of targets on the surface.

However, many of the same old problems were evident. Operational loss of aircraft and personnel was still a major problem—more men and planes were being lost operationally than to the guns of the enemy. No one seemed to want to face the real causes for much of this waste in lives and property—it was easier to blame it all on the capricious aspects of waging carrier war at sea.

The major nagging problem involved in much of this inefficiency was seldom discussed openly, but many were aware of it. Directly stated, too many incompetent persons were still slipping through the personnel assignment system into positions of authority and leadership. Men who might do little or no damage to the naval system in peacetime, or in a shore billet, could prove disastrous to that system in a combat assignment. By the time an error in leadership was found and corrected, extensive damage and loss of lives could occur.

For example, why did some carriers have a much higher rate of operational crashes during normal combat operations than others? Because a carrier tended to operate at the efficiency levels of the abilities and experiences of its leadership personnel at all levels—good people ran a good ship and lesser people a worse one. When mistakes in personnel assignments were found in a ship already in combat, the time it took to make a change could have a deadly effect.

II

As flight officer of VB-2, I spent much of my awake time, when not flying missions or on standby in the ready room, on either the flight or hangar decks checking the status of squadron aircraft availability. Repairs of battle damage and routine checks were important to maintaining a high level of combat readiness. I hoped that my presence showed my concerns about these vital matters and made for higher morale among the squadron's maintenance personnel—those unsung heroes who kept us flying combat strikes.

Coming from under the belly of an SB2C on the hangar deck, I was surprised to see Father Terrence McMahon, our Catholic chaplain, standing by the plane. The Padre, as everyone called him, was a quiet man of great dignity who was well-liked by all the crew, regardless of faith or beliefs. While I knew him, and we always exchanged greetings when we met, I was not especially close to him.

One of the Padre's characteristics was an almost perfect memory for names; if there was anyone in *Hornet* who knew every member of the crew it was Father McMahon. Thus, it did not surprise me when he addressed me by mine:

"Harold, may I ask you a personal question?"

"Of course, Padre. I hope that I know the answer," I replied.

His eyes were gentle and full of concern. "I have noted that you bless yourself with the sign of the cross when you taxi your plane into the takeoff spot before applying full throttle and leaving the deck. In fact you are the only pilot that never fails to do this. Does this mean that you are, perhaps, a Catholic? I never see you at Mass."

I was taken off guard by this direct query. What Father McMahon had noted, from his general quarters station in the ship's island flight deck area, was a personal ritual I always performed before takeoff.

"Padre, I am not a Catholic. In fact my father was a Methodist minister at the time of his death when I was three years old. I guess you could call me a good example of a WASP from Iowa.

224

Early in this war, right after the Coral Sea battle, I began crossing myself before takeoff. I never thought of the act as being particularly a Catholic one, but you do make a point."

The Padre smiled. "Harold, asking God's blessing of yourself is certainly not just for Catholics and I wish more of them out here would seriously do so, too. However, I have a final question: Just what do you ask God when you bless yourself? Do you ask for protection of your life and a safe return?"

I pondered this for a few moments. The Padre was asking a very serious question—one that I had thought about from the first battles of the war when friends, good Christians, began getting killed. I knew that many who had given their lives were better men than myself. They had believed in God and must have asked for his protection in battle. With such men being lost it made me wonder if God, in his infinite wisdom, even bothered to be interested in man's petty struggles, as reflected in mortal combat against fellow human beings. I gave the Padre this answer:

"Father McMahon, you have asked me a most difficult question. You may find this hard to believe, but I do not pray to God to spare my life, especially not at the expense of someone else. I ask God for two things when I leave this ship on a combat mission: Please keep my airplane engine running, and keep my guns and bombs firing. If God helps me in these two areas, I will have a fighting chance to protect myself—to get back safely to this ship. With my airplane flying and my guns firing, I willingly accept the responsibility for keeping myself alive."

The Padre smiled and gave me a farewell pat on the shoulder. "That is an unusual answer to my question and it is a good one. May God continue to bless you in the battles to come as he has in the past is my prayer for you."

As Father McMahon continued on his way, it suddenly came to me that I had forgotten to mention to him one other very important fact—the survival role of my guardian angel. I knew that I had one, and he never failed me when the going got rough. Although I had been reared in Christian surroundings in my formative years, I never considered myself particularly religious. But I had this feeling of trust and confidence in a spiritual aide that was so strong that I could not deny it—my guardian angel was real and always on duty!

Through the years since the war I have studied the subject of angels in religious, scientific, and even fictitious writings. I have not found an answer to explain either my wartime feelings or my still-prevalent beliefs regarding these supernatural beings. The postwar UFO sightings and further developments in the fields of atomic energy, space travel, solar energy, and dozens of other areas simply increased my curiosity.

Perhaps the best answer to the question of angels can be found in that literary miracle, the Bible. Reverend Billy Graham has made a fascinating study about them, entitled *Angels: God's Secret Agents,* which was published in 1975. Basing it primarily on the Bible itself, he also used other supportive sources in his research. One of these corroborated, in a sense, my own feelings about angels in war.

Graham cited a story, written by the English author Adela Rogers St. John, that describes an interesting aspect of the air war between the Royal Air Force and the German Luftwaffe in the Battle of Britain. She was present, along with the king, prime minister, and other dignitaries, at a celebration in London honoring Air Chief Marshal Sir Hugh Dowding:

> In his remarks, the Air Chief Marshal recounted the story of his legendary conflict where his pitifully small complement of men rarely slept, and their planes never stopped flying. He told about airmen on a mission who, having been hit, were either incapacitated or dead. Yet their planes kept flying and fighting; in fact, on occasion pilots in other planes would see a figure still operating the controls. What was the explanation? [Dowding] said he believed angels had actually flown some of the planes whose pilots sat dead in their cockpits. [4]

To have an airman with the stature of Sir Dowding state publicly his belief in angels assisting RAF pilots in their time of need is nothing short of astounding. Whether angels piloted planes for dead pilots obviously cannot be proven but the fact that the head man believed they did is an entrancing idea. It reinforces my own long-held belief in a guardian angel and benefactions in my behalf in times of peril.

Of course I am happy that my angel saw fit only to help me do the flying and fighting and did not replace me entirely, as related in Dowding's amazing story. And I sure want to give him the traditional Navy "well done!"

III

While the Navy under Admiral Nimitz was beginning to move through the Central Pacific by seizing the Marshalls, his counterpart in the Army, Gen. Douglas MacArthur, was preparing a leapfrog movement up the New Guinea coast on his way back to the Philippines—a move that would bypass thousands of Japanese troops, leaving them trapped in the eastern part of the island. He had picked Hollandia for a landing, but needed help from Task Force Fifty-eight to neutralize the Japanese Caroline Island bases and to support the actual landings. Also there were enemy installations to the west of the beachhead—Wakde, Sawar, and Sarmi—that would have to be nullified for a successful operation.

The Palau strikes were the first stage of naval support for this joint mission, and after refueling, rearming, and replacing losses, on 13 April, Jocko Clark took TG 58.1 to sea from Majuro for the invasion support phase. As promised by Vice Admiral Mitscher, Clark had been given command of a task group and was the youngest rear admiral commanding a fast carrier task group in the Pacific. He stated later: "I realized that only by turning in a top-notch performance could I hope to keep my job. My entire staff fell in with this line of thinking and to a man responded to meet the challenge." [5]

As the force approached the target area, our task group began daily searches, antisubmarine patrols, and combat air patrols. I was assigned a dawn search and had manned my designated plane on the starboard side near the catwalk just forward of the fantail. Aircraft engines had been started, preflight checks made, and the *Hornet* increased speed while turning into the wind for launch. At this moment, off the starboard beam, I saw the outline of a ship coming toward us in the darkness.

All ships were cruising under blackout conditions so the oncoming vessel was barely visible. Nonetheless, I could see enough of its shape to recognize it as a supply vessel of some sort. The distance remaining between our starboard side and the closing ship's bow made clearance possible by perhaps twenty yards—much too close for comfort. Fortunately the ship passed safely.

I picked up the radio intercom to talk to my gunner about the near miss. Suddenly, in almost the same area, but closer this time, another ship appeared off the *Hornet*'s starboard beam on a direct collision course. A large fleet tanker was bearing down on us in the early-morning light.

Pandemonium broke out in *Hornet*. Whistles, bells, and horns began blasting for emergency procedures throughout the ship. I quickly cut my plane's engine, unstrapped, and leaped from the cockpit, yelling to my gunner to get clear of the aircraft. The tanker was so close I thought the impact would be almost directly on top of us. From a position beside my plane, the onrushing ship's bow appeared as tall as our flight deck, which was more than sixty feet above the ocean's surface.

God's hand was surely on us that morning in April 1944. As the *Hornet* increased speed, the tanker went to full reverse, and the combination of the emergency actions of both ships made clearance possible. The tanker passed our stern with only inches to spare; I could have jumped from our fantail onto her bridge deck as she slid by. Some witnesses later swore that the two ships touched, but no evidence was found to confirm any contact.

Stories raced throughout the ship, retelling what happened on the bridge that morning. Junior officers present blamed only Browning, who was at the conn (the control area) during the incident, arguing that he simply would not listen to anyone—even when warned that he had turned onto a collision course. Rear Admiral Clark, who had run to the bridge in his bathrobe, was so angry that he got into a heated exchange with Browning in front of several junior officers. Clark, in discussing the incident later, said: "Captain Browning forgot about the tanker *Platte* directly astern. When I saw what was happening I ran for his bridge just in time to save him from being rammed broadside."[6] Clark had saved Browning for a third time—but the sand was running out.

In recounting the invasion support strikes of VB-2 I am using the diary notes I composed immediately after the actions:

USS Hornet *at sea, 22 April 1944.* This is a report of VB-2's part in Army landings at Hollandia, Tanahmerah Bay, and Humboldt Bay, and raids upon Wakde, Sawar, and Sarmi Point.

Our task group was assigned the targets of Wakde and Sawar airfields and enemy installations at Sarmi Point. We were to attack on D-1 day, which was 21 April 1944. My division of dive-bombers was a part of the first strike from *Hornet* [target was Sawar Airfield]. With the Skipper's seven, we had thirteen dive bombers, plus twelve fighters and six torpedo planes.

We approached Sawar from the east, coming along the coastline amid rain squalls and clouds, which broke up as we got close to the airport. We could see the target clearly from ten thousand feet and, as we passed Wakde Island, I saw many fires around the airfield and dispersal areas, which had been started by an attack group from *Yorktown*.

Our fighters had swept down over the target area, and CAG-2 Comdr. Roy Johnson had spotted a small AK (about two thousand tons) anchored in the harbor near Sarmi Point. He called the Skipper about this target; much to my surprise, it was assigned to my division to hit. As we turned toward the harbor where the ship was located we passed over Sawar Airfield and I observed heavy AA fire coming up from several prepared positions around the field. About the same time our torpedo planes dropped a series of incendiary bombs over that area, covering it completely.

We approached the ship from the southeast and dove from nine thousand feet; all six bombs were near misses clustered together in a beautiful pattern without a single direct hit. Half were very close, almost hitting the sides of the ship. Pulling out, I strafed a small boat that appeared to be beached on a nearby reef; there were no signs of life around it. My wingmen Dave and Jowls also strafed this small target.

Coming back, I passed close by the ship that we had attacked and found it was going down at the stern. Apparently the near misses had caved in the sides, opening holes below the waterline. Her sinking was verified later by pilots of other strikes and CAG also attested to her sinking condition.

At this point bad luck hit the squadron and never left us during the rest of the time in the target area. As Campbell's division [the Skipper] was rendezvousing about ten miles northeast of the airfield after their attack, Lt. (jg) Red Finger pulled up into Lt. (jg) Whiskey Watson in the join-up, both planes exploding in mid-air [there were no parachutes]. Both pilots and rearseatmen Ponzar and Flatt were killed. The remainder of the flight made it back to the ship, but my starboard wingman, Jowls Scheurer, had to crash-land aboard. His plane had thirty holes in it from small-caliber AA fired received as he pulled out of his dive on the ship; he had flown home without comment about the hits.

Back in the ready room we learned that two of strike 2B [the strike after ours] planes had crashed into the water while taking off with full loads. Lt. (jg) Jesse Bamber was saved by plane guard DD after the crash, but his gunner Foster drowned. Jesse told me that he was trapped in the cockpit and dragged thirty to forty feet below the surface before he could fight clear of the wreckage. The other crash was Lieutenant (jg) Bosworth, with Chartier as gunner, also going in on takeoff. Bos struck his head violently on the instrument panel when the SB2C hit the water almost out of control. After a successful pickup by plane guard DD, he died during the night from a skull fracture. Chartier survived. When this group returned after its desolating start, Lt. (jg) Karl Sherwood and gunner Henderson were missing in action, having last been seen entering a dive on the target. It had been a bad day for VB-2.

Digressing from the diary notes, I recall an interesting experience that occurred while we were returning from a close support strike during the D-day landings the next day. The Skipper did not appear at the rendezvous point after our attacks, so all aircraft joined up on me and we started home. Leaving the coast at about five thousand feet in a good defense formation, I spotted a twin-engined Japanese Betty flying low on the water heading northwest toward Rabaul. A loner, it apparently had been on a search mission to determine what was happening at Humboldt Bay and was now returning home.

This was the kind of opportunity that a bunch of dive-bomber pilots dream about. With an altitude advantage and nine to one odds, we had a chance of a lifetime. Without even considering a call to fighters in the area, I put the flight into a right echelon and led it down in column upon the unsuspecting bogey. Although only about fifty feet above the water, the Betty was in a perfect position for each of us to make a classic high-side run. Being careful not to fly into the water, I charged my twenty-millimeter cannons and swept in on the poor bastard from a five o'clock position, firing at point-blank range. I saw a few rounds come toward me from the top turret gun before my shells hit; the turret cover flew off the bomber like a cork from a bottle of champagne. Each following Helldiver poured twenty-millimeter cannon shells into the hapless Betty and it settled lower and lower until, still in level flight, it struck the water and exploded in a shower of debris.

Back aboard *Hornet* in the strike debriefing we had the problem of how to credit this kill. We decided to give joint credit to the two pilots who were firing the instant the Betty hit the water and exploded. These pilots were Lieutenants (jg) Garbler and Schaber and each got an Air Medal for the feat. But there was unanimity among us that the poor enemy bomber simply sank into the water from the weight of twenty-millimeter shell hits from all nine of the Sea Wolves formation. We also had some interesting discussions with our fighter pilot buddies of VF-2 about shooting down enemy aircraft, especially Betty-type snoopers, and offered our services as fighters if needed!

The kill of the Japanese Betty and credit for a ship sunk the previous day off Sarmi Point were badly needed by the personnel of VB-2 at the close of this two-day debacle. Morale was about as low as it could get, with five aircraft lost during the two days at a cost of four pilots and four gunners, and only one plane of five due to enemy action. The two aircraft going into the drink while attempting to take off with combat loads, after two previous losses the same way in the Palau operation, was beginning to indicate that something might be seriously wrong with air operations in *Hornet*. And there was the nagging problem of a skipper who was continually getting lost.

Two of the pilot losses hit me extra hard. I had known Walt Finger from when he had reported to VB-10 in *Enterprise* as a replacement ensign in the spring of 1943. He was from Illinois, a midwesterner like myself. As he had listed me as his effects inventory person in case of death, I had the sad duty of packing his things for return to his parents and writing letters of condolence to his family and girlfriend. As for Karl Sherwood, we had been good friends since first meeting back in Wildwood the previous summer and now, just ten months later, he was missing in action.

I summarized my feelings about these losses at the time in my diary: "All of these men were very good friends. It makes the price of war almost more than one can bear at times. I often wonder when my number will come up; I know one thing, losing such friends as these makes me hate the enemy more than ever."

IV

After two days of support to the MacArthur landings, Task Force Fifty-eight moved westward up the New Guinea coast in the general direction of the Philippines. We were looking for a good fight, but the Japanese did not come out in any sizeable force. After several days, word came to refuel all groups and proceed to Truk; in his dispatch orders to Jocko Clark, Mitscher joked a little, saying: "Plaster Truk with everything you have including empty beer bottles if you have any."[7] It was obvious that he wanted Truk reduced to impotence.

During this period, I decided to stick my neck out, bypassing my CO and going directly to CAG Johnson, because of what was happening within VB-2. We had two major problems and both were dynamite. The first was the perpetual lack of leadership being shown by our squadron CO and his inability to lead a wing of twelve aircraft on combat strikes. His lack of experience, evidenced by his continually getting lost and by the heavy losses within his division, made many of the pilots reluctant to fly with him. The second issue was the continuing loss of aircraft and crews during launches—someone had to take this problem forward to the ship's Air Department for serious discussion. Normally the squadron CO or its XO would have handled something like this, but in the case of VB-2 neither of these officers seemed aware that anything was even wrong, much less ready to do anything about it higher up. Thus this serious business was left to the third- and fourth-ranking flying officers in the squadron—Lieutenants Mike Micheel and Hal Buell.

Mike and I had discussed the losses on takeoff in detail, including all the known factors that cause such accidents. First and foremost was pilot error in handling an aircraft during takeoff with a full combat load. All pilots had been briefed about not pulling the aircraft into a climb off the bow, but to let speed build up before starting a climb. If the plane settled off the deck, pilots were instructed to use the altitude above the water to help build up sufficient flying speed, as there was about sixty feet that could be used to advantage before an airplane struck the water. Most important was to retract the landing gear as quickly as possible, not only to reduce the drag but to have the airplane in a clean condition if it struck the water. If wheels were still down the aircraft might flip over, trapping the crew inside. Of the ten crashes during takeoffs (for the total air group), pilot error had apparently been the cause in only one or two cases. Based upon other pilots' stories of near misses, we came to the conclusion that insufficient wind across the flight deck and too heavy a bomb load were the likely causes of most of the SB2C losses and perhaps the TBF ones, too. After coming to these conclusions, Mike and I recommended to the CAG that he ask the ship to give us more relative wind across the deck, and limit bomb loads to one 1,000-pounder in the bomb bay and two 250-pounders on the wings, for a total maximum load of 1,500 pounds.

CAG Roy Johnson agreed with our recommendations and, although realizing that taking on Captain Browning with these sensitive issues was potentially volatile, did so in our behalf. Browning gave him some flak, but we won the point and the wasteful losses of dive-bombers on takeoffs ended immediately. When the Skipper heard what we had done, he must have decided that the whole idea was mine. He took me to one side and made it clear that he considered what I had done as interference with his command responsibilities. He warned me that the next time it happened I would be sorry. I replied that I was only trying to stop the needless loss of aircraft and personnel—something that I would always do if those responsible did nothing. This really teed him off, and I came close to going into hack on the spot.

When the word was passed that the task force was headed for Truk to do battle, most of the pilots and gunners felt some apprehension. Unlike some of our recent targets, Truk was a Japanese stronghold with a fearsome reputation—its very name was enough to start hearts to beating a bit faster. Truk was Japan's Pearl Harbor and rated on a level with targets like Manila, Rabaul, and bases in the home islands for potential opposition to air attack. As we set up our strike schedules, we prepared for the worst.

Following what was becoming standard task force procedure, each carrier sent in a predawn fighter sweep on 29 April 1944 with gratifying results. Some sixty Japanese Zeros were caught airborne and shot down along with another thirty-four put to the torch on the ground and at harbor buoys. The sweep was followed by a series of dive-bomber and torpedo bomber attacks throughout the many island targets and a few auxiliary ships caught in the harbor. Like in Palau, units of the main fleet were gone from the area. My diary describes the action:

USS Hornet *at sea, 2 May 1944.* This is an account of VB-2's raids on Truk and Ponape from 29 April to 1 May 1944. I led strike 2C consisting of fourteen planes against AA emplacements on Param Island in Truk Lagoon. Returning pilots from strikes 2A and 2B told of heavy AA and some fighter opposition at the target. It turned out that they weren't kidding about the AA—we ran into the heaviest fire both at altitude and down low that had been encountered in raids to date.

I brought the flight in from the west at twelve thousand feet when high AA began to burst near as we came over the island, so we used some altitude for a high-speed approach and pushed over at about ten thousand. As the AA positions were our targets, and they were firing at us all the way down in the dives, it was not hard to pick out a good aiming point. We laid a good pattern down on the east-west ridge running across Param where the AA fire was the heaviest. One plane was hit, LaMoyne getting a large section of the port stabilizer of his rudder assembly shot away, but he returned safely to the ship.

Back at *Hornet* during debriefing I was ordered to the bridge—Rear Admiral Clark wanted to talk with me. He asked me how things were going at the target and I replied fine, except for the AA fire! He then told me we were doing a good job and gave me the traditional "well done."

My wing went into Param again in the afternoon. This time the target area was a town along the west side of the island. I came in almost exactly the same way as in the morning strike, and the attack went off smoothly. Again we got a good pattern of bombs into the target area and pilots reported later that my group set a large warehouse ablaze. AA fire was not as bad as earlier; we lost no aircraft; it was a good day's work.

The next day, 30 April, the attacks on Truk continued with control of the air completely in our hands. I was assigned Dublon Island as a target with gas dumps, the seaplane base, hangars, and buildings as specific objectives. Again coming from the west, we encountered heavy cloud coverage over most of Truk Atoll. Then I got a break and found a hole in the clouds. We plunged down through it right upon the target area. As the Japs never saw us until we were dropping our bombs, the AA fire was extraneous small stuff and very scattered as we were leaving. I never saw more devastation than I observed leaving this area, with Eten Island almost blown out of the water. We set new fires in an already badly beaten-up target area. With the weather closing in, our strike was the last one of the Truk operation.

The Truk raids of April 1944 proved what was becoming an obvious fact—Task Force Fifty-eight could go anywhere it wanted and had the power to seize and hold air superiority while there. The force lost twenty-six aircraft over Truk—all to the heavy AA fire encountered. The lifeguard submarine *Tang* combined with cruiser seaplanes to rescue most of the pilots and gunners shot down. One pilot, Lt. (jg) John Burns, landed his OS2U Kingfisher in the lagoon itself, picked up seven downed pilots, and then taxied out to where *Tang* was on station. Due to a rough sea, which prevented a takeoff, the seaplane had to be sunk by gunfire but all of the valuable airmen were saved—part of a total of twenty-two who lived to fight again. As for Truk, it never recovered from the pounding it received and ceased to be a threat to U.S. naval operations in the Central Pacific.

Just how important the new pilot lifesaving concepts were becoming was noted a short time later. Intelligence reports revealed that at least eight U.S. pilots who had been shot down over Truk in the first raid back in February had been executed by the Japanese after they were captured. (One of this group was the famous Lt. Smokey Stover of VF-5 fame on Guadalcanal.) If pilots had an escape valve like the lifeguard submarine, they had a chance for rescue if shot down, instead of surrendering and being ruthlessly killed by an unscrupulous enemy.

Leaving Truk, TF-58 moved in on Ponape on 1 May. I took an attack in about noon. We were assigned underground storage dumps along the eastern edge of an old airfield. Clouds covered the target, but the Japanese helped us find them by firing AA up through the clouds, enabling me to estimate about where the airfield was. Again finding a hole, we spotted the field and made our drops, but nothing happened—no secondary fires or explosions were observed. Later in the day cruisers and battleships of the force moved in near shore and shelled the entire area from the sea.

Mitscher was delighted with the Truk raids, and especially the conduct of his new task group commander Rear Admiral Clark. He personally gave Jocko a "well done" and we all went to Kwajalein for a few days of recreation while loading up to hit the Japanese again where they least expected it.

V

The bomb was hung up. No doubt about it. So what do you do now?

My division of six Helldivers was returning from a routine strike on the Japanese airfield at Ponape. It is the nature of combat pilots to "estimate the situation" when preparing for a mission and make a prestrike guess as to whether it will be rough, normal, or easy. After we briefed for this one—a routine milk run against a field where there were no aircraft, little expected AA fire, and no weather problems—the consensus was it would be a piece of cake.

Things went pretty much as planned and the whole affair began to have a carnival-like atmosphere as we rendezvoused to return home. There had been little ground fire and no fighter opposition; all planes were coming back into formation without injury; the open flight decks awaited us a short distance away on the shiny blue sea. We had that feeling of elation that always came when a mission was over and everything was going right.

At that point, in the rendezvous, a small problem presented itself—Jack Taylor, my second section leader, had a wing bomb still hanging from his starboard wing rack. One hundred pounds of fuse and explosive, squat and ugly, the GP bomb gleamed in the reflected sunlight. It was not supposed to be there; it should have dropped clear with its companions during the bombing run on the target. But there it was, and now things were not entirely right.

The small problem increased in size when all routine emergency procedures failed to get the bomb to release. But I didn't have any real concern at this point as safety features were built into all armaments, including bombs, to prevent their unwanted explosion. All bombs had an arming device in the form of a small propeller mounted to the nose fuse. This propeller would start to spin as the bomb fell from the aircraft rack, arming the fuse of the bomb so that it would explode upon contact with ground, water, or target. Normally a bomb had to travel at least 250 feet after release to arm itself, and there was no way to start the propeller turning until the bomb separated from its rack. In effect, this meant that any bomb still in place on a rack was not armed and would not explode under any circumstances during takeoff, flying, or landing of the aircraft.

The arming action was so safe that when I had a night crash

after being shot down during takeoff in my Dauntless on Guadalcanal, the five-hundred-pound GP bomb I was carrying when I crashed simply tore away from the main rack and rolled off to one side without exploding! Because of this experience, I had considerable confidence in the bomb's arming system.

Arriving back at the task force I called Ripper Base to report on the wayward bomb in detail. I was told to stay with the problem aircraft, have all other planes from the strike land, and repeat all emergency procedures for such a situation. Jack Taylor, with both Dave Stear and me flying on his wing, followed the orders with no apparent success—the rogue bomb was still firmly attached to the starboard wing rack. Meanwhile, as we performed these maneuvers, all other aircraft in the strike group landed safely. *Hornet* control finally ordered us to land, with Taylor to come in last.

I had landed and was taxiing forward toward the pack when Dad Taylor made his landing among the arresting cables. It was a normal carrier arrested landing in every way except one: the one-hundred-pound bomb, which had resisted all attempts to jettison it in the air, detached itself from the wing rack and dropped to the carrier deck. The bomb then bounced both forward and upward, arching into the air about twenty feet before returning back to the deck. When it struck the second time it exploded.

Because there is so much noise on a carrier deck during a recovery, I do not remember ever hearing the explosion itself but was aware that the bomb had detonated when its shock wave struck me in my open cockpit, and a fragment neatly severed my radio antenna pole located just forward and about two feet above my head on the engine mount. I also noted that the man who was directing the movement of my aircraft suddenly pitched forward on the deck. The crash horn started blasting, and deck personnel began running past my plane back toward the arresting gear area with foam and fire hoses. Another plane director started moving my aircraft forward again while the fallen one lay motionless on the deck. He was slightly curled on his side in a fetal position, almost as if asleep. I saw a growing pool of blood emerge from under his waist as his comrades hurried to him with a wire stretcher. He had been hit with a bomb fragment and killed instantly. Another deck man was hit in the legs, losing both but surviving. The most unusual casualty was a man lying asleep under an aircraft on the hangar deck far below. A piece of shrapnel went down through the main deck and spaces, finally striking him with enough velocity to end his life at a considerable distance from the explosion. Several others were injured but survived.

It was accidents like this one that made flight deck operations one of the most dangerous forms of work that anyone could take part in. No one ever knew when something might go wrong. The reason for the bomb exploding was never determined and the event proved again the mysterious workings of fate in determining who lived and who died in war.

VI

The problem of Captain Browning and his negative impact upon the performance of the *Hornet* would not go away, and Clark knew this. He would say later: "Mitscher, having heard of some of my difficulties with Miles Browning, kept telling me that *Hornet* would never be right so long as Browning remained the captain. I concurred but pointed out, how can I do anything until he commits an overt act?"[8]

That overt act finally occurred while the *Hornet* was anchored at Eniwetok, and it must rank as one of the most bizarre happenings on any U.S. warship in World War II. As standard ship's routine—when war conditions permitted—movies were shown on the hangar deck after the evening meal. All hands, from the admiral down to the junior seaman, could attend these movies except members of the duty watch section. Folding chairs were arranged in an open area aft of the forward elevator, the screen was dropped down from the overhead, all lights were extinguished, and the movie appeared on screen—just like a theater.

On the evening of the movie incident Rear Admiral Clark and most of his staff were in attendance—as well as Browning, the ship's officers, and air group pilots. Front-row seats were provided for the admiral's group. I was seated four rows behind them, between two of my flight division pilots, Lts. (jg) Jack Taylor and Dave Stear. We were in the right section of seats, next to the starboard hangar bulkhead. Behind us were seated hundreds of ship's crew and squadron personnel. In addition to the chairs, people were sitting on aircraft wings, the overhead catwalks, engine stands, and other places of opportunity. Approximately two thousand men were packed into the viewing area.

A short cartoon had started prior to the main feature in the darkened area, when a loud hissing noise was heard coming from the rear of the audience. Someone had accidentally actuated a carbon dioxide fire extinguisher, creating an unusual sound. A cry of "It's a bomb" started a human tidal wave action rolling from the rear toward the front of the area where we were seated. As we heard the rumble and stood up, we were engulfed by the moving crowd. I yelled to Jack and Dave: "Get up against the bulkhead!" We turned our backs against the nearby side of the hangar and, using hands, elbows, knees, and feet, fended off the terrified herd crowding around us. We kept shouting over and over, "Be calm, everything is okay!"

Fortunately, in a few moments, someone turned on the overhead lights. Once people could see, they calmed down and the riot ended as suddenly as it had started. Rear Admiral Clark was amazed by the panic he had witnessed on his flagship: "People were knocked down and trampled all around me. More than thirty had to be sent to sick bay. My guess was that as they came close to me and realized I was the admiral they backed away; otherwise I too would have been crushed."[9]

The admiral guessed wrong. No one could see anyone's rank in the darkness. What saved Clark from injury was his location at the front edge of the audience, and the fact that he had several dozen strong, young officer-pilots between him and the main body of the mob. These men were combat-experienced and did not panic in this frenzied situation. They kept their feet and fought back the surging crowd by instinct. The crest of the human wave never reached either Clark or Browning.

Captain Browning's actions during the next fifteen minutes sealed his fate. One man had fallen through a side opening into the water and was pulled out. This man said he thought there was another man in the water; the duty officer ordered a small-boat search around the ship; the captain countermanded the order. Rear Admiral Clark recommended both a boat search and crew muster, but these instructions were ignored. Browning had the injured taken to sick bay, the seats were reset, and the movie was continued as if nothing had happened.

Unfortunately, there was a second man overboard—his body was found floating in the harbor two days later. Rear Admiral Clark had his overt act. After hearing the story, Vice Admiral Mitscher immediately ordered a court of inquiry to be convened. Browning was found guilty of negligence and Mitscher ordered him to be relieved as captain of the *Hornet*. He was replaced by Capt. William D. Sample, a strong yet gentle officer, almost fatherly, who soon had the ship's company operating in an excellent and professional manner.

Captain Browning quickly disappeared from the carrier navy he had served for more than a quarter of a century. He was ordered to the naval air station at Leavenworth, Kansas, which incidentally is also the site of a large federal prison. One pilot, thinking the worst when he heard of Browning's orders, said: "Leavenworth! I didn't think they would do that to him." Clark observed that Browning, although a brilliant officer who had many fine qualities, was his own worst enemy. Back in Washington, the top naval officer, Adm. Ernie King, who had disliked Browning for a long time, was at last satisfied—an irritation had been removed.

As for Browning, when snowstorms swept across the Kansas prairies in the winter of 1944, sending wind chill factors to 30 degrees below zero, he probably realized that he was in America's Siberia and recalled the balmy Pacific winds blowing across the flight deck of the *Hornet*. Under such circumstances, few would blame the "architect of victory at Midway" for a teardrop or two in his scotch-and-soda during happy hour at the officers' club.

Along with the removal of Browning as captain of *Hornet*, another event occurred at about the same time that had a positive effect upon the competency of both the ship and VB-2. *Hornet* got a new air officer who was one of us; he was appointed by Rear Admiral Clark, who described his thinking at the time:

> In *Hornet*'s air group I had recognized in [Comdr.] Roy L.
> Johnson a high type of leadership. When a vacancy occurred for
> *Hornet*'s air department head, I nominated Johnson for the post,
> and as his successor in the air group I nominated [Lt. Comdr.]
> J. D. Arnold. These two changes produced much greater
> effectiveness in the operation of *Hornet*, which soon came to be
> known as a crack ship. Johnson fleeted up to executive officer in
> due time.[10]

Things were looking better for both the *Hornet* and Air Group Two.

VII

A squadron in action had losses that required assignment of replacement aircraft and aircrews to maintain a maximum level of combat readiness. New planes were often obtained from small escort aircraft carriers at sea right after an action; replacement pilots and gunners usually came to the squadron when it returned to a major port such as Eniwetok or Majuro.

As the squadron's air officer, it was one of my duties to welcome these neophytes to our ranks and verbally prepare them for their combat baptism. The following is a briefing that I gave to a group of replacement pilots in the summer of 1944, put together from old notes and memory.

Gentlemen, welcome to Bombing Squadron Two, flying from Rear Adm. Jocko Clark's flagship *Hornet.* I am the squadron air officer, Hal Buell. I presume that you are all eager to get into combat and kill lots of Japs before this war ends—you do not have to go home without attaining hero status! I can assure you that you have come to the right place if you want combat action. Our ship and Rear Admiral Clark both have reputations for hard-hitting action against the enemy as Task Group 58.1, a part of Vice Admiral Mitscher's famous Task Force Fifty-eight. You are now a part of that group, and therefore of that reputation. Consider yourselves fortunate to have been ordered to this outfit —one of the best of many dive-bombing squadrons flying from decks of TF-58 carriers.

However, there is a side to your new status here that is often not even discussed in many squadrons because it is too agonizing a subject and thus lies hidden and unspoken. The painful fact is that you are replacement pilots sent here to fill the places of men who were killed last week or the week before. Some of those men were old squadron hands who had been with VB-2 since it was commissioned more than a year ago in Quonset Point, Rhode Island. But many of our losses are from among men just like yourselves who are sent here to bring our squadron back up to a full complement of fighting personnel.

I am not telling you this to put you down in any way, but to simply state the facts as to how things have been working out for us here. Believe me, we are all very glad you are here to help us. You are commissioned naval officers and aviators who have finished strenuous flight- and ground-training courses to prepare you for your duties here. You will all be assigned places in combat sections of divisions and be rotated on the strike schedule just as every other pilot in this squadron. Unlike the situation that exists when a squadron is first organized and begins training back in the States, we do not have the time to carefully check each of you out in all aspects of the many and varied combat missions we will be flying within a few days. You will have to learn a lot of new things related to combat quickly, and make no mistakes operationally, or you may not survive. Frankly, if we can get each of you through your first five missions successfully, there is a good chance you may be around to return with the squadron to Uncle Sugar when our combat tour ends.

To help accomplish this I am assigning each of you to fly wing on an experienced section leader, with the other wingman in the section also experienced. Thus you will have not only a leader but also a friend with you when you first "meet the elephant." [This was an old Civil War term used by vets when advising new recruits before their first battle.] We are carefully briefed by intelligence officers here before each mission, and make detailed plans for each strike based upon the latest information available about the target. We try to stick with this premission plan if possible, changing to an alternative one only when circumstances or targets make it necessary. You won't have to worry about changes however, as your job is to fly wing and support your leader and section in whatever he does. Flying combat and staying alive is a team effort and this effort is one of the main reasons why we have far fewer losses when we hit the Japs than they have when they hit us.

A discussion of team effort invariably leads to lengthy lists of what a pilot should do in almost any situation that arises. I am not against this sound concept, which includes checkoff lists, emergency procedures, safety checks, and other programs. But I have a theory that takes this idea a step further. It's really quite simple—you must also know what not to do. Often the best way to keep from getting hurt is to know what not to do!

Assuming that each of you already knows, or thinks he knows, most of the things to do regarding operational flying procedures, basic tactics, use of weapons, and dozens of other procedures too numerous to cover in this briefing, I am going to spend the remainder of this talk stressing some things you must never do and give you good solid reasons why.

First, do not ever be a loner. Whenever you are alone in a Japanese target area you become the number one target of both

242

enemy fighters and anti-aircraft fire. Our dive-bombing tactics are designed to keep us together up to the individual dives, and bring us back together quickly after each bomb is fired. Any carelessness during this time—any individual variation from squadron tactical team doctrine to do your own thing—may be fatal to you. You may be surprised to know that the observation most often made at a debriefing, when discussing a missing pilot, is: "The last time that I saw him was in the breakup for the dive." If you get lost from your section at this time, and see other friendly planes, go join up and return to the force with them. Our strengths against fighter attacks are close formation flying and good gunnery from both our rear gunners and our front-firing cannons. So keep your leader in sight, even in your dive; get back into formation quickly; do not get caught alone.

Second, do not press any attacks too low. The moment you get low sets the stage for several adverse things to happen. Your plane (and you) can be blown apart from bomb blast or a secondary explosion of enemy ammunition or fuel under attack. I learned this lesson at Tulagi-Gavutu on 7 August 1942 when an ammunition dump I was strafing exploded in front of me and almost got me at two hundred feet altitude. Going too low may find you striking strange objects such as trees, hillsides, or the surface of the ground or sea—a quite permanent type of error. If you are too low and take a hit you do not have that extra margin of altitude to help you make it to the lifeguard submarine pickup point, and you need five hundred feet to bail out safely. In a dive-bomber the low flyer often becomes a slow flyer and this leads to disaster from any gun fired by anyone below.

Third, do not get careless in your operational flying at any time. A high percentage of our losses have been operational ones —going in on takeoff, midair collisions, and bad landings. You are just as dead from an operational crash, and a loss to our efforts, as if you were shot down by an enemy fighter or AA fire. A simple error in performing your checkoff lists properly can result in an operational loss. Never take a chance unless there is real need to.

I will close with this thought. When we go on a mission, no matter how successful it may be, something is lost from that success if we lose a plane. It is especially bad for both the guy lost and his next-of-kin back home. You are part of a team and vital to it, so you are of no value to that team dead. We have two sayings around here: (1) take care of your ass first, then do something for the flag, and (2) a little ditty that goes like this:

He who drops his bomb and runs away,
Lives to drop a bomb another day.

I cannot say that these things you do not do will bring you back from a mission—but they should help. Welcome aboard.

VIII

The next mission for Task Force Fifty-eight was to be a big one —support the invasion and capture of the Marianas Islands of Saipan, Tinian, Rota, and Guam. First landings would take place at Saipan on 15 June 1944 with preinvasion softening-up raids scheduled to begin on the twelfth. *Hornet* was assigned the town of Agana and the airfield at Orote Point on Guam as targets.

As the task force approached the Marianas, a variation of the dawn fighter sweep was made by our fighters. Instead of waiting for dawn of the twelfth, an afternoon launch of 212 F6Fs went in from about 175 miles east the day before. The fighters were accompanied by ten Helldivers carrying special life-raft kits to drop to any pilots shot down; I flew one of them. Lt. Comdr. Bill Dean, CO of VF-2, led his flight to the airfields on Rota and Guam. About 30 Zeros were shot down at Orote by our fighters and, in all, approximately 150 Japanese planes were destroyed by task group fighters throughout the islands. The cost was eleven Hellcats with three pilots rescued. This was the first of several big days that VF-2 would have in the Marianas and Bonins areas in shooting down record numbers of enemy aircraft.

I led a strike on each of two days, 12 and 13 June 1944. The Japanese AA fire at Orote was some of the heaviest we had encountered since starting this war cruise in March. In the two days, TF-58 destroyed all the existing aircraft operating from the fields in the Marianas complex and what little shipping that was around. On the second day, my division found an AK (cargo ship) underway near Guam, we dove on it, scoring hits that caused the ship to blow apart and sink. There was no doubt about this one as we brought home pictures showing it going down—a confirmed kill. Because pictures ended any arguments about hits or sinkings, I had at least one K-20 camera along in my division at all times to take photos, if target conditions permitted, of any damage done. When enemy fighters were about we seldom got pictures, as we never hung around a target under the threat of fighter interception.

After only two days in the Marianas, Clark and TG-58.1 received orders, along with Rear Adm. W. K. "Keen" Harrill commanding TG-58.4, to move north and hit the Bonins as the Japanese were staging additional planes down from the home islands in an attempt to resist the Saipan invasion just starting. With these orders, the first of the famous "Jocko Jima" raids was about to begin.

The word *jima* means island in Japanese. Islands such as Chichi, Haha, Muko, and Iwo were all part of the Nanpo Shoto, a chain that begins at the entrance of Tokyo Bay and runs southerly roughly along the 140-degree-west longitudinal line. At around six hundred miles from Tokyo you come to the Bonins with Chichi, Haha, and Muko Jimas; another one hundred miles more or less and you are at Iwo Jima, a part of the Volcano group. These first attacks on the Jimas had us almost in the Emperor's back pocket and were the closest anyone had been to Japan since the Doolittle Tokyo Raid in April 1942.

Unknown to any of us junior officers at the time, a drama of some magnitude was going on behind the scenes between Harrill and Clark regarding the orders received from Mitscher. Using as excuses the possibility of the main Japanese carrier fleet coming out for battle and heavy weather predictions for the Bonins area, Harrill told Clark "he did not want to go north to hit the Jimas." Our admiral was concerned by this action, and went to *Essex* (Harrill's flagship) for a conference; Clark describes this meeting:

> [Harrill's] reluctance to carry out [Mitscher's] orders surprised me. Formerly a top flight officer, he now seemed to have lost his zip. After spending hours trying to convince him of the importance of stopping the Japanese air threat from the north, I finally said in exasperation: If you do not join me in this job I will do it all myself. After that remark he agreed to participate, but he provided only token assistance. Nevertheless, seven carriers were better than four, and though concerned about Harrill, I returned to my flagship satisfied. [11]

Moving north quickly, planes from Jocko's four carriers hit Chichi Jima and Iwo Jima on the afternoon of 15 June, while Harrill's carriers provided combat air patrol over the forces. Our fighters, with VF-2 having another good day, shot down twenty-four Zeros over the targets and destroyed more on the airfield ramps.

My strike was against the harbor area installations of Chichi Jima, a target that proved difficult because of the terrain. The harbor was completely surrounded by rugged hills, with only a small opening to the west for escape. To attack targets in the harbor required dives into a bowl-like area nicknamed the "punch bowl." The AA fire here was heavy and unique—one could get shot at both from below and from hillside emplacements. The shells would come downward toward our planes from the hills as we withdrew across the bay to exit through the opening to the west, as well as from ships and shore batteries below. VB-2 lost Lt. Dan Galvin on one of the first raids and he was to survive in a Japanese prisoner-of-war camp in Japan. I never knew if his gunner made it or not. Chichi Jima was a tough, dirty target that always scared the hell out of me and left me feeling like I hadn't accomplished anything except to stay alive when I got safely outside the bowl again. I preferred to hit Iwo Jima—at least its AA fire only came from one direction.

After two days of hitting anything that moved and some things that didn't on and around the Bonins, we departed to the southwest. The Jimas were located midway between Japan and the Marianas, where the invasion of Saipan was proceeding on schedule. We were sailing to rejoin the other half of Task Force Fifty-eight in the Marianas area.

The latest intelligence reports indicated that a large part of the Japanese carrier fleet had left its bases and was headed toward the invasion site. It was a reported enemy force of as many as nine carriers and 450 aircraft. Clark launched a twelve-plane search out 350 miles to the west on 17 June; I flew one of the sectors with a F6F escort, a five-hour flight in which we made no contacts as the Japanese fleet was still seven hundred miles to the west.

Admiral Clark revealed in his autobiography that he almost took his Task Group 58.1 on a continuing southwestward course toward the advancing Japanese fleet that night of 17 June 1944. When Harrill refused to accompany him with Task Group 58.4, Jocko had second thoughts about taking on the Japanese with only his four carriers and finally turned to a southeast heading to join the rest of Task Force Fifty-eight west of Guam. If Clark had gotten Harrill to keep going with him to the Japanese fleet, the Marianas Turkey Shoot coming up on 19–20 June would probably never have happened as it did; instead a true carrier-versus-carrier battle at sea would have taken place.

Until his dying day, Clark felt that a great opportunity to smash the approaching Japanese carriers was lost. A chance to get the enemy between two U.S. carrier forces west of the Marianas was not taken and instead we waited for the Japanese to come to us. Clark also stated that he did not want to embarrass Mitscher before Spruance, who was supreme commander of the Fifth Fleet. So instead of a decisive final carrier-versus-carrier battle, we had the Turkey Shoot, an almost suicidal mission into darkness that, while breaking the back of Japan's naval air power, left four enemy carriers to embark (without aircraft) one last time four months later at Leyte Gulf.

11

THE TURKEY SHOOT

I

ON 19 June, the first Japanese carrier planes arrived at TF-58 in the early morning. All day long these dive-bombers and fighters kept coming, and our fighters kept shooting them down. The few that made it through the interceptions to attack our ships were promptly downed with AA fire.

This Japanese tactic of sending in attacks from outside our range of approximately 275 miles, and then landing the aircraft at airfields in the Marianas to rearm and refuel before attacking again and returning to the carriers, was an excellent one. It was a carbon copy of what the Americans did on 13–16 November 1942 with Air Group Ten off *Enterprise,* using Henderson Field, in the final defense of Guadalcanal with considerable success, only on a lesser scale. For the Japanese Navy, the operation became one of tactical execution against a combination of superb fighter direction radar-controlled intercepts, with U.S. pilots flying sound tactics and gunnery in their Hellcats and bombing the island airfields with their Helldivers and Avengers.

In conjunction with this tactical policy of keeping the Japanese airfields bombed out, I took a final late afternoon flight against Orote Point field on Guam. It was a routine mission to crater the runways and bomb out any aircraft that might have arrived unobserved since the last strike earlier. I had two divisions of fighters with me, led by Lt. Russ Reiserer, an old friend from Big E days in 1942, who was CO of a small unit that usually flew night missions only. With VF-2 getting many kills around the forces that day, Russ had talked *Hornet* brass into letting him get a chance at some day kills.

We were rendezvousing after bombing the field when a large flight of Japanese aircraft appeared and began breaking for landings. It was a group of carrier-type Vals and Zeros that had somehow missed the task groups to the west and now needed to land and refuel before attacking. Flight leaders tally-hoed these bandits and Reiserer's flight went to work. He dropped into the landing pattern and started firing into the circling aircraft; when he was through he had scored five kills. A VF-2 pilot, Ens. Wilbur "Spider" Webb, shot down six, while two others in the flight got four each. Thus four *Hornet*-based pilots downed nineteen Japanese aircraft in a few minutes of action.

Recently I met Spider Webb at a *Hornet* club reunion and we got to talking about his tremendous feat at Orote on 19 June 1944. I asked him for his own story about this action to include in this book. He sent me some materials, including an article that appeared some years ago in *Scuttlebutt*, a Silver Eagles Association journal. I have edited it for inclusion here.

II

Late in the day of the Marianas Turkey Shoot all pilots of AG-2 had flown one or two strikes against Guam, or patrols over the task force. When a last strike was scheduled, Ens. Spider Webb volunteered to go, and was tail-end Charlie of a high-cover division from VF-2.

As the group was leaving the target area, Spider spotted a downed pilot in a one-man raft about one hundred yards off the tip of Orote Peninsula. There was also an OS2U cruiser plane on the water about three miles out, apparently picking up another downed pilot. Webb asked permission to drop down and cover the man in the raft, and his section leader went to protect the OS2U.

He circled the downed pilot, marking the area with two packets of dye, and then decided to try to throw him a life raft as a spare. While thus engaged, Spider spotted a long line of aircraft low over the mountains heading for the Orote airstrip. The big red meatballs on the sides and wings meant that these were more Japanese aircraft arriving from their carriers to the west.

Turning toward this mass of aircraft, Spider made one of the famous radio transmissions of the Pacific war: "Any American fighter near Orote Peninsula, I have forty Jap planes surrounded and need a little help." He also called his section leader, saying that he was going to attack as the Japanese had not yet seen him; he was less than one hundred yards from a section of Vals and below them as they were letting down to land.

Sliding into the traffic pattern of Japanese aircraft, he positioned himself behind a three-plane section of Vals and opened fire on the left plane. After a short burst the plane exploded and he moved behind the center one. It too exploded at the left wing root. Spider was so close to these victims that he had to skid his plane to remain behind them. He then moved to the third plane in the section—it exploded at the right wing root and fell apart.

The rear gunners of the Vals had already housed their guns for landing, and the ground gunners could not fire at Webb without hitting their own planes, so the greatest danger was debris from exploding targets at point-blank range. Webb moved behind a second section of three Vals and opened up again. The rear gunners were frantically clearing their guns and starting to fire. With only four of his .50s now firing, Spider hit the left plane gunner and pilot, flames covered the center section of the plane, and it nosed down and crashed into the water below. A second plane did not want to burn, and if it had not exploded, he would have collided with it. Pieces of this fifth plane hit his Hellcat. These planes were shot down at below five hundred feet altitude and at a point-blank range of one hundred feet or less.

With guns starting to malfunction, Webb broke away to clear them. He then hit a sixth, lone Val turning on final landing approach, flaming it with a short burst that sent it into the rock ledge of Orote Peninsula. Pulling up to three hundred feet he attacked two more Vals still in formation, fired both, but did not see them go in. With no gun camera film left to verify these runs, he was not credited with kills—only probables. (Personally, I think that he got both.)

Vice Admiral Mitscher must have thought so too. He recommended Ensign Webb for a Congressional Medal of Honor. He ended up with a Navy Cross for this action. When he landed back on *Hornet,* his landing gear had been partly shot away, he had no canopy, and his goggles had been shot off his flight helmet. Without a scratch Spider climbed down from a plane with 147 bullet holes in it. After it was stripped for spare parts, his sturdy steed was given a proper burial at sea.

III

By day's end Task Force Fifty-eight had eliminated at least 385 enemy aircraft, with Jocko's task group downing 109 and VF-2 getting 51 of the total, a new high for a squadron in one day's combat efforts. (VF-2 would beat this total five days later over Iwo Jima with 67 victories in one day.) The Turkey Shoot was the single greatest aerial victory of the Pacific war. Forty F6Fs were lost, with many pilots rescued; this worked out to a ratio of almost ten to one in our favor. Not one U.S. aircraft carrier was damaged.

But this battle was not over. The twentieth of June found task force scouts hunting 325 miles to the west for the Japanese carriers from which the attacks of the previous day had originated. We spent the day in the ready room on combat alert, dressed in full flight gear, waiting to man planes of the scheduled attack group. I was to lead my division of six with the Skipper set to go with nine. I did not like going on a key strike with Soupy along, but as CO he was determined to go. This was probably my last chance to dive on a Japanese carrier so I briefed my flight carefully; we would operate as a unit of six—to hell with whatever foul-up the CO might get into—we would hit a Japanese carrier if there was one within range.

Hours of tense waiting passed slowly. By 1530 in the afternoon I had about come to the conclusion that the Japanese would not be found with time enough left to attack them before darkness. Then exciting news from air plot to our ready room: The main Japanese carrier fleet had been found! Lt. Robert S. Nelson, in a TBF from *Wasp,* had located the Japanese bearing 290 degrees, distance 275 miles.

I had inscribed a large circle on my plotting board with a radius of 250 miles, the maximum distance I felt that I could take my division on a strike and return with enough fuel to get everyone back aboard safely. When I plotted the reported contact it fell outside my safe circle. Then the contact position was moved still further west until we would be going at least three hundred miles to hit the Japanese carriers. Going beyond fuel range was only one part of the problem—due to the late hour we would barely get to the enemy in daylight, and faced night landings upon return.

The hardest decision Vice Adm. Marc Mitscher had to make in the Pacific war against the Japanese was this one: "Launch first deckloads as soon as possible," with a final admonishment to all pilots—"Get the carriers!" At 1624 the first of 240 aircraft from eleven aircraft carriers took off and by 1636 a superbly executed launch was completed. "Fourteen of these aborted for various reasons and returned to their ships. Of the planes that continued, 95 were Hellcats (some carrying 500-pounders), 54 were Avengers (only a few carried torpedoes, the rest four 500-pounders), 51 were Helldivers with 1,500-pound loads, and the remaining 26 planes were Dauntlesses flying on their last carrier battle. [1]

From a purely personal viewpoint, I have always thought that the most amazing thing about this mission was that it ever took place at all. Almost all the pilots leaving the carriers, certainly all the flight leaders, knew they were going beyond normal gas range to hit the enemy. If the Japanese made such a strike against our fleet, we would dub it a suicide mission, but when U.S. leaders launched us on 20 June 1944, it was seriously considered an acceptable risk. It was, of course, much more, and the terrible losses in aircraft that resulted—losses in lives too that might have been still greater had rough seas caused ditchings and hampered the unprecedented rescue efforts—marks this as the costliest single mission in naval aviation history, except perhaps the Battle of Midway.

Yet, almost to a man, we went on the mission as ordered, knowing that chances of a safe return to a flight deck were at best severely limited. These young men, just as their brothers-in-arms had done two years before at Midway, departed with an eagerness to engage the enemy and to hell with the consequences. Unlike the Japanese foe, these Americans loved life and lived it to the hilt. There were no thoughts of suicide or hara-kiri, only a deep desire to take part in the big one—to win at all costs. The men who flew into the sunset on 20 June 1944 were perpetuating all those treasured traditions of the first naval aviators.

My division came together smoothly, and we began a slow fuel-saving climb on course toward the target. I had six aircraft and did not know that one of my regular pilots, Don Ransom, had not gotten off the deck and had been replaced by a standby, Lt. (jg) Art Doherty, who was destined to make this important strike with me. I did not know where the Skipper was with the rest of VB-2's aircraft and could not spare the time or fuel to look for him. We were leading the bombers from TG-58.1; we had fighter cover; I was in radio contact with Comdr. Jackson D. Arnold, our CAG; and we were on our way to bomb the Japanese fleet.

As we flew along, I remembered another mission into darkness made on 24 August 1942. That time I was an ensign flying wing on Skipper Turner Caldwell; we missed the Japanese fleet and went to Guadalcanal's Henderson Field as a lifesaving alternative to the battle-damaged Big E. This time I was a division leader with my own flight, headed northwest in the waning daylight again looking for the Japanese fleet, but with one big difference—there was no safety valve in the form of an island airfield. I said a short prayer: Please, God, help me lead my flight to an enemy carrier for a successful attack and then safely home.

I felt a surge of confidence pass through me—my guardian angel was on duty and had heard my prayer. Scanning ahead to the horizon for the Japanese fleet that I now knew would be there, we six killer angels flew on.

IV

As the strike formation of aircraft from Task Group 58.1 approached the armada of Japanese warships heading into the afternoon sunset, it was a formidable group. In the lead was *Hornet*'s AG-2, followed by *Yorktown*'s AG-1, *Bataan*'s AG-50, and *Belleau Wood*'s AG-24. In charge of this mass flight of seventy-five aircraft from four U.S. carriers was my CAG, Comdr. Jackson D. Arnold.

Of the two Japanese carrier divisions spread out on the ocean far below, Arnold picked Ozawa's Division One flagship as the target for attack. Switching on his voice radio, he ordered all Ripper (AG-2) planes to attack *Zuikaku*. He reported later: "I told them that that was their ticket home."

In excellent position to initiate an immediate dive, I requested from Arnold: "This is Ripper Hal. I request permission to dive now." His reply was: "Go ahead Hal, show them how it's done."

Receiving this clearance from Ripper Strike Leader, I moved down and away with my division of six Helldivers and bored straight in with a high-speed approach. The thought going through my mind was that, at last, I had a large enemy aircraft carrier below me and my own division of dive-bombers to take down on it. By moving in first, some surprise might be achieved, but more importantly I wanted to get some bombs on that big deck before anyone else—after more than two years of sea combat, and many dives upon enemy warships but no carrier, this enemy flattop was mine!

Words cannot describe the AA fire that began coming up from the huge circular Japanese task force formation of eleven ships as my Helldiver group moved into a break position for our dives. In the lead plane I was a focal point, and with the mass of shells passing all about me, I felt like I was diving into an Iowa plains hailstorm. In addition to tracer ammunition, the enemy ships were using shells that exploded in a variety of bright colors. Some threw out long tentacles of flaming white phosphorus unlike anything I had ever seen before.

As I pushed over into my final dive at about twelve thousand feet, the AA fire became so intense in my immediate vicinity that I saw no way of getting through it. I had never encountered such flak. My dive brakes were already open and I was well into a good dive, but because of the potent defensive fire, I felt like I was moving in slow motion in quicksand. I would never make it. At this point I did something I had never done before in a dive—I closed my dive brakes. My plane responded by dropping like a stone toward the target below, leaving the heavy AA fire behind.

So much for that problem but now I had another more serious one. My speed was building up and, in the clean condition without flaps, I could never expect to pull the plane out of the dive after firing my bomb. Shouting a prayer to my guardian angel, at six thousand feet I placed the dive brake selector back into the open position. The wing dive brakes did what no manufacturing specs said they would—they opened! It was as if a giant hand grabbed my plane by the tail, my headlong plunge slowed, and there was the enemy carrier dead in my sight below me, turning into my flight path along its lengthwise axis. At a point-blank range of two thousand feet, I fired my bombs.

After release I broke my dive and started the pullout, closed the wing flaps, and bent over in the cockpit to activate the bomb bay doors lever, which was mounted on the deck of the plane. At that precise instant, while bent forward and down in the cockpit, my Helldiver and I were struck a savage blow—a direct hit from an enemy AA shell.

The shell struck underneath the starboard wing about eight feet out from the side of the plane, and then traveled up through before exploding two or three feet above the upper surface. A large fragment of shell passed through the open cockpit enclosure, striking me in the back where I was hunched up from bending over. This shrapnel piece passed diagonally right to left across my back from lower right rib cage area to my upper left shoulder, just close enough to slice open my flight suit like the cut of a razor. The force of the blow from this shell fragment, as it tore through my protruding parachute backpack, was like being clubbed from behind with a baseball bat. At the same instant as the blow, I felt a searing stab of pain like a hot iron being pressed against my back. I straightened up in the cockpit and the thought flashed through my mind: "Oh God, I've been hit bad." The burning pain was from a minute bit of the bigger piece of shell, about the size of a .45-caliber bullet, which had buried itself in the middle of my back.

Continuing the pullout, I leveled my stricken Beast at fifty to one hundred feet above the water, and moved between destroyers in the screen who kept blasting away as I passed. The damaged wing was on fire, with a hole about one foot in diameter that was gradually enlarging in size as the edges burned away with a white glow. I still had aileron control with the stick but immediately began having trouble holding the wing up as the size of the burning hole quickly increased. I had to get that fire out fast, before the wing burned away enough to cause loss of control, or structural failure, but how?

The intensity of the heat of the fire burning the aluminum skin of the wing, and thus enlarging the size of the hole, made it white hot in color. Where had I seen this color before? Then I remembered: It was identical to the intense white glow I'd seen many times as a young boy, in a blacksmith's forge, while watching Bill Wern working at his trade back in Plymouth. White heat was caused by forcing air into the burning area by a bellows. Airflow over the wing was having this effect on the hole as the aircraft raced across the waves, taking me away from the Japanese task force. If I reduced the speed of my Helldiver drastically, thus cutting down the force of air passage through the hole, I might get the fire out.

Already outside the screen of Japanese destroyers, one of my wingmen, Dave Stear, joined up with two other aircraft. I turned to port a bit for a homeward heading and began slowing down. By climbing slightly and cutting engine power, I gradually reduced escape speed. But the wing continued to burn and, as the hole grew larger, it became increasingly harder for me to hold the wing up in level flight. I was becoming really concerned when, at 125 knots airspeed, the fire suddenly snuffed out. By this time the hole was nearly a yard across and, even with full trim tab, I was forced to hold the stick far to the left in order to maintain level flight. In the fading twilight, the outer wing beyond the hole was flexing slightly as we flew along. As there was nothing that could be done about it, I offered up a small prayer that the wing would remain intact.

With the fire out, and the plane on a homeward heading and still flying, I could now think of myself. How bad was the wound? I was feeling little actual pain, and was not dizzy or faint, but that could be because my body was still running on natural adrenaline from the excitement of the attack. Reaching behind with my left hand, I felt my lower back—it was wet and sticky. My hand came away covered with blood! While there was a considerable amount of it, I realized that the wound must not be a serious one as I was not feeling weak or having the kind of pain that a major one would cause. Apparently it was something that I could live with.

Setting my feet firmly on the cockpit deck, I unbuckled the seat belt and shoulder harness and raised myself up from the aircraft seat. The result of this action was for the severed parachute backpack and harness to fall away. There would be no bailing out —any emergency would mean a water landing.

When I stood up in the cockpit in the fading daylight, my wingman Dave Stear became concerned. Over my earphones came his urgent voice: "Ripper Hal from Ripper Dave. Don't bail out, Hal, you're too low. Your plane is OK—stay with it—don't bail out!" The sight of me rising up in the cockpit appeared to Dave as a preparation for bailing out, which was the furthest thing from my mind at that point, but I appreciated his concern.

So, with engine settings at maximum cruise and most fuel economy, the forlorn little formation of five planes settled down for the long flight home, as complete darkness enveloped us in its ebony folds.

What had been the results of the attack that I had so brashly led my division into? *Zuikaku* was steaming northwest at twenty-four knots when we dove. William T. Y'Blood describes the attack in his book *Red Sun Setting* as follows:

> On each side of her bow, 1,600 yards away, were the *Myoko* and *Haguro*. In an approximately 2,200-yard circle around the carrier were the *Yahagi* and seven destroyers. Although not supposed to lead the attack, Lt. H. L. Buell's division was in the best position to make a run on the *Zuikaku,* and so he was given permission to lead the way. In an 80-degree dive, Buell led the first six Bombing 2 Helldivers down. The enemy ships opened up with a colorful pyrotechnic display. Into the fiery show the planes dove, releasing their thousand-pounders at about 2,500 feet. The flattop was slewing around in a hard starboard turn as Buell's group dropped on her and presented a "good lengthwise stem-to-stern target." The fliers thought they had made two or three solid hits on the ship, for explosions and fires were seen to start on her.
>
> [Lt. Comdr.] G. B. Campbell led his group of eight planes around a large cloud just north of A Force. . . . These planes pushed over from 12,000 feet and also released their 1,000-pound GP and SAP bombs at 2,500 feet. As Campbell attacked, he saw "one big hole with a fire down inside near the island." Most of the crews noticed large fires raging from amidships forward. Like the pilots of the other division, these Helldiver fliers thought they had scored telling hits on *Zuikaku*.[2]

After VB-2 had finished their attack and scored several hits, Arnold sent Lt. Comdr. J. W. Runyan, CO of VB-1 from *Yorktown,* with thirteen more Helldivers, down on *Zuikaku* to finish her off. Runyan reported seeing a large hole in the carrier with fire coming up from the hangar deck below. Three more hits were tallied as well as several near misses. The ship was burning and smoking so badly that the last two pilots moved their dives over to a nearby cruiser.

Six Avenger planes from our VT-2 then made coordinated runs on the damaged carrier. No hits were scored by torpedoes from these planes, but all made it through the intense AA fire—a miracle in itself. The total attack effort was completed when several fighters from the light carrier *Bataan* made runs with five-hundred-pound bombs. During this phase of the action, one section of these bomb-carrying Hellcats suddenly became involved with fifteen to twenty Zeros, and had to jettison the bombs to fight for their lives as fighters. The leader of this section, a friend named Lt. Cliff Fanning, although wounded and with his F6F badly shot up, made it back to our forces and survived.

The attacks by planes from Task Force 58.1, commanded by Comdr. Jack Arnold, put *Zuikaku* out of the action. The Helldivers of VB-1 and VB-2 had scored eight hits and many near misses. Japanese battle reports examined after the war indicate that fires on the hangar deck got out of control rapidly and damage control parties were forced to use hand fire extinguishers as the water mains were knocked out. An order to abandon ship was given, and Admiral Ozawa was preparing to leave the battered carrier, when damage control personnel began to make headway against the fires, bringing them under control. *Zuikaku* was able to leave the area and eventually made it back to Japan for extensive repairs. She would come out one last time in October 1944 for "Bull's Run," and be sent to the bottom at last in that action, but not as an operational carrier: Her last fight with aircraft aboard, in a carrier-versus-carrier battle, had just been completed here in the Philippine Sea.

One highlight of this action for Buell & Company was a photograph taken by a crewman in a TBF from several thousand feet above the scene. The picture was shot at exactly the moment my division had completed its attack, and shows a mauled and burning *Zuikaku* running for her life. The screening vessels are frantically turning in formation, attempting to stay with the obviously badly hit carrier. The panoramic view has frozen a brief moment of combat time forever in the fading sunlight, a vista of the Japanese empire's "red sun setting." This symbolic picture was widely published at the time, joining other great photographs of the Pacific war that would become historical treasures.

V

I do not remember much about the flight back to Task Force Fifty-eight that night, nor even how many planes were in the small formation following me in the darkness. I think there were at least four, including both Dave Stear and Ralph Yaussi. As we flew along, the voices of other returning pilots kept coming over the air to report they were out of fuel and landing in the water.

Trying not to think about my steadily falling fuel gauge needle, I concentrated on maintaining a direct course back to *Hornet* at the most economic engine settings. I could no longer see my damaged wing and the slow flexing of the outer section in the darkness but could feel the movement in the controls and it was frightening. Continuing to hold the stick in a far left position to main level flight, I kept shifting it between left and right hands as each arm became tired from the strain. The wing might fail without warning, resulting in an uncontrolled crash into the water below, but as time passed I put this possibility out of my mind, and I lived each minute of continuing flight, sipping them like fine cognac.

I do not recall the time passing on the return homeward from the attack. There was little communication with either my wingman Dave Stear or gunner Red Lakey. We flew along in a sort of grim, quiet silence, almost as if in a time warp, the glow from our engine exhausts giving us hope. Lakey had tuned in the homer, and a letter started coming into my earphones—a faint signal but the right one: We were dead on course. There was nothing to be seen yet on the distant horizon, but the signal indicated we were making a direct intercept with *Hornet*.

Since we were among the first planes to make an attack, we were also with the first to arrive back over the task force. Radios came to life as anxious pilots began calling the various carriers for instructions to land. Soon the air was filled with frantic voices all trying to talk at once—each was an emergency due to a low fuel state. Using the air group frequency, I told my flight to pick a carrier and land. The other planes dropped away, leaving Dave and me a solitary pair in the night sky.

From here on events moved swiftly and are a blur in my memory. I picked a large carrier below me and swung around to enter the traffic pattern, telling Dave to break first to land. After he left, and before making any landing preparations, an aircraft appeared from above and dropped across in front of me, almost hitting the plane. I realized that my wing lights were not working and I was hard to see. With so little fuel the engine might quit at any moment —time was running out.

At this instant the ships below began turning searchlights into the sky. I had seen some lights come on a short time before off to my right and now the ships below me were also lighting up. The first lights were Jocko Clark illuminating *Hornet;* the lights below were from *Lexington* as Mitscher gave his famous order to "turn on the lights." Soon the ocean was covered with lighted ships speeding through the night. From above it looked like Coney Island on the Fourth of July.

Not knowing one carrier from another in the darkness, I turned into the landing pattern ahead of the carrier below, and informed Lakey to be prepared for a water landing if the engine should quit. His reply was a frantic plea to get us on the deck as he was a poor swimmer and afraid he could not make it in the water. Heading downwind I decided to try to get aboard, so I put the tail hook down and, holding my breath, moved the wheel indicator to DOWN.

I was not sure what would happen when the big SB2C landing gear dropped because of the drag it would induce. Drastically increasing power to keep flying, I found that to hold up the damaged wing now required full left aileron and all the strength in my right arm. With hook indicating down and full RPM set, I eased around into a final turn up the groove toward the carrier fantail, and put the flaps into the landing position.

As the landing flaps started down, the Beast shuddered and almost spun in. I stopped the flaps at the halfway point and went to full power. My new problem was a complete flap surface on the port wing but only half a surface starboard—the outer part of that flap had burned away. This worked slightly in my favor as the additional drag on the port side, and the rudder needed to compensate, helped me hold the damaged wing in level flight. However, approaching the carrier's ramp, I was in a precarious situation— at full power to keep flying just above a stall, there was no engine power left for a wave off.

I could see that the deck ahead of me was open, my signal was a roger, and I was still flying. Broadcasting my condition, I emphasized that I could not take a late wave off. Due to the cluttered radio traffic, the call was probably not heard, and no signal to stop my landing attempt came. With the breakdown of communications around the task force that night, any individual control by radio was impossible. I continued an approach with my critically damaged Helldiver—still on roger without a wave off.

I was at the ramp in cut position on a roger when suddenly,

without warning, the LSO gave me a last-second wave off. This signal would provoke a crisis if one was in a good airplane in broad daylight, and many a fine pilot has crashed trying to answer it. In my wounded condition at the ramp, a late wave off was telling me to commit suicide. With no power reserve and staggering just above stall, to lower either wing to turn away would put me into the ramp, the spud locker (stern of the ship), or an uncontrolled spiral dive to the ocean. I did the only thing that would give Lakey and myself a chance to survive—I closed the throttle and landed straight ahead on the open deck.

The plane came down squarely amid the arresting cables, but instead of engaging one of them, the hook bounced (this is called a bolter) and so did the Helldiver. We soared just high enough to clear the first two barriers, came down on top of the final one, then tore loose and slid up the deck toward the pack. Dave had landed ahead of me and was still moving into a tie-down spot when we came crashing into his tail. Gunner A2c. W. E. Redman was killed by the impact, and a sailor was also killed in the ship's port catwalk.

Fortunately there was no fire. I cut all engine switches as the crash occurred and, with empty tanks, there was not enough fuel to ignite. The flight deck personnel covered the planes with foam, and began getting us out of the wreckage. Since I was pinned down in the cockpit, it took some moments for the deck crew to release me from the tangled metal, but except for minor cuts and bruises I was freed uninjured, as was Lakey from the rear cockpit. The wrecks were then jettisoned over the side and landings resumed.

When clear of the wreckage, I saw two stretchers containing covered bodies near the carrier's island. I asked someone nearby about them. He replied in an unfeeling way: "Those are the two men you killed with your airplane." A feeling of anguish swept over me as I realized that the crash had been the unwilling cause of the loss of two lives, one a squadron shipmate.

At that moment a marine orderly came up and said that the admiral wanted to see me at once. I followed him into the island and up several ladders, groping in the darkness until we emerged into a night-lighted space. I did not have any idea what carrier this was but knew it wasn't *Hornet* because there was not a single familiar face around me.

I was in Vice Admiral Mitscher's flag operations in *Lexington*. A commander came up to me and I recognized him as Gus Widhelm, air officer on the admiral's staff; we knew each other from the early days of combat in 1942. He was with Capt. Arleigh Burke, chief of staff to Mitscher. Excitedly, Gus grabbed me by the arm and said: "Hal, did you attack a Japanese carrier?"

As calmly as possible, I told them that I had led my division of six Helldivers, followed by my CO with eight more, down on a large carrier of the *Shokaku* class and was sure that several hits were made. Two other carriers nearby were also attacked but, because I took a hit and left the area in my burning plane, I could not confirm anything definite as to damage or whether they had been sunk.

I must have been a pathetic figure standing there in my tattered flight suit, covered with gore and grime from the crash, trying to answer their agitated questions. I was near exhaustion but still on my feet, probably because of the adrenaline still flowing as a result of the situation that led to the crash. Both Widhelm and Burke continued to ply me with questions.

After a brief time, with me at a point of near collapse, the rasping voice of "Fabulous" Marc Mitscher came from the semi-darkness at one end of a divan. Mitscher was famous for compassion for his pilots, and he showed this characteristic now. In a low voice, barely discernible, he spoke:

"Gentlemen, you have questioned the lieutenant enough. Can't you see that he has been hurt and is terribly tired? Young man, you go to sick bay immediately, get yourself checked over, have a couple of brandies, and get a good night's sleep. Further debriefing can wait until tomorrow. Well done in your efforts to sink the enemy's carriers on a tough mission."

I thanked the admiral and departed with an aide to the sick bay. Here a somewhat harassed young doctor gave my back a cursory examination, taped a bandage over the wound, and told me that I had been very lucky—the shell had only grazed me. Departing with three small bottles of cognac, I did not question him about the pain my back had been giving me—if he said it was a minor scratch, so be it.

VI

There is only a hairline's difference between a Navy Cross and a general court-martial.

—LT. GEN. LEWIS B. "CHESTY" PULLER, USMC,
FIVE-TIME WINNER OF THE NAVY CROSS

I ended up rooming for the night with Lt. Jim Seybert, a fighter pilot in VF-16 who was from my home town Ottumwa. Jim was about three years older than me, and thus we had not known each other very well in our high school years. He liked to play country music on a guitar, and I joined in on a harmonica; he helped me get through that night on the *Lexington*. I was feeling despondent about the crash, and Redman was the first man I had lost from a formation under my leadership, so the effect was devastating. I was also worried about the fate of the other aircraft of my division, as I was on a strange ship and was not getting information on losses, as I would have in *Hornet*. Of course, little was yet known about men who went down in the water or who had been rescued, but it was becoming clear that the mission had ended in disaster, with about a hundred planes lost to crashes on decks and into the water from fuel exhaustion.

After a fitful night's sleep and breakfast the next morning, I was summoned to PriFly in the carrier's island. Here I was greeted by a duo of irate regular-Navy officers—the air officer of *Lexington* and the dive-bomber squadron CO. Both proceeded to tear my ass to shreds, using profanity for emphasis, for having crashed on deck the night before after receiving a wave-off from the signal officer. I tried my best to explain the reason for my actions, which had been based upon a battle-damaged Helldiver and an intense desire to survive a situation not of my making. I pointed out that without the unfortunate hook bounce I would have made a successful arrested landing under very adverse conditions.

Neither of the two officers was in a mood to listen to anything that I had to say in my defense. At this point the air officer (I don't remember his name) stated that he was recommending me for a court-martial. His use of profanity had already raised my dander —the threatened court-martial charge got me mad. Using a few choice words myself, I told him to go ahead if he wished. I would ask my captain and admiral in *Hornet* to be judged by my peers—

fighting pilots with the same amount of combat flying time as I had —if they could find enough such pilots for the job. Fuming with anger, I left PriFly.

One sad assignment remained to be discharged before Lakey, Stear, and I could move by destroyer back to *Hornet*. Early that afternoon the bodies of Redman and the deck sailor killed in the crash were prepared for burial at sea. The three of us plus one chief from *Lexington* served as escorts for Redman. The flag-draped bodies were placed on low platforms on the port side deck-edge elevator at hangar deck level. The elevator was then raised to the flight deck, where ship's company and air group personnel stood at attention while burial rites, including rifle volleys and taps, were conducted. On signal we lifted the inboard end of the plat-form board, tilting it so that the wrapped, weighted remains slid from under the flag cover and dropped over the side into the sea. Although trying desperately to keep my emotions under control while serving as burial escort leader for a fallen comrade, tears ran down my face as the body disappeared into the blue Pacific.

The episode with the two officers, combined with the burial ceremony, had me close to an emotional breaking point when I climbed from the destroyer's bosun chair onto the deck of *Hornet*. And I was beginning to have pain in the form of a throbbing irrita-tion from my "scratch" back wound. Hundreds of *Hornet*'s officers and crew were milling about congratulating us, patting us and grasping our hands. We were like football players receiving acco-lades from fans after a winning touchdown in the championship game. I winced each time my back was struck.

Part of the reason for this display of emotion was that VB-2 had been officially credited with sinking a *Shokaku*-class Japanese car-rier in the mission of 20 June, now being called "Mitscher's Sunday Punch" by newspaper correspondents, along with the sobriquet of "Marianas Turkey Shoot" for the two-day battle. Attacks by two squadrons of Helldivers on *Zuikaku* had scored at least eight credited hits and several near misses and she was believed to have gone down. And all of my division had been accounted for without a loss, except for Redman.

The air boss of *Hornet*, Comdr. Roy Johnson, immediately took me up to the admiral's bridge, where Jocko gave me a personal handshake and a well done. Then I related to Johnson my sad tale about the threatened court-martial. He became quite angry and promised me that he would take care of the matter. It seems that the *Lexington* air officer was a friend and classmate of his. Years later Admiral Johnson told me that he had kept his promise to me through direct contact with the officer, and no charge was ever brought against me. All I knew was that nothing more was said about the event. (The *Lexington* officer involved was killed a short time later in an airplane crash.)

Leaving the flag bridge, I headed for the sick bay and looked up our air group flight surgeon, Lt. Comdr. Doc Stratton. I told him that my back was bothering me, and took off my shirt and undershirt for an examination. He gave a low whistle and an oath when he saw my bare back as he removed the adhesive bandage. An angry red circle of infection about the size of a salad plate surrounded the oozing wound. Using a probe and tweezers, he found the small fragment of shell embedded in my flesh and removed it. A few stitches, some sulfa powder and pills, and a day's rest found me feeling as if I had never been hit. I have the suspicion that when Doc Stratton's medical report about the incident went forward, a certain young medic in *Lexington* probably needed first aid for wounds to his posterior.

Leading the attack on *Zuikaku* in the first battle of the Philippine Sea was clearly my greatest achievement in three combat war cruises against the Japanese in the Pacific war. Last of the original enemy aircraft carriers that took part in the infamous Pearl Harbor defeat, her near destruction in this attack gave me a deep sense of satisfaction. After being present at all four previous carrier-versus-carrier battles without getting a crack at a Japanese carrier, I had led my division, and VB-2, in one of the most successful attacks against a major one, scoring more confirmed hits than had been made against most such targets in the past four of these battles. The fact that *Zuikaku* did not sink took nothing away from the efficiency of our attack but, rather, was a credit to the Japanese crew who kept fighting the fires and saved their ship.

The attack had been costly to VB-2, especially in aircraft. In addition to Redman, we lost Lt. (jg) Jack H. Wells and A2c. Jacob V. Crout, an experienced crew flying in the skipper's second section. Their plane was last seen entering an attack dive. They may have been shot down by the intense AA fire, or by one of the many Zeros marauding about the Japanese carriers attacking loners after the dives. It is quite certain they were lost at the target

—our only casualty to enemy action—and not later in a water landing.

Of fourteen VB-2 Helldivers that took off for the mission into darkness, only five—Campbell, Hiigel, Looney, Stear, and I—landed back aboard a deck, with three of these suffering strike damages. In addition to one shot down, eight went into the drink on the flight back and at various points around the task forces; these planes were piloted by Sonnenberg, McGee, Bush, Scheurer, Ewing, Doherty, Taylor, and Yaussi. All of these pilots and their gunners were saved by destroyers in an elaborate rescue effort that began that night around the task forces and continued for several days afterward. Mitscher and Spruance gave up pursuit of the fleeing Japanese fleet to save the men who had given everything to carry out a suicide strike against it.

Aircraft losses in Task Force Fifty-eight for the mission into darkness beyond fuel range were sobering. The Belote brothers, in their book *Titans of the Seas,* summarize the attack as follows:

> By [Vice Admiral] Mitscher's reckoning only six fighters, ten dive bombers, and four torpedo planes, 20 aircraft altogether, had been lost in combat. But 17 fighters, 35 dive bombers, and 28 Avengers had been lost in deck crashes and water landings. Exactly 100 planes of 216 reaching the target area had been lost. Yet personnel losses had hardly been greater than in the Turkey Shoot the day before. The final count came to 16 pilots, 22 air crew, two deck officers, and four ships' enlisted crewmen killed or missing.[3]

It did not take long for Task Force Fifty-eight to return to full strength after its losses. CVE carriers loaded with replacement aircraft rendezvoused with the force within days and several AG-2 pilots left *Hornet* to bring planes back from them. I assigned myself to this ferry group and on 30 June flew a new Helldiver from *Copahee* to augment our squadron complement; it was my first flight since the crash.

When I was catapulted from the CVE to fly to *Hornet,* I felt exhilarated at being in the air again. Yet while the crash on the *Lexington* had not left me with a fear of flying, it had shaken my prior feeling of invincibility. Deep inside I had always felt that I would make it through a mission and firmly believed that sound flying principles helped in this effort. A great division who flew well together, we were getting good results in our efforts against the enemy. I lived pretty much day to day, took each mission as it came without worry beforehand, and had as much fun as possible during liberty times. There were still comely girls to chase (and sometimes catch), lots of booze to drink, and no end to Japanese targets yet in sight.

But because of the close call in the mission into darkness, the realization that I could be hit and hurt just like anyone else would not entirely leave my mind. I knew that I could not let this feeling of vulnerability affect me lest it influence my division and strike leadership capabilities.

So I accepted it. Another old cliche came to mind—my life has been seriously affected by cliches—this one written by Shakespeare:

> *Cowards die many times before their deaths;*
> *The valiant never taste of death but once.*

I still believed in my guardian angel, and credited him for helping me through the tragic Philippine Sea adventure. But I also came to the rather morbid conclusion that it was just a matter of time before I would be hit again, perhaps for good. With a sense of finality, rather than worry excessively about my coming demise, I simply put the thought from my mind, went back to flying and fighting as before, and prayed a little harder that I could keep going and not let down my comrades who were depending upon me for direction and leadership.

Considerate squadron and ship friends helped me through this period. I did not receive a single negative word about the crash from Rear Admiral Clark or his staff. I was recommended, along with others, for a Navy Cross for leading the attack. I learned later from Clark's autobiography that he, as a young pilot, had gone through a time of stress due to the loss of several friends in aviation accidents:

Duke Ramsey's words came to my mind: "Even though you crash and even though somebody gets killed, it's incident to service. If we stop flying because of mistakes, there will be no progress. Aviation must carry on." Those of us who were left strove to make certain that the others did not die in vain.[4]

Pilots crashed all over the fleet that night—some with fatal results. Many took their own cuts; *Enterprise* scored a first ever with two aircraft in the deck gear simultaneously without a scratch to either. CAG Arnold crashed through the *Hornet*'s barriers, his F6F caught fire, and the aircraft, with valuable photographs in its cameras, had to be jettisoned over the side. Most of the crashes, including those into the water, involved planes that were running out of fuel, not battle-damaged ones like mine. As I went over the episode in my mind, one nagging question kept coming up: After flying all the way to a cut position, and with a clear deck ahead, why had I received a "graveyard wave off" at the ramp?

VII

An answer to this obstinate question came in an unexpected manner some ten weeks later. Enclosed in a letter from my sister Edith Newell was a news story from the *Ottumwa Courier* that had appeared in August. It had been written by a correspondent in *Lexington*, released by the Navy, and contained an interesting account of that fateful night in June:

Aboard Carrier Flagship Off Marianas.—It was a nightmare aboard [*Lexington*], landing signal officers said, when American planes came back from sinking some of Japan's finest carriers west of the Marianas islands.

They were all in a tremendous rush to find a carrier and land before they ran out of gas. They came in five or six at a time. "All I could do," a signal officer said, "was wave them off. And then there'd be another bunch."

Some planes had no lights. The signal officer tried desperately to judge their position in the groove—the path up which the planes must come if they are to land safely—by the dim flicker of their exhausts. *Speed is judged by listening intently to the sound of the engines.* [my italics] Another signal officer was standing by with a spotlight to see whether each plane had wheels down and flaps set.

Once two bombers came up the groove together. Only one saw the signaled wave-off; the other tried to land. Several more came rushing along behind it. "We hit the deck fast" the signal

268

officer recalled. "Three or four went over us so low it seemed they almost grazed us, flat as we were."

So there was the explanation. In the darkness, with no lights to help determine my plane's attitude (staggering just above stall at the ramp, with full engine power roaring), the signal officer had assumed from the sound that I was too fast and had waved me off. I do not blame him for this choice. The sad part of it was that, under this set of circumstances in my battle-damaged Helldiver in the dark, I would never have received a cut no matter how perfect an approach I flew. After taking a forced cut to survive, I had to have some luck and catch a landing wire for an arrested landing, rather than have a hook bounce followed by a ricochet and partial barrier crash. Fate determined the latter ending to this sequel, two men died in the crash, and I have had to carry the burden of the tragedy since.

I want to say a few words about survival at this point. I guess all pilots have this instinct to a higher degree than most men performing less-demanding tasks. I know that aviators doing test work, or in combat, develop a high survival sense or they don't make it to old age. Recently I found a description of what this business of flying and surviving has always meant to me. Written by Gen. Chuck Yeager, a combat fighter ace and probably the foremost test pilot of his generation, he puts into words the enigmatic emotion that is called the survival instinct:

> You learn all you can about [a plane] and its systems. . . . You know when you're in sync with the machine, so plugged into its instruments and controls that your mind and your hand become the heart of its operating system. You can make that airplane talk, and like a good horse, the machine knows when it's in competent hands. You know what you can get away with. And you can be wrong only once. You smile reading newspaper stories about a pilot in a disabled plane that maneuvered to miss a schoolyard before he hit the ground. That's crap. In an emergency situation, a pilot thinks only about one thing—survival. You battle to survive right down to the ground; you think about nothing else. Your concentration is riveted on what to try next . . . you aren't even aware that a schoolyard exists. That's exactly how it is. . . . You count on your experience, concentration, and instincts to pull you through. And luck. Without luck . . .[5]

What Yeager calls luck, I might call a guardian angel.

The *Lexington* crash was to be the only time I would damage an airplane in approximately 450 carrier landings during my career as a tailhooker. Flying both prop and jet fighters and attack aircraft, doing day, night, and all-weather carrier operations over the years, I watched with increasing concern as the aircraft got heavier, the landing speeds faster, and the fragile link between the LSO and pilot deteriorate into near chaos. There was no longer enough time for two men, only one the actual pilot in control, to exchange landing information in an approach and consistently bring a carrier jet to a safe landing, under all conditions of weather and darkness, aboard a straight-deck carrier. The accident rates soared, with prohibitive costs in both human lives and treasure; the tailhook Navy was in serious trouble.

At this critical point a major breakthrough in carrier design—the angled-deck concept—solved the problem. With a barrier-free angled deck, a landing mirror, and the LSO in an advisory capacity, the pilot was in sole control of landing his plane aboard a carrier deck just as when landing on an airfield.[6] Exactly nine years after my crash on *Lexington*, as CO of VF-84 and CAG of a group of aircraft that completed the testing of America's first angled-deck carrier *Antietam*, we demonstrated the concept to the British Navy, originators of the idea, in June and July 1953. To celebrate this happy occasion, I composed the following limerick:

> *A tailhooker fresh out of tech,*
> *Asked God to help save his neck.*
> *The Lord heard his plea,*
> *From far out at sea,*
> *And sent him the first angled deck.*

12

THE JOCKO JIMAS AND THE PHILIPPINES

I

AT THE command of the ever-aggressive Jocko Clark, our task group, although short in attack aircraft after the mission into darkness, made a quick strike against the Japanese-held island of Pagan, then Iwo Jima, on 24 June while passing by on the way back to Eniwetok. VB-2 sent a strike into Pagan and found nothing worth the trip. But when VF-2's Hellcat fighter sweep arrived at Iwo, Jocko's luck in finding Japanese planes to destroy held. About 70 aircraft of 122 at the fields took off; in the ensuing battle, twenty-four enemy fighters and five torpedo bombers were shot down at a loss of six F6Fs. A second strike of forty-one enemy planes then came out, were intercepted, and seventeen shot down. Thus, counting snoopers and isolated planes, more than seventy Japanese aircraft were destroyed in this one-day foray.

During the brief rest period back in port several visiting journalists from the big news syndicates came aboard *Hornet* for stories about AG-2. VB-2's attack of *Zuikaku* in the night mission, combined with the fantastic kill scores by VF-2 against enemy aircraft, made the air group hot copy. The fighter XO, Tex Harris, an old friend from Big E days in 1942, called me to come to the fighter ready room. A photographer was there from Associated Press and he wanted a shot of "that crazy guy who dove first on the Japs."

He ended up taking a picture of Dad Taylor and me shaking hands and grinning.

I never thought much about the episode until a few weeks later, when letters from relatives and friends containing the photo began arriving. The shot, and an accompanying story by Charles Arnot, was picked up by newspapers and Dad and I were famous for two days—11 and 12 July 1944—coast to coast!

It was reorganization time for TF-58, and many individual ships and high-level commanders began to be relieved, being replaced by new ships and leadership. But things in *Hornet,* and for AG-2, remained the same and we left port to return to the Jimas again after refueling and replenishment.

We hit all the Jimas with an old-fashioned Fourth of July barn-burning celebration. In my first strike since the Sunday Punch, I took twelve Helldivers to Chichi Jima to attack shipping there. At the prebriefing, Lt. Pete "Owl" Brown, our squadron intelligence officer, told me about an unusual possible target. While studying photographs of the island, he had found what he believed to be a large ship, about cruiser size, under camouflage, at anchor in a small inlet south of the main harbor entrance. He showed me the spot; I picked a couple of geographic landmarks that might help me locate the inlet, and the target, if it was there. I vowed to pick this juicy plum if we found it.

Coming onto the western coast of Chichi Jima at twelve thousand feet as planned, I found my landmarks. Then, to my delight, there was our objective—a large ship hidden in the inlet just as Brown had detected from his photos. Instructing the flight to loosen up enough in the dive to be able to drop their bombs on my explosion, I planned to put a hit right on the covered target. Some of the pilots might not actually see the ship as a combination of netting and actual vegetation had been used to hide it—an excellent job of camouflage.

As the flight turned from the sea toward the target, AA fire abruptly started bursting around us. Looking down I could see that the ship was surrounded with AA positions that, with the ship's guns, were firing at us with no regard about being seen. The firing was so intense that for a moment I was concerned lest we were diving into a deliberately set flak trap. It was too late to second-guess the situation—we were committed to an attack. The best course of action now was to bore on in and knock it out.

While nothing compared to the AA encountered at the Japanese fleet, we had to pass through a much heavier concentration of defensive fire than usual for this type of target. With the ship growing larger in the bombsight, I went down to two thousand feet and fired. Banking up and away, I saw the first of a series of explosions start after my bomb went off—the ship began blowing itself apart. The pattern of bombs was so concentrated that no one really missed.

It was a jubilant dozen Helldivers that rendezvoused after the dives, with some whooping and hollering back and forth over the squadron radio attack channel, until I told them to knock it off. Part of the reason for the revelry was that this highly successful attack had come back-to-back, so to speak, with the attack on *Zuikaku*. We took some pictures and headed for home—all planes and crews intact, safe and sound. The action photos revealed that we had attacked and sunk a cruiser-minelayer—a major ship target.

There was one sour note in the otherwise happy feeling of success in the mission; for some reason my gunner, Chief Aviation Radioman Red Lakey, had been silent for the entire flight. When he had said nothing before takeoff, I had decided that he was finding it difficult to muster enthusiasm for this first mission after our last disastrous one, so I, too, remained silent. After the attack, with the enemy ship on fire and sinking at its moorings, I called him on intercom to check to see if he was okay, because he made no comment about our success. His reply, in a voice that did not sound normal, was he wanted to get back to the ship as soon as possible.

After we landed and were safely tied down, we dismounted from our Helldiver. Without saying a word to me, Lakey walked away from the plane and went below to the gunners' ready room. In his debriefing, he told the intelligence officer that he had flown his last mission as a gunner in a Helldiver. Red Lakey was serious—he never flew from a carrier deck again.

Something snapped in Lakey and he knew that he could not continue. I do not know what happened to him, or exactly what brought on his final decision. Later, he apologized to me for quitting, and I told him that I understood and held no hard feelings. But the truth was that I did not understand, and never had, how some men would keep going and others would not.

I was told later that Lakey said that when he saw the AA fire coming up again, just like in the Philippine Sea, he knew that he would be killed if he kept on flying, especially with me. Apparently he firmly believed that I was going to keep diving through Japanese AA fire until I was killed, and he didn't want to be a part of it any longer. We had flown together since he had first asked to be my gunner back in Wildwood, New Jersey, in the summer of 1943. Here just exactly one year later he'd had enough.

I would not be telling the truth if I said that this whole thing didn't hurt. I respected Red Lakey, and always had confidence in him. Now he was quitting, and for some reason I blamed myself for his departure.

As air officer of the squadron I could have selected a top gunner and ordered him to fly with me. But I didn't take that way out. Instead I had Dave Stear pick up a gunner at random from the standby pool each time I flew a mission. Gunners Ingersol, Clark, Albertelli, Begley, Donelan, Bottrell, Fisher, and Safford flew strikes with me during the rest of July—some more than one.

After several weeks of no permanently assigned gunner I got the result that I had been waiting for. A few days after Vice Admiral Mitscher had been aboard and presented decorations to pilots and aircrewmen, a young gunner named Frank Bolac approached me at my flight office. An airman second class, he had no assigned pilot. His request was simple: Could he be my permanent gunner for the rest of the cruise? He said that he wanted to be where the action was and not have to worry about who he might get assigned to fly with. He realized that he was a junior gunner, but would I give him a chance?

I told Bolac that he had the main quality I wanted in a gunner—he was willing voluntarily to take his chances with me. He was one of the best gunners I had during the war, and we genuinely enjoyed flying and fighting together. When the squadron broke up in November 1944, we parted company. (I heard in 1989 that Frank had died recently after a happy and prosperous life.)

Upon return from the latest raids on the Jimas, our task group joined the rest of Task Force Fifty-eight to support the invasion of Guam. With Saipan under control, taking Guam would wrap up the Marianas into a neat American package. VB-2 began daily strikes against the town of Agana and the airfields on Rota and Orote Point.

Something new and interesting was always happening aboard a flagship, incidents that brought some excitement into our daily shipboard routine. Two Betty snoopers were shot down by our ever-vigilant CAP, one making a controlled crash near the task group screen. A U.S. destroyer got to the scene immediately and managed to rescue five Japanese airmen as well as parts of the plane and its contents. Among the stuff picked up was a bag containing charts and information about several Japanese airfields and bases that proved to be quite valuable.

The five survivors were brought to *Hornet* for interrogation and safekeeping until we could get back to port. The pilot was an officer, and he began exhibiting all the characteristics of a samurai —he would not eat or drink, and refused to say anything to anyone. As he was injured slightly, he was put into a bunk in the sick bay. The interpreter was afraid the man would attempt suicide, so restraints were used to tie him to the bed frame.

For several hours the man lay there, with the interpreter asking an occasional question and getting no answer. Sometime in the middle of the night a marine guard noted that blood was running out of one corner of the prisoner's mouth. A doctor was called. In the examination he found that the pilot had bitten through his own tongue and was slowly bleeding to death from a severed artery. Prompt medical action saved his life.

When he had recovered sufficiently, the samurai finally talked to the interpreter. He explained that his code of conduct required him to act as he had. To his family, friends, and country he was a dead man—there was no such thing as a prisoner-of-war status for captured Japanese officers. His sincere attempt to commit hara-kiri was his final disruptive act. He was now ready to cooperate with his captors in any reasonable way. But we must always remember that he was a dead man and could never return to his home and family.

This man's brave act within his set of rules of conduct brought forth several hours of discussion in the ship's wardroom and squadron ready room. Many of us went down to see this stoic man lying in the sick bay and he would smile and nod his head when we wished him well. Much as I hated the Japanese, I had to admire a man who could conduct himself in the presence of his enemies as this man was doing. And we began to realize how little we really knew about the Japanese, especially the pilot-officer samurai

caste. The use of kamikaze units in large numbers against the
U.S. fleet was still in the future, but we had a better understanding
of the morale of these special airmen from exposure to this one
solitary pilot. He left the ship when we next hit port, and I suppose
that he went to a prisoner-of-war camp somewhere. I'm sure that
he never attempted to kill himself again—his sense of honor was
no doubt satisfied with his attempt when tied to a bunk in *Hornet*'s
sick bay. I've often wondered what happened to him: Did he ever
return to Japan?

We were to attack the Jocko Jimas one last time. The most
successful of four raids came on 4–5 August when a reconnaissance plane reported a convoy of Japanese ships headed for the
Bonins. "It looks like a fine day for scavengers," Clark remarked
as he asked for and received the go-ahead from Mitscher to make
a high-speed run on his favorite target.

We found the convoy and began strikes. The weather did not
cooperate, with heavy overcast, winds, and rain making dive-
bombing difficult. My flight hit one transport ship, which did not
go down immediately (it sank later in the day). The torpeckers got
into the act with torpedoes, the fighters strafed, and several cruisers and destroyers were detached from the screen to go in to
finish off any damaged stragglers. By day's end everybody's
combined efforts had sunk eleven Japanese cargo-type ships and
escorts totaling some twenty thousand tons. With little air opposition, only three enemy aircraft were shot down, with two dozen
destroyed on the ground at Iwo Jima.

Rear Admiral Clark, the Oppressor of the Jimas, received the
traditional accolades from higher authority. Nimitz wired "Congratulations on the thorough scavenging of Chichi Jima and Iwo
Jima. Well done to all concerned." Even the top boss in Washington noted the effort: Ernie King sent a terse "I most heartily
concur."

Back in the lagoon at Eniwetok on 9 August, Vice Adm. Marc
Mitscher showed his appreciation of the efforts of both *Hornet* and
Air Group Two with over 250 awards to personnel. I had the honor
of receiving a Navy Cross for the Philippine Sea attack on *Zuikaku*
right after Rear Adm. Jocko Clark received one for the recent
Bonins operations—both from the hands of Mitscher—and our
citations both read "for extraordinary heroism in operations
against the enemy." Dave Stear, Snarls Scheurer, and Dad Taylor

of my division also received Navy Crosses. It was a proud day for all of us.

Partly in jest, but not without considerable logic, the Volcanos and Bonins became known among *Hornet* and air group personnel as "Jocko Jima Retto—Clark Island Group." This led to the organization of the Jocko Jima Development Corporation, a real estate firm of no legal status dealing in "exclusive sites in the Bonin Islands." Shareholders were given printed certificates, which indicated ownership of "choice locations of all types in Iwo, Chichi, Haha, and Muko Jima—only 500 miles from downtown Tokyo."

Rear Admiral Clark signed each certificate as president of the corporation. He enjoyed this rapport with his pilots and talked about the event years later. "When I was chosen president of the corporation, I asked that share No. One be issued to [Admiral] Mitscher. My own share was No. Two. I felt highly honored to be the recipient of such a fitting souvenir."[1] Membership became a highly coveted honor even among people in high places who usually didn't bother to collect souvenirs. For my contributions to "establishing" the corporation, I became the proud possessor of share no. 20.

II

September 1944 found Air Group Two finishing up what had been a long, hot summer. VF-2 was the top fighter squadron in the Pacific, with more planes shot down and more ace pilots (five or more individual victories), than any fighter squadron had compiled in the war to date. (The record of 264 aircraft shot down and approximately 275 destroyed on the ground, plus 11 shot down by the night fighters, VFN-76, and 28 aces in a pilot complement of 50, is one of the top records of the Pacific war.) VT-2 had a solid record of sinkings and missions against targets, especially in total tonnage dropped on ground facilities and installations. My squadron, VB-2, had one of the best records against enemy shipping and warships, both sunk and damaged, ever compiled by a dive-bomber squadron. Within VB-2, my division of six and flight of twelve, nicknamed Buell & Company by Rear Adm. Jocko Clark, had amassed the highest enemy ship attack record for such groups. Pilots in the air group were proud of these records, but were tired of combat and had one main desire—to go home.

Somewhere back in Nimitz's Pearl Harbor headquarters, the

decision was made to get one last combat effort out of AG-2 before relief. This verdict turned loose one of the most destructive, battle-experienced air groups then flying from any U.S. aircraft carrier for a last fling against the Japanese. Task Force Fifty-eight, with a new Task Force Thirty-eight number and Admirals Halsey and McCain, would attack the Philippines to see just how tough the Japanese still were after the maulings of the past summer.

In preparation for the planned first strikes in a return to the Philippines, a major change was made in the complement of VB-2 in both aircraft type and pilots assigned. Helldivers were reduced from thirty-six aircraft to twenty-four, with an additional twelve F6Fs brought aboard *Hornet* to be used as fighter-bombers. Eighteen pilots from our squadron were hastily checked out in the F6F during the last week of August to fly these fighter-bombers. Lt. Mike Micheel was put in charge of these aircraft, and the pilots picked for this choice assignment considered themselves the luckiest alive.

This was the first actual assignment of fighter-bombers on a carrier—it represented a major change in thinking relative to air group squadron composition. It was done suddenly, apparently in answer to a need for more fighter-type aircraft to be available for the expected heavy fighting in the Philippines as we hit large Japanese bases in this area for the first time. There were some shortcomings in the plan: A major one was that most of these pilots were not trained in fighter tactics if they were called upon to be used in an interceptor role. But they did know how to bomb and strafe and, as this was to be their major mission, no one expected any difficulty. So eighteen dive-bombing comrades of VB-2 realized the dream of a lifetime by getting to fly fighter-type aircraft in combat in place of the Beast—much to the envy of their friends who continued to dive in the Helldiver.

During this last week of August, while the new Task Force Thirty-eight was forming up at Eniwetok, all pilots were given daily liberty on the island for the purpose of meeting old friends from other ships and to have a few drinks to help forget the war. We would go ashore from *Hornet* in either the ship's boat or the captain's gig. There was a large dock where all the boats from the various ships would unload their cargos of officers. Leaving the dock, a footpath ran a short distance before splitting into two lanes. All junior officers from ensign to lieutenant commander went left to their drinking area—the senior officers from commander through admiral went to the right.

A sizeable bunch of us from *Hornet* had been at the junior officers' bar for most of the afternoon and were gathered at the dock waiting for the boat to arrive to take us back to the ship for evening chow. Pilots and ship's officers from several other ships were also present. During some friendly horseplay, two or three men went off the dock into the water of the lagoon, which was about chest deep. When they got back on the dock, they proceeded to push others into the drink, until dozens of officers were standing around completely soaked. It was not long before each new arrival at the dock who had not been into the brine was greeted with a baptismal heave.

I was one of the early ones tossed in, and decided to enter the spirit of the occasion. After all, it was good clean fun, and the water helped to shake off the effects of an afternoon of imbibing. A group of six of us were catching dry victims and giving them a ceremonial one-two-three type of swing before letting them go into the water. By this time the game was out of control, and all ranks from ensigns to captains were voluntarily or involuntarily involved.

A fresh group had just arrived, and we were up to the count of three on a small man, when I noticed that the person we were launching into space was Vice Adm. J. S. McCain. Shouting a warning, which was too late, I dove with a couple of others into the water to retrieve him, arriving almost before he'd had a chance to hit. As we got hold of him and helped him to his feet, he was gasping and wheezing and said: "Get my hat, boys, get my hat." The hat, a special version of a field fatigue hat with the gold band and scrambled eggs almost all green from salt air, was his lucky hat and well-known among the fleet pilots. We retrieved the hat, got the admiral back up on the dock, and expressed our deepest regrets for our conduct.

What a great little guy he was! Vice Admiral McCain had just arrived in the area to relieve Vice Admiral Mitscher as commander of TF-38 after a shakedown cruise in September. He was a small man, almost fragile, and looked like a strong wind could blow him away. Dripping salt water, seaweed, and coral sand, he kept grinning as he shook hands with each of us while we continued making our apologies. He asked for a dry cigarette, lit up, and started telling us how good it was to be back with his "fighting men." With blue eyes twinkling from a wrinkled face, dominated by both a nose and ears of heroic proportions, McCain looked for all the world like a leprechaun.

As the boats began to arrive, one of the first was McCain's motor launch. Completely white, spotless, with brass gleaming and three-star blue flag flying, it was a beautiful sight. The admiral was now having fun with his boys, and didn't want it to end. So he asked us to join him on the boat; he would take each of us to our ship. To the dismay of the spotless boat's crew, a dozen or more dirty, bedraggled pilots came aboard with the admiral.

We then wound our way through the mass of warships in the harbor delivering each pilot to his ship. There were three of us for *Hornet*. As the launch would approach a carrier's gangway, the OOD (officer of the day, who sees everyone on and off the ship) would spot the admiral's three-star flag. Thinking a visiting admiral was coming to call, he would prepare to give honors on the quarterdeck. When we hit the *Hornet* gangway, with bells ringing and bullhorns crackling, the deck personnel saw a grimy lieutenant and two lieutenants (jg) leave the launch and come up the ladder. For a brief moment, we got the full VIP treatment before the whole thing became clear. We thought it was very funny, but the OOD of *Hornet* was not amused.

III

The Philippine Islands lie roughly east of Viet Nam, north of Indonesia, and southeast of China, with the China Sea on one side and the Philippine Sea on the other. Stretching north-northwest to south-southeast, this chain of islands extends more than one thousand miles, with the larger islands of Luzon in the north and Mindanao in the south and smaller islands—Mindoro, Panay, Negros, Cebu, Leyte, and Samar—in between. The group is over six hundred miles wide at the Palawan–Sulu Sea–Mindanao area.

The newly designated Task Force Thirty-eight sortied from Eniwetok on 28 August with eight large carriers and eight light carriers carrying over a thousand airplanes to "return to the Philippines." It was an awesome force, and by now a very confident one. There was little doubt in most minds that we could go anywhere we wanted in the Philippines and handle any Japanese forces that we might find.

The top brass had decided to start hitting Japanese airfields and installations in Mindanao and gradually work up to Manila. My first strike was leading a deck launch of twelve fighters, twelve dive-bombers, and ten torpedo planes across Davao Gulf and into the island itself. It was a new type of strike for us in that we were not heading for a predetermined objective, but rather would attack targets of opportunity as we came to them. We found a couple of small trawlers in Davao Gulf, which were easily disposed of, and we also hit a few aircraft on the ground at Sassa Airfield. An oil dump was fired, sending up huge clouds of black smoke that could be seen for miles. By the next day we found little in worthwhile targets, and were ordered to proceed further north into the central areas of Cebu and Negros.

I recall one experience that happened during the two-day attacks on Mindanao. A little way inland from the town of Davao was a small, winding river. We had been briefed that we might find some boat traffic on the river, and that it was fair game. Sure enough I spotted a sizeable barge, or scow, slowly moving downriver. But before I could set up an attack with some of my flight, I saw a lone F6F fighter flying very low over the water toward the target. He was not one of the *Hornet* group. I opened up on the attack channel and advised the plane that he was much too low in his run and to break off his attack. I had no more than finished those remarks when the fighter opened up at point-blank range with his six .50-calibers and, as he passed over the barge, it exploded into a million pieces. Unfortunately the Hellcat simply disappeared in a ball of flame too. He had ignited a bargeload of ammunition (that was good) but had made the mistake of not anticipating what the results of his run might be and got himself too low and close (that was bad).

The whole thing went into my combat debriefing back on *Hornet*. I never found out, probably no one ever did, just who the hapless young man was. He merely became another statistic among those missing in action. To me the sad part was that a barge of ammo was not worth the life of a fine young American pilot. If anything good could be said about the episode, it did provide a graphic example to my entire flight of what a little carelessness could do to you. Now they knew why I harped on the subject of getting too low over a target.

IV

After hitting Davao Gulf and Mindanao Island bases and shipping, Task Force Thirty-eight moved quickly northward toward the central Philippines. This move caught the air defense commander of the islands in the midst of a fatal error. Masatake Okumiya, graduate of the Japanese Naval Academy, naval aviator, and fifteen-year veteran of the Japanese conquests and Pacific war with the United States, has given us an insight into Japanese thinking at that time in his book *Zero*.

As commander of the air defense of the Philippines, Okumiya ordered Zero fighters based at Clark Field on Luzon Island to come south immediately to Cebu Airfield. These fighters arrived too late to defend against our raids at Davao and Mindanao, but were still at Cebu and Negros airfields two days later when we came roaring in from our carriers at sea to the east.

I was leading a strike group from *Hornet* that morning of 12 September, consisting of twelve dive-bombers, ten torpedo bombers, and twelve fighters. As we approached the target I saw what was, to a dive-bomber pilot, a dream come true: there on the runways and parking aprons were dozens of aircraft! I could see the dust swirling about far below, indicating that the Japanese pilots were desperately starting their engines and striving to get airborne to intercept us. We had succeeded in surprising them completely.

When approaching an airfield in a dive-bomber, one rarely ever saw aircraft taxiing about or in the open on the ground. A fighter sweep almost always preceded the dive-bombers' arrival and parked aircraft would be burned-out hulks by the time we did our dives. However, aircraft in hangars or revetments and those camouflaged around the field could be blasted out with bombs and often became casualties in this manner.

We rushed to the pushover point of our dives as I realized that there was extreme danger in this juicy target. If many of the enemy fighters milling about to take off could get airborne, there would be swarms of them in pursuit of us after our dives, hacking away at our formations as we left the area. As *Hornet* strike leader, I immediately released my fighter escort of Hellcats who dove to intercept the Zeros making scrambling takeoffs in pairs from the east-west runway. We had kicked open an anthill of enemy fighters.

We went into dives from a high-speed break. I pushed over and was well into my dive when I saw two aircraft below start down the runway in a formation takeoff. Moving ahead of them with ample lead, I fired my total bomb load of a 1,000-pounder in the bomb bay and the two 250-pounders on the wings. The bombs struck among the two fighters just as they were leaving the ground. The leader veered right into the jungle in a flaming arc; the other exploded at the end of the runway. Frankly, I believe both of those Zeros were airborne when destroyed for a neat double, but I had to settle for two "destroyed on the ground" in the debrief back at *Hornet*.

My flight pounded bombs into the parked and taxiing aircraft with reckless abandon. The Ripper fighter leader begged me, by VHF, to let the Japanese pilots take off so that they could shoot them down in the air to raise their scores. I refused this request, for I wasn't about to allow these deadly fighters to get airborne if we could get them like sitting ducks. Sportsmanship had no place in the serious business of killing that we were engaged in at the moment.

Cebu Airfield became a three-ring circus of whirling, diving, and strafing aircraft—mostly ours but also a few of theirs. Under conditions like these, I got the flight back together in formation as quickly as possible, and out of the immediate area, to deter fighter attacks, leaving the arena to the fighters and fighter-bombers who were with the strike. Planes from another carrier arrived to join in the melee, and the destruction of Japanese airpower continued unabated.

Strange things can happen in the heat of action such as this, especially to an aircraft flying about alone. One of our pilots, Lt. Lyle Felderman, flying by himself in a Hellcat fighter-bomber on a run over the field, began receiving direct hits from the rear. Taking violent evasive action, he turned enough to see that the "enemy" firing on him was another Hellcat! The pursuing American pilot apparently realized his mistake at the last moment, broke off his run, and flew away but not before seriously crippling Feldy's plane. Nursing the damaged F6F back to the task force he landed it aboard, but the aircraft was so badly shot up it was ruled strike damaged and jettisoned over the side. The armor-plated seat and self-sealing gas tanks of the sturdy F6F had saved Felderman from becoming another "meatball" flag on an overzealous fighter pilot's airplane.

Okumiya, the Japanese pilot I mentioned earlier as involved in the air defense planning of the Philippines, happened to be flying into Cebu Airfield from Davao at the exact time of our attack. In his book *Zero*, he describes it:

> My transport plane arrived on the scene almost simultaneously with the first wave of enemy fighters and bombers. Our pilot swung clear of the field lest we be caught by the Hellcats, which would quickly have shot us out of the sky. We were able to see, before the transport fled the area, the dive bombers plunging from the sky, and the fighter planes as they screamed back and forth over the field, their wing guns spitting tracers into the parked Zeros. Within minutes Cebu became utter confusion. The American pilots were remarkably accurate, and the flames and black smoke boiling from the burning Zeros reminded me of a crematorium . . . ours.[2]

Okumiya estimated that of about one hundred Zero fighters sitting on Cebu's runways, more than fifty were either burned or blown to pieces: "It was a loss of great magnitude; in a single stroke the [Americans] destroyed nearly two thirds of the entire serviceable fighter plane force in the Philippines, and left in damaged condition many other Zeros."[3]

Of the dozens of attacks I made upon enemy bases, airfields, and other land targets during three years of combat against the Japanese, this September raid into the central Philippines at Cebu was by far the most successful. In a matter of a few minutes, a major attempt by the enemy to build up an interceptor fighter force in the Philippines was wiped out. The whole Philippine air defense system was proving to be a hollow shell—the U.S. timetable for a return invasion of these islands could be moved ahead by months.

Masatake Okumiya called the Cebu raid a crematorium where Japan's air power turned to ashes; to Ripper Air Group Two, and especially Buell & Company, it was to be remembered as the "Cebu Barbecue."

During these raids of 12–13 September in the central Philippines, Ens. Thomas C. Tillar, a fighter pilot in VF-2, was shot down. After bailout, he was rescued by local natives, who told him that nearby Leyte had no Japanese garrisons and thus would be an ideal place for the United States to make landings when they returned. And they were coming soon, weren't they, with all the airplanes now flying about?

When Tillar was flown back by PBY to the *Hornet* anchorage a few days later, he told his valuable story to Rear Admiral Clark and staff. This was exactly the kind of intelligence that Jocko liked —right from the horse's mouth. He quickly forwarded the message to Halsey, who sent a recommendation on up to the top allied strategic planners (King, Marshall, Roosevelt, and Churchill) via Admiral Nimitz: Why not change the coming Philippine invasion landings to Leyte rather than Mindanao as now planned? Halsey also pointed out that the Philippine defenses, especially air, were much weaker than anticipated, so the invasion should be carried out as soon as possible.

Much to everyone's surprise the impossible happened, and plans were changed at the highest levels for the invasion site to be moved to Leyte, and the date moved up by several weeks to 20 October 1944. The move both shortened the war and made the initial invasion landings almost unopposed—and this saved lives. How many persons were blessed by the intelligence report of a young ensign after being rescued can only be estimated.

V

After the immense success of the Cebu Barbecue, I took my group back to the same area the next day. Almost as an anticlimax, we found a large Japanese AK in the harbor near Negros, and pounced upon it, blowing it apart in flames with several direct hits. The coordination and accuracy of our dive-bombing attacks against shipping was attracting Jocko Clark's attention and it was about this time that he began using the term Buell & Company for my flight.

We withdrew from the central Philippines during the night of the thirteenth, moving back south along the eastern coast of Mindanao. About midmorning on the fourteenth, the admiral decided to send a strike to the Davao Gulf area to see if anything in the way of shipping had come back since the raids of the week before. My wing was given the strike assignment and, in addition to eleven

Helldivers, I had eight torpeckers and eight fighters, the latter under the command of Lt. Comdr. Leroy "Tex" Harris, XO of VF-2.

It turned out to be a lucky day. Ranging ahead of the main formation, Tex spotted a destroyer cruising in a southeasterly heading away from the main harbor area of Davao Gulf. It was alone: apparently it had completed some sort of mission at Davao and was departing the area at maximum speed. Tex called me by VHF and gave me its location, and in a few minutes I saw the target below in the bright sunlight, a gleaming new destroyer of the *Teratsuki* class. I decided to attack with my dive-bombers, using the TBFs if needed.

As we approached, the ship began shooting defiantly with its AA, more as an attempt to scare us rather than effectively shoot down our aircraft. In a perfectly coordinated attack, I sent four escort fighters that were with us down in flak-depressing runs, with the dive-bombers timing their dives to arrive on the fighters' tails. The Japanese destroyer skipper made the standard defensive maneuver by entering a maximum turn to starboard. We were diving from about eleven thousand feet with exact spacing between aircraft. With the ship turning at full speed, I had to use a point-of-aim in the open water where I estimated the ship would be when my bomb arrived. In what was probably the finest dive-bombing shot that I ever made, my one-thousand-pound armor-piercing weapon struck the doomed vessel about forty feet back from the bow and squarely amidships. With a delayed-action fuse, the bomb penetrated down into the ship for twenty or so feet before exploding, and the blast removed fifty feet of the bow cleanly, as if a giant cleaver had chopped it off. The wild turn ceased and the badly wounded ship straightened on course as its speed fell off drastically.

I had a wristwatch with a timing feature that allowed me to use it as a stopwatch. I started timing when I fired my bomb, and then pulled out in a sweeping circle to watch the show. Each plane fired a good shot, the near misses and hits so close together it was hard to tell who got the actual hits. As my bomb had removed the bow, the ship was now moving straight ahead and slowing down until it became almost a stationary target. When the last plane fired its bomb and pulled out, I pushed the timing switch again on my watch —eighty-two seconds had elapsed.

The devastation was instantaneous and complete. All that was left on the water were pieces of debris, some still falling from the explosions, and a few men swimming about—personnel who had jumped or been blown over the side from topside battle stations. It was a scene of absolute destruction, which gave me a feeling that combined the revulsion of instant death with the satisfaction of completing a perfect attack without losing a man.

Shipmate leaders flying with us came on their radios with congratulations; members of Buell & Company were exhilarated by their complete success, yet subdued by the finality of the attack. It was not easy being executioners of other human beings, even when they were a hated enemy. The role of avenging angels of death was more than a western movie of good guys in white hats versus bad guys in black ones; we were beginning to feel some guilt from all the killing of the past few weeks because it was inhumane conduct, even though it was done for a just cause—for country and for our way of life.

Someone came on the air suggesting that we "crack a few coconuts" (a rather crude term given to strafing enemy personnel in the water—their heads resembled floating coconuts). I ordered no strafing. We were too close to witnesses on shore, and possible prisoner-of-war camps, to do anything that might bring reprisals against helpless comrades in captivity. Besides, the men in the water were too far from land to have much chance of survival in any case.

As my formation of Helldivers headed back to *Hornet,* I made a radio call to the admiral, using his private designator. I knew his birthday was in early November, very near to my own (the fourth). I stated in my call that we wanted the ship we had just sunk to be an early birthday present to him from all of us in the Ripper air group and that we hoped that he had many more happy birthdays in the future. With all of his harsh exterior, the admiral was really quite a sentimentalist, and my birthday gift proffered ahead of time made a big hit. He got on the bullhorn and announced to the ship's company that we had just sunk a ship for him and we landed to a hero's welcome from all hands. Later that night Lieutenant Blair, who had led the AA strafing fighters, and I, at the insistence of *Hornet's* new captain, A. K. Doyle, related the day's experience over the ship's speaker system to the crew. It was a night to remember.

I still have a copy of the dispatch that was sent to Commander Carrier, Division Five (COMCARDIV FIVE) reporting this successful attack:

```
From:   HORNET                                    9/14/44
Action: CTG 38.1
Info:   COMCARDIV 5

        DD BELIEVED TERATSUKI CLASS SUNK
        CENTER DAVAO GULF GRID JIG TEN
        XRAY ZERO ZERO X TWO DIRECT HALF TON
        BOMB HITS VB TWO X BLEW UP SANK
        IMMEDIATELY X MANY NIP SURVIVORS IN
        WATER X
```

It turned out that this attack caught the attention of the Navy's public relations people, and a news release was put out when Air Group Two returned to the states in November. I was home on leave when the following story appeared nationwide on the Associated Press wire:

HELPS SINK JAP SHIP IN THREE MINUTES

Fighters and bombers of the Navy's top Air Group Two, now home on leave, which sent more than 122,000 tons of Japanese shipping beneath the waves, teamed up on an enemy destroyer in Davao Gulf on September 14 and sank it in three minutes after it was sighted.

This little model of the perfectly coordinated fighter-bomber attack was led by Lt. Harold Lloyd Buell, USNR, 420 Chester Avenue, Ottumwa, Iowa, dive bomber pilot, and Lt. Comdr. LeRoy E. Harris, USN, 5360 East Broadway, Long Beach, California, then executive officer of the group's fighter squadron.

Eleven bombers led by Lt. Buell were winging over Davao Gulf that morning when the enemy destroyer was sighted running full speed. It immediately put up a terrific barrage of anti-aircraft fire, and as promptly the bombers and fighters prepared for the attack.

Lt. Buell dove first and scored a direct hit on the bow, knocking the destroyer around on its course. The next seven bombs were damaging near misses, and the last three struck the doomed vessel squarely amidships, causing tremendous explosions. The Jap warship was under the surface three minutes after she was sighted, less than 90 seconds after the attack was instituted.

When the ship was first sighted, Lt. Comdr. Harris radioed the task force flagship and the force commander wanted to know the exact position. Harris looked over at the Helldivers peeling off and radioed back: "In less than five minutes, I'll tell you exactly where she was." He overestimated by two minutes.

In addition to the Associated Press release above, *Time* magazine ran a story entitled "The Rippers" in the 23 October 1944 issue. It was directed mostly to Fighting Squadron Two's exploits, but was also complimentary of the entire air group and reflected the high regard the Navy had for Air Group Two in the fall of 1944. However, the position of "top group in the Navy" was of short duration and, after the Battle of Leyte Gulf, several more air groups claimed better total scores than ours, based upon numerous Japanese warships sunk in that battle.

Recently, I mentioned to historians John B. Lundstrom and James Sawruk that I had been unable to find any information about the Japanese ship we had so totally destroyed in Davao Gulf on 14 September 1944. At the time it had been identified as a destroyer of the *Teratsuki* class, but no record showed a destroyer being sunk at that location. Lundstrom said that he had sources to make identification possible.

He found the answer in Hansgeorg Jentschura's *Warships of the Imperial Japanese Navy, 1869–1945*. The vessel was T.5, a fast (over twenty-five knots), powerfully armed landing ship designed to carry landing craft and amphibious tanks. It was 315 feet long with a beam of 33 feet and displaced 1,800 tons. Armament included twenty-six 25-millimeter AA guns and five 13-millimeter machine guns. We had one thing right in our identification: The ship was a new one, having just been launched a few weeks before we sank it in the gulf on what may have been its first mission of war. In defense of thinking that T.5 was a destroyer, it was about the same size, and had a silhouette much like a destroyer except that its stern sloped to the water aft.

T.5 was a versatile ship as to loadings: Alternative loads were seven type two amphibious tanks and 220 tons of cargo, two Koryu midget submarines and 184 tons of cargo, six Kaiten human torpedoes and 243 tons of cargo, 450–500 tons of cargo, or 480 marines.

VI

There were a few Japanese targets in the Pacific that could make one's heart beat faster just hearing the names spoken. One of these was Rabaul. Another was Truk. And then there was Manila Bay.

In September 1944, Rabaul and Truk had both been neutralized and no longer caused sweaty palms among naval aviators. But Manila Bay, and Clark Field loaded with Zeros, was still a mystery. Except for search flights near its confines, it had not been attacked in any force. On 21 September 1944 Task Force Thirty-eight arrived offshore and, like Rabaul and Truk previously, Manila Bay would never be the same again.

The now-familiar routine of a fighter sweep of dozens of F6Fs arriving at dawn, closely followed by dive-bombers and torpedo bombers meant that all the fighting took place in and around Manila. Not a single Japanese aircraft made it out to our task force that day. We didn't find any major fleet units, but there were plenty of destroyers and transport-type ships in the harbor to keep the first strike wave busy.

I was scheduled to take in a second strike from *Hornet*—the usual twelve dive-bombers, eight torpedo bombers, and twelve fighters. We were preparing to man planes, when I was called to the admiral's area; Lt. Comdr. Bill Dean, CO of VF-2, had just returned from the dawn fighter sweep. He reported to the admiral that there was a Japanese destroyer in the harbor cruising at top speed, shooting down planes as they attacked, and making no effort to leave or escape to sea. This type of conduct was certainly worth noting, and our admiral Jocko Clark had an answer: He told me to take Buell & Company to Manila Bay, find this maverick, and give it the same treatment that we had given the one in Davao Gulf just one week earlier. I told him we would do our best, saluted, and departed.

Flying in toward Luzon, I realized that we were under the gun this time. Here we were headed toward an assigned target with a direct order to sink it. There would be plenty of witnesses to our attempt who would know whether we were successful. The tough part about the assignment was that Japanese destroyers aren't normally easy to hit and sink, and this particular one appeared to be an unusually hardy adversary. Of course, we might get a break and find the ship already sunk or gone when we got to the harbor.

Luzon Island is quite mountainous and covered with heavy jungle. In our briefings we had been told that large areas up in the hills were controlled by Philippine guerrilla bands, and maps showing these "safe spots" had been prepared for us to memorize locations. We were also instructed that these men would be burning fires in their areas, so if hit one should head for the nearest column of smoke rising from the trees and bail out over it. As we approached Manila I could see dozens of smoke beacons in the mountains as promised. In addition to these extra safety features, the usual lifeguard submarine was on station a short distance at sea from the entrance to the bay.

Arriving at Manila Bay we found the defiant destroyer still afloat and firing at any plane that came near. She was maintaining a sea position that kept her within range of numerous shore batteries, so that the combined AA fire from both ship and shore sources was intimidating and deadly to any attackers.

In what was becoming a smooth attack pattern, we came in over the ship at twelve thousand feet and began our dives. It was a repeat performance of the previous week: I started the action again with a bow hit followed by a deluge of Buell & Company hits and near misses that blew the ship into pieces rather than simply sinking it. When twelve thousand-pound bombs are exploded in such a close pattern, no destroyer-sized ship is capable of surviving. As I was retiring to the rendezvous point, a small steam vessel appeared in my path. I had all four twenty-millimeter cannons charged and gave this target a long burst before breaking clear, leaving it dead in the water and afire. In spite of heavy AA fire all around us, especially from the shore placements, not a single shell struck a Helldiver, and a joyful band headed back to the sanctuary of *Hornet*.

Both Jentschura and Paul S. Dull list the Japanese destroyer sunk that day as the *Satsuki*, a *Mutsuki*-class destroyer launched 25 March 1925. This old veteran was 338 feet long, had a beam of 30 feet, with 1,772 tons displacement and a top speed of about 35 knots.

Rear Adm. Jocko Clark, on his last war cruise before taking a break, was delighted with our attack. He must have said something to his new boss, Vice Adm. John McCain—in a few months I received a Distinguished Flying Cross for leading the mission. But worth more than a medal to me were the superb performances that were now becoming commonplace with Buell & Company; we had been put on the spot by Clark and not been found wanting. We were sinking ships almost every time we dove on them and returning home without losing a man. Let's face it—that was what this particular game was all about!

VII

By sundown on the twenty-first, after a continuous pounding by aircraft of TF-38, there was no enemy air opposition in or around Manila. All hands out at sea to the east slept soundly, with no nightmares of aerial visitors at midnight.

The next morning found us in *Hornet* preparing for a second day of attacks to clean up any targets left from the previous day's actions. I was assigned to lead a deck load strike and had manned my Helldiver parked on the port side aft, with a 1,000-pounder in the bomb bay, a 250-pounder on each wing and a full load of twenty-millimeter cannon shells for four guns. We had started our engines, and the launch was about to begin.

Hornet was cruising under a thin overcast at eight hundred feet, which was starting to burn off from the morning sun. TF-38.1 had a defensive CAP already airborne, which had been launched at dawn, relieving the night fighters. These fighters were above the overcast. As there had been no enemy planes around, it was a surprise when the general quarters sirens started, and the bull-horn announced that we had an incoming bogey on the radar screen.

I saw him almost immediately, just under the clouds, flying toward us up the wake of the ship. It was obvious that he had picked *Hornet* as a target, and was making his run. The Japanese plane was a Zero carrying what looked like a five-hundred-pound bomb on a belly rack. He was moving fast, and diving toward the stern of the ship. He then flew up the centerline of the carrier at about fifty feet altitude. He was rolling slightly from side to side as he passed over us—apparently he was trying desperately to get his bomb to drop from its rack. By the grace of God, his bomb hung up and did not drop. At the point-blank range of his attack, if it had dropped, it would have fallen into the pack of aircraft we were preparing to launch. As we were all loaded with bombs, ammo, and fuel, a single bomb hit among us would have started a chain reaction of explosions that would have killed us all and destroyed the *Hornet*.

As the rogue plane passed the bow, the pilot heeled over into a sharp wingover to port. While making this maneuver, the bomb disengaged and fell harmlessly into the water with a violent explosion. By this time every gun on *Hornet*, and the ships nearby, were blasting away at the plane, while it continued its turn. I could see that the pilot intended to swing around and come in for another run up the ship from a stern position. Cutting my engine I unstrapped from the cockpit, yelled to my gunner Frank Bolac to get clear, and took cover in the nearby catwalk, but Bolac stayed with his now-ready guns.

By this time the pilot was boring in again from the stern, with guns and cannon firing, flying just high enough to clear the deck and its load of aircraft. He stitched a neat path right up through the pack, holing several planes and causing some casualties but no explosions. Again, every gun of the force that could get a shot in was firing—I saw pieces fly off the aircraft as it was hit but not downed.

Unbelievably, as the Zero reached the bow, the pilot again put his craft into a chandelle turn to port and came around for a third run. In a display of bravery and determination, this single antagonist headed in again with all guns firing, holing more aircraft as he passed. And again he ran the gauntlet of heavy AA fire without going down.

At this point in the drama, as the Zero was completing its third run on *Hornet*, an F6F from the CAP came charging onto the scene. He flew in behind the enemy plane and began firing, so the Japanese pilot pulled back on his control stick and disappeared straight up into the overcast. With some misgivings I watched the F6F follow him. Normally, an F6F could not stay with a Zero in this type of maneuver, especially with a skilled Japanese pilot at the controls.

A few moments later a plane came diving from the overcast, striking the water and exploding a short distance from a screening destroyer to our port side. A cheer went up as everyone assumed that the crashed plane was the Japanese, but unfortunately it was the F6F, falling out of control. Then as a final gesture from a great pilot, the Zero descended out of the clouds, flew by the ship while performing a slow roll, and departed in a heading toward Clark Field with all AA guns still firing away at his retreating form.

The performance of this unknown Japanese pilot was the bravest and most skilled bit of enemy flying that I saw in the Pacific war. All of us in *Hornet* could be thankful for two things: The pilot was not a kamikaze who could have dived unopposed into our helpless ship, and he was not wounded seriously enough to make him decide to perform hara-kiri by taking us with him. Instead he put on an air show that can only be described as spectacular.

When I was a small boy, I loved to listen to stories about the Indians in Iowa, as told to me by a man more than ninety years old at that time, whom everyone called Grandpa McMillan. One of his stories was about how certain warriors would sometimes perform a strange rite in battle called "doing coup." The act consisted of an Indian touching his enemy with his hand, or his weapon, without hurting or killing him. Grandpa McMillan did not like Indians, but he admired one who had performed coup on him in a fight. When he told me about the exploit, he closed the story with "that was one brave Indian."

To the unknown Japanese pilot who came out to the *Hornet* on 22 September 1944 and put on his air show I give Grandpa McMillan's greatest compliment: You were one brave Indian!

VIII

Departing Manila Bay, Task Force Thirty-eight headed southeast. McCain decided to send one last strike across the central Philippines west to Coron, a distance of 325 miles, to catch any ships that might have fled there from Manila Bay. Using wing tanks for the first time, I led this strike on 24 September—the last one for both myself and the squadron. In what was almost routine, we dove on a large minesweeper, sinking it with the now-familiar pattern of hits and near misses. This kill gave us a total of five ships sunk in the last ten days of our combat cruise—an impressive finish for the Sea Wolves and Ripper Air Group.

On 29 September 1944, Air Group Two was relieved by Air Group Eleven at Manus in the Admiralty Islands. We were headed for home after over six months of heavy combat. As it would turn out in fewer than thirty days, we left at just the right time. The Battle of Leyte Gulf on 23–26 October 1944 was the last of the great naval battles of World War II—and it took place without AG-2's participation. Who knows how many lives were saved in our group by this fortunate timing by the gods of war?

Leyte Gulf was to see the first deliberate use of organized kamikaze attacks. What a weapon it was! Here was a flying bomb with a perfect guidance system—human mind and eyes for radar and human hands to move the controls. The destruction caused our naval forces by this weapon during the coming months was to have horrible consequences, and it most certainly helped to make the decision to use the atomic bomb an easier one for American leaders in the summer of 1945.

But this is a story about Dauntless Helldivers and how they sank ships by diving on them, not about kamikazes or atomic bombs. The battle of Leyte Gulf on 24 October 1944 was probably the most concentrated destruction of Japanese warships by dive-bombers in World War II. In an awesome display of power, Task Force Thirty-eight destroyed the last of the Japanese Imperial Navy.

It was a struggle almost too large to describe adequately. Japan lost the superbattleship *Musashi* and two lesser ones, the *Yama-shiro* and *Fuso;* one large carrier, the *Zuikaku* (back from her Philippine sea wounds) and three light carriers; six heavy cruisers, four light ones, and nine destroyers. U.S. losses in this epic battle were the light carrier *Princeton,* two escort carriers, *Gambier Bay* and *St Lo,* two destroyers, and one destroyer-escort.

Several great dive-bomber squadrons took part in the sinking of the last four Japanese aircraft carriers to sail in harm's way. Although these carriers had no aircraft aboard to attack our carriers, and thus were decoys, their sinking was no less valorous an achievement. The AA fire braved by U.S. naval attack pilots was both heavy and accurate. Samuel Eliot Morison wrote that Ozawa's ships' fire "was perhaps the most deadly on either side in the Pacific War." Many brave men, both pilots and gunners, made their last dive on this day.

Essex's VB-15, under the leadership of Comdr. Jim Mini and CAG Dave McCampbell, top ace fighter pilot in the Navy, were there. Comdr. T. Hugh Winters, CAG of AG-19 in *Lexington,* and his wingman are the only naval aviators to watch three enemy aircraft carriers sink in one day. (Hugh was target coordinator for several hours over the Japanese carriers.) An old comrade from

Yorktown and VS-5, Art "Goocher" Downing, XO flying from *Wasp* with VB-14, earned a third Navy Cross. Close to home, a classmate from Ottumwa High School, class of 1937, Lt. George B. Searle, flying from *Intrepid* with VB-18, won himself a Navy Cross, along with Lt. Ben Preston, a second-time-around veteran of the battles of 1942. There was a Norfolk Deck Dodger present —Lt. John David Bridgers of VB-15. (It is interesting that VB-15 was the squadron that VB-2 replaced in the *Hornet*, back in March 1944, at the request of the tyrannical Browning.) And I must not forget Lt. Edwin "Big Ed" Wilson, flying in VB-11 from *Hornet*, who missed his goal of a lifetime—to dive-bomb a Japanese carrier —because TG-38.1 was away being refueled and arrived back too late to take part against the enemy flattops. (They were already sunk!)

One of the top dive-bombing squadrons at Leyte Gulf was VB-13, flying from *Franklin*. In their last strikes after several months of heavy combat, they were involved in the sinking of three carriers and two battleships in this action. An old shipmate from Air Group Ten in *Enterprise*, Lt. Jack Finrow, USNR, won a Navy Cross with a direct hit on the battleship *Musashi* but received it posthumously, because he was lost the next day attacking a carrier. My good friend Lt. E. John Weil, USNR, hit *Zuiho*, earning a Navy Cross. He gave me the following account:

> From fourteen thousand feet in clear weather with light wind I led my division down on a Nip carrier with a meatball painted on the deck. Halfway down I was in a slight skid, which would cause a miss, so I fought the controls until the ball was back on center and the sight on target. This brought my drop altitude considerably below procedure, but I wanted a hit at that moment more than anything else in the world! Amid unbelievable AA fire, I released and pulled out, leveling at about six hundred feet. My gunner, A3c. Louis A. Horton, USN, shouted over the intercom: "Direct hit, direct hit!" I was jinking and headed for the deck when I passed right alongside one of the battle wagons; its pagoda masts and varieties of firepower were awesome.

Weil's squadron mate, Lt. Dutch Bomberger, USNR, also hit a carrier and won the Navy Cross, and Lt. Dick Harding, USNR, assisted and received a Silver Star. One of the most decorated squadrons of the Pacific war, VB-13 airmen were awarded 22 Navy Crosses, a Silver Star, 25 Distinguished Flying Crosses, and 149 Air Medals. Bomberger, Harding, Weil, and I ended up together at Cecil Field as instructors in the Training Command in 1945.

There were bloody trials at Okinawa and Iwo Jima still to undergo, including the terrors of kamikaze planes and Baka bombs, and raids on tough targets in the Japanese homeland itself, before surrender would take place on *Missouri* in Tokyo Bay, but Leyte Gulf ended Nippon's naval air power forever. It is an inspiring saga that amplifies the gallant efforts of all those Dauntless Helldivers who combined their efforts in sinking the last of the Emperor's major warships.

I have always considered it extremely fortunate that I was assigned to VB-2 in Air Group Two aboard *Hornet* during the summer of 1944. The assignment allowed me to serve under several naval officers whom I admire greatly, including Rear Adm. C. H. Duerfeldt, Vice Adm. Jackson D. Arnold, Adm. Roy L. Johnson, and Adm. A. K. Doyle. Best of all, I got to serve in the flagship of the most tenacious task group commander of all those who fought under Adm. Marc Mitscher—Adm. J. J. Clark.

Adm. William A. Moffett is credited with saying that "life is a matter of timing." I agree, and thank a divine power that timed my life so that I could be a part of those historical days when we all "did our thing" to the Japanese with the irrepressible Jocko!

13

PREPARATION THREE

I

AIR GROUP Two broke up in San Francisco, and we scattered to the four corners of the country. Dave Stear and Ralph Yaussi immediately went down to Los Angeles and married their waiting sweethearts; it was my twenty-fifth birthday, 4 November 1944. I caught a train for Ottumwa and began a thirty-day leave.

I arrived at the Jacksonville Naval Air Station, my new posting, in the Gray Gremlin on 11 December 1944. It was hard to believe this was the same place that I had visited back in early 1941 before the war. The barren, sand-swept airfield with its temporary buildings had become a beautiful permanent base with every convenience. It was now headquarters for the Naval Air Operational Training Command and several fleet air squadrons.

In addition to the main base on the St. Johns River, an outlying airfield had just been completed about fifteen miles west and a bit south of the city. Called Cecil Field, it was to be my new home, and the combat training of dive-bomber pilots for the fleet was my new assignment. One of three new airfields built along the eastern seaboard of the United States, Cecil Field was a forerunner of the large naval air bases that would extend naval aviation into the jet era.

Like all new airfields, Cecil Field left quite a bit to be desired as to living and recreational facilities. As there was no on-base housing, all married personnel had to find a place to live in the surrounding countryside. There were a large number of bachelors among both the instructor-pilots and trainees, the latter being, for the most part, newly commissioned ensigns. The Navy provided housing for both groups with a senior BOQ for instructors and a junior one for the student ensigns. The main officers' club was still under construction so a small bar called the Ground Loop in the senior BOQ was an oasis for thirsty naval aviators.

There were several ingredients that made up this combination living and recreational spa. Bring together a bar, comfortable sleeping rooms, and a pleasant dining area, loosely run within circumscribed naval guidelines at a nominal cost, and put them in the middle of an airfield base built on Florida panhandle farmland. Limit transportation to the nearest city to a few buses and personal automobiles, with gasoline rationing in effect. Sprinkle this mixture with a liberal number (especially on weekends) of women of all sizes, shapes, and ages, both local and traveling through, who were allowed aboard the base as visitors. Add to all of this a volatile group of hard-flying combat veteran naval aviator instructors, most in their mid- to late twenties, who believed in playing as hard as they flew, that is, at full throttle until the engine either quit or blew up. Put this concoction into a blender that ran twenty-four hours a day, seven days a week and you have the Cecil Field BOQ in the spring of 1945.

Commanding officer of the Naval Auxiliary Air Station, Cecil Field, when I arrived for duty on 17 December 1944, was Capt. H. P. "Bags" Bagdanovich, the same officer I had first known as a student aviator at Opa-Locka in the fall of 1941. Bags was the perfect CO for Cecil Field at the time; he understood this bunch of maverick instructors who had been assigned to do the important job of preparing the dive-bomber pilots needed to fly the carrier-based planes in air support of the coming invasion of Japan. It was an atmosphere much like the one he had been part of as a lieutenant instructor before the war, only wilder, with most of the participants reserve rather than regular naval aviation officers. At least four of us were old students of his who had gone forth, battled the Japanese successfully, and returned to serve with him again. He was proud of us, called us "Bags' boys," and never missed a Friday-afternoon happy hour at the Ground Loop to swap combat sea stories. It was a situation that required understanding and the ability to temper Navy regulations with tolerant use of common sense. Bags had these qualities in abundance.

To illustrate this point, I have recreated a typical Bagdanovich memorandum that was issued and posted in the BOQ in answer to a problem:

U. S. NAVAL AUXILIARY AIR STATION
Cecil Field, Florida

MEMORANDUM

It has come to the attention of the Commanding Officer that numerous guests of BOQ resident officers have been requesting breakfast after the scheduled time for such services has passed. Attention is directed to the hours of meals, especially breakfast, that are posted in the BOQ dining area; any officer or guest requesting meal service outside of these posted times will be refused such service.

H. P. BAGDANOVICH
Captain, U. S. Navy
Commanding

The intent of this memo was to handle a complaint from the personnel running the dining room at the BOQ. They were tired of women coming in at 0900 or 1000, long after the pilots had eaten breakfast and left to fly, to order a complete eye-opening meal of eggs, grits, bacon, toast, juice, and coffee, and then to sign a guest meal chit with their host's name. This memo handled the problem effectively without making an issue of a greater one—the cohabitation from time to time of civilian women with pilots of the U.S. Navy in a Navy facility on a naval base! Fortunately for those involved, the real issue never came to a head, and the morale of many was enhanced by this careful overlooking of existing naval regulations.

II

In some ways, living in the Cecil Field BOQ in early 1945 was a bit like being a resident in a bustling apartment house in a small town. Everyone knew each other and helped handle any problems

300

that came up. As housing was in short supply, and overnight or weekend sleeping rooms at a premium, planning ahead was necessary. Our wide-open facility became a haven and refuge for many women, especially on weekends and after big dances and parties, who might be in need of temporary shelter from the strife and storms of life in the outside world around our base.

A typical case that comes to mind is one of a lieutenant (jg) instructor who arrived for duty with a new bride and no place to live. They were put into a nice room, and a schedule was set for the blushing bride to use the community-type shower in that wing of the building without intrusion. The newlyweds spent at least a month under these makeshift conditions until a proper place off base was found for them to live. I don't believe I ever saw a happier bride, and she did repair sewing jobs for all of us to show her appreciation.

I encountered a new dimension of naval life at Cecil in the form of Waves. As I had been out of the country on aircraft carriers or at remote airfields for three years, I was not familiar with the increasing role of women in the Navy. They now constituted a sizeable part of the naval personnel at most shore bases. I was not surprised to see large numbers of Waves in administrative positions formerly held by male yeomen, and doing office work much like secretarial jobs in industry. However, I was taken aback by the numbers of women to be found working as mechanics on the aircraft in the hangars. Everywhere one looked were petite grease monkeys toiling away on everything from engines to hydraulic systems. Dressed in tight-fitting coveralls, with ponytails falling from fatigue caps, I never got used to seeing these curvaceous sailors crawling about a SB2C without mentally losing some of my officerlike reserve that was supposed to separate officers from the enlisted personnel of the Navy.

I honestly can say that fraternization between pilots and enlisted women sailors was not a problem in those days. Every officer knew that he or she had to maintain the required distance between himself or herself and enlisted personnel on duty especially those under his or her direct command. But men are men and some say women are glad of it. There were many very attractive enlisted Waves about, and everyone went on liberty sooner or later. Meetings were discreetly set up and took place between naval aviators and their women shipmates with no appreciable damage done to "good order and discipline of the United States Navy." I know this is true because I took part in these activities myself.

To combat pilots like those instructing at Cecil Field in the spring of 1945, one lived to fly, to drink, and to go on liberty. Each new day was a gift to be savored and enjoyed. We were a happy-go-lucky bunch that liked a good joke, especially if it was on a friend.

Almost anything could happen and often did. One must remember that in early 1945 the war was still going strong in the Pacific, with an invasion of the Japanese homeland considered necessary and being planned. Some combat veterans would be asked to go out as leaders of the hundreds of new pilots like these to whom we were so patiently teaching combat skills in daily flights from Cecil Field. I had no illusions about my chances of returning from a fourth war cruise to the Far East against Nippon. As a dive-bomber's life could be short, and it was good to be alive, one took what pleasure he could from the opportunities that came along, often not realizing or even caring about the pain that these relationships might cause others who became involved. I never deliberately hurt anyone during those days, especially the bonny young women who came by from time to time to brighten my life.

III

The flying being done at Cecil Field was as nearly like a fleet squadron as we could make it. Each senior lieutenant was assigned a group of ten newly commissioned and designated naval aviator ensigns. A lieutenant (jg) was also assigned as assistant and second-division flight leader. Called a flight, these twelve pilots with twelve gunners and aircraft operated just like a small squadron. We had our own ready room where we gathered for briefings, debriefings, and lounging around between flight assignments. We had a squadron organization of sections and divisions, flew flights of different numbers of aircraft up to twelve, with lots of gunnery over the ocean to the east and dive-bombing on targets in the area. All flights were conducted as if we were a fleet outfit, and I was a hard taskmaster in the air, demanding a best effort at all times. I was like a squadron skipper and my lieutenant (jg) aide, a Texan named Pingray, was my XO. It was the nearest thing to fleet squadron duty one could be involved with and still be on shore duty in the training command.

Comdr. Ralph Weymouth was in charge of all training at Cecil Field and his head flight officer was Lt. J. D. Bridgers. J. D. was an old friend of mine from cadet training days before the war and one of the original Norfolk Deck Dodgers. A two-tour combat man like most of us, including Weymouth, he had a mean streak that had gotten even worse during the war. He loved to make fun of others, but like many practical jokers he was not very good at taking a joke on himself. His position as head flight officer under Weymouth allowed him to indulge in his favorite pastime of practical joking with little fear of retaliation.

Weymouth did not like me and, in all fairness, I understood why. He had been CO of VB-16 aboard *Lexington,* where I had crashed the night of the first Battle of the Philippine Sea, 20 June 1944. When I reported to him in his Cecil Field office, we had a frank talk. I told him that he was entitled to his opinion of me but perhaps he did not know the whole story, and proceeded to tell him my side of it. I then promised to do a good job for him in this assignment, but told him I would leave just as soon as I could get orders away from his command. This seemed to be an adequate explanation to Weymouth, and we parted without animosity.

The Helldivers we were flying at Cecil Field were not all products of Curtiss Aircraft. Some were being assembled by Grumman and others at a plant in Canada. It did not make much difference where it was put together—the Beast was still a lot of airplane for youngsters, with characteristics that could kill a pilot in a hurry. Thus my XO Pingray and I spent a good bit of our time stressing safety and proper respect for the airplane, and it paid off. We did not have a serious accident during the five-month training cycle.

This group of young ensigns was unusual in that practically all were noncollege men. Shortly after Midway, with its high losses, a few personnel people in high places pushed through a decision to take bright young men into naval aviation training directly from high school. Because the other selection requirements were maintained at a very high level, this lack of formal higher education proved to have little or no impact upon the final product. The men taken in were the best in the population, and their training was so intense that they learned everything they needed to know "the Navy way."

A feature of dive-bombing training at Cecil Field was a fancy new target built out in the piney woods south of the field. The target consisted of a bull's-eye in white about fifty feet across, superimposed upon a large plus sign with its arms running north-south and east-west. About two hundred yards to the north and east of the target center, two semiunderground bunkers were built with openings facing the bombing area. Inside each bunker a crew of two sat with a surveyor's-type device, which they used to measure both bearing and distance to where a practice bomb struck. When both observations were drawn on a chart, the exact point of a bomb's impact could be marked within inches. No longer were hits or misses a pilot's best guess, an estimate, or the observation of a witness circling the target. Now hits could be carefully recorded, with no room for question or argument. This new accuracy was a boon for those who were good bombers, and for students to learn from their mistakes, but quickly exposed the average (or less) dive-bombing abilities of others, who had been able to cover up in the past with verbiage.

Gathering together the best dive-bomber pilots in the Navy in a bar such as the Ground Loop, with the spirits flowing, could bring out sea stories, with appropriate exaggerations about great bomb hits of the past. We respected each other's bombing abilities for the most part, but there were few shrinking violets in this group. Deep down inside, each thought that he was the best dive-bomber pilot in the Navy, or among the top few. Confirmed hits scored on Japanese warships in combat, and one's bombing abilities as described by others in the peer group, were criteria used in judgment. How many medals a person had was never used as a factor because of the wide differences in standards that awards reflected. Good bombers may have not received credit for hits because they had not spoken up, or someone else, often senior to them, had taken credit for their hit. When enough booze had been ingested these small injustices inherent to the Navy's system of decorations were brought out, and even good friends could come close to blows in the discussions.

With a foolproof target for scoring, we ended up with a dive-bombing shootout. I made the best score in a close contest and was declared the first dive-bombing champion of the Operational Training Command, East Coast, given a Navy E award appropriately signed, and the well-wishes of my peers at the Ground Loop. As a fringe benefit I was designated to lead a flight of twelve senior dive-bombing instructors in a combat attack demonstration against a target set up in the center of Cecil Field—a summer show for a class of midshipmen from the Naval Academy.

IV

The dive-bombing demonstration flight on 22 June 1945 was to be my final one at Cecil Field. Keeping the promise that I had made to Weymouth, I was successful in getting myself a set of orders to another part of the Operational Training Command located at nearby Daytona Beach. Thanks to a close friend and fellow dive-bombing instructor, Lt. E. John Weil, I heard about a call for two highly experienced combat lieutenants to volunteer to move to VBF-1, a crack outfit forming up at Daytona Beach Naval Air Station. We put in for this choice assignment and were the lucky ones picked.

On 28 June 1945 I checked out of the wacky Cecil Field BOQ, scene of many a wild adventure during my six months residence there. I went by the office of Commander Weymouth to say farewell. He greeted me with genuine cordiality, told me I had become a valuable instructor, and had proved that my system of dive-bombing at the fleet operational level worked. I thanked him and departed.

V

I arrived at Daytona Beach just prior to a Fourth of July holiday. Everything that I owned in the world was packed into the Gray Gremlin, and there was room to spare. I looked up E. John Weil, who had moved into a small garage apartment in the northern part of town. E. John graciously agreed to let me share the place with him, splitting the cost. Looking back on those days, I can honestly say that the next three months spent in those diminutive quarters was one of the happiest periods of my naval career.

The Daytona Beach Naval Air Station and airfield were located approximately five miles west of the city. It was not a large base with multitudes of aircraft, but a small one with our fighter-bomber training squadron the reason for its existence. We were still flying Beasts, but were to get F6Fs soon and new F8Fs in the future.

The mission of the squadron was to develop fighter-bomber tactics and skills for new fleet squadrons of fighter-bombers flying from escort carriers. With the invasion of Japan coming in the fall, commanders in high places had decided to provide air support from

305

dozens of CVEs equipped with only one type of aircraft—a fighter that could be used for defense against kamikazes with its guns and could also carry bombs and rockets for use in troop support against land targets. Having only one kind of aircraft aboard would end many existing problems of supply, maintenance, and replacement of aircraft on the CVEs, with each carrier operating about forty aircraft (two squadrons).

To accomplish this mission, the Navy had collected together some of the finest combat veteran fighter and dive-bomber pilots on the East Coast. All were volunteers for the squadron and for the assignments that would be made in a matter of a few weeks. From the combination of these talents would come the squadron commanders of the fighter-bomber outfits aboard the CVEs.

VI

The Bomb ended the war. If we had had to invade Japan, a million soldiers on both sides would have been killed and a million more would have been maimed for life. It was as simple as that.

—PRESIDENT HARRY S TRUMAN

On 6 August 1945 the U.S. Army Air Corps dropped the first atomic bomb on Hiroshima, followed on the ninth with a second one on Nagasaki. These attacks were made at the direct order of the commander-in-chief of our armed forces, the president of the United States, from airfields located in the Marianas. Within one week after the second drop, the Japanese surrendered unconditionally, ending the war in the Pacific.

I clearly recall what a surprise it was to all of us at Daytona when we heard about the atomic bomb. However, although it was an event of great magnitude, none of us realized that day just how important the impact would be. No one really understood what an atomic explosion was or had the vaguest idea of the death and destruction this new weapon involved. To most of us, it was just a new kind of bomb with a big bang for the B-29 boys to play with —a superblockbuster like those that had been used earlier against German cities in the European theatre.

So our lives proceeded along for a few days at the same pace as before the Hiroshima drop. On the night of the second bomb drop, a dispatch came in with a routine training assignment.

It ordered six of us to fly to Wildwood for a training session in conjunction with VB-97. Specifically, we would be firing a new type of rocket from wing racks of our SB2Cs, utilizing a fancy rocket target that had been erected at Wildwood. Personnel of VB-97 would provide us the support services necessary. As I was the senior lieutenant of the group I was acting CO of this division, with Lt. Edwin "Big Ed" Wilson leading the second section. I was given verbal orders to have the flight back to Daytona in no more than one working week.

After parking our Beasts at Wildwood, Big Ed and I hit the beach for liberty. It was the first time I had been back in the area since VB-2 days in the summer of 1943. Big Ed Wilson was, if anything, a bigger liberty hound than myself. Although we were having a good time at Wildwood, it was, after all, a lot like Daytona Beach. We decided that what we needed was a quick liberty trip to that queen of cities, New York.

By pushing ourselves, we finished all of the assigned ground-training and rocket-firing flights during the eleventh and twelfth. On the afternoon of the thirteenth, we headed our planes for Floyd Bennett Naval Air Station, and by nightfall Big Ed and I had checked into the Commodore Hotel and were doing Manhattan, including the Copacabana Club, at full throttle.

We had been so busy flying and having fun that neither of us had bothered to read a newspaper or listen to a radio news report for days. Thus we had no idea what was happening in the Pacific since the second atomic bomb drop on Nagasaki and the resulting peace overtures from Emperor Hirohito.

VII

On the morning of 14 August 1945 we were awakened by loud noises drifting up from the streets below. A quick check with the hotel phone operator informed us that the commotion was coming from some kind of a celebration in Times Square; here's Big Ed's version of what happened next:

Hal and I put on our khaki uniforms, complete with wings and combat ribbons, and proceeded to Times Square. We found the area throbbing with excitement. As we milled about, the big ticker tape electric sign on the angle building in the Square started flashing over and over, "Japs Surrender." With that good

307

news people poured into the streets and Times Square became packed with humanity. We two naval aviator combat veteran lieutenants became instant celebrities. We were patted, pawed, kissed, and cheered. A woman came out of a store with her arms filled with cold, opened beer bottles screaming: "The war is over and my son is alive." Needless to say we each had a cold beer; this started our celebration. Every bar we went into someone would buy us a drink. Even bartenders in tough New York gave us free drinks. We were interviewed by all the movie news services, and local press reporters. We had a ball; what a spectacular place to be when the Pacific war ended.

The twenty-four hours from when Big Ed and I were awakened on 14 August until we took off from Floyd Bennett the next day about noon were wild. Among the beautiful people we met as we bounded about Manhattan Island was a lovely Irish lass named Nancy Malone, who worked in one of the offices that simply closed shop for the day. I talked her into missing her train home to continue doing the town—what a time we had! With Big Ed and a young woman he'd met, we stayed up all night hitting one night spot after another, until we finally parted on separate trains the morning of the fifteenth. A tall, lovely brunette with green eyes, dimples, and full of Irish wit, she was a delightful companion to share what to me was one of the most important dates in my life —the end of the Pacific war.

14

OMEGA

I

WHEN BIG Ed and I returned to Daytona with our six Helldivers from the rocket-firing assignment and our Times Square frolic, we found the squadron in a state of agitated confusion. With the war finally over and won at last the nation's emotions, held in check for almost four years of conflict, gave way. Suddenly everyone in the various services (except the career regulars) wanted simply to go home to continue their lives in peace, free from the danger of death. Each mother, wife, and sweetheart demanded from both political and military leaders that their loved ones be released and brought home immediately.

With over ten million citizens in uniform, the problems associated with dismantling America's war machine were complex ones. For the millions of men overseas, especially in the Pacific, discharge procedures could not even begin until they were safely transported back to the States—a gigantic task in itself. To those of us stationed at bases within the country, separation and return home would be a much easier effort for the military brass to handle. But wherever a service person was located, his or her discharge would ultimately depend upon a unique numbers game that had been created especially for the occasion.

The great numbers game of 1945 was not a lottery or game of

chance like the original selection of draftee numbers had been before the start of the war. Rather it was a discharge process based upon a score each man had earned that combined many factors of his record compiled since enlisting or being drafted into service. Points were credited for total time in uniform, months overseas, actual combat actions, and there were even points for decorations received in combat.

The total points an individual earned gave him a number, with the highest numbers getting discharged first. The pilots stationed at Daytona Beach were, for the most part, men with high numbers. In spite of intense competition, I emerged with one of the highest and was among the first sent to nearby Jacksonville Naval Air Station for release to inactive duty.

The importance of an early discharge was readily apparent—I planned to return to Parsons College to continue my undergraduate premed work, which had been interrupted by my departure into naval aviation in December 1940. If I could get into college classes by the first of October, although a late-entry student, I would not have to wait until midyear to resume studies.

Looking back on those days, I realize that I acted hastily in departing from my naval career in this almost callous fashion. Like many young men of the time, I did not realize how much my extensive combat experiences and the disciplined, yet carefree life of the naval aviator had changed me in a period of approximately five years. All that I thought about was that I was now five years older and still not set on a career; indeed, I was apprehensive as to the hard work and lack of immediate promise that my future seemed to hold.

Yet it was a logical course of action for a war-weary pilot to return to the Mid West—to the scenes of childhood—and to the pursuits that had been dropped to go to war. An ardent desire to see family and friends dominated my perspective. The intense motivation to become a military aviator was gone, replaced with a quiet confidence in my ability to fly and fight in airplanes. However, I still loved military flying, especially with the tailhook Navy, and was going to find out very quickly that life without this challenge was not for me.

NAVAL AIR OPERATIONAL TRAINING COMMAND
Headquarters

UNITED STATES NAVAL AIR STATION
Jacksonville, Florida

20 September 1945

From: CNAOpTra

To: Lt. Harold L. BUELL, (A1), USNR, 104297
               Naval Air Station
               Daytona Beach, Florida

Via: Commanding Officer

Subj: Release from Active Duty.

Ref: (a)ALNav 252-45
              (b)ALNav 198-45
              (c)CNAOpTra Dispatch 042035 of
              September 1945

1. Your Commanding Officer is directed to withhold delivery of these orders until he has obtained clearance from the Director of Distribution of the Naval District Headquarters in which your station is located for you to proceed to the Separation Center listed below.

2. Upon receipt of such clearance and when directed by your Commanding Officer you will consider yourself detached from your present duty and from such other duty as may have been assigned to you; will proceed to Naval Air Station, Jacksonville, Florida, and report to the Commanding Officer, U. S. Personnel Separation Center for temporary duty in connection with your release from active duty.

3. Upon the completion of this temporary duty you will, when directed by the Commanding Officer, U. S. Naval Personnel Separation Center, regard yourself detached and proceed to Ottumwa, Iowa, which you have stated to be your home of record at the time you were called to active duty, for release

from active duty in accordance with instructions to be issued by Commanding Officer of the Personnel Separation Center.

RALPH DAVISON
Rear Admiral, USN
CNAOpTra

cc: DNI, Navy Dept.
BuPers
Comdt., 9th Naval Dist. (Officer's Home District)
Disb. Off. NAS, Daytona Beach, Fla.
PSC NAS, Jacksonville, Fla.

II

After a planning flight to the Separation center at Jacksonville on 24 September to set up my appointment time, I checked out of the squadron. Having loaded the Grey Gremlin with my worldly possessions. I went to the personnel office to pick up my final set of orders. I planned to give the traditional farewell to the commanding officer as my departing act. When I presented myself to his secretary, I was advised that Captain Woods wanted to talk to me, and I was ushered into his presence.

I did not know R. W. D. Woods very well, never having served with him during the war—he was not a carrier-type aviator—and my time at Daytona had been so short I had not met him socially. We shook hands and he began talking:

"Hal, I am happy to get this chance to talk to you about something that is very important to both the Navy and to naval aviators like yourself. I am sorry that I didn't get with you sooner about this matter, and hope that I'm not too late with this significant information.

"The Navy is very concerned about losing most of its combat know-how, as represented by men such as yourself, to release to inactive duty. It realizes that you will remain on call in the reserves for several more years, and be available for service in case of an emergency. But this arrangement does not help the permanent regular Navy retain its combat edge both as a force-in-being and as a training organization for pilots to come. The only way this can be achieved is to induce certain key combat pilots like yourself to become a part of the regular-Navy establishment.

"While a few such pilots have already asked to be augmented into the regular Navy, there have not been enough of them do so to fill the Navy's needs, especially for the number of aircraft carriers that will remain in active service. So BUPERS [Bureau of Naval Personnel] in Washington has contacted COs of bases like this one and instructed us to bring certain facts about the regular Navy to the attention of young reserve aviators like yourself. It is hoped that when you hear these plans you might consider making the regular Navy a career."

He paused, placed his fingertips together, then continued:

"The Navy has just received congressional approval to augment three thousand reserve naval aviators into the regular Navy immediately. These men, for the most part, will come from the ranks of lieutenants (jg) and lieutenants with your time in the service, and most will have combat experience. The more combat experience the pilot has, especially in carriers, the better his chance of being selected. Frankly, Hal, a man with your qualifications should be almost a certainty for selection.

"I have also been advised that there will be a general ALNAV promotion from lieutenant to lieutenant commander, for officers with your time in rank, in about two weeks. This October list will be the last of the wartime-type promotions without selection boards—a tremendous advantage for lieutenants like yourself in that you will have attained mandatory retirement rights, under existing laws, without ever facing a selection board operating within a limiting promotional percentage requirement. Your first real selection will come in several years when you come up for commander. I also have been told that persons given regular commissions under this plan who have not completed a four-year college degree will be educated later, either in a college or a naval facility, to the equivalence of a Bachelor of Science degree at the Academy; this additional higher education will be so that the man being augmented can compete with his Academy-graduate peer group."

Captain Woods paused in his soliloquy, rose from a seat behind his desk, and moved toward me as I stood up from my chair. He smiled and said: "Hal, have I interested you enough to stop these orders for your discharge?"

The information that Captain Woods had presented to me was not only surprising—it was important as well. There had been considerable conjecture about promotions for lieutenants during the summer of 1945; we were sure we would be made lieutenant commanders to command the squadrons that had been planned for the invasion of Japan. But with the war ending suddenly in August, the logical conclusion was that all ranks would be frozen until demobilization was over and the size of the peacetime naval establishment could be determined. Now I had just been advised that promotion to lieutenant commander was only two to four weeks away!

The fact that the Navy had approval to select three thousand volunteers from naval aviation reserve ranks for regular commissions was also significant news. Augmenting the regular Navy by bringing in reserve personnel had been going on continuously, but always in a rather hit-or-miss fashion, with limited opportunity because of the small numbers involved. A commitment of three thousand selections was a real personnel policy change and indicated that the Navy was serious about a postwar carrier aviation force-in-being built around its combat-experienced reserve aviators.

Providing for further higher education for those selected was a final enticement that made the entire package an attractive offer. One of the serious drawbacks to a regular Navy career, to many combat veterans like myself who had dropped out of college to join naval aviation, was our inability to compete for the higher ranks against an Academy-trained peer group. The two- and three-year college dropout would have little chance for commander, captain, or admiral selection without a college degree. If the Navy kept its promise to educate selected officers to the level of the Academy graduate (a four-year college degree) it was removing a major obstruction to a reserve candidate for regular-Navy selection. The promotion to lieutenant commander by ALNAV, combined with the promise of education to a four-year college degree level, if one selected, made this offer for augmentation a truly fine career opportunity.

"Captain Woods, I wish that I had known about this new naval aviation augmentation program sooner. What you have just outlined to me looks like a good deal, especially to people in my age and length of service group. However, I have already made commitments to many persons back home, and have been promised immediate college entry early next week when I get to Fairfield, Iowa. I don't want to delay these plans by remaining on active duty now for several months while the Navy processes a request for a regular commission, makes a selection decision, and gives me an answer. Thank you for the briefing."

I picked up my briefcase containing my discharge orders and stuck out my hand for a final handshake. Captain Woods took it, smiled, and said:

"Hal, I don't want to give up on you. I have a final offer for you that will not change your present plans one iota. I took the liberty to have a set of application forms made out for your signature. You can sign them, go home as you planned, and the Navy will do the rest. I will send in the request, it will be processed, and you will be notified if you are selected. You can then decide whether you want to accept or decline a regular commission. You should hear something around the first of the year. How about it?"

The proposal looked like the best of two worlds to me that day, and I sat down, carefully read the papers, and signed them. It turned out that, because of the persistence of Captain Woods, I signed a paper that was destined to change the direction of my life forever.

At 0800, 29 September 1945, I reported to the Naval Personnel Separation Center, Jacksonville Naval Air Station, for release from active duty in the Navy. It was a well-run operation and, as I had a set of retirement papers with no hidden problems or errors, I was completely processed and on my way out of town by noon. Heading north, my immediate objective was Columbia, South Carolina, where I had set up a rendezvous with a pretty rebel lass. After a brief pause there, I planned to continue nonstop the rest of the way to Ottumwa.

Thinking back about this discharge, it is funny what lingers most in my memory. First of all, I received a pleasant surprise financially—$100 "mustering-out pay" and a travel mileage payment of $72.37. These funds augmented my final Navy paycheck handsomely. I was allowed to keep my leather flight jacket and helmet; the chief at the flight gear loft winked and said: "Lieutenant, you'll need these if the Navy calls you back to active duty for an emergency!" I was given two lapel pins—one was an attractive USNR logo, and the other the official discharge eagle. The latter became known to naval veterans as "the ruptured duck." I never wore these pins but I still have them. I also kept a practically new Colt

.45 that had been with me on my combat missions during the three war cruises. It meant a lot to me and I kept it in a special holster under the car seat.

After spending a fun evening at Columbia, I pushed on home. In many ways it was anticlimactic as I was pressed for time and could not visit anyone but my family in the old hometown. My sister Elsie Bryant had what civilian clothes I still owned ready to wear. I off-loaded my uniforms from the car, put in the civvies, and headed for classes at Parsons College, twenty-five miles down the road at Fairfield.

The sudden change from naval aviator warrior to college student in a matter of a weekend was turbulent and required adjustments. The first day on campus the football coach, Bill Urban, found me and talked me into coming out for practice that afternoon. With a few vets arriving back from service each week, he was ecstatically filling gaps in his team of teenagers with us older, mature youths. I told him that I would try to help, but being out of condition for college-level athletics, I would need some time before I could play. My playing positions were right guard on offense and roving linebacker on defense. Phil Willson arrived back and moved in at right tackle alongside me. I tried to get Jack Mayo, just back from the Navy, to play center (his old position before the war), but he was married with a daughter and no longer interested in spending his time on the gridiron. He told me he thought I was crazy playing again with a bunch of kids, and he was right.

So, in a weekend transformation, I settled into the old prewar order of attending classes, football practices, and study in the library. In many ways it was a dull routine in an environment that was no longer satisfying to me or my interests; I plugged along in silence. But it was Indian summer—the most beautiful time of the year in the heartland—with the foliage changing colors daily as I squired young lasses around in my convertible with the top down, amid the falling leaves, in the crisp, fall air. I was only a year away from frightful warfare in the Pacific, and already the harsh memories were beginning to fade from my immediate thoughts and I was finding peace within myself.

III

Where the wild rose tints the prairie
With its summer sheen,

Stand our noble Alma Mater
Of the rose and green.

—PARSONS COLLEGE ALMA MATER SONG

Like most colleges and universities in America, Parsons College had an annual fall homecoming—an event of some magnitude with campus decorations, parties, a parade, football game, and a gala dance complete with a queen. In addition to being fun for the students, the main purpose of the affair was to get alumni to return to the campus during the festive weekend. Homecoming for 1945 fell on the third weekend of October, after I had been back for two weeks.

This event is as good a place as any to end this saga about dive-bombers with golden wings in World War II. School officials asked to use my car, with the top down, to transport the homecoming queen in the parade; I gave permission providing that they would shine it up for the occasion. Both the car and queen, Elaine Barnes, looked radiant. In the football game against Carthage College from nearby Illinois, we won a tough one by a score of 7-6.

I continued my classes with little enthusiasm. My former guardian, Dr. Donald McElderry, was delighted with my premed studies and arranged a transfer to the medical school at the University of Iowa at the end of the school year in May 1946. While progress was being made, my heart was not in my new activities—I missed my shipmates.

In January 1946 fate sent me a reprieve. As Captain Woods had said back at Daytona Beach, the Navy would do its job, and I received word that I'd been selected for regular Navy. Happily leaving Parsons for Anacostia Naval Air Station in Washington, D.C., I was promoted to lieutenant commander, sworn in, then ordered to the nearby Pentagon to begin sixteen more years of active duty as an officer, aviator, and gentleman.

But that is another story.

EPILOGUE

I have often been fortunate to have been in the right place at the right time—blessed in that way—a sense of timing almost an instinct. But timing is made by a man, I think, and therefore he creates his own destiny. Take it or leave it, my timing was right; I accept that with gratitude, whether it was man-made or God-made.

—SIR LAURENCE OLIVIER

When I started this story some pages ago, I promised to tell you about "Dauntless Helldivers with wings of gold." Except for a few side roads, I hope I have kept that promise.

I also hope that you agree with me that it was a story worth the telling. Dive-bombing to destroy a target was a combat tactic that was an accurate offensive weapon of both the Japanese and American carrier navies in World War II. It was also successfully used by the Germans, with the Stuka dive-bomber a valuable weapon in close support of ground troops, especially as a tank-destroyer on the Russian front. The British Royal Navy used the tactic on selected occasions.

The dive-bomber continued flying in our Navy in Korea and Vietnam with that wonderful machine the AD Skyraider, known affectionately as the "Flying Dump Truck." It was the epitome of this type of plane, with all of the rugged features learned in World War II in its design, and it did the job until the newer jet types, combined with "smart bombs," powerful rockets, and electronic wonders finally ended the old-fashioned methods of bomb delivery in person. Like all things, new ideas and methods replaced the old, and naval aviation is better for it.

Old Dauntless Helldivers are justifiably proud of themselves. When the mighty Task Force Thirty-eight/Fifty-eight went to sea in the final stages of the Pacific war in 1944 and 1945, the fist of its air arm was the dive-bomber. With fighters to clear the skies of enemy aircraft, these planes, and their companions in the TBFs, had the power to hit and destroy any target that could be reached from the sea, anywhere in the world. The task force could destroy any naval force then in existence that might try to stop it, and did so several times. It could land the U.S. Marines on the beaches of hell itself—and did so at Iwo Jima. It could defend itself from land-based air attacks including the dreaded kamikaze. The U.S. carrier task force with its aircraft had become the most powerful naval weapon ever designed by man.

So the fighters controlled the air, the torpeckers roamed at will, and friendly submarines had a field day sinking ships. But when the real chips were bet in a face-to-face showdown, carrier-versus-carrier, there came a time in the game when the outcome had to be decided.

That was when those Dauntless Helldivers with wings of gold went out and did their duty. We are sure the world will never see such a force again.

APPENDIX A

Major Battles, Invasions and Raids
of
Harold L. Buell

FIRST WAR CRUISE—SCOUTING SQUADRON FIVE

Coral Sea	USS *Yorktown* (CV-5)	4–8 May 1942
Midway	USS *Saratoga* (CV-3)	3–12 June 1942
Guadalcanal-Tulagi landings	USS *Enterprise* (CV-6)	7–9 August 1942
Capture-defense Guadalcanal	USS *Enterprise* (CV-6)	August 1942–February 1943
Eastern Solomons	USS *Enterprise* (CV-6)	23–24 August 1942

SECOND WAR CRUISE—BOMBING SQUADRON TEN

Santa Cruz	USS *Enterprise* (CV-6)	25–26 October 1942
Battle of Guadalcanal	USS *Enterprise* (CV-6)	12–15 November 1942
Rennell Island	USS *Enterprise* (CV-6)	29–30 January 1943

THIRD WAR CRUISE—BOMBING SQUADRON TWO

Palau, Woleai, Yap	USS *Hornet* (CV-12)	30 March–1 April 1944
Hollandia occupation	USS *Hornet* (CV-12)	20–24 April 1944
Truk Island raids	USS *Hornet* (CV-12)	29–30 April 1944
Marianas occupation	USS *Hornet* (CV-12)	11 June–5 July 1944
Battle Philippine Sea	USS *Hornet* (CV-12)	19–20 June 1944
Bonin Island raids	USS *Hornet* (CV-12)	July–August 1944
Occupation of Palau	USS *Hornet* (CV-12)	September 1944
First Philippine Island raids	USS *Hornet* (CV-12)	9–24 September 1944

APPENDIX B

Pilot Rosters

PILOT ROSTER OF VS-5 IN *YORKTOWN*—APRIL 1942

Lt. Comdr. W. O. Burch, Jr., CO

Lt. T. F. Caldwell, Jr., XO

Lt. S. B. Strong, Operations Officer

Lt. R. B. Woodhull, Flight Officer

Lt. (jg) A. L. Downing

Lt. (jg) F. L. Faulkner

Lt. (jg) E. V. Johnson

Lt. (jg) H. W. Nicholson

Lt. (jg) S. W. Vejtasa

Ens. W. A. Austin

Ens. W. E. Brown, Jr.

Ens. H. L. Buell

Ens. K. C. Campbell

Ens. W. W. Coolbaugh

Ens. H. N. Ervin

Ens. R. H. Goddard

Ens. J. H. Jorgenson

Ens. E. B. Kinzer

Ens. E. Maul

Ens. L. G. Traynor

Ens. S. J. Underhill

PILOT ROSTER OF VS-5 IN *ENTERPRISE*—JULY 1942

Lt. T. F. Caldwell, Jr.

Lt. A. L. Downing

Lt. H. W. Nicholson

Lt. S. B. Strong

Lt. R. B. Woodhull

Lt. (jg) W. A. Austin

Ens. J. T. Barker

Ens. W. E. Brown, Jr.

Ens. H. L. Buell

Ens. H. N. Ervin

Ens. E. A. Conzett

Ens. W. W. Coolbaugh

Ens. H. N. Ervin

Ens. G. G. Estes

Ens. J. H. Jorgenson

Ens. E. Maul

Ens. A. C. Pfautz

Ens. J. F. Richey

Ens. L. G. Traynor

PILOT ROSTER OF VB-10 IN *ENTERPRISE*—OCTOBER 1942

Lt. Comdr. J. A. Thomas
Lt. V. W. Welch
Lt. (jg) H. L. Buell
Lt. (jg) R. D. Gibson
Lt. (jg) R. H. Goddard
Lt. (jg) J. L. Griffith
Lt. (jg) J. G. Leonard
Lt. (jg) B. A. McGraw
Lt. (jg) J. D. Wakeham
Lt. (jg) F. R. West

Ens. R. M. Buchanan
Ens. J. H. Carroum
Ens. D. H. Frissell
Ens. P. M. Halloran
Ens. R. A. Hoogerwerf
Ens. G. C. Nelson
Ens. L. Robinson
Ens. E. J. Stevens
Ens. N. E. Wiggins

APPENDIX C

Bombing Squadron Two
Squadron Tactical Organization, Pilots and
Gunners—24 March 1944

WING A

Division One

41 Lt. Comdr. Campbell Kline
42 Lt. (jg) Hardin Hills
43 Ens. McGee Cressy
44 Lt. (jg) Finger Ponzar
45 Ens. Bush Secrest
46 Ens. Wells Crout

Supernumeraries
   Lt. (jg) Watson Flatt
   Ens. Reynolds Youmans

Division Two

47 Lt. Buell Lakey
48 Ens. Stear Redman
49 Ens. Scheurer Davis
50 Lt. (jg) Taylor Case
51 Lt. (jg) LaMoyne Donelan
52 Ens. Ransom Howard

Supernumeraries
   Ens. Yaussi Curry
    Husted

WING B

53 Lt. Smith Wilks
54 Lt. (jg) Maxson Chigas
55 Ens. Sills McDonald
56 Lt. (jg) Houston Freeman
57 Ens. Bosworth Cubetz
58 Ens. Moore Germuska

Supernumeraries
   Lt. (jg) Garbler Brigantino
   Ens. Wynn Lee

59 Lt. (jg) Felderman Pattillo
60 Lt. (jg) Fritts Bates
61 Ens. Tull MacElroy
62 Lt. (jg) Garbe Bolac
63 Ens. Richey Stanley
64 Lt. (jg) Powers Charles

Supernumeraries
   Ens. Doherty Berliner
    Chartier

WING C

65	Lt. Micheel	Hart	71	Lt. (jg) Bamber	Foster
66	Lt. Galvin	Long	72	Ens. Ricks	Calpass
67	Ens. Armstrong	Maxwell	73	Ens. Robertson	Hastings
68	Lt. (jg) Russom	Harrison	74	Lt. (jg) Sherwood	Henderson
69	Lt. (jg) Dane	Cooper	75	Ens. Schaber	Durako
70	Ens. Harrsen	McGowan	76	Ens. Finnell	Meyer

Supernumeraries   *Supernumeraries*

     Ens. Isabella   Fanok   Ens. Norris   Albertelli

APPENDIX D

USS *Hornet* (CV-12)
Record of Air Group Two
15 March–24 September 1944

MISSIONS

1. Palau
2. Woleai
3. New Guinea
4. Truk
5. Ponape
6. Guam and Rota
7. Kazans and Bonins
8. Marianas Turkey Shoot
9. Fleet action
10. Pagan
11. Kazans and Bonins
12. Kazans and Bonins
13. Guam and Rota
14. Yap, Ulithi, and Fais
15. Kazans and Bonins
16. Palau
17. Mindanao
18. Visayas
19. Morotai and Halmahera
20. Manila
21. Visayas

SORTIES

	VF	VT	VB	Total
	3,971	1,330	1,947	7,248

HOURS

	13,638	4,043	5,521	23,202

ENEMY PLANES DESTROYED

In air	275
On ground (approximately)	275

[Note: In air includes eleven aircraft shot down by VFN-76, operating from *Hornet* with Air Group Two.]

ENEMY SHIPPING

Sunk	27
Probably sunk	22
Damaged	128

TONNAGE SUNK

1 CV	30,000
2 DD (*Fubuki/Mutsuki* classes)	3,500
2 CM	4,000
1 AK (large)	7,000
9 AK (medium)	45,000
5 AK (small)	7,200
2 AO ([oiler] large)	18,000
1 AO (small)	2,000
1 AO (medium)	5,000
2 Luggers (small cargo ship)	600
1 Sampan	50
Total	122,350

PROBABLY SUNK

1 CM (minelayer)	2,000
2 AK (large)	17,000
8 AK (medium)	40,500
1 AO (medium)	4,000
5 Coastal craft	500
5 Luggers	250
Total	64,250

[Note: At this point in the original report, a list of 128 more damaged ships of varied size and type are listed, totaling an additional 215,450 tons.]

Total sunk, probably sunk, and damaged: 402,050 tons

APPENDIX D

GROUND INSTALLATIONS DAMAGED OR DESTROYED

1. Airfield runways, dispersal areas, and installations
2. Seaplane and submarine base facilities
3. Coastal-defense guns, antiaircraft batteries, other guns
4. Ammunition and fuel dumps
5. Buildings, including barracks, supply, offices, and warehouses
6. Pillboxes, and other defense installations
7. Radio and radar installations
8. Docks, jetties, and other harbor facilities

BOMBS DROPPED (TONS):   1393

TORPEDOES DROPPED: 53

AMMUNITION EXPENDED (ROUNDS)

20 mm	129,560
.50 cal	1,499,905
.30 cal	160,278

[Note: This is an edited copy of the "Record of Air Group Two" that was created in October 1944, when the group returned to the United States for reassignment. It is a summary of the combat actions of all three of the group's squadrons.]

NOTES

Chapter 2   PREPARATION ONE

1. Vern Haugland, *The Eagle Squadrons,* New York, Ziff-Davis Flying Books, 1979, pp. 14–15.

2. Ibid., p. xii.

Chapter 3   ODYSSEY

1. Gordon W. Prange, *At Dawn We Slept,* New York, McGraw-Hill, 1981, Chapter 2.

2. Ibid., p. 516.

3. E. B. Potter, *Nimitz,* Annapolis, Maryland, Naval Institute Press, 1976, photo #5 after preface.

Chapter 4   CORAL SEA

1. Gordon W. Prange with Donald M. Goldstein and Katherine V. Dillon, *Miracle at Midway,* New York, McGraw-Hill, 1982, p. 290.

2. Robert Cressman, *That Gallant Ship,* Missoula, Montana, Pictorial Histories Publishing Company, 1985, p. 85.

3. Ibid., p. 91.

4. Ibid., p. 94.

5. John B. Lundstrom and James C. Sawruk, "Courage and Devotion to Duty," *The Hook,* Winter 1988, pp. 26–29.

6. *Nimitz,* p. 76.

7. John B. Lundstrom, *The First Team,* Annapolis, Maryland, Naval Institute Press, 1984, pp. 343–344.

8. *The Hook,* "Courage and Devotion," p. 36.

Chapter 5   MIDWAY

1. Edward P. Stafford, *The Big E,* New York, Dell, 1964, p. 106.

2. *The First Team,* pp. 539–547.

3. *Nimitz,* p. 107.

4. James H. and William M. Belote, *Titans of the Seas,* New York, Harper & Row, 1975, p. 185.

Chapter 6   EASTERN SOLOMONS

1. Saburo Sakai, with Martin Caidin and Fred Saito, *Samurai!* Garden City, New York, Nelson Doubleday, 1957.

2. *Titans of the Seas,* p. 145.

3. Ibid., p. 146.

4. Eugene Burns, *Then There Was One,* New York, Harcourt, Brace, 1944, p. 75.

Chapter 7   CACTUS

1. Adm. William F. Halsey and J. Bryan III, *Admiral Halsey's Story,* New York, McGraw-Hill, 1947, p. 123.

Chapter 8   VB-10

1. *Titans of the Seas,* p. 167.

2. Ibid., pp. 178–179.

3. David C. Evans, ed., *The Japanese Navy in World War II,* Annapolis, Maryland, Naval Institute Press, 1969, p. 192.

Chapter 9   PREPARATION TWO

1. Stephen E. Ambrose, *Nixon,* New York, Simon and Schuster, 1987, pp. 105–106.

2. Carroll V. Glines, *The Doolittle Raid,* New York, Orion Books, 1988, pp. 85–87.

Chapter 10   ISLAND RAIDS

1. Thomas B. Buell, *The Quiet Warrior,* Boston, Little, Brown, 1974, p. 126.

2. Adm. J. J. "Jocko" Clark with Clark G. Reynolds, *Carrier Admiral,* New York, David McKay, 1967, p. 149.

3. Ibid., p. 150.

4. Billy Graham, *Angels: God's Secret Agents,* New York, Doubleday, Pocket Book Edition, 1975, pp. 175–176.

5. *Carrier Admiral*, p. 152.

6. Ibid., p. 154.

7. Ibid., p. 155.

8. Ibid., p. 157.

9. Ibid., p. 157.

10. Ibid., p. 158.

11. Ibid., pp. 162–163.

Chapter 11   THE TURKEY SHOOT

1. William T. Y'Blood, *Red Sun Setting*, Annapolis, Maryland, Naval Institute Press, 1981, p. 153. Note: Like many stats of Pacific battles, there are differences in the aircraft totals for this one. Of the accounts I have researched, I like data contained in Y'Blood's Appendix 4 and have used them here. Many historians have a total of only 216 aircraft taking part in this action —ten fewer Hellcat fighters.

2. *Red Sun Setting*, p. 159.

3. *Titans of the Seas*, p. 357.

4. *Carrier Admiral*, p. 51.

5. Gen. Chuck Yeager with Leo Janos, *Yeager*, New York, Bantam Books, 1985, p. 119.

6. See my article "The Angled Deck Concept—Savior of the Tailhook Navy," *The Hook*, Fall, 1987.

Chapter 12   THE JOCKO JIMAS AND THE PHILIPPINES

1. *Carrier Admiral*, p. 179.

2. Masatake Okumiya and Jiro Horikoshi with Martin Caidin, *Zero!* New York, Ballantine Books, 1956, pp. 242–243.

3. Ibid., p. 242.

BIBLIOGRAPHY

Books

Ambrose, Stephen E. *Nixon.* New York: Simon and Schuster, 1987. The education of a politician, 1913–62.

Belote, James H. and William M. *Titans of the Seas.* New York: Harper & Row, 1975. Good coverage of carrier-vs.-carrier war.

——. *Typhoon of Steel: The Battle for Okinawa.* New York: Harper & Row, 1970. Paperback reprint. New York: Bantam Books, 1984.

Berry, Henry. *Semper Fi, Mac.* New York: Arbor House, 1982. Memories of the U.S. Marines in World War II.

Blackburn, Tom. *The Jolly Rogers.* New York: Orion Books, 1989. The story of Blackburn and VF-17.

Boyington, "Pappy." *Baa Baa Blacksheep.* New York: Dell, 1958.

Buell, Thomas B. *The Quiet Warrior.* Boston: Little, Brown, 1974. A biography of Adm. Raymond A. Spruance.

——. *Master of Sea Power.* Boston: Little, Brown, 1980. A biography of Adm. Ernest J. King.

Burns, Eugene. *Then There Was One.* New York: Harcourt, Brace, 1944. Personal account of the first year of war on USS *Enterprise.*

Caidin, Martin. *Golden Wings.* New York: Random House, 1960. A pictorial history of the U.S. Navy and Marine Corps in the air.

Clark, Adm. J. J. "Jocko," with Clark G. Reynolds. *Carrier Admiral.* New York: David McKay, 1967. Excellent book on carrier task force operations in two wars.

Cressman, Robert. *That Gallant Ship, USS* Yorktown *(CV-5).* Missoula, Montana: Pictorial Histories Publishing Company, 1985.

Dull, Paul. *A Battle History of the Imperial Japanese Navy (1941–1945)*. Annapolis, Maryland: Naval Institute Press, 1976.

Evans, David C., ed. *The Japanese Navy in World War II*. Annapolis, Maryland: Naval Institute Press, 1969. Japanese naval officers' account.

Ewing, Steve. *The USS* Enterprise *(CV-6)*. Missoula, Montana: Pictorial Histories Publishing Company, 1982. Most decorated ship of World War II.

Fahey, James C. *The Ships and Aircraft of the United States Fleet*. 4 vols. New York: Ships and Aircraft, 1945.

Fuchida, Mitsuo, and Masetake Okumiya. *Midway: The Battle That Doomed Japan*. Annapolis, Maryland: Naval Institute Press, 1955.

Glines, Carroll V. *The Doolittle Raid*. New York: Orion Books, 1988.

Graham, Billy. *Angels: God's Secret Agents*. New York: Doubleday, Pocket Book Edition, 1975.

Gregg, Charles T. *Tarawa*. Briarcliff Manor, New York: Stein and Day, 1984.

Griffin, W. E. B. *The New Breed*. New York: G. P. Putnam's Sons, 1987.

Griffith, Samuel B. *The Battle for Guadalcanal*. New York: Bantam Books, 1963.

Halsey, Adm. William F., and J. Bryan III. *Admiral Halsey's Story*. New York: McGraw-Hill, 1947.

Hammel, Eric. *Guadalcanal: Starvation Island*. New York: Crown, 1987.

———. *Guadalcanal: The Carrier Battles*. New York: Crown, 1987.

———. *Guadalcanal: Decision at Sea*. New York: Crown, 1988.

Haugland, Vern. *The Eagle Squadrons*. New York: Ziff-Davis Flying Books, 1979. Yanks in the RAF, 1940–42.

Hoyt, Edwin F. *The Battle of Leyte Gulf: The Death Knell of the Japanese Fleet*. New York: Weybright and Talley , 1972.

———. *Blue Skies and Blood*. New York: Paul S. Eriksson, 1975.

———. *Storm over the Gilberts*. New York: Mason/Charter, 1978. War in the central Pacific, 1943.

———. *To the Marianas*. New York: Van Nostrand Reinhold, 1980. War in the central Pacific, 1944.

———. *McCampbell's Heroes*. New York: Van Nostrand Reinhold, 1983.

Hynes, Samuel. *Flights of Passage*. Annapolis, Maryland: Naval Institute Press, 1988. Reflections of a World War II marine aviator.

Inoguchi, Capt. Rikihei, and Cdr. Tadashi Nakajima, with Roger Pineau. *The Divine Wind*. New York: Bantam Books, 1958.

Jablonski, E. *Airwar*. 2 vols. New York: Doubleday, 1971.

Jentschura, Hansgeorg, et al. *Warships of the Imperial Japanese Navy, 1869–1945*. London: Arms & Armour Press, 1977.

Johnson, Stanley. *Queen of the Flattops*. New York: Dutton, 1942.

———. *The Grim Reapers*. New York: Dutton, 1943.

Kaplan, Philip, and Collier, Richard. *Their Finest Hour.* New York: Abbeville Press, 1989.

Krulak, Gen. Victor H. *First to Fight.* Annapolis, Maryland: Naval Institute Press, 1984. An inside view of the U.S. Marine Corps.

Kuwahara, Yasuo, and Gordon T. Allred. *Kamikaze.* New York: Ballantine Books, 1957. Japanese pilot's story of suicide squadrons.

Lawson, Robert, ed. *The History of U.S. Naval Air Power.* New York: Military Press, 1985. Outstanding collection of photographs.

Lindbergh, Charles A. *The Spirit of St. Louis.* New York: Charles Scribner's Sons, 1953.

Lord, Walter. *Day of Infamy.* New York: Holt, Rinehart, 1957.

———. *Incredible Victory.* New York: Harper & Row, 1967. Best book ever written about the Battle of Midway.

———. *Lonely Vigil.* New York: Viking, 1977.

Lundstrom, John B. *The First Team.* Annapolis, Maryland: Naval Institute Press, 1984. Pacific naval air combat from Pearl Harbor to Midway. Best work done on the fighter war.

Manchester, William. *American Caesar.* Boston: Little, Brown, 1978. Biography of Douglas MacArthur, 1880–1964.

———. *Goodbye, Darkness.* New York: Dell, 1979.

Manning, Robert, ed. *Above and Beyond.* Boston: Boston Printing Company, 1985. History of the Medal of Honor.

Merillat, Herbert C. *Guadalcanal Remembered.* New York: Dodd, Mead, 1982.

Miller, Merle. *Plain Speaking.* New York: Berkley and G. P. Putnam's Sons, 1973. Oral biography of Harry Truman.

Miller, Nathan. *The U.S. Navy: An Illustrated History.* Annapolis, Maryland: Naval Institute and American Heritage, 1977.

Miller, Thomas G., Jr. *The Cactus Air Force.* New York: Harper & Row, 1969. Paperback reprint. New York: Bantam Books, 1981. Great book on Guadalcanal air operations, August–November 1942.

Morison, Samuel E. *History of United States Naval Operations in World War II.* 15 vols. Boston: Little, Brown, 1947. A classic.

———. *The Two-Ocean War.* Boston: Little, Brown, 1963.

Naito, Hatsuho. *Thunder Gods.* New York: Kodansha International, 1989. Kamikaze pilots tell their story (translated from Japanese).

Okumiya, Masatake, and Jiro Horikoshi, with Martin Caidin. *Zero!* New York: Ballantine Books, 1956.

Parry, Col. Francis Fox. *Three-War Marine: Pacific-Korea-Vietnam.* Pacifica, California: Pacifica Press, 1987.

Parsons College. The yearbook *Peira* and newspaper *Portfolio,* 1939–46.

Pensacola and Jacksonville Naval Air Station. *Flight Jacket, 1941.* Montgomery, Alabama: Paragon Press, 1941.

Porter, Col. R. Bruce, with Eric Hammel. *Ace!* Pacifica, California: Pacifica Press, 1985. A book about Marine shore-based night fighters.

Potter, E. B. *Nimitz*. Annapolis, Maryland: Naval Institute Press, 1976.
———. *Bull Halsey: A Biography*. Annapolis, Maryland: Naval Institute Press, 1985.
———. *Admiral Arleigh Burke*. Annapolis, Maryland: Naval Institute Press, 1990.
Prange, Gordon. *At Dawn We Slept*. New York: McGraw-Hill, 1981. Outstanding book on the Pearl Harbor attack.
———, with Donald M. Goldstein and Katherine V. Dillon. *Miracle at Midway*. New York: McGraw-Hill, 1982.
———, with Donald M. Goldstein and Katherine V. Dillon. *Pearl Harbor: The Verdict of History*. New York: McGraw-Hill, 1986.
Ross, Bill D. *Iwo Jima: Legacy of Valor*. New York: Vanguard, 1985.
Rudel, Hans Ulrich. *Stuka Pilot*. New York: Bantam Books, 1958. German use of dive-bombers.
Russ, Martin. *Line of Departure: Tarawa*. New York: Doubleday, 1975. Dramatic story of annihilating seventy-six-hour battle.
Sakai, Saburo, with Martin Caidin and Fred Saito. *Samurai!* Garden City, New York: Nelson Doubleday, 1957.
Schultz, Duane. *Wake Island*. New York: St. Martin's Press, 1978.
Shaara, Michael. *The Killer Angels*. New York: David McKay, 1974.
Sherrod, Robert. *History of Marine Corps Aviation in World War II*. Washington, D.C.: Combat Forces Press, 1952.
Shores, Christopher. *Duel for the Sky*. Garden City, New York: Doubleday, 1985. Crucial air battles of World War II.
Sims, Edward H. *Greatest Fighter Missions*. New York: Ballantine Books, 1962.
Sledge, E. B. *With the Old Breed at Peleliu and Okinawa*. Novato, California: Presidio Press, 1981.
Smith, Peter C. *The History of Dive Bombing*. Annapolis, Maryland: The Nautical & Aviation Publishing Company of America, 1981. Only book on dive-bombing history in England, Germany, Japan, and U.S. Navy.
Spector, Ronald H. *Eagle Against the Sun*. New York: Macmillan, The Free Press, 1985.
Spurr, Russell. *A Glorious Way to Die*. New York: Newmarket Press, 1981. The kamikaze mission of Yamato in April 1945.
Stafford, Edward P. *The Big E*. New York: Random House, 1962. Paperback reprint. New York: Dell, 1964. Best *Enterprise* book.
Stewart, Adrian. *The Battle of Leyte Gulf*. New York: Charles Scribner's Sons, 1980.
Tillman, Barrett. *The Dauntless Dive Bomber of World War II*. Annapolis, Maryland: Naval Institute Press, 1976.
———. *Hellcat: The F6F in World War II*. Annapolis, Maryland: Naval Institute Press, 1979.
———. *Corsair*. Annapolis, Maryland: Naval Institute Press, 1979.
Toland, John. *Infamy*. Garden City, New York: Doubleday, 1982
———. *Gods of War*. Garden City, New York: Doubleday, 1985.

Tregaskis, Richard. *Guadalcanal Diary*. New York: Random House, 1943.

U.S. Strategic Bombing Survey. *The Campaigns of the Pacific War*. Washington, D.C.: U.S. Government Printing Office, 1946.

VB-2 Pilots, eds. *Chock to Chock*. Limited ed. Private Printing, 1945. A chronicle, including photographs, of VB-2 and Air Group Two from June 1943 to November 1944.

Wagner, Ray. *American Combat Planes*. Garden City, New York: Doubleday, 1982. A comprehensive history of the development of our military aircraft (over 1,400 photographs).

Wakeman, Frederic. *Shore Leave*. New York: Signet Books, 1948.

Wheeler, Richard. *Iwo*. New York: Lippincott & Crowell, 1980.

———. *A Special Valor*. New York: Harper & Row, 1983.

Wilson, Jim. *Retreat, Hell!* New York: William Morrow, 1988.

Winslow, W. G. *The Fleet the Gods Forgot*. Annapolis, Maryland: Naval Institute Press, 1982. The U.S. Asiatic Fleet in World War II.

Winters, Capt. Hugh. *Skipper*. Mesa, Arizona: Champlin Fighter Museum Press, 1985.

Wolfe, Tom. *The Right Stuff*. New York: Farrar, Straus, Giroux, 1979.

Wouk, Herman. *The Winds of War* and *War and Remembrance*. 2 vols. New York: Pocket Books, 1971, 1978.

Y'Blood, William T. *Red Sun Setting*. Annapolis, Maryland: Naval Institute Press, 1981. A definitive account of the first battle of Philippine Sea.

———. *The Little Giants*. Annapolis, Maryland: Naval Institute Press, 1987. About CVEs.

Yeager, Gen. Chuck, with Leo Janos. *Yeager*. New York: Bantam Books, 1985. The autobiography of America's greatest test pilot.

Articles

Adams, Capt. John P. "The First Use of the Thach Weave in Combat." Naval Aviation Museum, *Foundation*, Spring 1988.

Arbes, Capt. James D. "The Incomparable John G. Crommelin—My First Skipper." Naval Aviation Museum, *Foundation*, Spring 1987.

Bloch, Harry. "Only a Sky Full of Hellcats." *World War II Times*, July 1988.

Buell, Dr. Harold L. "Death of a Captain." United States Naval Institute, *Proceedings*, February 1986.

———. "The Angled Deck Concept—Savior of the Tailhook Navy." The Tailhook Association, *The Hook*, Fall 1987.

———. "Elimination Base Training." Naval Aviation Museum, *Foundation*, Fall 1987.

———. "Yorktown's Crucial Dash to Midway." Naval Aviation Museum, *Foundation*, Spring 1988.

Cagle, Vice Adm. M. W. "The Saga of Radioman Wiley." Naval Aviation Museum, *Foundation*, Fall 1988.

———. "The Crommelin Brothers Five." Naval Aviation Museum, *Foundation*, Fall 1988.

Cagle, Capt. Maury. "Bombing 5 [sic] at Midway: The Battle and Its Aftermath." Naval Aviation Museum, *Foundation*, Spring 1988.

Caldwell, Vice Adm. Turner F. "The Stranded *Enterprise* Aviators on Guadalcanal." Naval Aviation Museum, *Foundation*, Spring 1986.

———. "A Naval Aviator in Wartime Hollywood." Naval Aviation Museum, *Foundation*, Spring 1987.

Coffin, Scoofer. "Buzzard Brigade Blasted Away at Santa Cruz." *World War II Times*, September 1986.

Cressman, Robert J. "Marine Air at Midway." Naval Aviation Museum, *Foundation*, Spring 1988.

Emerson, William. "A Rather Full Day." *Naval Aviation News* and *All Hands*, February 1945.

Gay, George. "The TBD-1 Devastator." Naval Aviation Museum, *Foundation*, Spring 1988.

Gray, William P. "Jocko Clark." *Life* magazine, January 1945.

Harris, Maynard. "America's First Hero." *World War II Times*, November 1988.

"Japanese Fleet." *Life* magazine, July 1944.

Laub, Rear Adm. Robert E. "The American Torpedo Attacks at Midway." Naval Aviation Museum, *Foundation*, Spring 1988.

Mangrum, Lt. Col. Richard C. "Guadalcanal Diary." *American Magazine*, February 1943.

McCuskey, Capt. E. Scott, and Capt. John P. Adams. "VF-42 Wildcats at Midway." Naval Aviation Museum, *Foundation*, Spring 1988.

Palmer, Comdr. Carlton D. "The Pioneer Days of Naval Aviation." Naval Aviation Museum, *Foundation*, Fall 1985.

Rausa, Capt. Rosario. "Pride of the Navy." Naval Aviation Museum, *Foundation*, Spring 1987.

Redifer, Rex. "That Date of Infamy." *World War II Times*, November 1988.

Riley, William A. "Enlisted Pilots at Midway." Naval Aviation Museum, *Foundation*, Spring 1988.

Rothenberg, Comdr. Allan. "That Little Ensign in the Back." Naval Aviation Museum, *Foundation*, Spring 1988.

"Sealebrity." *The Scuttlebutt*, July 1985.

Tamburello, Dr. G. B. "Tsushin Choho." Naval Aviation Museum, *Foundation*, Spring 1988.

"The Rippers." *Time* magazine, October 1944.

"The Saga of Smokey Stover." *World War II Times*, May 1988.

"U.S. Fights for the Solomons." *Life* magazine, November 1942.

U.S. Navy Department. *War Communiques*, October 1942.

Watson, Elbert. "Ensign Gay Needed His Deer Rifle." *World War II Times*, November 1987.

Williams, Audra. "He Led the Attack on Pearl Harbor: Captain Fuchida's Midway Observations." *World War II Times,* April–May 1987.

Williams, Brad. "Firing Pearl Harbor's First Shot." *World War II Times,* July 1987.

Winters, Capt. T. Hugh. "Recollections of the Battle of Leyte Gulf." Naval Aviation Museum, *Foundation,* Fall 1985.

INDEX

339